# An Invitation to Learning and Memory

JOHN F. HALL, *Pennsylvania State University*

ALLYN AND BACON, INC.

Boston   London   Sydney   Toronto

**Library of Congress Cataloging in Publication Data**

Hall, John Fry, birthdate-
  An invitation to learning and memory.

    Bibliography: p.
    Includes index.
    1. Learning, Psychology of. 2. Memory. I. Title.
BF 318.H34        513.1        81-15030
ISBN 0-205-07608-4        AACR2

Printed in the United States of America.

10  9  8  7  6  5  4  3  2  1      86  85  84  83  82

This book is dedicated with affection
to my wife, Jean

# Contents

# Preface

The learning and memory literature is so extensive that many authors decide to limit their coverage to a single area or to a selected number of topics. I believe, however, that the introductory student should have the opportunity to examine most of the basic topics that have been traditionally encompassed in the learning and memory area. Thus, my objective in writing this text has been to present as broad a picture of learning and memory as possible within the confines of a single book suitable for a one-semester course.

Fifteen years ago, when writing a similar text, I was convinced that learning principles were basically the same regardless of the type of task used by the investigator; the organization of that volume reflected such a bias. Now I am not as sanguine that such is the case. As a result, I have adopted the working hypothesis that it is best to separately examine the learning paradigms and general areas of investigation that most current experimenters have used in their examination of this area of psychology.

This organization permits some rearrangement of the material, if desired by the instructor. After the introductory chapter has been completed, it is possible to have students then read the material on verbal learning and retention found in Chapters 9–12, or motor skills learning in Chapter 13, prior to examining classical and instrumental conditioning in Chapters 2–8.

Students frequently express doubt that learning principles generated from laboratory studies have relevance for human behavior. I have addressed such student criticism by attempting to show, wherever possible, the applicability of the experimental studies that have been discussed.

An instructor's manual accompanies this text. The manual provides a short description of films appropriate for class presentation, a short summary of articles in popular periodicals which may be used for outside reading assignments, and a variety of questions which will aid the instructor in constructing examinations.

I am indebted to many individuals for their help in writing this text. In particular, I would like to thank Arno F. Wittig, Chris D. Anderson, Shirley C. Brown, F. Robert Brush, Charles I. Brooks, and Michael Best for their many helpful comments. Sally Lifland did an excellent job in making the manuscript much more readable. Finally, I would like to give special thanks to my wife, Jean, whose help began with the transcribing of original notes and continued through the compilation of the indexes.

J.F.H.

# CHAPTER ONE

# Introduction

It is likely that the emergence of Homo sapiens as the most complex organism on this planet has stemmed from superior development of the learning process. And as our culture grows even more complex, the importance of learning will undoubtedly increase.

The rise of technical schools and the host of other educational institutions found in the Western culture is testimony to the importance of learning. But the contribution of this process extends far beyond formal educational experiences. Books on improving memory make the best sellers' list. Ways have been developed to control physiological responses, e.g., blood pressure, heart rate, as well as emotional responses (particularly those which are debilitating). It is generally accepted, for example, that many of our fears and phobias have been learned, and a variety of practitioners attempt to help their patients unlearn them. It is interesting to note that the medical community has recently indicated that researchers searching for ways of increasing human longevity should direct their efforts to learning how to modify behavior so people will want to have sound health habits—such as not smoking, limiting alcohol intake, eating properly, and engaging in appropriate exercise patterns.

In summary, the comprehension and control of the learning process has been posited by some as an elixir to solve many of our problems. Are these claims valid? What do we actually know about learning? As a first step in attempting to answer these questions, let us trace the development of interest in the learning process.

## HISTORY OF THE STUDY OF LEARNING

Interest in learning and memory can be traced to the Greeks, whose concern with memory focused on the study of mnemonics. (A mnemonic is a technique or procedure used to improve memory.) In an age before printing, with the spoken word the basic form of communication, it was necessary for Greek orators to memorize their material. What could be more helpful than methods that would assist in this demanding endeavor, particularly since one's speech might last for hours? The mnemonic techniques the Greeks used have been passed on, and even now continue to be employed as the foundation for many current "memory" systems.

One system, identified as the method of loci, has the individual associate items or ideas with discrete geographical locations, preferably familiar places. For example, each item in a list of groceries to be purchased might be associated with the varying rooms in your house. First, entering the kitchen, you might visualize a loaf of bread placed in the middle of the floor, while a bottle of milk dangles from the ceiling. Moving to the dining room, you would see a bottle of mustard had been spilled over the dining room table. Proceeding to the living room, you might envision a large light bulb protruding from one of the chairs, and so on. At the supermarket, you would visually "walk" through your house, recalling the items associated with each of the rooms.

However, the study of mnemonics did not play a role in the early *experimental* examination of learning and memory. Rather, the antecedent for this development is found in the work of Gustav Theodore Fechner, a German physiologist and physicist who published the *Elements of Psychophysics* in 1860.

Fechner's general objective was to work out the precise relationship existing between mind and body, a problem which at that time occupied the attention of many philosophers. Fechner's approach was to relate the physical characteristics of a stimulus—visual, auditory, or tactual—to the sensation that was perceived by the subject. His experimental studies resulted in the establishment of the Weber-Fechner law, which states that the strength of the sensation perceived by an individual is proportional to the logarithm of the stimulus used to elicit the sensation.

The fundamental importance of Fechner's work was not only that it represented the first successful instance of quantifying a mental phenomenon (sensation), but also that it inspired Hermann Ebbinghaus, another German scientist, to work on the quantification of the mental processes of learning and memory. In the years 1879–80 and 1883–84, Ebbinghaus undertook an extensive series of experiments designed to measure these processes.

The experimental task he used was the learning of a list of nonsense syllables.[1] Influenced by the English philosophers who had held that the principle of repetition was a law of association and basic in understanding how ideas were linked together, Ebbinghaus used the number of repetitions necessary to reproduce the list as a measure of learning. By noting how many fewer repetitions were required to master the same material at a later time, he was able to measure retention. Ebbinghaus's (1913) work culminated in the publication of a monograph, *Memory.*

In this monograph, Ebbinghaus acknowledged that many sayings regarding the role of learning, e.g., "He who learns quickly also forgets quickly," should be experimentally investigated. He believed, however, that it was necessary to first examine basic variables. In one series of experiments, he attempted to determine how the rate of learning was related to the number of syllables that comprised the list. In a second series of studies, he examined the retention of lists of syllables as a function of the length of the retention interval, with intervals ranging from 20 minutes to 31 days.

Not all of the early experimental investigations of learning were directed at determining how humans learn. A little more than a decade after Ebbinghaus's work, the experimental studies of Pavlov and Bechterev made substantial contributions to an understanding of the learning process.

Ivan Petrovich Pavlov was a Russian physiologist who would later win the Nobel prize for his studies of the physiology of digestion. While examining the contribution of salivation to the digestive process, Pavlov noted that the sound of his footsteps as he walked across the laboratory floor would elicit salivation in dogs who had frequently served as his experimental subjects. He identified salivation in response to such a stimulus as a psychic secretion, so designated to differentiate it from salivation elicited by traditionally used stimuli—meat powder or a weak solution of acid placed on the animal's tongue.

The discovery that salivation could be elicited by a "neutral" stimulus so aroused Pavlov's interest that he devoted the remainder of his life to studying this phenomenon.

Basic to such study was the establishment of a laboratory methodology to examine how such a response was acquired. The procedure he devised was to present a tone (produced by a tuning fork) along with a small quantity of meat powder. After presenting both stimuli on a number of occasions, he found that the presentation of the tone alone would elicit salivation—a response that he identified as a conditioned reflex. The conditioned reflex —or conditioned response, as it has now been identified—is used to infer the existence of a learning process, since the organism, after training, responds to a stimulus that previously was ineffective in eliciting that response.

Working at about the same time as Pavlov was another Russian investigator, Vladimir Bechterev, whose methodology was similar to that used by Pavlov. Bechterev noted that if a cold stimulus was suddenly applied to the skin of a dog the animal would catch its breath, a familiar reflex. It was then noted that if another stimulus was repeatedly applied at the same time as the cold, the other stimulus would serve as a substitute for the "natural" stimulus in eliciting the reflex. Another series of experiments followed, in which shock was used as the "natural" stimulus and the response elicited was voluntary—foot withdrawal. Bechterev found that if a neutral stimulus, such as a bell, was presented just prior to the onset of shock, the response of withdrawing the limb in order to avoid the painful stimulus was rapidly acquired. Bechterev's finding indicated that skeletal responses could be investigated—responses of a voluntary nature in contrast to salivation, an involuntary response. Bechterev's work also represented an early examination of avoidance learning, a paradigm that many subsequent experimenters have used.

By the 1900s, investigators in the United States became interested in examining the nature of the learning process, but their experimental procedures differed markedly from those of their European counterparts; the studies of Ebbinghaus, Pavlov, and Bechterev had not been translated into English, so few details of their work were known. E. L. Thorndike of Columbia University was probably the most prominent of these investigators. His early experiments have been widely cited.

Thorndike was interested in much more complex behavior than the simple kinds of responses examined by the Russian investigators. One apparatus he used was a puzzle box, a specially designed wooden cage with a latched door that could be opened from the inside if the animal pulled on a loop of string hanging from the top. See Figure 1-1. (Other mechanisms to open the door were also used in some experiments.) Hungry cats were placed inside the box and were "motivated" to get out when the experimenter placed a piece of fish in full view just outside the door. Animals responded with a variety of behaviors, such as clawing and scratching, and eventually they would come into contact with the looped string and release the door. The cats, on subsequent trials, would confine their responses to the general location of the string; thus the pulling of the loop and the opening of the door took place in progressively shorter periods of time. The behavior of Thorndike's cats was described as trial and error and was accepted by many psychologists as a basic form of animal learning.

Paralleling Thorndike's work with cats was Small's (1899, 1900) pioneer investigation of the white rat's ability to learn the correct path through a maze. His original maze was patterned after the human maze found in the Hampton Court Palace, England. The maze subsequently became a very popular type of learning task for many investigators using rats as their experimental subjects. Early types of mazes were quite complex, but these have been replaced by simpler types; investigators today most frequently use the T-maze.

Two notable contributions to learning and memory were made in the 1930s by B. F. Skinner and Sir Frederick Bartlett. Skinner invented an apparatus called the Skinner box. This apparatus consists of a small compartment containing a lever which operates a mechanism to dispense small food pellets into a food tray. The task for the experimental

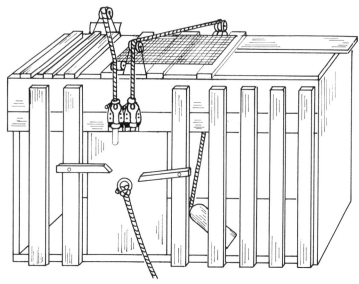

FIGURE 1-1.  Thorndike's puzzle box for studying instrumental behavior of cats. Escape from the box was made contingent on various responses.

subject, a rat, was to learn to press the lever in order to activate the mechanism that would deliver a pellet of food. Some years later the apparatus was modified for use with pigeons. The birds learned to peck small plastic disks placed on one wall of the apparatus in order to obtain a reward. See Figure 1-2 for a current version of the Skinner box.

The Skinner box task differs from most learning tasks since it is possible for the experimental subject to make a response, receive and consume a reward, and be in a position to repeat this procedure without being handled by the experimenter. As the coming chapters will show, it has been extensively used by many investigators.

Bartlett's contribution was in the area of memory. Unlike Ebbinghaus and other verbal learning experimenters who were interested in examining how lists of verbal items were learned and remembered, Bartlett used prose in the form of folktales as his experimental material. See page 229 for an illustration of the material he used. His subjects were asked to read the material; then, after varying intervals of time, e.g., hours, days, or months, they were asked to remember what they had read. As investigators have become increas-

ingly interested in the learning and remembering of prose, Bartlett's work has assumed greater importance.

The quizzical reader may wonder why early learning investigators were not more interested in examining motor skills. Not a great deal of interest was manifested in such learning during early years, although Bryan and Harter (1897, 1899) did become interested in determining how individuals send telegraphic code, a motor skills task of some complexity. With the advent of World War II, the need to select and train thousands of inductees to fly airplanes was responsible for stimulating interest in motor skills learning.

Since the early experimental studies of Ebbinghaus, thousands of learning and memory experiments have been conducted. Many different types of subjects have been used, ranging from paramecia to humans, with the kinds of learning tasks employed limited only by the imagination of the experimenters. The learning experiments that have been described were selected because they represent landmarks in the history of learning—the types of apparatus, materials, procedures, and methods used have served as models for many subsequent investigations.

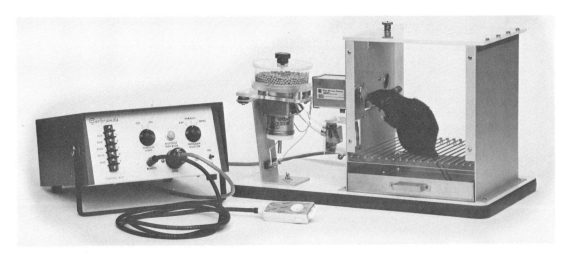

FIGURE 1-2.   A closeup of the experimental chamber used with the rat or small squirrel monkey. Courtesy of Gerbrands Corporation, Arlington, Massachusetts.

## A DEFINITION OF LEARNING

Although a variety of learning experiments have been described, learning has not yet been defined. Learning, like respiration or digestion, is a biological process, undoubtedly of a neurological nature, the operation of which is inferred from changes taking place in the organism's behavior. But all changes in behavior cannot be used to infer the learning process. Such processes as maturation and fatigue, for example, may result in behavior changes, and yet they differ from the learning process.

We shall not discuss in any detail the criteria investigators use to differentiate learning from these other processes. As noted in the learning experiments described in the previous section, repetition or practice appears to be a basic condition required for learning to take place. In most experiments, practice consists of providing the experimental subject with learning trials. However, the concept of practice or trials does not encompass all of the operations that result in learning. For example, an experimental subject may simply observe another subject making the learned response. Rats, cats, and monkeys, in addition to humans, all have been able to learn when their only "practice" consisted of watching another organism successfully perform the response to be learned. As a result, it seems more appropriate to use the term *experience*, which includes, but is not limited to, the concept of practice. See Box 1-1.

Some students may have wondered why we have not indicated that learning should be reflected in changes in the organism's conscious content or mental activity. Intuitively, we are aware that our mental content has been changed when we study the multiplication table, a list of words to be subsequently defined, or an array of Civil War dates. The problem is that this awareness is a private event; experimenters have no way of knowing if, or when, such changes have taken place. Science deals only with events that can be confirmed by others. In the future, we may be able to obtain public measures of these conscious content changes. Until such time, however, behavioral changes must be used to infer the operation of the learning process.

In summary, learning is an organismic process that arises from experience and is inferred from changes in the organism's behavior. Such a definition is admittedly imprecise. It does not say anything about the kind of organismic process, does not indicate the specific characteristics of the experience that will result in learning, nor does it specify the nature of the behavior change from which the learning process is inferred. These are the questions that some current investigators have been at-

BOX 1-1

Thorndike (1898) was interested in determining if cats and chickens could learn to escape from a puzzle box or a confined area by observing a previously trained subject perform an appropriate escape response. He was unable to determine that any of his animals had learned by observing the responses of others. However, other experimenters have reported positive findings. Kinnaman (1902) provided one monkey with a box that could be opened only by pulling out a plug which secured the lid. His subject failed to work the mechanism and gave up in despair. A second monkey was able to open the box by seizing the end of the plug with his teeth and pulling it out. The first monkey, after observing the action of the second, immediately solved the problem when given a second try. Later experimenters have over the years confirmed Kinnaman's findings that animals can learn by observation; see Warden and Jackson (1935), Herbert and Harsh (1944), Corson (1967), Powell, Saunders, and Thompson (1968), Jacoby and Dawson (1969), Menzel (1978).

Observational learning, or what Kling (1971) has described as exposure learning, never entered the mainstream of learning theory. One reason was the difficulty in assimilating observing behavior into the familiar stimulus-response paradigm, which emphasizes the importance of reinforcement for the acquisition of S-R relationships.

tempting to answer, and it is likely that their findings may contribute to a more adequate definition of learning.

Our inability to provide a precise definition of learning is not as great an obstacle as some might believe, a point noted by Hilgard (1951) some years ago. Hilgard wrote that "a precise definition of learning is not necessary, so long as we agree that the inference to learning is made from changes in performance that are a result of training . . . The experiments themselves define the field . . ." (p. 518). The latter statement is of fundamental importance. As long as there is agreement by workers in the field on the type of experimental operations used and the kinds of behavior changes to be measured, the study of the learning process can proceed.[2]

### Learning and Performance

It has been readily apparent to many investigators that a change in the organism's behavior cannot always be used to infer that learning has taken place. There is not always an identity between learning and performance. Students who have learned material for a course examination may find the test situation so traumatic that they are unable to remember

any of the material they learned. Or one may be unable to remember a person's name upon meeting that person on the street, only to find a few minutes later that the name "comes to mind." In these instances, the material had been learned, but that was not immediately evident from the individual's performance.

An experimental example of the learning-performance distinction is provided by an early but revealing study conducted by Blodgett (1929). Blodgett gave three groups of rats one trial a day on a six-unit multiple T-maze. One group (control) was run for seven days, with each animal permitted to eat food in the goal box for three minutes on each trial. A second group (Experimental Group I) was also run for seven days. For the first two days this group did not find food in the goal box, but on the third day and each day thereafter food was present. A third group (Experimental Group II) was treated similarly to Experimental Group I, except that reward was omitted for the first six days and introduced on the seventh. These animals were then run two additional days, with food in the goal box each day. Results are illustrated in Figure 1-3.

It may be noted that the discovery of food by Experimental Group I at the end of Trial 3 resulted in reduction in the error score

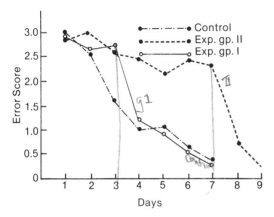

FIGURE 1-3. The influence of reward on maze learning. The control group has been reinforced on every trial. Experimental Group I had reward introduced on Trial 3, while Experimental Group II had reward introduced on Trial 7. Adapted from H. C. Blodgett, "The effect of the introduction of reward upon the maze performance of rats." *University of California Publications in Psychology*, 1929, Vol. 4, No. 8, pp. 113–134. Reprinted by permission of the University of California Press.

on Trial 4, not unlike that found for the control group for Trial 4. This change in performance as a function of finding reward on a single trial is even more dramatically revealed by the reduction of error scores made by Experimental Group II on Trial 8. Since the control group's gradual reduction in errors gives rise to the inference that the learning process does not take place rapidly, the results of Blodgett's study have been used to distinguish between learning and performance. Learning was obviously taking place for all animals; changes in performance were related to the presence or absence of reward.

## Acquisition and Maintenance

Having distinguished between the concepts of learning and performance, we should note two specific aspects of performance, namely, acquisition and maintenance. A look at a typical performance curve, as shown in Figure 1-4, reveals two phases. The first (A) has been designated as acquisition and consists of

the organism gradually approaching a performance asymptote. The next phase (B) consists of the subject, after nearing asymptote, continuing to respond at approximately this level of performance. This second performance phase has been designated maintenance behavior or steady-state responding.

Most learning experimenters have been interested in the acquisition phase, since it includes change in the organism's performance over trials, from which the learning process has been inferred. Referring back to Figure 1-3, the control group's reduction in errors over trials was used by Blodgett (1929) to make the inference that these animals were learning to make the correct response at each choice point in the maze. But maintenance behavior has also interested investigators. Most human behavior is maintenance behavior—behavior that has been acquired and continues to be maintained in order to enable individuals to successfully operate in their environment.

The basic task of the psychologist has been to identify those variables that influence acquisition as well as maintenance. But how should such an investigation proceed? Before answering this question, we must first consider the framework within which most current learning experiments have been conducted—a framework that can be described as behavioristic.

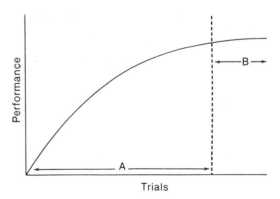

FIGURE 1-4. Hypothetical learning curve revealing acquisition phase (A) and maintenance phase (B).

## THE LEGACY OF BEHAVIORISM

Behaviorism, as a school of psychology, was founded by John B. Watson more than sixty years ago. Watson defined psychology not as the science of the mind, the then popular point of view, but rather as the science of behavior. Two basic tenets emerged from Watson's position. First, he stated that investigators should begin with what they can observe and postulate as little as possible beyond that. He rejected introspection as a method and abandoned the use of mentalistic and/or subjective constructs, which had been considered by many earlier psychologists to make up an individual's mind or conscious content. Watson argued that no one can "see" the thoughts and feelings of another individual, so these processes available only to the individual cannot be used as subject matter for a science. Such constructs as images, feelings, and memory were all considered "private" and unsuitable for use in a science of psychology.[3]

Second, Watson proposed that the scientific investigation of behavior be conducted by analyzing any act, whether learned or innate, in terms of a stimulus and a response. The environment provided a stimulus that elicited a response in the organism. A response was defined as some movement of a muscle or secretion of a gland. The task of the psychologist was to (1) determine the stimulus that was responsible for eliciting a response, and (2) predict the response from one's knowledge of the nature of the stimulus.

It is difficult to convey the importance of Watson's work, not only for psychologists, but for the public as well. When one of Watson's (1924) books, *Behaviorism*, was reviewed, the *New York Tribune* indicated it to be perhaps the most important book ever written, while the *New York Times* reported that the book marked an epoch in the intellectual history of humanity.

Watson's position was not met by universal acceptance. Although all of the objections that critics have raised cannot be presented, a few can be cited. Watson's assumption that behavior, and learning in particular, consisted of an association between an external stimulus and an overt response has been likened to the operation of an old-fashioned telephone switchboard where one caller gets "hooked up" with another on a one-to-one basis. This position has been regarded by most investigators as either a gross oversimplification of most human behavior or patently false. Such a position cannot explain the flexibility of response that is so characteristic of humans when placed in new situations. Much of our problem-solving behavior, for example, reflects an originality of responding that contradicts a theoretical framework of relatively rigid associative connections between a stimulus and a response.

Moreover, many experimenters believe that we must examine cognitive constructs if we are to adequately understand the learning process. These investigators have noted the importance of such concepts as images, plans, and strategies in providing a more adequate understanding of how learning takes place; although admittedly the definition, manipulation, and control of cognitive variables is difficult.

## A CURRENT POINT OF VIEW

"Stimulus" and "response" are concepts frequently found in the psychological literature, but most investigators today use these terms only to provide a framework for the study of learning. Experimenters are concerned with the prediction of behavior, so the organism's overt responses are obviously of major importance; in fact, these responses represent the dependent variable, or measure from which learning is inferred. Since such behavior takes place within the context of a stimulus situation, it is necessary to examine this aspect of learning as well. (The word "stimulus" is used only as a synonym for the term task or event—the environmental setting within which the learning process takes place.)

In addition to stimulus and response, we can add a third construct—the organism's central state or internal environment. Thus, investigators study those variables and/or processes that take place within the experimental subject and make a contribution to the nature of the learned response. The importance of recognizing the contribution of organismic or central state variables was pointed out by Woodworth and Schlosberg (1954) more than two decades ago; they wrote that the aim of the experimenter is to discover what goes on in the organism between the stimulus and the motor response.

Three constructs—the stimulus or task, the central state of the organism, and the response—provide a general framework for examining the learning process. Let us look at each of these in more detail.

### The Task or Stimulus Situation

The learning task can be described as an event or stimulus situation that is presented to the subject by the experimenter. Early investigators were concerned with examining some aspect of the task in an effort to determine its effect on learning. Verbal-learning investigators, for example, attempted to determine whether the characteristics of the nonsense syllables on the experimental list, an obvious task variable, played a role in the subject's acquisition of the list.

Although the learning task can be described in terms of the external stimuli presented to the subject, it is now obvious that the subject responds to only a few of the many stimuli presented. Since there is a difference between the stimuli that make up the task and the specific stimuli that the subject responds to, many psychologists have distinguished between them. The stimuli provided to the subject by the experimenter have been designated nominal stimuli, whereas functional stimuli are the stimuli as perceived and responded to by the subject. Each investigator hopes that there is an identity between the nominal and functional stimuli. But such is not always the case. One example of this disparity is found in a verbal-learning study reported by Underwood (1963). The task consisted of subjects learning to associate a trigram—three unrelated letters, such as XFT—with a three-letter word, e.g., GAS. Eight of these trigram-word combinations made up the list. There was no

physical similarity among the trigrams, since twenty-four different letters were used in constructing them. Following the completion of the task, the subjects were questioned as to how they had formed associations between each pair of items on the list. Underwood reported that a majority of the subjects stated that they had used only the first letter of the trigram as the stimulus to cue the response. Although the nominal stimulus consisted of three letters, the functional stimulus for most subjects was only the initial one.

### The Organism's Central State

Many experimenters now believe that they must examine the organism's central state, cognitive variables, if an adequate understanding of the learning process is to be achieved. Experiments that deal only with the analysis of external stimulus–overt response relationships are believed to be too limited in their approach to adequately describe the learning process. But if one acknowledges Watson's concern about working only with events that are observable, how does one go about investigating those constructs that are inaccessible to the experimenter?

One answer to this problem stems from the work of Hull (1943), who stressed the role of intervening variables or hypothetical constructs in behavior theory. Hull pointed out that physical and biological scientists have frequently used intervening variables to represent entities that cannot be physically seen or measured directly, but nonetheless can be hypothesized to account for certain events (such as electrons, genes, etc.). Hull emphasized that behavioral scientists must do the same. He recognized, however, that when such constructs are posited, they must be anchored or related to some antecedent (stimulus) condition that can be measured, as well as to a consequent condition (namely, the organism's response) that, of course, can also be measured.

The use of an intervening-variable approach has been of inestimable value in the psychologist's attempt to work with central-state variables, particularly those which have been designated as cognitive and motivational. Let us examine one example.

Intuitively, most people acknowledge that motivation makes an important contribution to behavior—the success individuals have in school, in athletics, or on the job is frequently attributed to motivation. Webster defines a motive as "a need or desire which prompts an organism to act in a certain way." Since needs and desires are not subject to direct observation and measurement, the psychologist's approach has been to conceptualize motivation as an intervening variable, anchored to both specific antecedent and consequent conditions.

Since organisms need nourishment to survive, depriving an organism of food for a specific number of hours (the antecedent condition) and then measuring some resultant behavior (the consequent condition) represented a first step in studying motivation. An early experiment of this type was conducted by Richter (1922), who found that the activity of the rat, as measured on an exercise or activity wheel, could be related to the length of time it was deprived of food.

Many psychologists after Richter adopted this approach in studying motivation—or drive, as they frequently termed this motivational construct. The word *drive* was used to emphasize that biological needs appeared to "drive" the organism to activity. Since motivation or drive was grounded in specific deprivation and behavioral measurements, it is not surprising that motivation, at least as related to the organism's biological need states, was acknowledged to be an appropriate construct in the behaviorist's analysis of behavior.

The problem of analyzing motivation grows more complex when attempts are made to identify and measure constructs that do not appear to be tied to the biological requirements of the organism. However, this section is not meant to provide a systematic examination of motivation, but only to demonstrate how it is possible to study central-state or organismic variables that influence behavior.

Cognitive processes represent a second central-state variable that demands consideration if one is to understand the nature of learn-ing. A cognitive process is defined as a subject's ideas, images, expectancies, hypotheses, strategies, etc.—our concern with them is how they contribute to learning.

Although Watson and the early behaviorists did not believe that cognitive variables or processes should be included in the study of behavior, many investigators today have pointed out that excluding their contribution may do irreparable harm to the understanding of the learning process. Razran (1971), for example, has written that recourse to cognitive variables is essential to the meaningful comprehension of the principles of learning. He suggested that, at a minimum, awareness, affect, images, and meanings must be studied for such comprehension. His twenty-five years of experimental work in conditioning human subjects suggests the importance of identifying such processes in order to understand even this simple type of learning task. Many psychologists would not agree on the importance of the specific cognitive constructs that Razran has delineated, but they would acknowledge that the identification of cognitive variables is necessary for any adequate examination of learning.

Since cognitive variables are private events, there is a problem in identifying and measuring them. But like motivational variables, they can be conceptualized as intervening variables, with their measurement tied to specific conditions and consequent behavior. The search for appropriate consequent behavior or public indicators of these cognitive variables has been an active one. When humans are used as subjects, verbal behavior becomes one such indicator. Although use of such overt responding is not without its problems, it can provide the experimenter with some valuable insights about the role of cognitive processing in human learning. There is hope that other response measures, perhaps of a physiological nature, will also contribute to solving this problem.[4]

### The Response

As we have stated earlier, the psychologist must use changes in the organism's response or effector system to infer the presence of the learning process. The responses from which such an inference is made will vary markedly in complexity and kind. In some studies, the response may be quite complex—for instance, a college student solving a difficult mathematical problem. In other instances, the response may be as simple as a rat pressing a bar, or a student closing an eye.

In addition to differing in complexity, responses differ as to the kind of effector innervated. Responses have been differentiated on the basis of whether the effector is controlled by the central nervous system or the autonomic nervous system. The autonomic nervous system exercises control over the functioning of glands and smooth muscles, e.g., salivation, dilation or constriction of the pupil, whereas the central nervous system controls responses involving our striped musculature. Although subjects can exercise direct control over the striped muscles, it has been accepted by most experimenters that control over autonomic responses is not possible, at least without a period of training.

Some learning theorists have not been concerned by the distinctions enumerated here. That is, they have assumed that the principles governing the learning process and the modification of behavior are quite general and may be inferred from either simple or complex responses and without regard to the specific nervous system involved.

Other theorists, however, have assumed that the learning principles involved are different, depending on whether the learned response is controlled by the central or autonomic nervous system. It is not our intent to discuss these theoretical considerations, since this is an issue that transcends any discussion of response measures. However, it should be pointed out that the theoretical predilection of the investigator may play an important role in determining the kind of response used to infer the learning process.

## LEARNING TAXONOMIES

A recurring problem in the investigation of learning has been the lack of a taxonomy—an arrangement or classification scheme enabling investigators to study their subject matter with maximum efficiency. The early naturalists could identify thousands of plants and animals, but their inability to provide a universally accepted classification system led to considerable confusion. Since the naturalists of each country had their own system, effective communication among them was impossible. It was not until the middle of the eighteenth century that a Swedish naturalist, Linnaeus, introduced the binomial method of scientific nomenclature that has become the basis of the classification system used today. In chemistry, it was a Russian, Mendeleev, who classified the known chemical elements in an arrangement now known as the periodic table. With this classification, Mendeleev was able to predict the existence of elements yet to be discovered.

Psychology has not had its Linnaeus or Mendeleev, and as a result there is no single taxonomy accepted by most investigators as a completely adequate way to classify tasks and/or processes found in the study of learning. This is not to say that classification schemes have not been proposed. Some have been based on the type of task used to examine the learning process, obvious examples being problem-solving or motor-skills tasks. Other investigators have suggested a taxonomy based on whether the response is controlled by the autonomic or central nervous system. Still others have provided taxonomies based on the kinds of experimental operations utilized.

Some of these classifications have proved satisfactory for handling a limited number of studies, but no single taxonomy has successfully classified all of the experimental investigations in the learning area. And yet, it is necessary to provide some classification or ordering, if for no other reason than to provide the reader with an appropriate development and/or logical succession of topics to be covered.

The organization of this text reflects most of the major topics found in current examinations of learning. In Chapter 2, the kinds of learning tasks used by Pavlov, Bechterev, Thorndike, Skinner, and others are described in some detail, and with reference to classical and instrumental conditioning. In Chapters 3 and 4, the contribution of a variety of experimental variables to the ease or difficulty of such conditioning is examined.

Discrimination learning is discussed in Chapter 5. Although frequently included within the classical and instrumental conditioning framework, it has been given separate consideration here since many of the experimental studies and the theoretical explanations for this type of learning task stand apart from those described in earlier chapters.

In Chapters 6 and 7 two processes, experimental extinction and stimulus generalization, are examined. These processes operate in all of the tasks described and play an important role in learning. Chapter 8 discusses the applicability for human beings of learning principles that have been found to operate with animals.

Chapters 9 through 12 describe verbal-learning and memory tasks. Many investigators, beginning with Ebbinghaus, have been concerned primarily with the learning and remembering of lists of verbal materials. Chapters 9 and 10 describe some of the experimental work that has been carried out in this tradition. Chapters 11 and 12 present a different approach to the study of verbal learning. Investigators have likened the organism's memory to a computer, with encoding, storage, and retrieval representing the basic constructs to be examined. The verbal-learning and memory area is concluded in Chapter 12 with a discussion of memory for two kinds of material, prose and faces. Finally, in Chapter 13 experimental work examining the learning of motor skills is discussed.

## SUMMARY

Learning occupies a central place in the lives of most individuals. Its contribution extends far beyond the role it plays in our formal educational experiences. The experimental investigation of learning began with the work of a German scientist, Ebbinghaus. Ebbinghaus was inspired by the work of an earlier German philosopher and physicist, Gustav Fechner, who had developed a method for measuring the mental process of sensation. Ebbinghaus was interested in determining how the process of learning could be examined. For his experimental work, he used the nonsense syllable. The task Ebbinghaus set for himself was to learn varying lists of these units and then examine how a number of conditions (e.g., length of the list) contributed to learning. List learning thus became a basic task in the study of verbal learning.

A decade after Ebbinghaus began his experimental studies, the Russian physiologist Pavlov, while examining the digestive process, found that one of the elements of digestion, salivation, could be elicited in dogs by the footsteps of the caretaker walking across the floor. The capacity of such "neutral" stimuli to elicit salivation aroused Pavlov's interest. He identified the response elicited by such neutral stimuli as being "conditioned" and devoted the remainder of his life to studying this phenomenon.

American investigators became interested in animal learning around the turn of the century. Thorndike had cats and chickens learn to escape from problem or puzzle boxes, whereas another experimenter, Small, investigated maze learning with rats. Some years later, Skinner invented the Skinner box, a basic apparatus in which rats learn to press a bar in order to secure food or water.

A description of the basic learning experiments does not, however, define the concept of learning. There has been some controversy regarding an appropriate definition of this construct. Investigators have adopted a definition stating that learning is an organismic process arising from the organism's experience and inferred from changes in the organism's behavior. Although the definition is admittedly imprecise, this is not a serious handicap. If experimenters can agree on the type of experimental operation to be used and the kind of behavior change to be measured, the study of learning can proceed.

## NOTES

1. Nonsense syllables used by Ebbinghaus and current investigators consist of consonant-vowel-consonant units that do not form a word, and are called CVCs. Examples are WIJ, JAF, XEG, YIC. Ebbinghaus believed these units were devoid of associations and thus were equivalent in the ease with which they could be learned. Further discussion of the properties of CVCs is found in Chapter 9.

2. This approach brings to mind the controversy among physicists regarding the nature of light. For some, light was defined by reference to wave theory; others preferred to define light in terms of quantum theory. The failure to agree on a definition did not preclude research in the area.

3. The puzzled reader may ask how Watson hoped to investigate behavior without using these entities—concepts that all of us use from time to time to "explain" our behavior. Watson denied the existence of some of these concepts; others he preferred to conceptualize in terms of overt behavior. Two examples can be provided. Mental images were denied altogether—they were only the ghosts of sensations. People were deluding themselves, Watson wrote, if they believed they had images. Thinking, on the other hand, was considered nothing more than subvocal speech, with Watson writing that what psychologists had hitherto called thought was in short nothing but talking to ourselves. The validity of Watson's assertions has, of course, been challenged.

4. Increased interest in dreaming, certainly a most private kind of event, has been largely attributable to Dement and Kleitman's (1957) discovery that rapid-eye movements during sleep (a public indicant) are correlated with subjective reports of dreaming.

# CHAPTER TWO

# Classical and Instrumental Conditioning: General Considerations

The experimental procedure utilized by Pavlov consisted of presenting his dogs with a tone followed a few seconds later by meat powder which elicited salivation and chewing movements. Pavlov found that after a number of such pairings of stimuli, the presentation of the tone would elicit salivation. In contrast, the procedure used by Thorndike consisted of providing reward only after his subjects had made an appropriate response; his cats had to first pull a string that opened a cage door prior to receiving food. It was only after a number of trials that the animals learned to pull the string soon after being placed in the cage.

Until the end of the 1930s, the term conditioning was used to describe the types of learning tasks utilized by both Pavlov and Thorndike. But Skinner (1938), and then Hilgard and Marquis (1940), proposed that a distinction be made between these types of learning tasks. Hilgard and Marquis's distinction, which is similar to Skinner's, has been the most frequently used. These authors proposed that Pavlovian type tasks be designated as classical conditioning. The procedure used in such tasks was a consistent presentation of the two stimuli (tone and meat powder in Pavlov's experiments) regardless of the response made by the experimental subject. Instrumental conditioning was used to identify Thorn-

dikian type tasks. Here, reward was provided only after the subject had made an appropriate response; thus, the response was instrumental to securing reward.

The difference between classical and instrumental conditioning can be related to what investigators have described as response contingency (or noncontingency), aptly illustrated in a study conducted by Wahlsten and Cole (1972). Their experimental procedure involved suspending a dog in a canvas hammock, with four holes in the canvas permitting the animal to extend its legs so that the feet were several inches off the floor. An electrode was attached to one paw to provide a mild shock, which in turn elicited a paw flexing response. The Pavlovian or classical conditioning procedure consisted of the presentation of a tone for 2 seconds, *always* followed by a .5 second shock. After a number of presentations of tone and shock, the tone would elicit the flexing response.

The instrumental conditioning operation also used tone and shock. The conditions were so arranged, however, that if the flexion response took place within the 2 second presentation of the tone, shock was omitted. Here, the omission of shock was *contingent* on whether the appropriate response was made. Both procedures resulted in the experimental animals learning to flex their paws to the tone, but significant differences in responding were noted. The percentage of conditioned responses exhibited over the first eight training periods and near asymptote was significantly higher for the instrumental conditioning group. In addition, an examination of conditioned response latencies revealed different distributions for the two groups. Latencies for the classical conditioning group were quite skewed, with most responses taking place just prior to the US (unconditioned stimulus); for the instrumental group, responses occurred most frequently just following the onset of the CS (conditioned stimulus). Figures 2-1 and 2-2 present these data.

The different operations used in classical and instrumental conditioning and the different experimental findings have caused some investigators to decide that each procedure re-

flects the operation of a different learning principle. It has been suggested, for example, that classical conditioning involves the principle of contiguity and is responsible for the modification of glandular and visceral responses that are largely controlled by the autonomic nervous system. The contiguity principle states that stimuli which are closely paired in time become associated one with the other.

Instrumental conditioning has been assumed to be responsible for the modification of skeletal responses, which are controlled by the somatic nervous system, and involves the principle of reinforcement. This principle states that the probability of a response being made in the learning task will increase if it is followed by reinforcement, although a precise definition of reinforcement has not been agreed upon. The skeletal response that

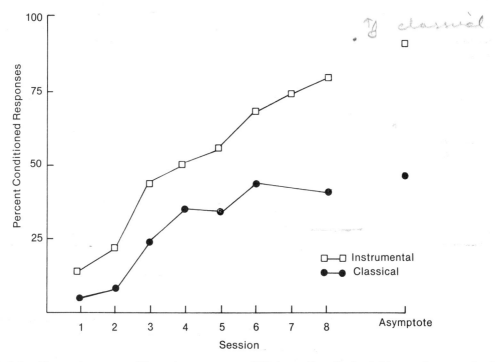

FIGURE 2-1. Percentage conditioned responses (CRs) on the first eight sessions and at asymptote for the classical and instrumental training groups. Adapted from Douglas L. Wahlsten and Michael Cole, "Classical and Avoidance Training of Leg Flexion in the Dog," in *Classical Conditioning II: Current Research and Theory*, © 1972, pp. 379–408. Reprinted by permission of Prentice-Hall, Inc., Englewood Cliffs, N.J.

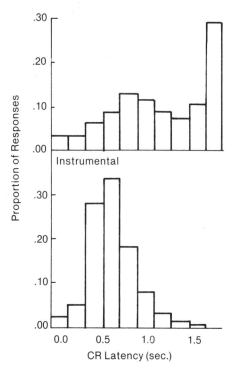

FIGURE 2-2. Distributions of CR latencies for the classical and instrumental conditioning groups. Adapted from Douglas L. Wahlsten and Michael Cole, "Classical and Avoidance Training of Leg Flexion in the Dog," in *Classical Conditioning II: Current Research and Theory*, © 1972, pp. 378–408. Reprinted by permission of Prentice-Hall, Inc., Englewood Cliffs, N.J.

Thorndike's cats acquired in order to escape from the puzzle box was learned because it was followed by reinforcement.

Other investigators have assumed that only a single principle is necessary to account for the learning of both skeletal and autonomic responses. The controversy has been a long and continuing one, as Hearst's (1975) examination of the issue reveals. Although many "critical" experiments have been conducted to demonstrate the failure or inadequacy of one position or the other, it seems evident that the controversy will remain with us for some time. Few controversies in psychology are settled by "crucial" experiments;

invariably investigators who support the discredited position can point to deficiencies in the "crucial" experiment or modify their position in order to account for the findings that are not in keeping with their position.

Regardless of the number of principles operating, the end product obtained in both classical and instrumental conditioning is the subject's establishment of associative relationships among the events that comprise each task. Thus, classical and instrumental conditioning tasks must be viewed as reflecting only different operations that experimenters have used in an effort to examine how varying experimental conditions influence the associative process. However, since each task employs different operations, it seems reasonable to examine them separately.

## CLASSICAL CONDITIONING

Pavlov's work, which was described briefly in Chapter 1, was the first *experimental* investigation of classical conditioning. Note that we have emphasized the word "experimental," since many individuals were aware of this procedure long before Pavlov conducted his experiments. For example, Bernard, in his lecture series in Paris circa 1885, described the salivary conditioning of a horse; see Rosenzweig (1959).

Pavlov's technique consisted of surgically transplanting the opening of the dog's salivary ducts from inside the mouth to outside. Such an operation permitted the animal's salivation to be measured more easily. After the effect of the surgery had worn off, Pavlov trained his animals to stand quietly in a loose harness on a table in a sound-deadened room. Seven or eight seconds after the sounding of a metronome or tuning fork, a small quantity of meat powder was moved within reach of the animal's mouth. The first presentation of the sound did not elicit salivation; but after a number of pairings of the two stimuli, Pavlov noted that salivation was elicited by the tone. A conditioned response had been established.

◼ BOX 2-1 ◼

Some secondary sources have given credit for the discovery of the conditioned response to an American, E. B. Twitmyer. Twitmyer (1902), a graduate student at the
University of Pennsylvania, published a Ph.D. dissertation describing his accidental
discovery of the conditioned response. Twitmyer was interested in investigating the
nature of the knee jerk. He used the ringing of a bell to prepare his subjects to receive simultaneous blows on each patellar tendon, which in turn elicited this response in both legs. Twitmyer described his discovery as follows:

> During the adjustment of the apparatus for an earlier group of experiments with one
> subject (Subject A) a decided kick of both legs was observed to follow a tap of the signal
> bell occurring without the usual blow of the hammers on the tendons. It was at first be-
> lieved that the subject had merely voluntarily kicked out the legs, but upon being ques-
> tioned, he stated that although quite conscious of the movement as it was taking place,
> it had not been caused by a volitional effort, and further, that the subjective feeling
> accompanying the movement was similar to the feeling of the movement following the
> blow on the tendons with the exception that he was quite conscious that the tendons
> had not been struck. Two alternatives presented themselves. Either (1) the subject was
> in error in his introspective observation and had voluntarily moved his legs, or (2) the
> true knee jerk (or a movement resembling it in appearance) had been produced by a
> stimulus other than the usual one. (p. 1059)

Twitmyer found that many of his other subjects responded similarly and concluded that "The occurrence of the kick without the blow on the tendons cannot be
explained as a mere accidental movement on the part of the subjects. On the contrary, the phenomenon occurs with sufficient frequency and regularity to demand
an inquiry as to its nature" (p. 1061). Unfortunately, American investigators were not
sufficiently curious to further examine this phenomenon.

However, Pavlov had been examining salivary conditioning for some time prior
to Twitmyer's accidental discovery of the conditioned knee jerk response. Pavlov's
discussion of a variety of conditioning phenomena, given to the plenary session of
the International Medical Congress in Madrid in 1903, would indicate that his experimental investigations undoubtedly commenced prior to 1900.

Pavlov's experiments were of basic importance since they enabled him to study a
higher nervous system activity, learning, by
purely objective means, and without speculation about the conscious experience of his animals. The salivary response, which he described as a rather inconsequential function,
served only as an objective measure from
which the properties of the nervous system
could be inferred. Pavlov's emphasis on objec-
tivity was not unique but in keeping with the
position of many other scientists of his time,
such as Beer, Bethe, and von Uexküll, all of
whom had called for the use of completely objective methods in studying behavior.

Pavlov believed that it was important to
provide specific designations for the stimuli
and responses used in his procedure, and sub-

sequent experimenters have continued to employ his terminology. In the experiment cited,
the two stimuli Pavlov utilized were designated as the unconditioned stimulus (US) and
the conditioned stimulus (CS). The unconditioned stimulus was the meat powder; more
generally, the US is defined as a stimulus that
will elicit a regular and measurable response
over an extended series of presentations. The
conditioned stimulus that Pavlov paired with
the US was the tone. By definition, conditioned stimuli are neutral; that is, they are not
capable at the beginning of the experiment of
eliciting any of the responses that can be
elicited by the US.

Pavlov observed three different responses. First, he noted that his animals frequently looked at the tuning fork or metro-

US → CS → UR.

nome which produced the CS. Pavlov termed such "looking" an investigatory reflex, although current investigators describe it as an orienting response (OR). Experimenters now point out that all of the varying skeletal and autonomic responses elicited by the CS should be identified as orienting responses. The contribution of orienting responses to the conditioning procedure is being investigated. For example, Vinogradova (1965) has suggested that a stimulus must be capable of eliciting an orienting response if that stimulus is to later serve as a successful CS—a CS which, after pairing with a US, will have the capacity to elicit a CR.

He called the second response, which was elicited by the US, the unconditioned response (UR). In Pavlov's experiments, the salivation and all of the other responses elicited by the meat powder, e.g., tongue and jaw movements, chewing, etc., would be identified as unconditioned responses.

The third response is the conditioned response (CR), which in Pavlov's study consisted of the dog salivating to the tone. Early investigators made the assumption that the conditioned response was either the same as the unconditioned response or a component part of it. For example, salivation is a part of the more complex eating response elicited by the meat powder. Figure 2-3 illustrates this point of view. Both the CS and US appear to elicit the same response.

Most investigators now consider classical conditioning merely an operation in which the pairing of the CS and US results in the CS eliciting a response different from that which the CS could elicit prior to the pairing oper-

ation. Such a consideration does not require that there be an identity or similarity between the CR and UR, although frequently this is the case.

**Experimental Extinction and Spontaneous Recovery**    Pavlov's experimental investigations extended for more than two decades. One basic problem which concerned him was how conditioned responses could be eliminated. He found that following the establishment of a conditioned response, the repeated presentation of the tone without the meat powder led to a decrease in conditioned responding. After a number of CS alone trials, the CR could no longer be elicited by presenting the CS. Pavlov termed this decline in responding **experimental extinction**. The term is now used not only to describe the operation (presenting the CS without pairing it with the US), but also to indicate the decrement in responding which takes place as a function of the CS alone trials. An example of the extinction of a conditioned salivary response, as reported by Pavlov, is found in Figure 2-4.

Pavlov also found that if his subjects were provided with a rest period following the response decrement, which arose from the extinction operation, the presentation of the CS would once again result in the conditioned response being elicited. The strength of this response was somewhat diminished. This recovery of an extinguished response after an interval of rest was termed **spontaneous recovery**.

Since Pavlov was interested in how the nervous system functioned, it is not surprising that he speculated about the physiological processes that he believed were responsible for the acquisition and extinction of the conditioned response. Pavlov assumed there was the growth and development of an excitatory process during the presentation of CS-US trials. He speculated that a pathway was established in the brain between the neural representation of the CS and the CR. Extinction trials resulted in the development of an inhibitory process. The presentation of the CS alone trials resulted in the growth of an inhibitory state, which accumulated in sufficient strength

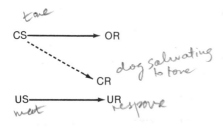

FIGURE 2-3.    Typical diagram depicting the classical conditioning procedure.

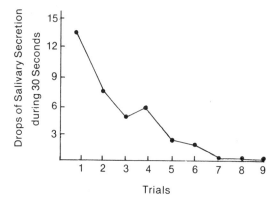

FIGURE 2-4.   The conditioned stimulus (CS) was presented once every 3 minutes without the unconditioned stimulus. Plotted from data provided by Pavlov (1927).

in the brain to temporarily block the previously established CS-CR pathway. But this inhibitory state dissipated with rest, so that eventually the CS would again elicit the CR. Pavlov's theory of inhibition was quite complex, involving inhibition arising from both internal and external sources. Although current physiologists have found little neurological evidence to support Pavlov's theorizing, the interested reader can refer to Kimble (1961) or Hall (1976) for Pavlov's description of the operation of these processes.

**Higher Order Conditioning**   A final conditioning phenomenon has been identified as higher order conditioning. Following the establishment of a conditioned response, the experimenter may provide the subject with additional trials in which a new CS (CS$_2$) is paired with the previously utilized CS (CS$_1$). In effect, the original CS serves as a US. After a number of pairings of CS$_2$-CS$_1$, the CS$_2$ becomes capable of eliciting the CR, with the phenomenon being identified as higher order conditioning.

An illustration of the procedure is found in one of Pavlov's early experiments. The ticking of a metronome (CS) followed by the presentation of meat powder (US) resulted in the metronome eliciting salivation. Following

such training, a visual stimulus in the form of a black square (CS$_2$) was paired with the metronome (CS). By the tenth pairing, the black square was capable of eliciting salivation, although the response was only half as strong as that elicited by the original CS.

The capacity of a CS$_2$ to elicit the CR has been also identified as second order conditioning. Third order conditioning procedures would involve the presentation of a CS$_3$ paired with the CS$_2$, which in turn had been previously paired with a CS$_1$.

Higher order conditioning generated little enthusiasm among investigators in the United States until the 1970s, when Rescorla and his associates became interested in this type of conditioning procedure. The stability of second order conditioned responses, which Pavlov (1927) had earlier assumed to be quite fragile, was demonstrated in a series of conditioning experiments using both aversive and appetitive unconditioned stimuli; see Rizley and Rescorla (1972), Holland and Rescorla (1975).

In the latter study, first order conditioning was established by presenting hungry rats with a light flashing off and on for 12 seconds. Ten seconds after light onset, two food pellets were presented. The animal's response to the delivery of food in the experimental cage was increased activity; such activity, the CR, was measured as the animal moved around in its cage.

Following a training period in which the experimental animals received 84 light-food presentations over a period of eleven days, second order conditioning was undertaken. The animals received a total of 16 presentations of 10 seconds of a clicker (CS$_2$) followed by 10 seconds of flashing light (CS$_1$).

The number of responses/minute elicited by the clicker increased steadily over the 16 trials, clearly demonstrating second order conditioning. Appropriate control groups, on the other hand, revealed a decline in responding.

The thrust of Rescorla's work has indicated that the learning principles observed to operate with second order conditioning are similar to those operating with first order conditioning, although marked differences can be observed. Such differences suggest that second order conditioning is not a weaker form of first order conditioning. Further discussion would take us too far afield in this introductory presentation, but Rescorla's findings do have relevance for a better understanding of the learning process involved in classical conditioning.

### Methodological Considerations

In our examination of classical conditioning, several methodological issues should be considered. These are (1) the nature of the CS-US presentations, (2) the measurement of the conditioned response, and (3) the characteristics of the control group.

**The Nature of the CS-US Presentation** Pavlov's conditioning procedure consisted of presenting the CS a few seconds prior to the presentation of the US. He became interested, as did subsequent investigators, in examining the role that this CS-US sequence played in the establishment of the conditioned response. The three basic CS-US sequences have been identified as (1) forward, (2) simultaneous, and (3) backward.

Forward conditioning is a procedure in which the onset of the CS occurs prior to the onset of the US, while simultaneous conditioning refers to simultaneous onset of the CS and the US. Backward conditioning, of course, refers to the onset of the US being provided prior to the onset of the CS.

With the forward conditioning paradigm, the termination of the CS can be manipulated, resulting in either a delayed or a trace procedure. Delayed conditioning, which is the most frequently employed procedure, consists of the CS continuing until the US is presented, at which time it may either be continued or be terminated.

The trace procedure consists of presenting and terminating the CS prior to the onset of the US. In this procedure, an interval of time occurs between the termination of the CS and the onset of the US. The term trace arises from the assumption that it is the neural trace

left by the presentation of the CS that actually serves as the CS. Figure 2-5 describes these varying CS-US relationships.

Studies examining the varying procedures have indicated that the simultaneous and backward paradigms are not very effective in establishing stable conditioned responses. In fact, some experimenters are of the opinion that conditioned responses cannot be acquired using the backward conditioning procedure. Pavlov's position on this issue was equivocal. He first indicated that with a backward pairing of stimuli the conditioned reflex could not be established at all, but shortly thereafter he revised his position, believing that such conditioning was possible though unstable. Current investigators have reported both success and failure in demonstrating backward conditioning. A working hypothesis would suggest that the backward conditioning procedure can be used to establish some kinds of conditioned responses but not others. Stern and Frey (1978) have not been able to demonstrate conditioning of the rabbit's eyelid response using a US-CS procedure, but some investigators have been successful in backward conditioning a generalized emotional response; see Heth and Rescorla (1973), or Mahoney and Ayres (1976).

When a forward conditioning experiment is undertaken, it is necessary to decide whether to use a delayed or a trace procedure. Manning, Schneiderman, and Lordahl (1969) found that delayed conditioning was superior to trace when conditioning the heart rate of the rabbit. The length of the trace was either 2, 9, or 26 seconds. On the other hand, Ross, Ross, and Werden (1974) examined trace and delayed procedures with human eyelid conditioning and found no differences in response between the two procedures. The length of the trace interval used by these investigators was quite short, ranging from .75 to 1.35 seconds.

These studies suggest that the critical feature in any comparison between the delay and trace procedures is the length of the trace. If the trace is long, delayed conditioning appears to be superior; if it is short, little difference may be observed between the two procedures.

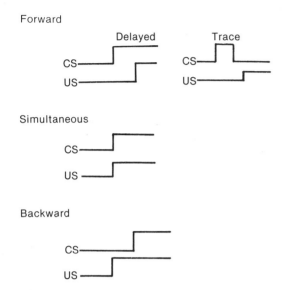

FIGURE 2-5. Forward, simultaneous, and backward conditioning paradigms, with the delayed and trace conditions illustrated.

**Response Measurement**   The second methodological issue is how the CR should be measured. Generally, CRs are measured during acquisition trials, with measures of (1) frequency, (2) latency, and (3) amplitude of the response being obtained. Frequency refers to the number or percentage of times that the CS is able to elicit the CR over the course of the CS-US presentations. **Latency** is the length of time it takes the CR to appear, as measured from the onset of the CS to the onset of the CR. **Amplitude** refers to the amount or size of the CR.

Investigators have also measured resistance to extinction. This is a convenient response measure, since the "conditioned" response cannot be influenced by the presentation of the US. However, the use of this measure is now on the wane. One reason for the decrease in use is that correlational studies revealed no relationship between the strength of conditioning, as measured by extinction, and response measures obtained during acquisition trials; see Brogden (1949), Hall and Kobrick (1952). An increasing number of ex-

perimenters have concluded that extinction appears to be a measure of persistence and not an indicator of the strength of the conditioned response.

*Measurement of More Than a Single Response*   It has been a common practice of experimenters to employ only a single response measure in their conditioning experiments. One recent development, however, has been the measurement of two or three responses. Such a practice demands that the same US be capable of eliciting all URs, in order for the accompanying CRs to be recorded.

A study by Yehle (1968) illustrates multiple response recording. Yehle used rabbits as his experimental subjects, with a classically conditioned discrimination task. With this type of classical conditioning, one CS (CS+), always followed by the US, is presented to the subject on some trials, while a different CS (CS−), which is never followed by the US, is presented on other trials. (See Chapter 5 for a fuller description of this type of task.) Different frequencies of a tone served as the CS+ and CS−, whereas shock was used as the US to elicit (a) the nictitating membrane response, (b) changes in heart rate, and (c) changes in respiration rate. (The nictitating membrane is a curved plate of cartilage which can be drawn laterally across the cornea in response to an airpuff directed at the eye.)

The percentages of conditioned responses to presentation of the CS+ are presented in Figure 2-6. As can be observed, heart rate responses appeared at full strength on the first 2 days of training, whereas nictitating membrane responses increased from almost 0 on Day 1 of training to a high value on Day 8. Respiration rate responses rose to a maximum on Days 2 and 3 and then exhibited a slow decline.

The implication of Yehle's findings is that no single type of acquisition curve will accommodate the "learning" of different responses even though each response has arisen from the same effector system. How rapidly a response can be "conditioned" not only is a function of the varying conditions present

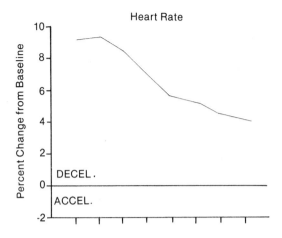

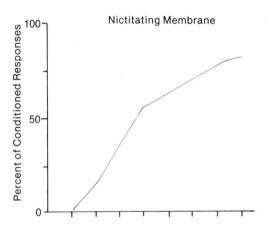

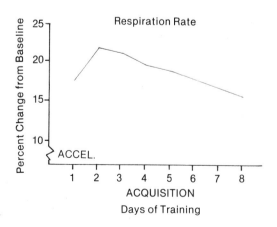

FIGURE 2-6.    Responses to the CS+ for each of three response systems. Adapted from A. L. Yehle (1968), "Divergencies among rabbit response systems during three-tone classical discrimination conditioning." *Journal of Experimental Psychology*, 1968, 77, 468–473. Copyright © 1968 by the American Psychological Association. Reprinted by permission.

during the conditioning trials (e.g., intensity of the CS), but also is determined by the kind of response measured.

**The Use of Control Groups**    The last methodological issue relates to the use of control groups. It has been assumed by many investigators that the establishment of a conditioned response results from a double stimulation procedure—the pairing of the CS with the US. But how do we know that conditioned responses are established because of such a pairing? Is it not possible that the CR may arise as a result of some particular experimental condition other than the pairing of stimuli?

In order to guard against this possibility, experimenters have compared the performance of the experimental group, the group receiving the CS-US pairings, with that of the control group. Traditionally, the control procedure has consisted of unpaired presentations of both the CS and the US, with these single presentations of stimuli occurring randomly. Other control procedures have occasionally been used, such as presentation of only the CS, but the unpaired presentation of the CS and US is by far the most frequently employed. The unpaired presentation procedure provides the control group with the opportunity to experience both the CS and the US, omitting only the paired presentation, which presumably is necessary for conditioning to take place. If the experimenter finds that the "conditioned" responses resulting from the paired presentation of stimuli cannot be distinguished from the responses arising from an unpaired presentation, the latter responses are identified as pseudoconditioned.

A provocative paper by Rescorla (1967) rejected the traditional assumption that the CR arises from the paired presentation of CS and US. Rescorla proposed that a CR was established because the experimental subject learned a contingency between the CS and US. A contingency differs from an association in that it is an association with a probability attached to it. The establishment of an association simply indicates that the US will follow the CS; the establishment of a contingency states that it is possible to assign some probability to the occurrence of the US following the CS.

The nature of the control group that an experimenter utilizes is related to the kinds of assumptions that are made about the learning process. Since Rescorla rejected the pairing operation as a necessary condition for the establishment of a conditioned response, he also rejected the use of the traditional control procedure described earlier. This procedure was methodologically inadequate, he pointed out, since the unpaired presentation of the CS and US provided control subjects with the opportunity to learn the contingency that the presentation of the CS would *not* be followed by the US. The learning of this contingency would produce inhibition, thus depressing the control group's performance; it would be a confounding variable in any comparison of the experimental group's and control group's performance.

In place of the traditional control group, Rescorla (1967) suggested the use of the "truly random" control. With this procedure ". . . both the CS and the US are presented to S [subject] but there is no contingency whatsoever between them. That is, the two events are programmed entirely randomly and independently in such a way that some 'pairings' of the CS and US may occur by chance alone" (p. 74).

More than a dozen investigators examining a variety of conditioned responses have been unable to find a difference in responses between the traditional control group and the truly random control group, thus suggesting that no methodological advantage is obtained when the latter type of control group is employed. In fact, Wasserman, Deich, Hunter, and Nagamatsu (1977) have indicated that the truly random control procedure may establish excitatory or inhibitory effects in the control group, thus nullifying its value as a control. One example is found in a study by Benedict

and Ayres (1972). They found that if the truly random control procedure fortuitously resulted in CS-US pairings early in the experimental session, some conditioning occurred.

Because many investigators have been unable to find any differences in performance between the traditional control group and the truly random control, the superiority of the latter type of control procedure remains to be established. It seems reasonable to suggest that both control procedures need to be investigated further in order to better understand the nature of their contribution to the experimental findings.

### What Responses Can Be Conditioned?

After Pavlov's experimental demonstration that the salivary response could be conditioned, a host of experimenters extended Pavlov's work and found a variety of other responses that could also be conditioned. Chief among these are the (1) galvanic skin or electrodermal response, (2) changes in the heart rate, (3) emotional responses, and (4) eyeblink and the movement of the nictitating membrane. Each of these responses will only be described briefly, since they will be discussed in subsequent chapters.

### The Galvanic Skin or Electrodermal Response

The galvanic skin or electrodermal response (GSR or EDR) is measured by placing two electrodes on the surface of the skin. When a weak direct current is provided, a voltage develops across these electrodes and it is possible to measure the skin's apparent resistance or conductance. It is a response measure often used in lie detection, since lying is generally an effective stimulus for its elicitation.

The GSR has two well-defined characteristics. First, it has a relatively long latency, ranging from 3 to 5 seconds, as measured from the onset of an eliciting stimulus. Second, the response is of long duration, requiring another 3 to 5 seconds in order to reach maximum amplitude.

An examination of the GSR response, as found in classical conditioning experiments that have used long CS presentations, reveals that it generally consists of three humps

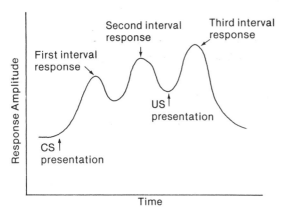

FIGURE 2-7.    Galvanic skin responses to the conditioned and unconditioned stimuli.

or components, as illustrated in Figure 2-7. The first component has been identified as an orientation response made first to the presentation of the CS, whereas the third component is elicited by the US. It is the second hump, often described as an anticipatory or second interval response, that has been acknowledged by many to reflect the "conditioned" response.[1] Many of the findings obtained in the early GSR conditioning studies are suspect, since these experimenters did not differentiate among the varying components. Thus, any "conditioned response" obtained was confounded by first and third interval components.

**Heart Rate**    The unusual aspect of heart rate conditioning is that the CR is represented by a *change* in rate. Watson (1916) made an early attempt to condition the heart rate in humans, but contemporary interest in conditioning this response began with a study by Notterman, Schoenfeld, and Bersh (1952), who used college students as subjects. The CS was a 750 Hz tone, with shock serving as the US. These experimenters found that after 11 CS-US pairings, they obtained a CR in the form of a reduction in the number of beats per minute. Many subsequent investigators working with animals as well as humans have reported successful attempts to condition heart rate. A puzzling aspect of these studies is that some experimenters have reported heart beat *acceleration* while others have found decelera-

tion. Still others have reported a biphasic cardiac response pattern. Here, during the initial seconds of the CS presentation, there is heart rate acceleration followed by deceleration during the terminal portion of CS presentation and prior to US onset. It is known, however, that the unconditioned response to an unconditioned stimulus of shock is an acceleration of the heart beat.

An interesting area of investigation has been the conditioning of heart rate when electrical stimulation to the brain is used as the US. Malmo (1964) has demonstrated that such stimulation to the lateral septal area of the rat's brain resulted in a slowing of the animal's heart rate. By pairing a tone with this kind of US, Malmo (1965) was able to demonstrate a conditioned response consisting of deceleration.

**Emotional Responses**    In contrast to the specificity of GSR and heart rate responses, the emotional response has been regarded as more complex and diffuse. It contains both autonomic and skeletal response components and is inferred from some behavioral indicator. The classical conditioning of such a response is found in the pioneer study of Watson and Rayner (1920). Their single subject, Albert, a child 11 months old, was not afraid of animals but had a distinct fear of loud noises. The experimental procedure consisted of presenting to Albert, who had been placed on a table, a white rat which served as a CS. A loud sound, produced by striking a steel bar with a hammer, served as the US. After just five presentations of the white rat and loud sound, the sight of the rat resulted in Albert's withdrawing and beginning to whimper. After two additional paired presentations, the authors report that the "instant the rat was shown alone, the baby began to cry. Almost instantly he turned sharply to the left, fell over on his left side, raised himself on all fours and began to crawl away so rapidly that he was caught with difficulty before reaching the edge of the table" (p. 5). It was evident that a conditioned emotional response had been established using a classical conditioning procedure.

The difficulties in obtaining human subjects to serve in emotional conditioning experiments of the type just described are obvious. In fact, psychologists now would not undertake this type of study because of ethical considerations. One alternative has been to use animals as subjects, but the question that immediately arises is how one measures emotionality in an animal. Estes and Skinner (1941) and Hunt and Brady (1951) have developed a widely used procedure for doing this.

Rats were first trained in a Skinner box to press a bar for food. Once the animals were bar pressing at a steady rate, the emotional conditioning stage of the experiment was instituted. The animals were placed in a different type of apparatus, and a tone (CS) was paired with the presentation of shock (US). The experimenters assumed that shock elicited an emotional response, so after the animals had been given a number of tone-shock pairings, the tone was expected to be capable of eliciting this response. Note, however, that no direct measurement of the emotional response was made. Following the conditioning trials, the animals were returned to the Skinner box, where they resumed pressing the bar for food. The tone (CS) was presented from time to time, with the experimenter noting how the rate of bar pressing changed as a function of the presentation of the tone. A comparison of the rate of bar pressing prior to the presentation of the tone with the rate of responding during tone presentation revealed a marked decline in the rate of responding during presentation of the tone. This decrement in responding has been termed response suppression. In summary, the rationale for classifying this procedure as emotional conditioning is that a double stimulation procedure, the presentation of the tone and shock, is assumed to result in the tone being able to elicit an emotional response. The presence of this response is inferred from the reduction or suppression of the previously learned instrumental response.

**The Eyeblink**    The skeletal response most frequently examined by investigators in the United States is the human eyeblink. Usually, the CS is a tone or a change in the illumination of a small glass window that is placed in front of the subject; the US is a puff of compressed air or nitrogen delivered to the cornea of the eye, which produces an eyeblink. In order to measure the blink, a thin wire is lightly cemented to the subject's eyelid so that the movement of the lid moves the wire, which in turn rotates the shaft of a microtorque potentiometer. The resistance changes obtained from the potentiometer are amplified and recorded.

Gormezano and his associates have indicated the feasibility of conditioning the eyeblink in the rabbit. This animal, because of its docility, large eyelid, and low spontaneous blink rate, makes an ideal subject. In an early study, Schneiderman, Fuentes, and Gormezano (1962), using an 800 Hz tone as the CS and a US of compressed nitrogen delivered to the cornea, were able to obtain typical conditioning curves. In a second study, Gormezano, Schneiderman, Deaux, and Fuentes (1962) demonstrated that it was also possible to condition the nictitating membrane of the rabbit using the same CS and US. It will be recalled that the nictitating membrane is the rabbit's "third" eyelid consisting of a curved plate of cartilage drawn laterally across the cornea.

**Other Responses That Can Be Classically Conditioned**    Our examination of classically conditioned responses has been limited to those responses investigators have used most frequently. However, many different responses can be conditioned. In fact, we are only now becoming aware of the variety of conditioned responses that can be established; this ability to condition responses may have important implications for humans in their attempt to control responses that at one time were assumed to be involuntary. Let us examine a few of these.

Investigators have reported the conditioning of a blocking of the alpha rhythm. A human who is awake but resting with eyes closed will reveal, using the EEG, a brain wave of about 8–10 cycles/second. This can be observed most prominently when recording from the occipital lobe. This rhythm can be suppressed by illuminating the retina, by asking the subject to solve a simple arithmetic problem, or by asking the subject to attend to almost any specific stimulus. Procedurally, the presentation of a CS with a US that blocks the alpha rhythm should, after a number of pairings, result in the CS being able to suppress the rhythm when presented alone. Putney, Erwin, and Smith (1972) have demonstrated such to be the case.

A second example of conditioning an involuntary response involves changes in the blood glucose level of the rat, as reported in a series of experiments by Woods, Makous, and Hutton (1968, 1969) and Hutton, Woods, and Makous (1970). On each trial their procedure consisted of first measuring the glucose level of both experimental and control animals by obtaining a blood sample, following which experimental subjects were injected with insulin. The insulin served as a US by reducing blood glucose level. Control animals were injected with physiological saline. Twenty minutes later, a second blood sample was obtained in order to measure any change in glucose level. Fifteen such trials were distributed over 33 days. On the first test day, two days following the last conditioning trial, the same procedure was followed except that experimental subjects were injected with physiological saline just as the control subjects were.

The experimental findings were as follows: No difference in blood glucose levels was noted between experimental and control animals *prior* to the experimental animals receiving their first injection of insulin. For each of the 15 conditioning trials, the injection of insulin in the experimental animals resulted in a decrease in glucose level ranging from 14 to 50 percent; the injection of saline in the control animals was followed by an increase in blood glucose in almost every instance. On the test day, the injection of saline in the experimental group resulted in a decrease in glucose level, while an increase was noted with the control animals—the difference between the groups was statistically significant. The procedure of injecting the animals served as a conditioned stimulus, which was capable of eliciting the change in blood sugar that previously had been associated with the action of the unconditioned stimulus, the insulin.[2]

## The Value of Classical Conditioning Experiments

What objectives are achieved by an investigator who classically conditions a college student's eyeblink, a dog's salivary response, or a rat's heart rate? There are several answers to this question.

Some investigators have been interested in analyzing the nature of associative learning. Dickinson and Mackintosh (1978) have written, "conditioning is . . . as simple a form of associative learning as we are likely to find" (p. 587). The excellent control that experimenters can exercise over the presentation of the stimuli and the preciseness of response measurement are fundamental reasons for selecting this type of learning task to examine how associative learning takes place.

Those physiological changes that someday will be identified as representing the neurological basis of learning will most likely be discovered through the study of classically conditioned responses. Thompson and his associates see the study of the classically conditioned nictitating membrane response of the rabbit as an extremely useful procedure for analyzing the relationship between brain mechanisms and learning. A series of studies by these investigators has made substantial progress in this important undertaking; see Patterson, Cegavske, and Thompson (1973), Cegavske, Thompson, Patterson, and Gormezano (1976).

Another objective has been to use the classical conditioning task as a model for a number of nonlaboratory or everyday learning experiences, recognizing, of course, that the thread which ties the laboratory experiment to these situations may be tenuous. The experimental work of Watson and Rayner (1920) in conditioning Albert to be afraid of a white rat suggests how some human emotional responses are learned. Quite possibly, severe emotional responses, described as phobic, may arise from situations similar to the classical conditioning task.

Experimenters have also been interested in determining how emotional responses can be eliminated. Although laboratory studies reveal that the elimination of conditioned responses can be achieved by using an extinction procedure, Masserman (1943) and Wolpe (1952) found the emotional responses of fear and anxiety did not appear to be eliminated by this procedure. This suggested that an appropriate way to treat anxiety might be counterconditioning, a technique that is now found in a variety of psychotherapeutic procedures.

The counterconditioning procedure consists of conditioning a new response that is incompatible with the emotional response. For example, suppose a rat fears a specific location in an experimental apparatus because the spot is associated with shock. The experimenter may make the animal hungry and place food at a place in the apparatus where the animal's fear response is sufficiently weak so the animal can eat. Each day the food can be placed progressively nearer to the location eliciting fear, so that eventually the animal will eat from the specific location which originally elicited fear. Since a positive affective state is generated from eating and is incompatible with fear, the counterconditioning procedure effectively eliminates the animal's fear of the apparatus.

Classical conditioning models have also been used in a effort to better understand drug addiction. Psychologists are indebted to Pavlov (1927) for his early work in demonstrating that it is possible to condition addictive behavior resulting from morphine injection. Krylov, as reported by Pavlov, found that when dogs received morphine injections regularly, the preliminaries associated with the injections were sufficient to produce all of the observable symptoms (nausea, salivation, vomiting, etc.) that arose from the injection of the drug itself. Krylov's findings have been replicated by early and current investigators; see Collins and Tatum (1925), Crisler (1930), and Wikler (1970).

It is not likely that classical conditioning plays an important role in accounting for drug seeking or the beginning of addictive behavior. As Jaffe (1970) has acknowledged, instrumental conditioning serves as a better paradigm since the euphoric reaction produced by the drug serves as a reward for the beginning addict. Later, reinforcement is provided by the reduction of the tension, anxiety, and pain

occasioned through the lack of the drug in the body. Much more feasible is the proposed role of classical conditioning in withdrawal responses accompanying therapy and contributing to the craving responsible for the addict's return to the habit.

It has been assumed that the subject's early withdrawal symptoms, which can be identified as URs, are produced by physiological factors (US) stemming from the absence of the drug in the nervous system. A variety of environmental stimuli are invariably associated with the US, so the withdrawal symptoms may be elicited by such stimuli long after the physiological factors cease to exist. Jaffe (1970) has written that narcotic addicts often report that they feel sensations very similar to withdrawal symptoms when they return to situations where drugs are available. He suggests that it is not unlikely that the alcoholic has similar experiences. Such conditioned abstinence phenomena may play a significant role in the frequent relapses that characterize the clinical picture of compulsive abuse. Wikler (1965) has demonstrated the eliciting of withdrawal symptoms by conditioned stimuli in his laboratory.

Several investigators have shown that allergic reactions that have a physiological base (such as the presence of an allergen which triggers the attack) can also be conditioned. Ottenberg, Stein, Lewis, and Hamilton (1958) and Justensen, Braun, Garrison, and Pendelton (1970) have been able to demonstrate the conditioning of bronchial asthma attacks in the guinea pig.

It is not surprising, then, that many investigators see the use of classical conditioning tasks as an effective way to examine the nature of associative learning, and also as a prototype for many learning situations which are experienced in everyday life.

## INSTRUMENTAL CONDITIONING

Thorndike's studies of cats learning to escape from a puzzle box were followed by a host of animal learning experiments, conducted principally in the United States over the next forty years.

Many species served as experimental subjects, and there were a variety of learning tasks utilized. In most of these studies, reward played a basic role in promoting the acquisition of the learned response.

In the late thirties, and prior to Hilgard and Marquis's (1940) text differentiating classical from instrumental conditioning, Skinner (1938) identified the Thorndikian learning situation as an operant conditioning task. He believed that the learned response made by the experimental subject was not elicited by identifiable stimuli—at least in the sense that the US elicits the UR in classical conditioning. Responses appearing in the operant conditioning task Skinner described as operants; later investigators have designated these responses as *free* operants, since the subject placed in the experimental apparatus is free to respond at any time.

Inasmuch as the organism's response is instrumental in securing reinforcement, operant conditioning has been considered by some to be an example of instrumental conditioning, and the terms instrumental conditioning and operant conditioning have been used interchangeably. Most experimenters, although acknowledging the role of reinforcement in operant tasks, have pointed to specific methodological procedures that set operant conditioning tasks apart from the typical instrumental conditioning task. Accordingly, operant conditioning shall be discussed later in the chapter.

### A Classification of Instrumental Learning Tasks

Hilgard and Marquis (1940) recognized that reward, as a basic component of the instrumental learning task, should be broadened to include relief from noxious or aversive stimulation. With this in mind, they proposed that instrumental learning tasks be categorized as: (1) reward, (2) secondary reward, (3) escape, and (4) avoidance.

**Reward Tasks**   Reward tasks can be illustrated by Thorndike's puzzle box situation—the cats had to make the correct response of pulling a string in order to open a cage door and receive food. Instrumental reward tasks have been quite varied. An often used task is having an experimental subject, usually a hungry or thirsty rat, traverse the length of an alley or runway in order to find food or water in the goal box.

**Secondary Reward Tasks**   Secondary reward tasks are similar in makeup to those in which food, water, or some other appetitive stimulus serves as reward. The basic difference is that a neutral stimulus acquires reward characteristics by being associated with the reward and is used as the goal object. An interesting example of a secondary reward study is an experiment by Cowles (1937). Chimps learned to insert poker chips into a slot machine that delivered a raisin for each poker chip inserted. This procedure resulted in the chimps establishing an associative relationship between raisins and poker chips; Cowles found that the poker chips would serve as an adequate reward for these chimps in subsequent learning studies. Token rewards are now designated as secondary reinforcing stimuli. A vast number of studies have been designed and conducted over the past three decades to answer empirical and theoretical questions related to the operation of such stimuli.

**Escape Tasks**   With escape tasks, an aversive stimulus is presented and the experimental subject must learn to make a response in order to reduce or escape from the painful stimulation. The reduction or termination of the pain serves as the reward. In a study by Trapold and Fowler (1960), rats were placed in a runway where they received shock through a grid floor. The animals learned to escape from this aversive stimulus by running down the alley into an uncharged goal box.

A shuttle box of the type illustrated in Figure 2-8 is often used for an escape task. One side of the box is charged; when the door separating the compartments is raised, the animal must jump the hurdle in order to escape to the uncharged or safe compartment.

Campbell and Masterson (1969) have shown that it is not necessary for the safe compartment to provide total reduction of shock in order for learning to take place. The

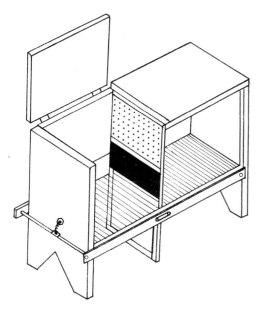

FIGURE 2-8. A shuttle box designed for the study of escape and avoidance learning with rats. When the shutter is raised, the rat can jump the hurdle to get into the other half of the apparatus.

instrumental response can be acquired as long as the "safe" compartment contains discriminably less shock than the compartment from which the animal escapes.

**Avoidance Tasks** The last type of instrumental task proposed by Hilgard and Marquis (1940) is the avoidance task. Here, the experimental subject's instrumental response enables it to avoid receiving the aversive stimulus. Present-day experimenters have divided avoidance learning into two types: active and passive avoidance.

A study by Church, Brush, and Solomon (1956) using dogs as experimental subjects illustrates an active avoidance situation. A shuttle box apparatus was used, with a CS of a buzzer sounding for 5, 10, or 20 seconds. The termination of the CS was followed by shock to the animals' feet (US). Animals learned to avoid the shock by jumping over a barrier and into the other compartment during the presentation of the CS.

Another type of active avoidance task has been designated as nondiscriminated or Sidman (1953) avoidance. There is no signal or CS to predict the onset of the aversive stimulation. Rather, shock is provided on a regular interval, but an instrumental response by the subject, such as bar pressing, will delay or postpone the shock for an arbitrary length of time set by the experimenter. The interval between shock presentations is known as the shock-shock interval, while the amount of time that the instrumental response delays presentation of shock is known as the response-shock interval. It is possible for the subject to learn to respond and greatly reduce the frequency of shock.

With passive avoidance, the subject is first trained to make some instrumental response. Following such training, the subject receives an aversive stimulus for continuing to make this response; as a result, it must learn to stop responding, or remain passive. Passive avoidance tasks are frequently designated as punishment tasks. A study by Kamin (1959) illustrates this. Rats were first trained to avoid shock by running from one compartment to another in a shuttle box. A buzzer served as the cue, and shock was administered 10 seconds following its onset. After the animal had learned to avoid the shock by responding when the buzzer sounded, the task was changed. When the buzzer sounded and the animals ran to the second compartment, they received shock. As a result, they had to learn to avoid shock by remaining in the first compartment and not responding when the buzzer was presented.

Since avoidance tasks have been placed in the instrumental learning category, investigators have wrestled with the problem of identifying the nature of the reward that presumably strengthens the instrumental response. It cannot be the termination of the aversive stimulus as would be found with escape tasks, since the noxious stimulus cannot be terminated if it has been avoided. The problem is a complex one, since theorists have rejected teleological or purposive explanations. Purposive or teleological explanations of avoidance behavior deal with the undesirable consequences that might have taken place if the avoidance response had not been made. For example, the statement "The mouse runs from the cat in order to avoid being caught" attributes to the words "in order to" the reason for the mouse's running response. But such an "explanation" provides no additional information beyond the basic fact that the mouse runs from the cat.

The reward, secondary reward, escape, and avoidance instrumental learning task classifications provided by Hilgard and Marquis (1940) mask a certain feature of these tasks that should be made explicit. This feature has to do with the nature of the cue or stimulus that forms a part of the task.

Many instrumental conditioning tasks can be categorized as simple or nonsignaled —with such tasks, the stimulus situation provides no specific cues (at least as manipulated by the experimenter) to indicate when a response will result in reinforcement. The task provides the organism with a general situational milieu, but specific stimuli to cue the instrumental response cannot be identified.

A second category of tasks can be described as signaled instrumental conditioning tasks. Here, the experimenter provides the subject with a signal or discriminative stimulus, and if the organism responds appropriately, reinforcement will be provided. Avoidance tasks are generally of this variety, since the organism must receive some cue in order to respond in time to avoid the aversive stimulus. But it is also possible to use this type of discriminative task when employing rewards. By placing a light above the lever in the Skinner box, the experimenter can arrange conditions so that reward is provided for lever pressing only during the presentation of the light. There is an obvious similarity between classical conditioning and signaled instrumental conditioning tasks, although there is no US in the latter paradigm to elicit the instrumental response.

To the nonsignaled and signaled tasks, we can add a third, the discrimination task. Here, two (or more) stimuli are presented and the subject learns to respond to the stimulus that is associated with reward, or relief from aversive stimulation.

Many of the learning variables examined have produced similar effects on both nonsignaled and signaled tasks, so this material will be combined in Chapters 3 and 4. Discrimination tasks and the resultant discrimination learning process have frequently been considered apart from these other tasks. In keeping with this precedent, such learning will be discussed in Chapter 5.

## Response Measurement

The measurement of responding in instrumental conditioning tasks is similar to that in classical conditioning in that response measures during acquisition include: (1) latency, (2) magnitude, and (3) frequency or probability of correct responding. Generally, nonsignaled instrumental tasks utilize latency measures—the time required for a rat to leave the starting box in a runway, or the speed with which the animal traverses the length of the alley. In contrast, signaled and discrimination tasks utilize response frequency or probability.

Latency and probability measures can also be obtained during extinction trials, but our bias, as noted previously, has been to stress response measures obtained during acquisition; extinction data must be regarded as suspect when used to infer strength of conditioning.

## Operant Conditioning

The kinds of apparatus used in operant conditioning experiments have been so designed that (1) the subject's response takes only a short time to make, and (2) reinforcement is received in proximity to where the response is made; after completing the response and receiving reinforcement, the subject is ready to respond again. The apparatus permits free responding, since the manipulandum is always available. An example of operant responding would be a pigeon pecking at a plastic disk thousands of times in a single experimental session.

Operant conditioning tasks differ from instrumental conditioning tasks along several procedural dimensions. One is that discrete learning trials, used with instrumental learning tasks, cannot be programmed with operant conditioning experiments. Thus, with operant tasks, subjects are provided with learning sessions; the animals are placed in the experimental apparatus for a fixed length of time—for instance, 30 minutes, or until they obtain a specific number of reinforcements. Such responding is called continuous.

The lack of discrete trials and the rapidity with which operant responses can be completed bring up two other considerations. One is that the subject cannot be provided with reinforcement after each response, as would frequently be the case with instrumental conditioning tasks. This results in operant investigators using reinforcement schedules, or programs detailing how reinforcement shall be provided. Second, the rapidity with which the responses may be made has resulted in investigators using the rate of response as their basic

response measure. Both of these topics will be discussed in the following sections.

In addition to these procedural distinctions between operant and instrumental learning tasks, other differences can be noted. Generally, operant experimenters have been primarily concerned with maintenance behavior; their interest is directed not toward an examination of variables that influence *acquisition* but rather toward how specific variables influence the maintenance of a behavior. After a bar pressing response has been acquired by a rat, for example, and the animal reveals a stable level of responding, the operant investigator would be interested in examining how such variables as type of reinforcement schedule influence the rate of responding.

A second difference is that operant investigators place much more emphasis on the analysis of individual responding so only a few experimental subjects need to be used. The basic strategy is to see if control can be exercised over the subject's behavior. If this can be accomplished, the experimenter's objective is achieved. (See Box 2-2.)

---

**BOX 2-2**

The horse has been used only infrequently in psychological experiments, but Myers and Mesker (1960) used a 10-year-old gelding as an experimental subject to demonstrate operant conditioning. The animal's task was to nudge with his lips a lever along a horizontal plane, with the experimenters using one-half cup of grain as reinforcement for responding. For the first 7 days of the experiment, the animal was placed on a continuous reinforcement schedule with reinforcement being provided after every response. Intermittent reinforcement schedules were then provided over the next 12 days. On Days 1–3, reinforcement was provided after every third response; Days 4–6, reinforcement was provided after every fifth response; Days 7–9, reinforcement was provided after every eleventh response. (These schedules have been identified as fixed ratio schedules of FR 3, FR 5, FR 8, and FR 11.)

The experimental findings indicated that as the fixed ratio schedule increased from FR 3 to FR 11, the animal's response rate also increased, so that by the time the animal was placed on an FR 11 schedule, a remarkably stable rate of response was evident. The experimenter's objective was achieved, since the experiment demonstrated that operant conditioning procedures could be applied to an unlikely kind of experimental subject, that the animal's response rate could be manipulated by changing the number of responses required to obtain reinforcement, and that a stable level of responding could be produced with this technique.

**Schedules of Reinforcement** As mentioned earlier, operant conditioning tasks frequently result in the experimental subject making a large number of responses within a very short period of time. Since it is not feasible to provide reinforcement after each response, it has been necessary to specify which responses will be reinforced through the use of a reinforcement schedule. Reinforcement may be provided after the subject has made a specified (or variable) number of responses, or after a specific (or variable) amount of time has elapsed since the last response was made. Four basic reinforcement schedules have been utilized: (1) fixed interval, (2) variable interval, (3) fixed ratio, and (4) variable ratio. These schedules have been defined as follows.

*Fixed Interval (FI)* With a fixed interval schedule, reinforcement is provided for the first response that the organism makes after some fixed period of time, measured from the last reinforcement, has elapsed. With a 20 second fixed interval (FI) schedule, reinforcement is provided for the first response that occurs 20 seconds or more following the previous reinforcement.

*Variable Interval (VI)* With the variable interval schedule, reinforcement is provided for the first response that is made after a variable, rather than a fixed, period of time has elapsed (as measured from the last reinforcement). A 20 second variable interval (VI) schedule consists of reinforcement administered for the first response that follows selected time intervals averaging 20 seconds in duration.

*Fixed Ratio (FR)* For the fixed ratio schedule, reinforcement is provided after every *n*th response. For example, a 10:1 fixed ratio (FR) schedule is defined as every tenth response being followed by reinforcement.

*Variable Ratio (VR)* With the variable ratio schedule, the number of responses needed in order to secure reinforcement varies, but the varying numbers of responses are averaged to provide a descriptive statement of the type of schedule utilized. A 10:1 variable ratio sched-

ule would be produced by the following: 4 responses followed by reinforcement; 14 responses followed by reinforcement; 10 responses followed by reinforcement; 6 responses followed by reinforcement; and 16 responses followed by reinforcement.

These varying reinforcement schedules can frequently be observed to influence human behavior. An example of the VR schedule is found in the operation of slot machines programmed to pay off on some average number of operations. Since the machine has been placed on this type of schedule, it is not possible to predict which particular play will pay off. One player may win twice in succession, while the next player may pull the lever twenty or thirty times without a payoff. Applied psychologists have often attempted to apply these reinforcement schedules to business, factory, and school settings with an appropriate scheduling of piecework systems, hourly wages, etc.

*Other Operant Reinforcement Schedules* In addition to the four basic reinforcement schedules described, a number of other and more complex schedules have been used. Three of these are (1) multiple, (2) chained, and (3) concurrent.

Multiple schedules consist of two or more schedules presented successively and correlated with external cues. A pigeon might be given a 30 second presentation of a red plastic disk, followed by a 30 second presentation of a yellow disk, and then a green one. Responding to the presentation of the red disk would be associated with a specific VI schedule, the yellow disk would be associated with a specific FI schedule, while the green disk would be associated with a VR schedule.

Chain schedules also consist of two or more cues presented successively to the subject; however, responding by the organism to the first stimulus results only in the presentation of the second stimulus. Responding to the second stimulus will result in reinforcement.

Concurrent schedules involve two or more responses, each reinforced by a separate schedule. For example, a pigeon may be reinforced for responding to a plastic disk placed on the right side of the box on a FI schedule, whereas its response to a plastic disk placed on the left side of the box will result in a VI schedule.

Two other reinforcement schedules that have been used by operant investigators are differential reinforcement for low rates (DRL) and differential reinforcement for high rates (DRH). With the DRL schedule, the more frequently used of the two, the organism's response is reinforced only if it is made *after* a specific time period has elapsed; responses made within the time interval are not reinforced. A practical illustration would be flooding your carburetor in attempting to start your car. You must wait a sufficient period of time before it can be successfully started. As would be expected, the DRL schedule results in a very low response rate and one that is related to the length of the interval set by the experimenter.

With the DRH schedule, reinforcement depends on the subject responding a specific number of times within a designated time period, say 20 pecks at a disk within 5 seconds. This schedule has been used only infrequently, since it is very difficult to control the subject's responding. Assume, for example, that the experimenter sets a DRH criterion of having a pigeon peck at a disk 10 times in 4 seconds. If responding takes place at this rate, reinforcement is received. If responding on an occasion should go below this number during the 4 second time period, reinforcement is not provided. This lack of reinforcement reduces the rate of responding still more, resulting in reinforcement being withheld, which in turn results in still fewer responses being made, etc. Eventually, the response may cease completely, since reinforcement has not been received.

**Rate of Responding**    The response measure used in all of the schedules is the rate of responding—the number of responses made by the organism within an experimental session. The plotting of these responses results in a cumulative curve: the number of responses made by the subject is plotted on the ordinate against time on the abscissa. Figure 2-9 shows how a cumulative record is obtained. Each time the organism responds, the pen moves vertically on the paper feeding through the apparatus.

Note that if the organism does not respond, a horizontal line occurs in the direction of the paper feed. The more frequently the organism responds, the more closely the record approaches verticality. Although the rate of

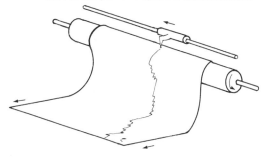

Each response made by the organism moves the pen one space in this direction.

FIGURE 2-9.    A picture of a commercial recorder and a sketch of its operation. Photo courtesy of Gerbrands Corporation, Arlington, Massachusetts.

responding is directly proportional to the slope of the curve, at slopes above 80° small differences in the angle represent very large differences in rate.

## The Value of Instrumental Conditioning

A discussion of the relevance of instrumental conditioning does not appear to be as necessary as an explanation of the value of classical conditioning, since most learned human behavior can be identified as instrumental. However, the kinds of simple instrumental conditioning experiments discussed, like classical conditioning studies, provide experimenters with an opportunity to analyze the nature of associative learning. Instrumental conditioning tasks generally place emphasis on the establishment of an association between the organism's response and reinforcement. Investigators are thus provided with an opportunity to examine the contribution of reinforcement variables in the establishment of this association.

Operant training procedures have been widely applied in attempts to modify the behavior of inmates in mental institutions. Use of a token economy, one of the most popular of these procedures, consists of reinforcing desirable patient behavior with tokens. These tokens can be exchanged for privileges or material goods the patient finds enjoyable, ranging from watching television to securing candy, cigarettes, etc. The usefulness of similar type programs has been demonstrated in normal school settings as well. See Chapter 8 for further discussion of this topic.

## Autoshaping

We would like to conclude this chapter by discussing a type of experimental operation identified as autoshaping. Some investigators have assumed autoshaping to be a type of classical conditioning operation, whereas others believe it to be an example of instrumental conditioning. Let us provide an illustration of this phenomenon.

Brown and Jenkins (1968) were interested in examining how the strength of a response was related to the manipulation of the conditional relationships among the stimulus, the response, and the presentation of reward. One procedure they used was to repeatedly pair an 8 second white key light with the presentation of food. Although the subjects were not required to respond in order to secure food, the experimenters were surprised to find that repeated pairing of the two stimuli resulted in the reliable emergence of pecking at the lighted key. A comparison of this group's responding with that of appropriate control groups indicated that the acquisition of the response was dependent on light-food pairing in that order.

The pairing of the lighted key and the presentation of the food mirrors the classical conditioning operation, but critics have argued that there was nothing in classical conditioning theory which would predict that the bird's response should be directed at the key. Nonetheless, experimental evidence has accumulated to indicate that there is an impressive parallel between classical conditioning and autoshaping.

In Brown and Jenkin's study, the kind of pecking response made by the pigeon to the lighted key can be viewed as a part of its consummatory response to food. If such is the case, one would predict that the response to the key would change if the reward (US) were changed, and Moore (1973) has provided experimental support for the correctness of this prediction. Moore found that if the pigeon was made thirsty and water was used as reward, a different type of pecking response to the lighted key was observed. When the lighted key was associated with food, the pecking response was short and forceful, with the beak open. When the key signaled water, the pigeon moved its head laterally across the key, with a slight opening and closing of the beak. In effect, the key was "eaten" or "drunk," depending on the kind of reward associated with it. In summary, the pigeon's autoconditioned response bears a marked similarity to the response made to the reward (or unconditioned stimulus), thus suggesting autoconditioning to be a type of classical conditioning task.

In addition, there is the suggestion that with the autoshaping procedure, the lighted key (CS) must predict the appearance of the reward (US), a relationship that is also noted with traditional classical conditioning operations. In an autoshaping experiment, Gamzu and Williams (1973) have found that if food is presented equally often with and without the lighted key, the pecking response does not increase above operant level.

Finally, support for considering autoshaping an example of classical conditioning can be found in a study by Williams and Williams (1969), who used an omission training procedure. With this type of task, the making of the conditioned or instrumental response is followed by the experimenter not presenting reward; thus, there is a negative response-reward contingency. In their experiment, the presentation of an illuminated key for 6 seconds was followed by the presentation of food for 4 seconds. But instead of the pigeon's key peck turning off the light and being followed by food, a negative response-reward contingency was introduced. When the lighted key was pecked, the peck turned off the key light but food was not presented. Nonetheless, substantial responding took place. If the pecking response, arising from the presentation of the lighted key and reward, was assumed to be an instance of instrumental conditioning, the omission of food should have resulted in the pigeons ceasing to respond, an outcome that was not obtained.

But two points deserve comment. First, although pecking appears to operate in a manner similar to a classical conditioned response in autoshaping experiments, this does not mean that the responses observed in many operant or instrumental conditioning experiments should also be identified as Pavlovian CRs. Key pecking can also serve as an instrumental response. Second, it may be that some of the experimental findings obtained with autoshaping have applicability only for the pigeon. For example, Sidman and Fletcher (1968) have pointed out that the topography of the monkey's key pressing response, obtained by the repeated pairing of a lighted key and the presentation of food, is much different from its consummatory response, a finding that would be expected if an instrumental conditioning procedure were used. And Gamzu and Schwam (1974), using monkeys as experimental subjects, were unable to confirm Williams and Williams's (1969) finding that omission training did not eliminate responding. Gamzu and Schwam found that the introduction of a negative contingency between the presentation of an illuminated key and reward markedly reduced responding. These authors have indicated that not all of the demonstrations of autoshaping can be considered to be under the control of those processes that are primarily responsible for the phenomena obtained in pigeons.

## SUMMARY

After examining the conditioning situations employed by Pavlov and Thorndike, Hilgard and Marquis (1940) differentiated two types of tasks. They designated Pavlovian type tasks as classical conditioning, and Thorndikian type tasks as instrumental.

The procedure used in classical conditioning consists of pairing a conditioned stimulus (CS) with an unconditioned stimulus (US). The US has the capacity to elicit from the experimental subject a regular and measurable response, designated as the unconditioned response (UR). The conditioned stimulus does not have this capacity. When the CS and US are paired, the CS is able to elicit a response, generally similar to the response elicited by the US, and identified as a conditioned response (CR).

After a CR has been established, the repeated presentation of the CS without the US results in experimental extinction—cessation of the conditioned response. If a rest period is placed between the last extinction trial and a subsequent presentation of the CS, the conditioned response reappears. This phenomenon has been identified as spontaneous recovery.

It has been generally assumed that conditioned responses are established as a result of the pairing operation, so that the control group used in classical conditioning studies consists of the random and single presentation of either the CS or the US. Some investigators have assumed that the conditioned response does not develop from the pairing operation, but arises from the subject learning a contingency between the CS and US—that the US will follow the CS. They have argued that the traditional control group receiving unpaired presentations of the CS and US also learns a contingency—that the US will never follow the CS. The result is that the experimental group's performance, as compared to the control group's, is overestimated.

Many different responses have been conditioned. Those most frequently examined in the laboratory include: (1) the galvanic skin response (GSR), (2) changes in heart rate, (3) emotional responses, and (4) the human eye-blink and movement of the nictitating membrane of the rabbit (the rabbit's third eyelid). Investigators have been able to condition a variety of other responses including blocking the alpha rhythm and changing blood glucose level.

The variety of instrumental learning tasks used has resulted in a number of classification systems being proposed. The most frequently cited was proposed by Hilgard and Marquis (1940). They divided instrumental learning tasks into (1) reward (2) secondary reward, (3) escape, and (4) avoidance tasks.

A special kind of instrumental task has been identified as the free operant, first described by Skinner (1938). Operant tasks differ from traditional instrumental tasks along a number of dimensions. The subject's instrumental response takes only a very short time to complete, with the experimental apparatus designed so that the subject is free to make this response throughout the entire experimental session. Discrete learning trials cannot be programmed with operant tasks, and reinforcement cannot be provided after every response.

One result has been that operant investigators employ reinforcement schedules, with the basic schedules being categorized as fixed interval (FI), variable interval (VI), fixed ratio (FR), and variable ratio (VR). In addition, the most frequent response measure utilized by operant investigators is rate of responding, with a cumulative recorder being used to measure the subject's frequent and rapid responding. Operant procedures have been used extensively in modifying human behavior.

An interesting phenomenon which appears to have some similarity to classical conditioning is known as autoshaping. Here, it was originally found that the reliable pairing of a lighted key with food resulted in pigeons pecking at the key although such responding was not instrumental in making the food available. The pairing of the lighted key and food mirrors the classical conditioning operation. Some investigators have used this procedure to further examine the nature of classical conditioning.

## NOTES

1. Some experimenters, however, believe that first interval responses can also be conditioned. Other investigators have assumed that the conditioned GSR is nothing more than the reappearance of an orienting response to the CS. See Prokasy (1977), Furedy, and Poulos (1977), Grings (1977), Stern and Walrath (1977), for a discussion of this issue.

2. Siegel (1972, 1975), also using insulin injection, has reported the conditioning of a hyperglycemic effect—an elevation in blood glucose level rather than a decline. It is not clear why findings contrary to those obtained by Woods et al. (1968, 1969) have been obtained. In Siegel's case, the increase in blood sugar represents an effect opposite to that produced by the insulin.

# CHAPTER THREE

# The Contribution of Stimulus and Motivation Variables to Classicial and Instrumental Conditioning

Learned responses differ markedly as a function of the kinds of experimental variables that are manipulated. For example, it has been found that the use of a very loud conditioned stimulus in contrast to a very soft one will result in an increased probability of eliciting a conditioned response. Similarly, placing a large pellet of food in the goal box at the end of the runway will cause rats to traverse the alley more rapidly than will placing a small pellet in the goal box. Some explanation is necessary to account for such differences in response strength; it is usually assumed that these differences reflect differences in the learning process.

These next two chapters will examine why there are differences in the strength of learned responses. Such differences can be observed as a function of (a) stimulus conditions, (b) motivational conditions, and (c) cognitive variables that have been manipulated in the task. This chapter will cover the role of stimulus and motivational variables, while cognitive variables will be discussed in Chapter 4. In a few instances we shall examine these variables as they influence discrimination learning; a complete examination of this type of learning task will be found in Chapter 5.

## STIMULUS VARIABLES

It is not surprising that experimenters have been interested in determining how learning is related to the characteristics of the conditioned or discriminative stimulus used in classical and instrumental conditioning operations, since such stimuli are readily observable and easily manipulated. Generally, a physical attribute has been manipulated; perhaps the most frequently examined one has been stimulus intensity.

### Stimulus Intensity

How does the intensity of a stimulus influence the learning process? Investigators have used the instrumental conditioning task only infrequently in examining this variable, with Kessen (1953) and Passey and Possenti (1956) finding that stimulus intensity contributed to increases in the strength of instrumental responding.

Stimulus intensity is most often examined through the use of classical conditioning tasks. Most current experimenters have found that increasing the intensity of the CS results in more rapid conditioning of, for example, flexion response in the dog (Walker, 1960), respiratory response in the fish (Woodward, 1971), heart rate in the pigeon (Cohen, 1974), eyeblink in the rabbit (Frey, 1969), nictitating membrane in the rabbit (Scavio and Gormezano, 1974), and conditioned emotional response in the rat (Kamin and Schaub, 1963; Jakubowski and Zielinski, 1978).

With classical conditioning tasks, most experimenters have found that the intensity effect will be accentuated if the experimental design provides for each subject to experience more than a single level of stimulus intensity. The procedure used to study this was a within-subjects design. It can be compared with the more frequently used between-subjects design, in which different intensity levels are presented to different groups of subjects. In a study by Grice and Hunter (1964) employing both of these experimental designs, the eyeblink response was conditioned for 100 trials to a tone (CS), with an airpuff serving as the US. A within-subjects group received 50 trials with a soft tone and 50 trials with a loud tone. Two between-subjects groups were used, one group being conditioned to the loud tone while the other group was conditioned to the soft. The findings for the last 60 trials to the loud and soft tones for the within- and between-subjects groups are presented in Figure 3-1. The presentation of two intensities of the CS to the same subject substantially increased the effect of the intensity variable.

However, Scavio and Gormezano (1974), when examining the nictitating membrane response of the rabbit, and Zielinski and Walasek (1977), when investigating the CER of the rat, were unable to obtain different intensity effects as a function of whether a between- or within-subjects experimental design was used.

Pavlov explained stimulus intensity effects by assuming that the presentation of an intense stimulus resulted in greater neural activity, which in turn resulted in more rapid conditioning. A similar approach was suggested by Hull's (1949) dynamism theory, which proposed that a basic property of the nervous system was to produce more vigorous responding with increased stimulus intensity.

Tangential support for Hull's position can be found in reaction time experiments

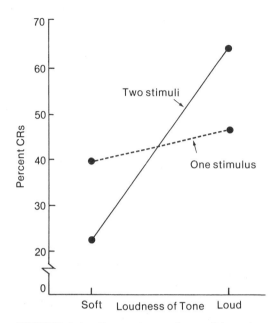

FIGURE 3-1. Percentage of conditioned responses during last 60 trials to the loud and soft tones under the one- and two-stimulus conditions. Adapted from G. R. Grice and J. J. Hunter, "Stimulus intensity effects depend upon the type of experimental design." *Psychological Review*, 1964, 71, 247–256. Copyright © 1964 by the American Psychological Association. Reprinted by permission.

—Grice and Hunter (1964) found that reaction time to a weak stimulus was significantly slower than reaction time to a more intense stimulus. But Hull's theory cannot explain adequately why the intensity effect is accentuated when different levels are used, as shown in the within- vs. between-subjects findings obtained by Grice and Hunter (1964).

Moreover, Kamin (1965) has shown that a large *decrease* in stimulus intensity will result in more rapid conditioning than a small decrement, a finding also not in keeping with Hull's theoretical analysis. In Kamin's (1965) experiment, a conditioned emotional response (CER) task was used, with an 80 db sound serving as background noise in the experimental chamber. The CS Kamin used was a reduction of the noise level from the 80 db level to either 70, 60, 50, 45, or 0 db. Five groups of rats each received a different reduction in noise level. Conditioned suppression was obtained in all groups, but it was largest for the two groups in which the CS was represented by a reduction in noise from 80 to 45 db or from 80 to 0 db. Thus, the largest decrease in noise intensity was accompanied by the most rapid conditioning. Kamin's findings suggest that intensity effects must be viewed within a context of stimulus change rather than intensity per se.

With Hull's (1949) theory of stimulus intensity effects discredited, Grice and Hunter (1964) proposed that the intensity effect is dependent upon the organism's adaptation level (AL). The adaptation level, as proposed by Helson (1948, 1964), refers to a frame of reference produced by the stimulation that the subject receives. This frame of reference determines, at least in part, how a specific stimulus will be perceived. For example, the judgment that a subject makes about the loudness of a test tone is related to whether the presentation of the tone was preceded by the subject hearing a series of soft tones or a series of loud tones. The adaptation level position posits that the series of tones preceding the test tone establishes within the subject a specific frame of reference against which the test tone is judged.

When two tones differing in intensity are used—e.g., high and low, as in the Grice and Hunter study (1964)—the subject's adaptation level or frame of reference for loudness lies between the two, so that exaggerated intensity effects are obtained. Presentation of the soft tone seems less intense than if only a single intensity had been presented, while the presentation of the loud tone seems more intense. Such perceived differences in intensity lead to the differences in conditioned responding.

In a subsequent examination of stimulus intensity effects, Grice (1968, 1972) has found his adaptation level theory difficult to integrate with other behavioral constructs. As a result, he has proposed a more elaborate explanation based on decision theory. Grice's theoretical position is beyond the scope of this discussion on intensity effects. It is apparent,

however, that the conflicting findings that have been obtained make any explanation of stimulus intensity effects premature.

### The CS-US Interval

The second stimulus variable is related to the interval of time separating the onset of the CS from the onset of the US, or the interstimulus interval (ISI). Wolfle (1930, 1932) and Kappauf and Schlosberg (1937) conditioned finger withdrawal and the galvanic skin response and found that optimal conditioning took place when a .5 second interstimulus interval was used. Hull (1943), using such experimental evidence, as well as neurological information related to the strength of the afferent impulse produced by the action of the conditioned stimulus, assumed that the optimal interval for all conditioning tasks was .5 second. This conclusion was echoed by many psychologists for the next several decades.

However, experimenters have become increasingly skeptical of this conclusion. An examination of the findings of many interstimulus interval studies—using both humans and animals and employing a variety of response measures—reveals that Hull was in error; optimal conditioning may take place with intervals that differ markedly from .5 second.

Using fish as their experimental subjects, Noble, Gruender, and Meyer (1959) and Noble and Adams (1963) found that the frequency of conditioned responding increased as the interstimulus interval was lengthened from .5 to 2.0 seconds, while further increases in the ISI resulted in a declining response frequency. Ost and Lauer (1965), examining ISIs of 2, 5, 10, and 15 seconds in their study of salivary conditioning in dogs, reported that "the highest response rates appear in the 5 and 15 second groups" (p. 203).

The examples provided certainly suggest that the optimal interstimulus interval will vary as a function of the type of response conditioned. But if further evidence is needed, Vandercar and Schneiderman (1967) conducted a most revealing classically conditioned discrimination experiment. (For a description of this type of classical conditioning task, see

Chapter 5.) The rabbit's nictitating membrane (NM) and heart rate were simultaneously conditioned, with a 550 Hz tone serving as the CS + and a 2400 Hz tone as the CS − . (For some subjects these conditions were reversed.) Shock, as the US, elicited both responses. Four groups of subjects received ISIs of either (a) .25, (b) .75, (c) 2.25, or (d) 6.75 seconds. Seven days of training, with 80 trials per day, was provided. Results revealed that the optimal interval for the nictitating membrane was an ISI of .75 second, while the optimal ISI for conditioning the heart rate was 2.25. Such findings provide compelling evidence that no single interval is optimal for all responses.

No satisfactory reason has been provided for why different response systems have different interstimulus intervals for optimal conditioning, although a number of investigators have wrestled with the problem; see Gormezano (1972), Mackintosh (1974). The response latency of the effector system examined plays an obvious role, but since the relationship between reaction time and the length of the interstimulus interval leading to optimal conditioning is not perfect, other unidentified variables must make a contribution.

## MOTIVATION

A teacher observes early in the term that one child seems eager to learn the material presented while another child could "care less." Since both children have about the same level of intelligence, the difference in learning is attributed to differences in their motivation. A reading of the sports page reveals that a professional tennis player loses a match to a player whom the professional has generally beaten, or that a weak college football team has defeated a much stronger opponent. Such sports upsets have often been attributed by coaches to a lack of "desire" or motivation on the part of the defeated players.

Thus, motivational variables may play an important role in learning and performance. In this section some of the evidence that has led to this conclusion will be reviewed; but first it is important to examine the construct of motivation itself.

### The Nature of Motivation

The concept of motivation is sufficiently complex that this section can only provide a brief overview of the construct, focusing particularly on its relevance to the area of learning. The reader is referred to Cofer and Appley (1964), Weiner (1972), and Korman (1974) for an extended examination of the topic.

Motivation has been defined as "a need or desire which prompts an organism to act in a certain way." A motive is thus seen by psychologists interested in learning as having an eliciting function—it prompts or initiates activity.

Motivational theorists have examined those events that satisfy the organism's needs or desires—events that can be designated as rewards or reinforcement. The function of reinforcement is to increase the probability that one response rather than another will be made. Some experimenters consider reinforcement to be distinct from the concept of a motive, as noted in the familiar phrase "motivation *and* reward." Others, however, have viewed reward as being an integral aspect of the motivational construct. In this text, we shall assume that motivation in the learning task has two functions: an eliciting function and a reinforcing function.

**The Eliciting Function**   Early investigators believed that the organism's needs were responsible for eliciting activity, and they used the construct of *drive* to describe this relationship. A drive was thus regarded as a primitive motivational construct. Need states were manipulated by depriving the organism of some basic physiological requirement, such as food or water, while activity was measured by the amount of activity exhibited by the animal in an exercise wheel. The early studies of Richter (1922, 1927) indicated that increasing the rat's need for food would result in increased amounts of activity. These experimental findings lent support to the position that drives, and more generally motives, had the function of initiating or eliciting behavior.

Over the years, investigators have noted some basic problems involved in the use of the construct of drive. First, some psychologists employed the term indiscriminately. Curiosity, exploration, and boredom have been posited as drive states, without experimenters identifying the appropriate antecedent condition necessary for their arousal. The use of the concept of drive in this way bears a marked similarity to the earlier employment of the concept of instinct, which was eventually abandoned because it contributed little to understanding behavior. In addition, experimental evidence has accumulated to dispute the position that an inherent characteristic of an organism's physiological need state was to produce activity.

Many studies have revealed that such needs were not always accompanied by increased activity; see Strong (1957), Bolles and deLorge (1962), Treichler and Hall (1962).

These difficulties have cast doubt on the usefulness of the drive concept. Wayner and Carey (1973) have written that ". . . the term drive has been bandied about to the point where it is not only useless but is actually meaningless and confusing in the literature. We believe that the term serves no scientific purpose and should be abandoned" (p. 54).

The difficulties with the concept of drive do not negate the eliciting function of a motive, since investigators have identified several stimulus conditions that do have this function. Aversive or noxious events—stimuli resulting in pain or unpleasant emotional states such as fear or anxiety—are motivating, in that they prompt the organism to escape or avoid these sources of stimulation. Rewards also contribute to a motive's eliciting function. If the organism has a need or desire for a goal object and anticipates receiving it, the goal object becomes an incentive and will prompt responding. For example, if the earlier responses of a deprived rat placed in an experimental situation resulted in its obtaining food, the hungry animal's anticipation of receiving food would elicit responding if the animal were placed in the experimental task on a subsequent occasion.

**The Reinforcing Function**   The reinforcing function of a motive has been commonly attributed to the role of reward or reinforcement; investigators are aware of its action in increasing the probability of a response. The termination of aversive stimulation also has a reinforcing function, identified as **negative reinforcement.**

Thus, learning theorists center their examination of motivation around the roles of aversive stimuli and rewards in eliciting and reinforcing responses observed in learning tasks.

## Motivation in Classical Conditioning

With classical conditioning tasks, the motivational functions of elicitation and reinforcement are attributed to the action of the unconditioned stimulus.[1] The manipulation of the US has taken the form of (1) varying the frequency with which the US has been paired with the CS, and (2) examining the role of US intensity.

**Frequency and Characteristics of the CS-US Presentations**   In most classical conditioning studies, conditioned responding is a function of the frequency of CS-US presentations. That is, as more and more CS-US presentations are provided, greater amounts of conditioning take place.

Does it follow then that the frequency of CS-US presentations is responsible for the establishment of a conditioned response? Some experimenters have denied such an interpretation. Rescorla (1967) has suggested that rather than the frequency of the pairings, it is the establishment of a contingency between the CS and US that is basic to CR learning. Rescorla's position has been supported by the work of Hupka, Kwaterski, and Moore (1970) and Leonard, Fishbein, and Monteau (1972). These investigators have found that when the number of CS-US presentations has been held constant, the presentation of additional US alone trials will retard acquisition.

In the Leonard et al. study, the nictitating membrane response of the rabbits was classically conditioned using a tone (CS) paired with shock (US). A control group received just 100 paired CS-US trials, while two experimental groups received 100 CS-US trials and also 100 US alone trials. For one group, the US alone trials were presented midway between a 60 second intertrial interval, while the second group received the US alone trials midway between a 120 second intertrial interval. Conditioning for the two experimental groups was significantly poorer than for the control, thus indicating that the addition of US alone trials reduced the probability or influenced the contingency that the US would always follow the CS. See Figure 3-2.

Further evidence of the role of US alone trials in influencing conditioning has been obtained by several other investigators. They found that the presentation of only the US prior to the CS-US trials (rather than during acquisition trials) also reduced the rate at which the conditioned response was acquired. Such an effect has been demonstrated with the conditioning of the eyeblink (Hobson, 1968), the

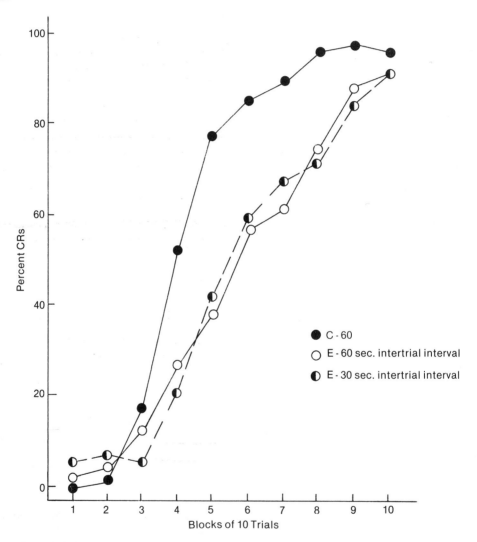

FIGURE 3-2.   Course of conditioned responding for the control group and the two experimental groups. Adapted from D. W. Leonard, L. C. Fishbein, and J. E. Monteau, "The effects of interpolated US alone (USa) presentations on classical membrane conditioning in rabbit (Oryctolagus cuniculus). *Conditional Reflex,*1972, 7, 107–114. Reprinted by permission of Lippincott/Harper Co.

nictitating membrane response of the rabbit (Mis and Moore, 1973), and the conditioned emotional response (Randich and LoLordo, 1979).

*Intermittent or Partial Reinforcement* Another method of studying conditioned response learning has been to omit the US on some trials, thus providing the subject with a number of CS alone trials during the acquisition series. When CS alone trials become a part of such a series, the procedure is called partial or intermittent reinforcement.[2]

Humphreys (1939) examined the role of partial reinforcement on the conditioned eyeblink. In his study, three groups of students were given the following training: 96 trials with 100 percent reinforcement; 96 trials with 50 percent reinforcement, with the 48 CS-US presentations randomly interspersed with the 48 CS alone trials; or 48 trials with 100 percent reinforcement. Humphreys reported no significant differences among the groups with regard to the number of conditioned responses or the magnitude of the CRs obtained during acquisition. However, after the first few trials the partial reinforcement group's responding never attained the same level as the 100 percent reinforcement group.

Many experimenters examining a variety of conditioned responses have confirmed Humphreys's findings of superior responding when continuously reinforced trials are provided. These responses include the eyeblink in humans (Grant and Schipper, 1952; Ross, 1959; Prokasy and Williams, 1979), heart rate in dogs (Fitzgerald, 1963), nictitating membrane in rabbits (Prokasy and Gormezano, 1979), and the conditioned emotional response in rats (Wagner, Siegel, and Fein, 1967).

But what of maintenance performance? After the subjects reach a level of performance approaching asymptote using a continuous reinforcement schedule, is it necessary to continue to use continuously reinforced trials in order to maintain their performance? Gibbs, Latham, and Gormezano (1978) examined this question by first establishing the conditioned nictitating membrane response in rabbits with 300 CS-US trials. Following such training, one group of subjects continued to receive continuously reinforced trials; other groups were provided partial reinforcement schedules—the US was presented on either 50, 25, 15, 5, or 0 percent of the 600 trials following the 300 training trials. Figure 3-3 presents the performance levels for all of these groups. A 50 percent reinforcement schedule maintains performance at a level comparable to that achieved by the continuously reinforced group. Moreover, a partial reinforcement schedule in which the US was presented on only 15 percent of the trials resulted in a conditioned response frequency level of 80 percent.

**The Intensity of the Unconditioned Stimulus**
Pavlov's early experiments indicated that the strength of a conditioned response was related to the intensity of the unconditioned stimulus used, and many later investigators have confirmed Pavlov's findings. Razran's (1957) review indicated that Russian investigators have found the CR latency and magnitude to vary directly with the magnitude of the US employed; many American investigators have obtained similar findings. For instance, Wagner, Siegel, Thomas, and Ellison (1964) conditioned the salivary response of the dog using either 1 or 6 food pellets as the US. After 11 days of eight training trials per day, they found that the 6 pellet group reached a higher level of conditioned responding.

A second method of manipulating US intensity has been to vary the intensity of shock. Smith (1968) examined the conditioned nictitating membrane of the rabbit using either a 1, 2, or 4 ma intensity shock. He found that the percentage of CR responses was a function of increasing US intensity. Similarly, Annau and Kamin (1961) and Kamin and Brimer (1963), in examining the conditioned emotional response, found that response suppression was a function of the intensity of the shock used as the US. In the Annau and Kamin (1961) study, four CS-US pairings per day for 10 days were provided. The CS was white noise and the US was either a .28, .49, .85, 1.55, or 2.91 ma shock. The suppression of bar pressing that

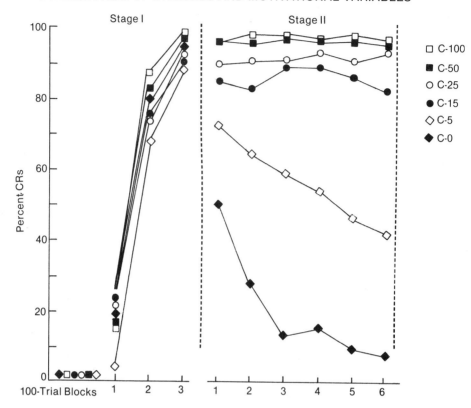

FIGURE 3-3.   Percent of conditioned responses as a function of the percentage of reinforcement provided in Stage II training, after all groups had received 100 percent reinforcement during Stage I. Adapted from C. M. Gibbs, S. B. Latham, and I. Gormezano, "Classical conditioning of the rabbit membrane response." *Animal Learning and Behavior,* 1978, 6, 209–215. Reprinted by permission of the Psychonomic Society.

took place in each test session following the CS-US trials is presented in Figure 3-4, and clearly reveals the role of US intensity.

But, how does the intensity of the unconditioned stimulus influence classical conditioned responding? The role of US intensity in such responding is quite complex. In order to indicate the nature of this complexity, it is first necessary to describe the theoretical position of Prokasy (1972), who suggested that classical conditioning can be related to four basic parameters:

1. the level of the subject's responding at the beginning of the CS-US trials
2. the trial during which the subject shifts from not responding to more consistent responding, thus giving evidence of learning

3. the growth or rate of responding during the CS-US trials provided
4. the asymptote or terminal level of responding.

Prokasy and Harsanyi (1968) found that when three intensities (weak, medium, strong) of an airpuff were used as the US in an eyeblink conditioning experiment, the parameters described were influenced in different ways. For example, the use of medium and strong unconditioned stimuli, in contrast to the weak unconditioned stimulus, resulted in subjects beginning to consistently respond to the CS earlier in the learning trials. In addition, different terminal levels of responding were noted, with the strong US producing the highest level, the medium US producing the

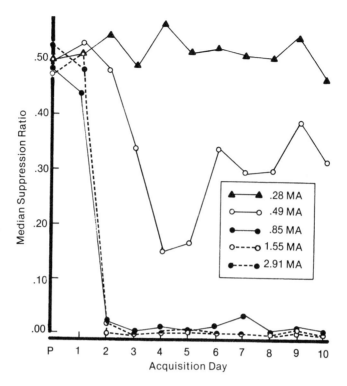

FIGURE 3-4.    Median suppression ratio as a function of day of acquisition training. Adapted from Z. Annau and L. J. Kamin, "The conditioned emotional response as a function of intensity of the US." *Journal of Comparative and Physiological Psychology*, 1961, 54, 428–432. Copyright © 1961 by the American Psychological Association. Reprinted by permission.

next highest level, and the weak US producing the lowest level of responding.

## Motivation in Instrumental Conditioning

How does motivation contribute to performance in instrumental conditioning? Investigators have concentrated on three motivational conditions:

1. the frequency and patterning of reinforced trials
2. the characteristics of the reinforcing agent
3. the time or delay interval between the making of the instrumental response and the receiving of reinforcement.

### Frequency and Patterning of Reinforcement

A commonplace finding in instrumental conditioning experiments has been that perfor-

mance during acquisition trials is related to the frequency with which continuously reinforced trials are provided. Although it is possible to examine how acquisition performance is related to the intermittency of reinforcement provided during training, few experimenters have chosen to examine this question. When such studies have been conducted, the standard method has been to examine the rat's performance in traversing a runway. However, the findings have been variable. In an early study, Weinstock (1958) found that performance (as measured by running time) of intermittently or partially reinforced animals was superior to that of animals provided with continuous reinforcement. This finding was also obtained by Goodrich (1959), Haggard (1959), and Wagner (1961). But later investigators found just the reverse. In these studies, continuously reinforced animals performed better than those receiving partial reinforcement; see Bacon (1962), Brown and Wagner (1964), Mikulka and Pavlik (1966), Wong (1978). The lack of consistent findings makes any theoretical explanation for one result or the other premature.

**Operant Reinforcement Schedules**  The basic procedure for examining the contribution of partial reinforcement with the operant task has been to use some type of reinforcement schedule. There is such extensive literature in this area that we can indicate only some of the important relationships existing between the type of schedule provided and the characteristics of the organism's performance. It is important to keep in mind that the subjects have already acquired the response being measured; the experimenter's objective has been to determine how different schedules of reinforcement influence *maintenance* behavior.

*Fixed Interval and Variable Interval Schedules*  It will be recalled from Chapter 2 that in the fixed interval (FI) schedule, the organism receives reinforcement for the first response made after a fixed or specific period of time. In the variable interval (VI) schedule, the time interval determining when reinforcement shall occur varies, with the value of the VI schedule being the average time between reinforcements.

A comparison of responding under FI and VI schedules reveals marked differences. Nevin (1973) has provided an interesting comparison of a rat's rate of lever pressing for water under a FI–1 minute and VI–1 minute schedule. (See Figure 3-5.) Under the FI–1 minute schedule, an animal makes relatively few responses at the beginning of the one minute interval but increases the rate of responding dramatically just prior to the time reinforcement is provided. This is a fundamental property of FI schedules; responding takes place at very low rates at the beginning of the interval but increases rapidly as the end of the interval approaches. The effect is clearly observed in a study by Dews (1962), who provided pigeons with a standard FI–500 second schedule. Dews noted the average number of responses made by his four subjects over each 50 second period making up the 500 second schedule. The differential rate of responding produces a scalloping effect, which can be noted in Figure 3-6.

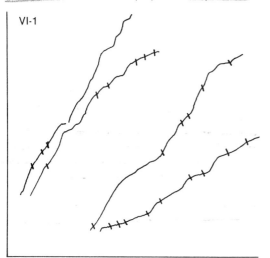

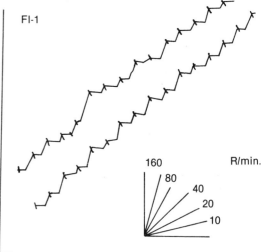

FIGURE 3-5.  Cumulative records of lever pressing by rats under a FI–1 and a VI–1 schedule of reinforcement. Presentation of reinforcement indicated by the diagonal marks. Adapted from *The Study of Behavior* by John A. Nevin. Copyright © 1973 by Scott, Foresman and Company. Reprinted by permission.

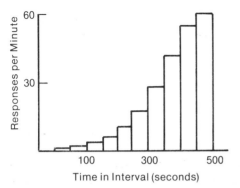

FIGURE 3-6. Rate of pecking in successive 50 second periods during a standard FI-500 second schedule of reinforcement. Adapted from P. B. Dews, "The effect of multiple S periods on responding on a fixed-interval schedule." *Journal of the Experimental Analysis of Behavior*, 1962, 5, 369–374. Copyright © 1962 by the Society for the Experimental Analysis of Behavior, Inc. Reprinted by permission.

A variable interval schedule eliminates the scalloping effect, as is revealed by data on Nevin's use of a VI-1 minute schedule, shown in Figure 3-5. The difference in rates of responding at the beginning and end of the interval, which characterized the FI schedule, is replaced by a relatively steady rate of responding with a VI schedule.

One similarity that exists between FI and VI responding is that the rate of responding is inversely related to the length of the interval. In a study by Wilson (1954), six groups of rats were trained at one of the following FI values—1/6, 1/3, 1, 2, 4, or 6 minutes—until 240 reinforcements had been received. Wilson found that the number of responses made per minute declined as a function of the length of the fixed interval.

Clark (1958) obtained similar findings using a variable interval schedule. Schedules of VI-1, VI-2, and VI-3 minutes were examined with different groups of rats placed under varying deprivation levels. At each level of deprivation, the VI-1 schedule provided the largest number of responses per minute, while the VI-3 schedule produced the smallest. (See Figure 3-7.)

*Fixed Ratio and Variable Ratio Schedules* A fixed ratio (FR) schedule is one in which the subject must make a fixed number of responses before receiving reinforcement, with the last response of the appropriate number resulting in reinforcement. The variable ratio (VR) schedule is one in which the number of responses determining when reinforcement will occur varies over the experimental session, with the value of the schedule being the average number of responses required for reinforcement. A comparison of an FR-45 with a VR-45 schedule can be found in a study by Nevin (1973), who used a rat's rate of lever pressing as the response measure. (See Figure 3-8.)

Under the FR schedule, pauses in responding may follow reinforcement, with the pause or rest on some occasions being fairly long. Once the animal begins to respond, the number of responses required to obtain reinforcement, provided it is not an excessive number, may be completed with a sustained burst of responding. In contrast, the cumulative record for the VR-45 schedule reveals that pauses in responding are not related to the receiving of reinforcement. Long pauses may appear either in midst of a sustained burst of responding or immediately after receiving reinforcement.

*Ratio vs. Interval Schedules* When a ratio schedule is employed, whether it be fixed or variable, the rate of responding directly determines the reinforcement rate. If an animal responds at a rate of 20 responses per minute and a FR-60 schedule is used, the animal will receive one reinforcement every three minutes, or 20 reinforcements per hour. But an increase to 30 responses per minute on a FR-60 schedule will result in one reinforcement every two minutes, or 30 reinforcements per hour. The increase in response rate will result in a greater number of reinforcements, which in turn will result in a greater number of responses, etc.

In contrast, the use of an interval schedule limits the amount of reinforcement received by the organism during any one in-

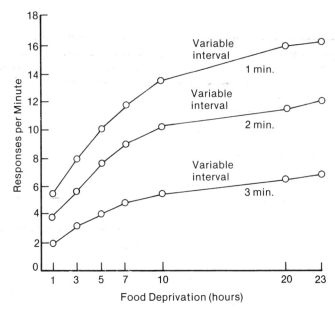

FIGURE 3-7.    Rate of bar pressing under three different schedules of reinforcement as a function of deprivation time. Adapted from F. C. Clark, "The effect of deprivation and frequency of rein-forcement on variable-interval responding." *Journal of the Experimental Analysis of Behavior,* 1958, 1, 221–228. Copyright © 1958 by the Society for the Experimental Analysis of Behavior. Re-printed by permission.

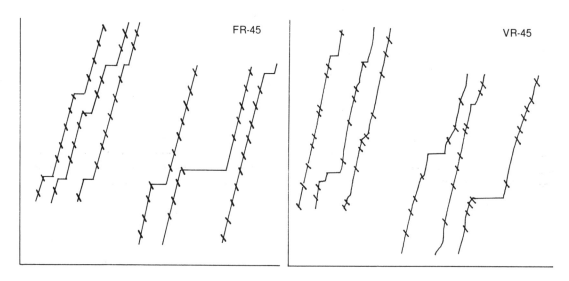

FIGURE 3-8.    Cumulative records of lever pressing by rats under a FR–45 and a VR–45 response schedule of reinforcement. Presentation of reinforcement is indicated by the diagonal marks. Adapted from *The Study of Behavior* by John A. Nevin. Copyright © 1973 by Scott, Foresman and Company. Reprinted by permission.

terval. Reinforcement can never be more frequent than the reinforcement value assigned to the interval, and is independent of the organism's rate of responding. A VI-1 minute schedule will result in no more than 60 reinforcements in an hour, regardless of whether the animal responds 20 times per minute or 60 times. It is not surprising, then, that ratio schedules will result in higher rates of responding than interval schedules since the organism can increase the amount of reinforcement received by increasing its rate of responding.

*The Matching Law*   One interesting finding has been noted by investigators who have examined reinforcement frequency with tasks employing concurrent schedules of reinforcement. It will be recalled from Chapter 2 that a concurrent schedule provides the subject with a choice of making one of two responses, each of which has been associated with a specific reinforcement schedule. For example, a pigeon in an experimental chamber may peck at a red key with reinforcement on a VI-1 minute schedule or it may peck at a green key with a VI-2 reinforcement schedule.

There is one methodological problem in using concurrent schedules. If the response made on one key is immediately followed by the subject receiving reinforcement for responding on the other key, the sequence of responding may be influenced. In order to maintain the independence of the two schedules, experimenters incorporate into their experimental procedure a changeover delay (COD) period. Such a delay prevents the reinforcement of a response that immediately follows a changeover from the other response.

When a concurrent schedule is used, the pigeons' rate of responding will remain relatively constant, but they will divide their time (and thus frequency of responding) between the two schedules in proportion to the frequency of reinforcement obtained from each schedule. In the example cited above, two-thirds of the reinforcements provided are associated with responding to the VI-1 minute key, so two-thirds of the pigeons' responses will be made to that key.

Herrnstein (1961) has found that this proportional relationship between responses and reinforcement holds over a wide range of variable interval values. For example, he found that if the proportion of reinforcements available to the pigeon on Key 1 was .25, the proportion of responses the pigeon would make to this key would also be .25. If, however, the proportion of reinforcements available on this key was increased to .75, the proportion of responding by the pigeon to this key would also increase to .75. This has led to the postulation of a matching law, which states that the relative frequency of a response will match the relative frequency of the reinforcement obtained by that response. This relationship has been expressed as follows:

$$\frac{\text{Response to Stimulus 1}}{\text{Responding to Stimulus 1} + \text{Responding to Stimulus 2}} = \frac{\text{Reinforcement obtained from Stimulus 1}}{\text{Reinforcement obtained from Stimulus 1} + \text{Reinforcement obtained from Stimulus 2}}$$

An interesting demonstration of the matching law, as it operates with humans, has been provided by Schroeder and Holland (1969), who used eye movements as a response measure. The task of the subject was to watch for deflections of a pointer, which could appear in any of four dials. Two dials were placed on the right side of the apparatus, and two dials were placed on the left side. The task of the subjects was to detect as many deflections as possible. When a deflection was noted, the subject used a button to reset the pointer, an act which could be considered reinforcement. Looking at the two dials on one side of the apparatus was considered to be equivalent to responding to a single key, whereas looking horizontally or diagonally was analogous to switching from one key to another, as would be done with a concurrent schedule. Varying numbers of deflections were provided on the right and left dials. The experimenters found that their subjects matched their rate of eye movement to the rate of reinforcement.

Some operant investigators have viewed the use of concurrent schedules and choice by the experimental subject as a basic procedure for examining other reinforcement variables, such as amount or delay of reinforcement. For example, it is possible to provide a four second delay of reinforcement when the pigeon responds to one key and an eight second delay of reinforcement for response made to the other key. Investigators have found that the subject's response to this procedure conforms to the matching law. DeVilliers (1977) has provided an interesting review of some of these experimental findings.

**Characteristics of the Reinforcing Agent**
Early experimenters were interested in determining how the amount of reward influenced learning. Grindley (1929), using chickens, and Crespi (1942), using rats, found that performance, as measured by speed of traversing an alley, increased as a function of the amount of food provided.

Beginning in the late forties, a host of investigators using the runway have confirmed the findings of Grindley and Crespi, demonstrating that the rate of responding is an increasing function of the amount of reward; see Zeaman (1949), D'Amato (1955), Armus (1959), Reynolds and Pavlik (1960), Hill and Wallace (1967), Wike and Chen (1971).

One methodological problem has been that when different amounts of food are used, the amount of eating time will vary, as will time spent in the goal box. Do these variables contribute to increased performance, independently of the amount of food serving as a reward? Some investigators, cognizant of this problem, have preferred to vary reward by using different concentrations of sucrose solution, thus keeping constant the amount of consummatory activity and time spent in the goal box.

The experimenters using differing concentrations of a sucrose solution have ob-

tained findings consistent with the results reported when amount of reward has been varied—namely, higher concentrations of sucrose lead to higher performance levels; see Guttman (1953), Butter and Thomas (1958), Goodrich (1960), Kraeling (1961). In a study by Kraeling (1961), three groups of rats were given one trial per day for 99 days on a runway, with one of three concentrations of sucrose, 2.5, 5.0, or 10.0 percent, serving as a reward. The running speed of her animals over blocks of nine trials, presented in Figure 3-9, indicates performance level to be a function of the concentration of sucrose used as a reward.

Differing reductions in shock intensity have been used to examine the contribution of negative reinforcement. A study by Trapold and Fowler (1960) illustrates the procedure and experimental findings. Five groups of rats were given 20 training trials to learn to escape a shock of either 120, 160, 240, 320, or 400 volts by traversing the charged runway to reach an uncharged goal box. The results, as indicated in Figure 3-10, show that running speed was related to the amount of shock reduction provided.

*Contrast Effects*   One interesting aspect of reward studies has been the investigation of how shifts in the amount of reward influence performance. Crespi (1942) examined this variable, giving rats 19 acquisition trials and providing either 16, 64, or 256 pellets as the reward for traversing a runway.[3] This was followed by a shift to a 16 pellet reward for all animals. In a second study, subjects were given 19 trials with a 1 or 4 pellet reward, followed by a shift to 16 pellets. In both studies, there were abrupt or sudden shifts in runway performance. For animals given the 16 pellet reward after experiencing a larger reward, running speed slowed down dramatically; however, when an animal was shifted to 16 pellets from just 1 or 4 pellets in previous trials, running speed suddenly became more rapid.

Crespi (1942) found that the running speed of animals shifted from 256 or 64 pellets to 16 was slower than that of a constant 16 pellet group at its asymptote or limit of prac-

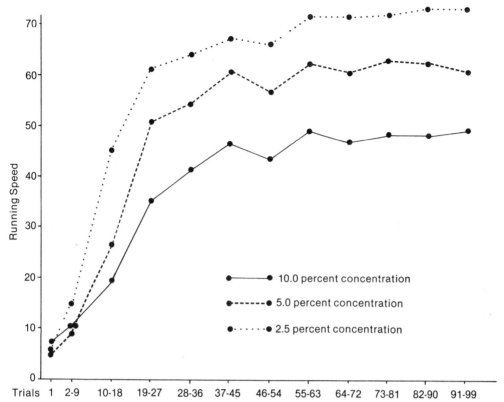

FIGURE 3-9.    Strength of instrumental response, broken down by concentration of sucrose solution. Adapted from D. Kraeling, "Analysis of amount of reward as a variable in learning." *Journal of Comparative and Physiological Psychology,* 1961, 54, 560–565. Copyright © 1961 by American Psychological Association. Reprinted by permission.

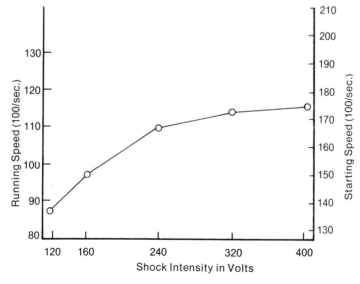

FIGURE 3-10.    Mean performance over the last eight trials as a function of shock intensity. Adapted from M. A. Trapold and H. Fowler, "Instrumental escape performance as a function of the intensity of noxious stimulation." *Journal of Experimental Psychology,* 1960, 6, 323–326. Copyright © 1960 by the American Psychological Association. Reprinted by permission.

tice. On the other hand, with those animals shifted from 1 or 4 pellets to 16, performance rose above the level characteristic of a constant 16 pellet group, which presumably had reached its asymptote of running speed. Increased performance as a result of going from a small to a large reward was termed a positive contrast or "elation" effect, whereas poorer performance associated with shifting from a larger to a smaller amount of reward was termed negative contrast or a "depression" effect. Subsequent findings have indicated the contrast effect to be transient, with the elevated and depressed performance levels eventually being replaced by levels similar to those reached by control animals, which had been provided only a single amount of reward. Figure 3-11 presents hypothetical performance curves illustrating this effect.

The early experimental findings on contrast effects were quite variable. Some individuals were able to replicate Crespi's findings, e.g., Zeaman (1949), Collier and Marx (1959), Ehrenfreund and Badia (1962), but others were unable to do so, e.g., Ashida and Birch (1964), Goodrich and Zaretsky (1962), Goldstein and Spence (1963). The problem for many experimenters was not in obtaining neg-

ative contrast, which appeared to be a reliable phenomenon, but in securing positive contrast effects. More recent research, such as that of Mellgren (1972), Lehr (1974), Shanab and Spencer (1978), and Spencer and Shanab (1979), suggests that positive contrast can be obtained.

One basic problem investigators have had in demonstrating positive contrast has been identified as a ceiling effect. That is, the experimental conditions used have generally resulted in the constant high reward group responding at the highest level of performance possible with this amount of reward. When the shift animals are switched from low to high reward, there is no opportunity for them to perform at a level higher than that achieved by the constant high reward subjects. One solution to this problem has been to manipulate the experimental conditions so as to lower the performance level of the high reward group. Thus, in Shanab and Spencer's (1978) study, the deprived animals had to wait for 20 seconds before receiving reward. As we shall note in the next section, such a delay in reinforcement results in a lowered performance level. With this modification of the experimental procedure, positive contrast effects were obtained.

How can contrast effects be explained? Crespi's (1942) identification of these effects in terms of "elation" and "depression" suggested that emotional states generated by the shifts in reward contributed to the findings. In keeping with this general explanation, many later investigators assumed that negative contrast effects could be accounted for by frustration. When animals were shifted from a high to a low reward, they became frustrated; this emotional state elicited responses incompatible with the instrumental response of running, thus leading to poorer performance. Control animals, having never experienced high reward, did not become emotional, so their performance was in keeping with the amount of reward provided.

Positive contrast effects have not been so easily accounted for. The early difficulty in consistently demonstrating this effect obviated the need for an explanation, but the posi-

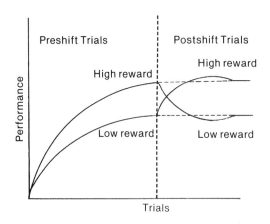

FIGURE 3-11. Hypothetical performance curves arising from a shift in the amount of reward and demonstrating positive and negative contrast effects.

tive findings obtained in later experimental studies as yet have not been adequately explained.

**Delay of Reinforcement** In instrumental conditioning, delay of reinforcement refers to the amount of time that elapses between the making of the response and the securing of reinforcement. Numerous investigators, beginning with Watson in 1917, have been interested in determining how this variable influences learning.

Perin (1943) found that when a delay of 30 seconds or more was introduced between the rat's pressing a bar and its receiving food, the animal was unable to learn this response. Renner's (1964) review of subsequent studies on the role of delay of reinforcement in instrumental learning tasks indicated the central importance of this variable. Contemporary investigators using nonsignaled instrumental tasks have continued to demonstrate its contribution to performance. Capaldi (1978), for example, trained rats to traverse a runway. He provided delays of 0, 10, 15, or 20 seconds between the time the animals entered the goal box and the time they received reinforcement.

Results indicated that the animals responded more rapidly as the delay interval approached 0.

Studies utilizing shock reduction or negative reinforcement have also indicated the importance of the delay interval. Fowler and Trapold (1962) have found that the speed of rats running a charged runway was significantly slower when shock reduction provided in the goal box was delayed. The delay interval used by these investigators was either 0, 1, 2, 3, 4, 6, or 16 seconds. Figure 3-12 presents these findings.

Tarpy and Koster (1970) noted an even more deleterious influence of delay. These experimenters provided rats with 60 shock-escape trials in which the termination of shock was delayed for either 0, 1.5, 3, or 6 seconds following the pressing of a lever. Although learning was obtained for the 0 and 1.5 second delay groups, learning did not take place when longer delay periods were used.

It may seem unusual to the reader that experimental subjects have difficulty in learning a task when the delay of reinforcement is measured in *seconds*. One reason for these unusual findings is that investigators have been

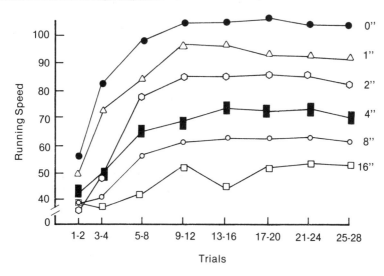

FIGURE 3-12. Running speed (100/time in sec.) as a function of the delay (in sec.) of shock termination. Adapted from H. Fowler and M. A. Trapold, "Escape performance as a function of delay of reinforcement." *Journal of Experimental Psychology*, 1962, 63, 464–467. Copyright © 1962 by the American Psychological Association. Reprinted by permission.

careful to control for the influence of secondary reinforcing stimuli (secondary rewards). It will be recalled from Chapter 2 that secondary reinforcing stimuli contribute to learning because they were previously associated with primary rewards such as food or water. If such stimuli are not controlled in the learning task, they can provide a "bridge" between the instrumental response and the securing of the delayed primary reward. Watson's (1917) early finding that rats could learn an instrumental response although reward was delayed for as long as 20 minutes has been attributed to the action of secondary rewards present in the task.

*Taste Aversion*  In light of the experimental evidence suggesting that relatively short delays of either reward or relief from aversive stimulation retard learning, a most provocative finding was obtained by Garcia and his associates (Garcia, Kimeldorf, and Koelling, 1955; Garcia and Kimeldorf, 1957). They noted that a taste aversion could be learned by rats even though the time interval between the response of drinking a liquid and a subsequent sickness was measured not in seconds but in hours. Smith and Roll's (1967) study illustrates the general procedure as well as typical findings. Rats were deprived of liquid for 24 hours and then given 20 minutes' access to saccharin. After either 0, .5, 1, 2, 3, 6, 12, or 24 hours, the experimental animals were irradiated, which produces nausea. Control subjects were given sham exposure for 200 seconds. Twenty-four hours later, each animal was given access to a bottle of saccharin and a bottle of water. The amount consumed from each bottle over a 48 hour period (expressed as a preference score) by each group of animals is found in Figure 3-13. The unusual aspect of Smith and Roll's (1967) result was that, although as long as 12 hours intervened between the presentation of the saccharin solution and the irradiation, the experimental animals avoided this liquid on the preference test.

The findings obtained by Garcia and his associates and those of Smith and Roll (1967) have raised a number of questions about the conditions responsible for establishing a taste aversion. One concern was whether any stimulus, external or internal, could serve as a cue (or discriminative stimulus) for the animal to avoid the saccharin associated with illness. A second question was whether an aversion would develop after associating the saccharin with any noxious stimulus, such as shock, or whether the aversion was dependent on the development of a gastric upset. Garcia and Koelling (1966) attempted to find answers to these questions by conducting a number of experiments, all using the same basic procedure. Rats were first trained to drink water with two characteristics: (a) the water was sweetened with saccharin (gustatory stimulus), with (b) flashes of light and a clicking noise (audiovisual stimuli) produced whenever the animal made contact with the drinking tube. For one group of animals, the drinking of the sweet, bright-noisy water was accompanied by shock to the feet. For a second group of animals, the sweet, bright-noisy water was mixed with lithium chloride or was followed by irradiation; either treatment subsequently produced severe illness.

In the second phase of the experiment, the experimenters were interested in determining if avoidance conditioning to the audiovisual and/or gustatory characteristics of the stimuli had taken place. The group of animals that had been made sick was provided with the opportunity to drink sweetened water unaccompanied by the light and click, or to drink unsweetened water in the presence of the light and click. Animals that had been shocked were given the opportunity to drink under either of these same conditions. Results indicated the selective character of the associative relationships established. Rats that had been made sick after drinking sweetened water avoided drinking it, but did not show an aversion to regular water accompanied by audiovisual stimuli. Rats that had been shocked did not avoid the sweetened water. Revusky and Garcia (1970) have commented on these findings, writing "if an animal wants to decide what made it sick, it will tend to ignore external events and carefully consider the flavors of previously consumed substances; if

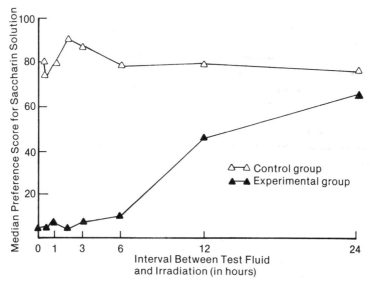

FIGURE 3-13.   The median preference score for each delay condition for the experimental and control subjects. Adapted from J. C. Smith and D. L. Roll, "Trace conditioning with X-rays as an aversive stimulus." *Psychonomic Science*, 1967, 9, 11–12. Reprinted by permission of the Psychonomic Society.

it wants to decide what produced an external event, it will tend to ignore flavor and will carefully consider the preceding exteroceptive stimuli" (p. 22).

Later studies have demonstrated that the ease of establishment of an associative relationship between a specific stimulus and a reinforcing event is dependent on the species examined. Wilcoxin, Dragoin, and Kral (1971) have found that birds learn to avoid eating toxic monarch butterflies by sight, suggesting that birds may be more disposed to associate nausea with visual cues than with gustatory ones. These investigators have experimentally demonstrated that quail readily learned to avoid blue water when this visual stimulus had been previously associated with illness; however, these birds did not learn to avoid sour water, a gustatory stimulus, although it too had been associated with illness. Rats, on the other hand, revealed an aversion to sour water but not colored water, after both types of water had been associated with nausea.

The study of taste aversion has been a popular one; a variety of experimental variables have been examined, only a few of which can be described here. Revusky and Bedarf (1967) have found that increasing the level of irradiation, which in turn increases the severity of the sickness, will strengthen the animal's aversion to the associated foodstuff. Studies by Smith and Birkle (1966), Dragoin (1971), and Barker (1976) have shown that increasing the strength or concentration of the liquid or foodstuff associated with nausea is also related to the strength of the avoidance response.

What contribution is provided by the experimental subject's experience with the foodstuff, or the toxic drug, and associated nausea? Here, most experimenters have found that preexposure to the foodstuff will weaken the taste aversion effect. In a study by Revusky and Bedarf (1967), one group of rats was provided with grape juice for 8 days, while a second group of animals was given condensed milk for the same period of time. On the treatment day, the two groups of animals were given 100 licks of each liquid so that each group was experiencing a familiar as well as a novel substance. An hour later, half of each group was irradiated (the other half served as control). Three days later, all animals were given 30 minutes of free access to both the milk and the grape juice. In examining the performance of the experimental animals, which consumed less of the liquids than the control subjects, the investigators found that significantly more of the experienced substance was consumed than the less experienced, thus demonstrating that novel foodstuffs were more strongly associated with toxicosis. Siegel (1974) has found that the experience with the foodstuff need be no greater than a single preexposure in order for the aversion to be reduced.

Other experimenters have centered their interest on the effects of preexposing the animal to the drug that causes nausea. In a series of studies, Braveman (1975) has found that preexposing the animal to injections of the drug alone will reduce the taste aversion effect. In one experiment, either 0, 1, or 3 injections of lithium chloride were provided. When multiple injections of lithium chloride were given, a recuperative period of 4 days was provided after each injection. Ten days after the last injection, the animals were given saccharin solution to drink, followed by an injection of lithium chloride. Three days later, the animals were presented with saccharin; it was observed that the amount consumed was a decreasing function of the number of pretraining injections that had been provided.

For students interested in the generality and relevance of laboratory findings, the taste aversion phenomenon has been demonstrated with a variety of organisms, including cats, mice, monkeys, ferrets, coyotes, birds, and reptiles, and with many different types of foodstuffs, such as sucrose, milk, grape juice, vinegar, and laboratory chow. See Box 3-1.

Gustavson, Garcia, Hankins, and Rusiniak (1974) have suggested that taste aversion procedures can be used in controlling predators. Sheep ranchers and environmentalists have argued over whether coyotes should be eliminated, since these animals have been responsible for killing sheep and thus causing substantial losses for the ranchers. Environmentalists, of course, have pointed out that indiscriminate killings could lead to another "endangered species." Gustavson et al. have proposed that sheep carcasses be laced with lithium chloride. The eating of the sheep meat would then result in the coyotes getting sick and subsequently avoiding this type of prey. Their experimental findings have demonstrated the effectiveness of such an approach. In this study, in which seven adult coyotes were used as experimental subjects, investigators found that only a single trial of lamb meat laced with lithium chloride was sufficient to establish a strong aversion, inhibiting the further eating of lambs. Such an aversion, however, did not generalize to the eating of rabbits.

*Can We Reconcile Taste Aversion Effects with the Findings Obtained with Delay of Reinforcement Studies?* We have noted that a taste aversion to a specific foodstuff can be acquired despite a long time interval between the ingestion of the foodstuff and a later illness. This result is contrary to the findings obtained with delay of reinforcement studies. Is it possible to reconcile findings from these two types of experiments?

Rozin and Kalat (1971) have argued that taste aversion findings can be accounted for by the postulation of a learning process or mechanism different from the one operating in typical laboratory learning tasks. Gustatory stimuli, consummatory responses, and unpleasant gastric consequences are all involved in the organism's feeding system—which these investigators have assumed involves a specialized adaptive system operating in its own distinct fashion. As they have written:

> Taste does not become a *signal* for poison in the sense that a tone or light becomes a signal for shock. In taste-aversion learning, the animal's perception of the taste itself or of its affective value may change. . . . The taste itself may become aversive or unacceptable, as if it were unpalatable. . . . By contrast, stimuli associated with shock do not themselves become aversive; they evoke little avoidance outside the training situation. (p. 478)

Rozin and Kalat's position has had some support from Garcia and Koelling (1966), whose experiment was reviewed earlier. It will be recalled that these investigators found that

Most of us have experienced taste aversion, but only a few investigators have used human subjects in experimentally validating this effect. Bernstein (1978) is one of these. In this study, a population of 41 children, ages 2 to 16, served as subjects, all of them being treated as outpatients in a hospital and clinic. Twenty-six of these children were receiving intravenous doses of chemotherapeutic drugs that produce gastrointestinal upset. Fourteen of these 26 subjects were given Mapletoff (an unusual ice cream prepared with maple and black walnut flavor extracts) to eat prior to their receiving the chemotherapeutic drug; the other 12 served as Control Group 1 and did not receive the ice cream. Control Group 2 consisted of 15 children who were receiving a drug that was nontoxic to the GI tract; these children were also given Mapletoff ice cream. Two to four weeks later, the acceptance (or rejection) of Mapletoff ice cream was measured by offering all 41 children a choice of either eating the ice cream or playing with a game. Results indicated that only 21 percent of the children receiving chemotherapeutic drugs chose the ice cream, in contrast to 67 percent for Control Group 1 and 73 percent for Control Group 2. Approximately 4½ months after this first preference test was provided, the subjects were given a second preference test. Here, patients were given a choice of either Mapletoff ice cream or another relatively novel ice cream, Hawaiian Delight. During this second testing, patients were asked to taste both ice cream flavors, indicate which they preferred, and eat as much as they wished. Results indicated that Mapletoff ice cream was preferred by 25 percent of the experimental group, in contrast to 66 percent and 50 percent of Control Groups 1 and 2. Aversion to the Mapletoff ice cream appeared to be a specific learned response. As Bernstein has noted, the demonstration of taste aversions in humans receiving chemotherapy treatments may be of importance to physicians who administer treatments that induce nausea. Such aversions may be one factor contributing to the anorexia and weight loss seen in patients with cancer.

an association between the taste of a liquid and sickness can be established when the delay interval is measured in hours, whereas the establishment of an associative relationship between an audiovisual stimulus and sickness is dependent on these events taking place in close temporal contiguity. The difficulty with Rozin and Kalat's position is that they have not provided us with any further information about the characteristics of the specialized learning process that operates in taste aversion acquisition.

The basis of a second explanation of taste aversion is found in the theoretical positions of Spence (1956) and Mowrer (1960). These investigators have posited that long delays of reinforcement provide the experimental subject with the opportunity to make other responses; these responses interfere with the subject's identification of the specific response that was responsible for securing reward. Revusky (1971) has suggested that by examin-

ing the characteristics of these interfering responses made by the experimental subject, the decremental effect of delayed reinforcement can be more adequately understood.

Revusky has posited that when two events to be associated, A and B, are separated in time, other environmental events, designated as C, may intervene. If the intervening event C becomes associated with either event A or B, these A-C, C-A, C-B, or B-C associations tend to block the association between A and B. But whether or not intervening events provide interference is dependent upon what Revusky (1971) has termed "situational relevance." Here, he hypothesized that subjects will readily associate events that take place in the same physical environment but not those occurring in different environments. According to this analysis, the difference between taste aversion and instrumental reward studies can be attributed to the characteristics of the intervening events in each experimental situation. For example, with taste aversion experiments, the responses made during the delay interval are not situationally relevant to the drinking of the flavored substance. The result is that little interference is provided by these responses, so the associative relationship between the flavored substance and sickness is readily acquired. In an instrumental reward study, a rat presses a bar in a Skinner box and after a delay obtains food. The responses made by the animal during the delay interval are situationally relevant and thus interfere with the acquisition of the bar pressing response. If situationally irrelevant responses could replace the relevant responses during the delay interval, it should be possible for the animal to learn instrumental reward tasks with very long delay intervals.

Lett (1973, 1974, 1975) has examined this last proposal in an experiment in which rats were trained to make a right-left position discrimination. Following a right or left turning response, they were picked up and placed in their home cage for either 1, 20, or 60 minutes. After one of these delay intervals, the animals were returned to the apparatus and placed in the start box, where they were either rewarded with a sucrose solution or not rewarded, depending on the correctness of their earlier response. One hundred trials (1 trial/day) were provided; the findings obtained in Experiment 1 (Lett, 1975) are shown in Figure 3-14. Learning has clearly taken place, in spite of a delay interval as long as 60 minutes between the making of the correct response and the securing of reward.

We should note that Lett used a discrimination task rather than an unsignaled task. But, as shall be shown in Chapter 5, the learning of discrimination tasks can also be subject to the deleterious effect of delay of reward. Lett's experimental studies, as well as those of later investigators using her procedure, thus seem relevent to the comparison of taste aversion findings with delay of reward studies.

Lett attributed the ability of her rats to learn with such long delay intervals to the fact that the responses made by the animals in their home cage were not situationally rele-

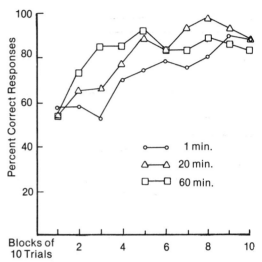

FIGURE 3-14. Percentage of correct responses during blocks of 10 trials for subjects after a delay of 1, 20, or 60 minutes for a right turn. Adapted from B. T. Lett, "Long delay learning in the T-maze." *Learning and Motivation*, 1975, 6, 80–90. Reprinted by permission.

vant and did not interfere with the response to be learned.

Lett's procedure dictated that the experimental animals be handled during each trial, since it was necessary to transfer these animals first from the apparatus to their home cages where they spent the delay interval, and then back to the apparatus in order to obtain (or not obtain) reward. Lieberman, McIntosh, and Thomas (1979) became interested in determining whether the handling and picking up of the animals contributed to Lett's findings. In their first experiment, similar to Lett's, a 60 second delay interval was used with rats learning a discrimination task. The picking up, handling, etc., of animals in the two experimental groups—the home cage group and experimental apparatus group—was the same; however, animals in the home cage group spent the delay interval in their home cage, whereas the experimental apparatus group spent the delay interval in the apparatus.

Findings indicated the *both* groups of rats learned the discrimination equally well.

Although Lett's (1975) findings that rats could learn a discrimination task with a long delay interval were confirmed, Leiberman et al.'s findings did not support Lett's position on the importance of where the animals spent the delay interval. Rather, handling appeared to be the critical variable. Other studies by Lieberman et al. confirmed the finding obtained in their first experiment. They demonstrated that if handling was delayed or omitted after the correct choice had been made, learning did not take place. Lieberman et al. found in a subsequent study (Experiment 4) that any unusual or salient stimulus presented after a correct discriminative response could mitigate the effects of delay. This finding indicated that handling was important only because it was a salient stimulus.

Lieberman et al. have suggested that the presentation of salient stimuli, such as handling, increased illumination, burst of noise, etc., following the making of a correct response in a discrimination experiment has a "marking" function. They wrote:

> . . . when a subject encounters a salient, unexpected stimulus, we believe that this leads the subject to search its memory in an attempt to identify causal responses. Any responses so identified are then more likely to be recalled during subsequent memory searches, as when the subject tries to recall preceding responses that could have produced food. (p. 240)

In spite of the encouraging beginning provided by Lett and Lieberman et al., experimenters are still having some difficulty reconciling the findings obtained in delay of reinforcement studies with the findings in taste aversion experiments. The studies on discrimination learning with long reward delays need confirmation; Roberts (1976), for example, using only a one minute reinforcement delay, was unable to replicate Lett's (1974) findings. Finally, the rapidity with which a taste aversion can be acquired despite delay intervals of up to 12 hours suggests that other explanations must be sought if these findings are to be reconciled with the results obtained with delay of reinforcement studies.

## SUMMARY

Experimenters examining nonsignaled and signaled conditioning tasks have been interested in how the learning process is influenced by the manipulation of three basic variables: stimulus conditions, motivational conditions, and cognitive variables.

Stimulus intensity has often been investigated. Most experimenters use classical conditioning tasks and find that the strength of the conditioned response is a function of the intensity of the conditioned stimulus. It has been noted that the intensity effect will be accentuated if the experimental design provides for each subject to experience more than a single level of stimulus intensity. The length of the CS-US interval is a second stimulus variable that has interested experimenters. Although early investigators believed that the optimal CS-US interval for all conditioning tasks was .5 second, it has since been demonstrated conclusively that the optimal CS-US interval will vary as a function of the type of response conditioned.

Motivational variables have been found to play an important role in determining the strength of the learned response. When classical conditioning tasks are used, the unconditioned stimulus serves as the source of motivation for the subject. It has been shown that the strength of the conditioned response increases as the strength or intensity of the unconditioned stimulus increases.

When instrumental conditioning tasks are used, three motivational variables have been examined: (1) the frequency or patterning of reinforced trials, (2) the characteristics of the reinforcing agent, and (3) the time or delay interval placed between the making of the instrumental response and the receiving of reinforcement.

The patterning of reinforcement has been investigated primarily with operant conditioning tasks. Fixed and variable interval and fixed and variable ratio reinforcement schedules are most often examined. Many comparisons among reinforcement schedules have been made; perhaps the most fundamental finding is that ratio schedules result in a more

rapid rate of responding than interval schedules.

The characteristics of the reinforcing
agent play a part in instrumental conditioning. Increasing the amount of reward causes
instrumental learning to take place more rapidly. An interesting aspect of these studies is
the finding of contrast effects. The presentation of a large reward followed by a small reward will result in the animal responding at a
performance level lower than the performance
level of an animal that was given the small reward from the beginning of the study. The
presentation of a small reward followed by a
large reward will result in the animal responding at a performance level higher than the performance level of an animal that was given the
large reward at the start of the learning trials.
These effects have been identified as negative
and positive contrast effects.

Experimenters examining delay of reinforcement have been interested in the effects
of varying the time interval between the making of the response and the securing of reward. Results reveal that as this interval
grows longer, learning declines. Investigators
have found, for example, that if the delay of
reinforcement interval is as long as 10 seconds, little learning will take place. Findings
contrary to these have been obtained with
taste aversion experiments, in which the animal is first fed a novel foodstuff and then
made sick either by injection of an illness-pro-
ducing drug, such as lithium chloride, or by
irradiation. Experimental results have indicated that a food aversion can be established
in animals with a delay interval of as long as
12 hours. Explanations for the divergent findings obtained in taste aversion studies and instrumental reward studies have been proposed, but at this time none of them are completely satisfactory.

## NOTES

1. There is some controversy regarding whether
unconditioned stimuli *must* have a motivational function but an examination of the experimental evidence bearing on this issue
would take us too far afield in this introductory presentation.
2. Most experimental interest has been directed
toward examining the role of partial reinforcement on extinction; we shall delay consideration of this topic until Chapter 6.
3. Crespi's procedure, in which animals have
been provided one amount of reward over a
series of trials followed by a shift to a different
amount, has been termed successive contrast.
Most investigators of contrast effects have
used this type of experimental design. It is also
possible, as Bower (1961) has done, to examine simultaneous contrast. Here, subjects
are concurrently presented with two different
amounts of reinforcement, with different cues
signaling the different amounts of reward
found in the goal box. Thus, a rat would receive eight pellets of food for traversing a
white runway but only one pellet for traversing a black runway. Trials on the black and
white runway are intermingled throughout
the training period.

# CHAPTER FOUR

# The Contribution of Cognitive Variables to Classical and Instrumental Conditioning

In this chapter, the review of variables contributing to classical and instrumental conditioning will be completed with an examination of the role of cognitive variables. In addition, two basic issues frequently raised in the examination of conditioning will be considered. One has to do with whether autonomic responses can be instrumentally conditioned; the second is concerned with the theoretical issue of what is learned in classical and instrumental conditioning tasks.

## COGNITIVE VARIABLES

Cognitive variables represent a class of central state or organismic variables that may contribute to learning and performance. Historically, Watson's pronouncement that cognitive variables were private, and therefore not appropriate for study, effectively prevented most learning psychologists from studying them. Nonetheless, a few psychologists did become interested in manipulating some experimental conditions that would be identified as cognitive. The positing of cognitive variables is more frequently found in discrimination tasks, where the greater complexity of learning demands that higher level mental processes be considered, than in nonsignaled and signaled learning tasks.

### The Contribution of Verbal Instructions and the Role of Awareness

A few early classical conditioning experimenters became interested in determining how the kinds of instructions given to subjects influenced the strength of the conditioned response. Since instructions can be viewed as a procedure for manipulating a cognitive process, these studies can be considered as precursors of the examination of cognitive variables.

Cook and Harris (1937) demonstrated that a conditioned galvanic skin response could be obtained merely by instructing the subject that shock would follow the presentation of a green light. Their experimental findings revealed that the presentation of 15 or 30 CS-US trials following such instructions did not increase the strength of the conditioned response beyond the strength obtained when only a single conditioning trial plus instructions was used. Deane (1961), conditioning heart rate, noted that "verbal instructions regarding when to expect shock were apparently more effective in bringing about the deceleration than actually receiving the shock itself" (p. 492).

The contribution of instructions has also been examined with the classical conditioning of skeletal responses. Unlike the autonomic conditioning studies of Cook and Harris

(1937) and Deane (1961), in which their subjects were told when to expect the presentation of the US, skeletal conditioning studies have used more indirect instructions, as illustrated in an eyelid conditioning study conducted by Nicholls and Kimble (1964). Here, two groups of subjects were provided with 40 conditioning trials. One group received "facilitative" instructions: "Relax and let your eye reactions take care of themselves. If you feel your eye close or about to close, do nothing to stop it." The second group received inhibitory instructions—the subject was asked to "Concentrate on not blinking until you feel the puff of air. That is, try not to blink after the light comes on until you feel the air puff." The percentages of CRs for the two groups, presented in Figure 4-1, clearly reveal the role of instructions in facilitating or inhibiting responding.

The facilitating and inhibiting effect of instructions to the subject on the conditioning of both autonomic and skeletal responses has been confirmed in more recent experiments; see Hill (1967), Swenson and Hill (1970), and Harvey and Wickens (1971, 1973). In summary, there seems to be little doubt that the strength of a simple classically conditioned response can be manipulated by the kinds of instructions provided. It seems reasonable to assume that such instructions are responsible for providing some change in the subject's cognitive structure, which in turn is responsible for determining the strength of the conditioned response.

### Cognitive Variables and Animal Learning

Can one study the role of cognitive variables in animal learning when the experimental subjects are handicapped by their inability to communicate with the experimenter? A few early investigators believed that it was possible to do so. Krechevsky (1932a) assumed that rats develop hypotheses in solving dis-

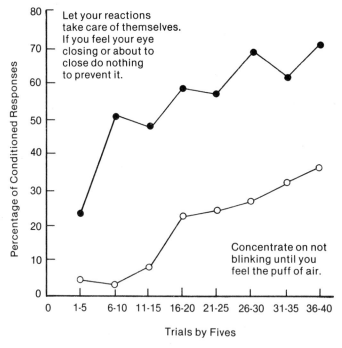

FIGURE 4-1.   Mean percentage of conditioned responses for subjects conditioned with facilitative and inhibitory instructions. Adapted from M. F. Nicholls and G. A. Kimble, "Effect of instruction upon eyelid conditioning." *Journal of Experimental Psychology*, 1964, 67, 400–402. Copyright © 1964 by the American Psychological Association. Reprinted by permission.

crimination problems, while Tolman (1932) attributed to his rats an expectancy of finding reward in the goal box of a multiple T-maze. See Box 4-1.

Most contemporaries of Krechevsky and Tolman believed that the postulation of cognitive constructs in animals was a step beyond serious scientific inquiry. Fowler (1978) described this position:

> An attitude dismissing, or even disavowing, animal cognition has long been prevalent among [these] investigators. . . . Mentalistic processes are not to be considered in the analysis of behavior; instead, the bodily reactions of the organism should be studied directly. Adopting this posture, the investigator can ensure public observation and replication of his data and, in so doing, promote the use of a scientific method. (p. 109)

During the past decade, experimenters have acknowledged that not only do cognitive processes exist in animals but their functioning must be identified if a complete account of animal learning is to be provided. (See Hulse, Fowler, and Honig's (1978) volume, *Cognitive Processes in Animal Behavior.*) Several examples can be cited.

**Cognitive Maps**   One cognitive process postulated is Menzel's (1978) "cognitive map." This cognitive construct has been inferred from the following behavior. A young chimpanzee is carried around in an open field and is able to view an experimenter hiding food in a number of different places—under leaves, in clumps of grass, etc. The animal is then returned to her cage but after an interval is released to find the food. With remarkable accuracy she visits the places where the food has been hidden. She does not retrace the experimenter's route in hiding the food but generally follows a shorter and more direct path. Clearly, the chimp must have learned a great deal from her initial observations, with such learning manifested in her behavior of finding the hidden food. The concept of a cognitive map has been posited by Menzel (1978) to describe the relationship between (a) the observation by his chimpanzees of where food had been hidden and (b) the kinds of behavior engaged in by the animals in finding the food.

**Learned Helplessness**   A more complex cognitive variable operating in animal learning has been described by Seligman and his as-

---

**BOX 4-1**

An early experiment conducted by Tinklepaugh (1928) illustrates his inference about the presence of a cognitive construct, expectancy, in monkeys learning a delayed response. In this study, a piece of banana was placed under one of two cups, while monkeys, serving as experimental subjects, observed where the food was placed. The animals were prevented from responding immediately, however, by a restraining board placed in front of the containers. After a few seconds' delay, the board was removed and the monkey was permitted to make a choice; responding to the baited cup was readily noted.

In what Tinklepaugh has described as a substitution test, the experimenter, without being observed by the monkey, substituted for the banana a piece of lettuce—a much less preferred food. Tinklepaugh reported what would happen when the monkey lifted the correct cup and found the lettuce:

> She looks at the lettuce but . . . does not touch it. She looks around the cup and behind the board. She stands up and looks under and around her. She picks the cup up and examines it thoroughly inside and out. She has on occasion turned toward observers present in the room and shrieked at them in apparent anger. (p. 224)

Tinklepaugh's explanation for such responding was that the animal *expected* to find food, with the animal's searching clearly revealing the operation of this cognitive variable.

sociates as learned helplessness. A study by Seligman and Maier (1967) described the experimental procedure and behavior that led to their positing of this construct.

The training phase of their experiment consisted of strapping dogs in hammocks which were so constructed that the animal's legs hung down below its body through holes cut in the canvas. The animal's head was held in position by two side panels. Three groups of subjects were run. An escape group was given 64 trials in which a five second shock was applied to the animal's hind leg on each trial. To escape from the shock the animal had to push one of the side panels. A second group received inescapable shock—when shock was presented, the panel pushing response (or any other response) would not terminate the shock. In order to equate shock duration for the escape and inescapable shock groups, each animal in the inescapable group was paired with an animal in the escape group. The amount of shock received by each animal in the escape group determined the amount of shock that was presented to the paired animal in the inescapable group. Thus, the only way in which the inescapable shock group differed from the escape group was in the lack of control it had over the termination of the shock. Finally, a control group was placed in the hammock but received no shock.

The test phase consisted of avoidance-escape training in the shuttle box. A darkening of the experimental chamber served as the CS, and 10 seconds later shock (US) was presented. Jumping over a shoulder-high barrier into an adjacent chamber during or after the 10 second CS-US interval enabled the animals to avoid or escape the shock. If the animal did not respond in 60 seconds following the onset of shock, the trial was terminated. Ten test trials were provided. The median latency of responding for the three groups is noted in Figure 4-2. The animals who had received inescapable shock during training were unable to learn the jumping response which would permit them to avoid or escape from the shock.

Maier and Seligman (1976) have provided an interesting description of the behav-

ior of dogs placed in this avoidance learning situation.

When placed in a shuttlebox an experimentally naive dog, at the onset of the first electric shock, runs frantically about, until it accidently scrambles over the barrier and escapes the shock. On the next trial, the dog, running frantically, crosses the barrier more quickly than on the preceding trial. Within a few trials the animal becomes very efficient in escaping and soon learns to avoid shock altogether. After about 50 trials the dog becomes nonchalant and stands in front of the barrier. At the onset of the signal for shock, the dog leaps gracefully across and rarely gets shocked again. But dogs first given inescapable shock in a Pavlovian hammock show a strikingly different pattern. Such a dog's first reactions to shock in the shuttle box are much the same as those of a naive dog. He runs around frantically for about 30 sec., but then stops moving, lies down, and quietly whines. After 1 min. of this, shock terminates automatically. The dog fails to cross the barrier and escape from shock. On the next trial, the dog again fails to escape. At first he struggles a bit and then, after a few seconds, seems to give up and passively accept the shock. On all succeeding trials, the dog continues to fail to escape. (p. 4)

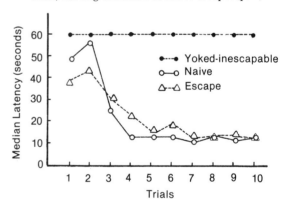

FIGURE 4-2.   Median response latency in a shuttle box for dogs given escapable, yoked inescapable, or no shock in a harness. Adapted from S. F. Maier and M. E. P. Seligman, "Learned helplessness: Theory and evidence." *Journal of Experimental Psychology: General*, 1976, 105, 3–46. Copyright © 1976 by the American Psychological Association. Reprinted by permission.

Seligman and his associates have inferred the concept of learned helplessness from the kind of behavior exhibited by the inescapable shock group. They assume that such a state arises when the experimental subject perceives that a particular outcome takes place independently of any response that might be made. We have considered learned helplessness to be a cognitive variable, although Maier and Seligman (1976) have suggested that motivational and emotional factors are also involved. Their description of learned helplessness involves (1) a motivational deficit, as revealed by the finding that the presentation of an aversive stimulus does not elicit responding during the test trial, (2) a cognitive deficit in which the earlier experience of uncontrolled shock interferes with the organism's capacity to perceive a contingent relationship between its behavior and an outcome, and (3) a modification of the organism's emotionality in which fear, originally elicited by the aversive state, is replaced by depression.

Learned helplessness has been demonstrated by experimenters using cats, rats, mice, dogs, and fish. Perhaps most interesting has been the finding of learned helplessness with humans. The procedure used with human subjects has been similar to that used with animals, although aversive stimuli other than shock, such as noise, have been used to motivate subjects.

In Hiroto's (1974) study, for example, pretreatment trials consisted of presenting a 110 db 3000 Hz tone to two groups of subjects. One group (Escapable) could escape from such stimulation by pushing a button which terminated the tone. For the second group (Inescapable) the button was inoperable so that pushing it did not control the termination of the tone. Both groups received 30 presentations of the tone. A third group (Control) did not receive the presentation of the tone during this part of the study.

All three groups were then presented with an avoidance/escape task. The apparatus used was described as a human analogue to the two-way shuttle box found in animal learned-helplessness studies. A 3 inch knob placed on the cover of the shuttle box could be moved from one side to the other along a 19 inch track. At the beginning of each trial, a red light was presented for 5 seconds, followed by the onset of the 110 db tone for 10 seconds. A correct response consisted of the subject moving the knob to one side of the apparatus on one trial, and sliding the knob in the opposite direction on the next trial. If such a response was made during the presentation of the red light, the tone was not presented, thus enabling the subject to avoid hearing the tone. Making this response after the tone was presented would terminate it, thus permitting the subject to escape. Results obtained for the 18 trials indicated that the inescapable tone group had longer response latencies and more failures to escape than either of the other two groups. The author has written, "Learned helplessness can be experimentally produced in man. Both animals and man show longer latencies and more failures to escape following inescapable aversive events than following escapable events or no pretreatment" (p. 192).

Many other investigators have also been able to demonstrate performance deficits arising from the inability of the subject to make an appropriate response during training trials; see Thornton and Jacobs (1971), Krantz, Glass, and Snyder (1974), Hiroto and Seligman (1975), or Klein and Seligman (1976). But it should be acknowledged that there have been replication failures as well; see Roth and Bootzin (1974), Roth and Kubal (1975). Miller and Norman (1979), in their review of the construct of learned helplessness, have concluded that "Seligman's theory of learned helplessness no longer offers a full and viable explanation for the results of the current research" (p. 106). They note that the theory is inadequate in the areas of (a) delineation of the varying conditions leading to learned helplessness; (b) determination of the varying experimental factors, e.g., the importance of the task that contributes to learned helplessness; and (c) assessment of the extent to which learned helplessness will generalize to other tasks. Although these are important issues, they should not detract from the contribution of this theory to a better understanding of human behavior.[1]

## Animal Communication

It has been generally assumed that complex communication behavior demands the operation of cognitive processes in the communicating organism. Over the past decade, comparative psychologists and ethologists have become interested in the area of animal communication and thus, indirectly, in an examination of cognitive processes in animals.

Griffin (1976), in his review of animal communication, has pointed out that Frisch's (1967, 1972, 1974) examination of the communication system of honey bees provides experimental evidence that bees communicate with each other by means of a waggle dance —the bees crawl rapidly over the vertical surface of the honeycomb inside the hive. One cycle of the dance consists of the bee making a very small circle, followed by a straight portion and then another circle in the opposite direction from the first, after which the straight segment is repeated.

This dance communication system is called into play when the colony is in need of food. Variations in the dance indicate the location, distance, and desirability of the food source. But the dance is not tightly linked to finding a source of food, as it can also be used by scouts to indicate the suitability of new locations for the colony. Griffin (1976) has written that individual scouts will exchange information about the suitability of potential hive locations. Only after many hours of such exchanges of information involving dozens of bees, and only when the dances of virtually all of the scouts indicate the same hive site, does the swarm as a whole fly off to the new location. This consensus results from communicative interaction among the individual bees, which alternately "speak" and "listen."

Perhaps the major breakthrough in the examination of communication has come from the studies of Gardner and Gardner (1969, 1971, 1974), Fouts (1972, 1977), Premack (1971), and Rumbaugh (1977), all of whom have taught chimpanzees to communicate with humans. Patterson (1978) has been conducting a similar project with a gorilla. The techniques used by these investigators have differed. Gardner and Gardner and Fouts have taught their subject Washoe the American sign language (Ameslan). Patterson is using Ameslan with KoKo, a baby gorilla. Premack had Sarah use colored plastic tokens as names for familiar objects. Rumbaugh had Lana press symbolic keys on a computer keyboard to communicate.

The varying projects have all yielded similar findings, revealing that apes can learn to use surprisingly large vocabularies to communicate. But since other animals can learn to use symbols, a critical aspect of these studies has been to demonstrate that apes can combine words (signs) to form new meanings. Examples are provided by Linden (1974), who has written that after tasting a radish, Washoe called out, "cry hurt food." She also identified a watermelon as a "candy drink" or as a "drink fruit." When asked "what that" in the presence of a swan, Washoe gave the sign "water bird."

An interesting example of communication is provided by Patterson (1978), who has raised a gorilla, KoKo, from infancy. By the time KoKo was 6½ years old, she had acquired 645 different signs, about 175 of which she used regularly. In one incident, KoKo bit Patterson. Three days after the event, the conversation regarding that incident went as follows (p. 459):

Patterson:  "What did you do to Penny?"
KoKo:       "Bite."
Patterson:  "You admit it?"
KoKo:       "Wrong bite."
Patterson:  "Why bite?"
KoKo:       "Because mad."
Patterson:  "Why mad?"
KoKo:       "Don't know."

Griffin (1976) believes that the varying kinds of communicative behavior reviewed here have much in common with human beings. He has suggested the existence of an evolutionary continuity in communication behavior and its underlying cognitive processes, which in turn supports the position that communication found in animals is not qualitatively different from that found in people.

This position has been also taken by Patterson (1978), who has written that language is no longer the exclusive domain of human beings.

There has been some problem in defining precisely what is meant by "language," but it has been generally agreed that two elements must be present in language behavior. First, the words or signs used must be symbols for something and be recognized as such by the user. Second, the user must combine the symbols or signs with one another to form novel combinations that can be understood by others.

All investigators have not been convinced that apes can learn a language. Seidenberg and Petitto (1978) have been quite critical of the language learning claims made by the investigators cited, while a lack of experimental support for such learning has come from Terrace, Petitto, Sanders, and Bever (1979). These experimenters have published an account of their attempt to teach Ameslan to Nim, a baby chimpanzee who was adopted when he was two weeks of age, and who served as an experimental subject for almost four years. During this time Nim was raised in a home environment and taught by a number of teachers, each for varying periods of time. During these teaching sessions, the teachers whispered into a miniature recorder the signs that Nim was using, their order, and whether they were spontaneous, prompted, modeled, or approximations of the correct sign. In addition, a number of videotapes and transcripts were made of Nim's Ameslan activities.

The findings of these investigators supported the conclusions drawn by other experimenters that apes can learn vocabularies of visual symbols, but these investigators suggested that the semantic competence attributed to apes using these symbols has been exaggerated. Thus, their findings, contrary to those reported by Gardner and Gardner (1969), Patterson (1978), etc., led them to conclude that the combinations of signs made by Nim were *not* primitive sentences. For example, they noted in their analysis of video-transcripts that Nim's combinations of utterances were often initiated by his teacher's sign

movements. Moreover, such utterances were only imitations of his teacher's preceding utterances.

The position of Terrace et al. (1979) has been supported by Thompson and Church (1980), who examined the language behavior of Rumbaugh's (1977) chimpanzee, Lana. Thompson and Church (1980) indicated that Lana's ability to communicate can be attributed to the operation of two basic processes—(1) paired-associate learning or the capacity to associate one sign with another and (2) a type of discrimination training —neither process representing the higher level mental process believed to be necessary for the display of language behavior.

In brief, the findings of Terrace et al. (1979) and Thompson and Church (1980) appear to refute the position that apes can use signs or symbols to create new meanings or to convey information. Rather, these investigators have assumed that the function of signs in an ape's vocabulary has been to satisfy a demand by the experimenter that the animal use that symbol in order to obtain some reward. Terrace et al. have concluded that

> For the moment, our detailed investigation suggests that an ape's language learning is severely restricted. Apes can learn many isolated symbols (as can dogs, horses and other nonhuman species), but they show no unequivocal evidence of mastering the conversational, semantic, or syntactic organization of language. (p. 901)

As Marx (1980) has indicated, the issue of whether language can be acquired by apes has not been resolved. Fouts, the Gardners, and Patterson have all taken issue with Terrace et al., maintaining that the manner in which Nim was trained was unnatural because it was carried out in a classroom, using techniques and procedures unlikely to elicit the spontaneous signing that characterizes language behavior. These investigators have also pointed to occasions in which their subjects have been observed signing to another chimpanzee, a situation in which reward for producing a sign was not present. It is obvious that the issue has not been settled.

**Summing Up**   Current investigators have been less reluctant than their predecessors to describe the operation of cognitive constructs. But a basic difficulty in cognitive research has been the lack of a classificatory scheme, a taxonomy, or perhaps some general theoretical orientation that seems necessary if some order is to be brought to the area. Cognitive processes have also been posited to operate in animal discrimination learning tasks. Further consideration of this topic will be delayed until Chapter 5.

## FURTHER CONSIDERATIONS IN CLASSICAL AND INSTRUMENTAL CONDITIONING

We have now completed our examination of some of the important variables or conditions contributing to the learning and maintenance of classically and instrumentally conditioned responses. But in this search, two basic issues frequently raised in the examination of conditioning have been neglected. One is the empirical question of whether autonomic responses can be instrumentally conditioned; the second deals with the more theoretical issue of what is learned in classical and instrumental conditioning tasks.

### Can Autonomic Nervous System Responses Be Instrumentally Conditioned?

A basic issue that has interested experimenters of classical and instrumental conditioning is what kinds of responses these operations can modify. Some early learning investigators hypothesized that responses innervated by the autonomic nervous system could be modified only by classical conditioning operations. Such a position is a part of the learning theories of Konorski and Miller (1937), Skinner (1938), and Mowrer (1950). The failures of Mowrer (1938) and Skinner (1938) to instrumentally condition the galvanic skin response

and vasoconstriction provided experimental support for this position.

In the early sixties, the problem of instrumentally conditioning autonomic responses was reopened by Kimmel and his associates. In a series of studies, many of which were summarized by Kimmel (1974), it was demonstrated that the GSR could be instrumentally conditioned. An early study by Kimmel and Kimmel (1963) illustrates the procedure. Experimental subjects, whose GSRs were monitored, were first provided with a 10 minute rest period, the last 5 minutes of which were used to establish a base level of GSR responding. Following this period, all GSRs emitted during a 16 minute test period were "reinforced" by the presentation of a light. A control or noncontingent group received the same number of light presentations, but light was never associated with a GSR. Clear evidence was obtained for the conditioning of the GSR, with the experimental group revealing increases of up to 120 percent of their initial resting level while the control group declined in rate of emission to below 80 percent.

The finding that various human autonomic responses can be modified using an instrumental conditioning operation has been confirmed in a host of studies—Engel and Hansen (1966) and Brener and Hothersall (1967) on heart rate; Snyder and Noble (1968) on vasoconstriction; and Frezza and Holland (1971) on salivary response.

Harris and Brady's (1974) survey of studies in which the autonomic responses of animals were instrumentally conditioned has provided confirmation of the results obtained with humans. Illustrative of the work with animals is an experiment conducted by Miller and Carmona (1967). Dogs who had been deprived of water for 16 hours were rewarded with water for salivating. The investigators first obtained a base rate of salivation, measured in number of drops per minute. During the experimental period, spontaneous bursts of salivation were reinforced with 20 ml of water. More specifically, water was first provided for every burst of salivation of one drop or more per 5 second period, with the performance criterion progressively increasing to 7 drops per 5 second period by the end of 40 days of training. In a second experiment, experimental animals learned *not* to salivate. Water was provided when the animal did not salivate for 2 seconds, with the time interval progressively increasing over training to 60 seconds. Figure 4-3 provides the results of Miller and Carmona's (1967) findings which convincingly demonstrate that salivation, an autonomic response, can be instrumentally conditioned.

A methodological problem that confronts the investigator conducting this type of instrumental conditioning experiment is the possibility of the subject exercising some control over an autonomic response through skeletal muscles (voluntary responding) or cognitive activity. Attempts to examine the role of such activity have taken the form of monitoring the subject's respiration rate and obtaining electromyographic (EMG) records during the experimental period. It is then possible to determine if changes in these responses have

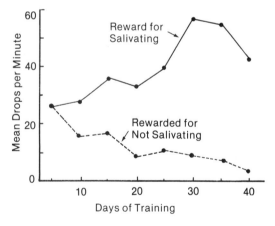

FIGURE 4-3.   Mean curves of instrumental learning by three thirsty dogs rewarded with water for increases or decreases in spontaneous salivation. Adapted from N. E. Miller and A. Carmona, "Modification of a visceral response, salivation in thirsty dogs, by instrumental training with water reward." *Journal of Comparative and Physiological Psychology,* 1967, 63, 1–6. Copyright © 1967 by the American Psychological Association. Reprinted by permission.

been correlated with the receiving of reinforcement. The presence of such changes suggests that the conditioning of the autonomic response has been mediated by skeletal responding. In addition, postexperimental interviews have been conducted with human subjects, in an effort to determine if they engaged in any cognitive activity that might be related to the receiving of reward.

Hall (1976) has reviewed many of the studies designed to examine the contribution of skeletal and cognitive mediators. He has concluded that the evidence is sufficiently controversial that it is impossible to come to any general conclusion regarding the role of skeletal and/or cognitive mediators in influencing autonomic conditioning. Goldstein (1979), in his review of instrumental cardiovascular conditioning, has expressed a similar point of view, writing that the lack of adequate controls for respiration and muscle tension has resulted in an incomplete understanding of the roles of voluntary somatic mediators.

Miller and his associates have suggested that one way to handle the problem of controlling muscular responses that might accompany autonomic responses would be to paralyze all skeletal muscles using the drug curare. Electrical stimulation of the brain, which Olds and Milner (1954) discovered to have reinforcing effects, could be used as reward. In a study conducted by Trowill (1967), curarized rats were first observed in order to measure their normal or base heart rate. Following this, one group of experimental animals received brain stimulation only if heart rate increased over the base rate, while a second group of animals received brain stimulation only if heart rate decreased below the base rate. Although rate changes were small, Trowill was able to demonstrate that heart rate could be either increased or decreased using brain stimulation as the reinforcing agent. Control animals receiving brain stimulation uncorrelated with increases or decreases of heart rate (yoked controls) failed to show the changes observed in their experimental counterparts.

In a subsequent study, Miller and DiCara (1967) attempted to discover if the small heart rate changes (5 percent) found by Trowill (1967) could be obtained by shaping the response—that is, by progressively shifting to a more difficult criterion after subjects had learned to achieve an easier one. Trowill's (1967) experimental procedure was replicated except that the experimental apparatus was so programmed that once a 2 percent heart rate increment (fast rate) or decrement (slow rate) was achieved, this new level of responding was considered to be the base rate and an additional 2 percent change was required to receive brain stimulation. The results, shown in Figure 4-4, clearly reveal increases or decreases in heart rate taking place as a function of reward.

The studies of Trowill (1967) and Miller and DiCara (1967) were confirmed in subsequent experiments conducted by Miller and Banuazizi (1968), DiCara and Miller (1968), and Miller and DiCara (1968). But, in the

early seventies, Miller and Dworkin (1974) made an extensive series of experiments and were unable to replicate the findings reported. Miller (1978) has concluded that "in the face of the much more extensive, careful studies that have failed to replicate the results of the original ones, it is prudent not to rely on any of the experiments on curarized animals for evidence on the instrumental learning of visceral responses" (p. 376).

This text cannot attempt to resolve the conflicting findings on instrumental conditioning of autonomic responses. It can be said, however, that it is probably not possible to control all of the skeletal and cognitive activity in the human subject in order to be sure that such responses are not mediators for any conditioning that takes place. Moreover, the findings of Obrist, Webb, Sutterer, and Howard (1970) and Goesling and Brener (1972) have suggested that central and autonomic nervous system activities, rather than being independent, represent two components of a general response system. If such is the case, any attempt to examine responses controlled by one system independent of the other is bound to fail.

### What Is Learned When Classical and Instrumental Conditioning Operations Are Used?

The many variables examined in Chapters 3 and 4 provide ample evidence that such variables can influence an organism's performance. The learning process has been inferred from such changes in performance. But precisely what has been learned in such situations?

Stimulus response psychologists have assumed that the learning taking place in classical and instrumental conditioning is associative in nature, and that the association is between a stimulus and a response. With classical conditioning, the familiar diagram with an arrow pointing from the CS to the CR indicates that the CS has become associated to the CR. (See Figure 2-3.)

With instrumental conditioning, the instrumental response is associated with a dis-

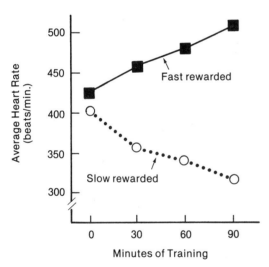

FIGURE 4-4. Instrumental learning of the heart in groups rewarded for fast or for slow rates. (Each point represents average of beats per minute during 5 min.) Adapted from N. E. Miller and L. DiCara, "Instrumental learning of heart-rate changes in curarized rats: shaping, and specificity to discriminative stimulus." *Journal of Comparative and Physiological Psychology*, 1967, 63, 12–19. Copyright © 1967 by the American Psychological Association. Reprinted by permission.

criminative stimulus in signaled tasks; in unsignaled tasks, the stimulus is left unspecified, although it is generally assumed that some part of the experimental apparatus provides the stimulus which is attached to the response.

Most current learning theorists have rejected the position that all of the associative relationships established in classical and instrumental learning tasks must take place between a stimulus and a response. Thompson (1972) has written, "The assumption that *behavioral* responses must occur to mediate learning . . . is an obsolete inheritance from early behaviorism. The evidence from many sources is now overwhelming that behavioral responses are not necessary for learning" (p. 123). Thompson's position suggests that any two events—stimuli, responses, or reinforcement—can be associated one with the other. Let us examine some of the evidence supporting this position.

Some investigators have demonstrated that in classical conditioning tasks, the US need not elicit an overt response in order for a CR to be established. Light and Gantt (1936) crushed the motor nerves of the rear leg of a dog and then "conditioned" the animal by using a buzzer as the CS, and shock, administered to the foot of the same leg, as the US. It was observed during the training trials that a UR could not be elicited by the US. However, after recovery of the damaged motor nerve, the animals were tested with the CS and the conditioned response of leg lifting was observed.

A more frequently used (as well as more humane) technique has been to prevent responding during training trials by injecting the subject with curare. Artificial respiration is then used to keep the animal alive. Instrumental avoidance experiments conducted by Solomon and Turner (1962) and Leaf (1964) have confirmed the findings of Light and Gantt (1936) that overt responding is not a necessary condition for learning to take place.

An early sensory preconditioning study conducted by Brogden (1939) provides experimental evidence supporting the position that an association between two stimuli can be established. In this experiment, dogs were given 200 pairings of a light and a bell presented simultaneously. A conditioning experiment was then conducted in which one of these stimuli was used as the CS, and shock, which elicited foot withdrawal, served as the US. A criterion of 20 consecutive CRs was established. Following such training, a transfer test was provided in which the other stimulus was presented to the subjects. A control group of animals was given similar conditioning and transfer trials; however, the preconditioning session of presentations of the light and bell was omitted. Results indicated that animals in the experimental group produced 78 conditioned responses during the transfer test while only 4 conditioned responses were made by the control animals. These findings resulted in Brogden concluding that the subjects had established an association between the two stimuli, the bell and the light, when they were presented during the preconditioning session. A large number of sensory preconditioning responses have all confirmed Brogden's findings; see Wickens and Briggs (1951), Silver and Meyer (1954), Hoffeld, Thompson, and Brogden (1958), Adamic and Melzack (1970).

Other studies suggest that during instrumental conditioning an associative relationship can be established between a response and the reward or outcome event. It will be recalled that in Chapter 1 we described an experiment conducted by Blodgett (1929), who found that rats would rapidly reduce their errors in a multiple T-maze when food was introduced into the goal box. Similarly, the positive and negative contrast studies beginning with Crespi (1942) indicate that a rat's responding can be modified dramatically by changing the amount of reward it receives.

Another kind of evidence, identified as latent extinction, also suggests the establishment of an association between a response and an outcome event. Seward and Levy (1949) found that a rat's response of traversing an alley to find food in a goal box could be extinguished quickly by placing the animal in the goal box which did not contain food prior to the extinction trials.

Some questions might be raised as to whether the term "association," rather than "contingency," should be used in describing these relationships. (It will be recalled that a contingency is an association with a probability attached.) Rescorla (1967) suggested that in classical conditioning studies the experimental subject learns a contingency between the CS and the US, and some experimental evidence has been obtained to support Rescorla's position. It would follow that the varying relationships that can be established among stimuli, responses, and outcome events should be described in terms of the learning of contingencies rather than associations. Unfortunately, all of the experimental evidence has not supported Rescorla's position, so additional evidence is needed to justify the exclusive use of one term or the other.

It is in the behavioristic tradition to conceptualize the learning process as the establishment of an association or contingency between or among stimuli, responses, and outcome events, since all of these events are observable. But during the last decade, many cognitive psychologists have suggested that what is learned in not an association between external events; rather, learning consists of a change in the organism's cognitive structure. Unfortunately, there has been considerable divergence among theorists regarding the nature of these changes, so that we shall not attempt to describe them. The interested reader can refer to Irwin (1971), Boneau (1974), Bindra (1978), Bolles (1979).

## SUMMARY

This chapter has examined the role of cognitive variables that may contribute to classical and instrumental conditioning. One such cognitive variable may be instructions to the subject. Investigators have indicated that instructions given to the experimental subject can facilitate or inhibit the classical conditioning of both autonomic and skeletal responses.

The examination of cognitive variables operating with animals learning classical and instrumental tasks becomes a difficult methodological problem, since the operation of these variables must be inferred from the organism's performance and without benefit of verbalization from the subject. Nonetheless, Menzel has posited the existence of a cognitive map operating in chimpanzees finding hidden foods. A second cognitive variable hypothesized to operate in animals has been identified as learned helplessness. Seligman and Maier have suggested that helplessness occurs when an experimental subject perceives that a particular outcome takes place independently of any response the subject makes. This creates a cognitive deficit, making animals unable to learn when placed in a second learning situation.

Animal communication has also interested experimenters. Some have taught chimpanzees to communicate using the American Sign Language or some other type of communication system independent of vocalization. There has been dispute among investigators as to whether the animals in such studies have learned a rudimentary language or whether they have learned only that specific symbols must be used in order to achieve a reward. To date, there has not been any resolution of this controversy.

A basic issue that has arisen in the examination of classical and instrumental conditioning is whether or not autonomic nervous system responses can be instrumentally conditioned. Although evidence indicates that such conditioning can take place, it is possible that the associative relationship is dependent on muscular responses mediating the learning of these visceral responses. Attempts to control muscular responses with curare have not been definitive. As one investigator has indicated, it is prudent not to rely on any of these experiments for evidence of the instrumental conditioning of visceral responses.

### NOTE

1. Revisions of the theory have been proposed, but their complexity has precluded our discussion of them in this presentation. The interested reader can consult Abramson, Seligman, and Teasdale (1978), Miller and Norman (1979), Maier and Jackson (1979), Alloy and Seligman (1979).

# CHAPTER FIVE

# Discrimination Learning

We have chosen to consider the learning of discrimination tasks separately from the learning of those tasks described as signaled and unsignaled. This division is arbitrary since, as Heinemann and Chase (1975) have pointed out, virtually all learning situations probably involve some kind of discrimination. But empirical as well as theoretical reasons can be cited for the distinction. An empirical reason is that some variables that contribute to discrimination learning do not operate in unsignaled and signaled learning situations. Theoretically, several of the explanations proposed have relevance primarily to how discrimination learning takes place. Thus, these variables and theories will be examined in this chapter.

## DISCRIMINATION OPERATIONS, TASKS, AND DISCRIMINANDA

Investigators examining discrimination task learning can use either classical or instrumental conditioning operations. With classical conditioning, two CSs are employed. On some trials, a positive stimulus (CS+) is followed by the presentation of the US; on other trials, a negative stimulus (CS−) is never followed by the US. This procedure, first used by Pavlov (1927), has been called **differential conditioning** or conditioned discrimination. Differential conditioning demands that a successive procedure be used—the CS+ and CS− must be presented singly and in random sequence over the conditioning trials.

When an instrumental conditioning operation is used in a two choice discrimination task, reinforcement follows the subject's responses to one stimulus (S+), but responses to the other stimulus (S−) are not reinforced. The S+ and S− may be presented on separate trials, but most investigators present the S+ and S− together so the subject must choose between them. Simple T-mazes, jumping stands, discrimination boxes, and the Wisconsin General Test Apparatus (WGTA) are the kinds of apparatuses most frequently used. Figure 5-1 illustrates a jumping stand of the type used by Lashley (1938) in examining the rat's visual capacity to discriminate between two levels of brightness. The WGTA is illustrated in Figure 5-2.

With the WGTA, two (or more) stimulus objects are placed on a stimulus tray, with each object covering a small food well. When the tray is placed in front of the subject, the subject responds by moving one of the objects to the side. If correct, the subject secures a reward found in the food well.

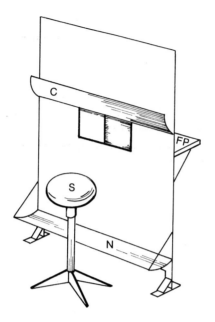

FIGURE 5-1. The Lashley jumping stand. The rat is trained to jump from the stand (S) to one of the doors. If the animal's response is correct, the door gives way and the rat is able to reach the food platform (FP). If the response is incorrect, the door remains fixed and the animal falls into the net below (N). The projecting cover (C) prevents the animal from jumping over the apparatus.

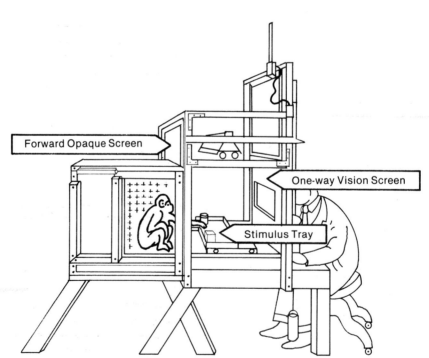

FIGURE 5-2. Wisconsin General Test Apparatus. Adapted from H. F. Harlow, "The formation of learning sets." *Psychological Review,* 1949, 56, 51–65. Copyright © 1949 by the American Psychological Association. Reprinted by permission.

More complex discrimination tasks have been identified as (1) oddity and (2) matching to sample. With the oddity task, three stimulus objects are presented together—two of these are identical, while the third stimulus is different. If the subject chooses the odd stimulus object, a reward is given.

In the matching to sample task, presentation of a single stimulus (sample) is followed by presentation of two stimuli, one of which is the same as the sample stimulus. The subject must learn to respond to the stimulus identical to the sample in order to receive a reward.

## THE NATURE OF THE DISCRIMINANDA

Simple discriminanda are used in most discrimination tasks, the specific type being adapted to the experimental subject and the kind of discrimination apparatus employed. Wooden objects of different shapes, sizes, and colors are used with monkeys in the WGTA. Illuminated keys or disks in a variety of colors generally serve as the discriminanda for pigeons, while the discrimination task apparatus for rats may utilize discriminanda consisting of flat pieces of light metal or cardboard that differ in brightness (e.g., black vs. white) or pattern (e.g., black and white vertical stripes vs. black and white horizontal stripes).

### Natural Concepts

The discriminanda used in laboratory studies are characterized by a simplicity that sets them apart from the kinds of stimuli confronting most organisms in natural discrimination situations. Laboratory stimuli will vary along only a few basic dimensions, such as color, shape, or size. In contrast, an open-ended variability characterizes the discriminanda found in natural settings. For example, we can discriminate dogs from all other animals, although dogs come in all shapes, sizes, colors, etc., and other animals may appear to have all of the attributes that characterize the dog.

Herrnstein and his associates have called such open-ended stimuli **natural concepts.** They have examined discrimination learning in pigeons using such stimuli; see Herrnstein and Loveland (1964), Herrnstein, Loveland, and Cable (1976), Herrnstein (1979). Herrnstein, Loveland, and Cable (1976) used 920 different pictures of trees, 880 different pictures of water, and 800 different pictures of a single person. Each group of pictures dealt with a natural concept—e.g., trees, water, a human being—which would serve as a S+ in the operant discrimination study. The pictures representing a single natural concept were quite diverse, with the concept photographed in whole or in part, from near or far, obstructed or unobstructed, etc. For example, the pictures of trees were of many different types of trees, and the pictures of water included everything from an aerial view of the Atlantic Ocean to a closeup of a very small puddle.

The photographs serving as negative stimuli (S−) were comparable to the positive stimuli (S+) except for the presence of the natural concept item. In Experiment 1, 920 negative pictures were combined with 920 pictures of trees to form a pool of 1840 photos. From this pool, sets of 40 S+ and 40 S− pictures were randomly drawn for use during each experimental session. Pools of pictures were also made up for the examination of water in Experiment 2 (1960 pictures) and a human being in Experiment 3 (1600 pictures).

The experimental procedure consisted of presenting a single picture, either an S+ or S−. If the pigeon pecked at the white key light placed below the picture when the S+ was presented, reinforcement was provided; pecking at the key light when the S− was presented did not result in reward. In each experiment pigeons were run for more than 100 sessions. Results clearly revealed the ability of pigeons to distinguish pictures of a tree, water, or a person from those not containing these natural concepts.

Findings such as these raise many questions for which psychologists, at least at the present time, have no ready answers. A traditional explanation for the ability of the pigeon to make these discriminations would be a theory in which trees, water, etc., were each identified as representing a class of stimuli (or a natural concept) because each photograph contained some element common to the concept. For example, all trees should have in common a particular color, shape, structure, etc., or possibly some combination of them. And yet, according to the experimenters, specific attributes were not common to all of the examples of a natural concept. In examining the pictures of trees, for example, the pigeons did not require that the tree be green, leafy, vertical, woody, branching, etc. Moreover, for a picture to be recognizable as a nontree, the picture did not have to eliminate greenness, woodiness, verticality, etc. Thus, a picture of a large stalk of celery, in spite of its many treelike characteristics, was consistently not responded to.

## VARIABLES INFLUENCING DISCRIMINATION LEARNING

In keeping with the general organization presented in Chapter 1, we will examine the contribution of stimulus or task variables, motivational variables, and cognitive variables to the learning of the discrimination task.

### Stimulus or Task Variables

**The Role of Stimulus Salience**    As the difference between the stimuli used in a discrimination task increases, the task becomes easier to learn. It takes the rat only a few trials to learn a black-white discrimination task; it has much more difficulty learning a light gray–medium gray discrimination. The characteristics of the discriminanda have been called **stimulus salience.**

To manipulate salience, physical characteristics of the stimuli have been changed. For example, Broadhurst (1957) provided three levels of difficulty in a discrimination task by differentially illuminating the two alleys of a Y-maze. The difference in illumination between these alleys was represented by the ratios of 1:300, 1:60, and 1:15. Broadhurst found that the discrimination task with the largest difference in illumination (1:300) yielded the most rapid learning, whereas the one with smallest difference (1:15) resulted in the slowest learning.

Another procedure for manipulating physical differences between stimuli has been to vary the number of elements comprising the discriminanda. In a study by Harlow (1945), monkeys were given training in discriminating between (a) three-dimensional stimulus objects (red pyramid vs. blue cube) and (b) two-dimensional stimulus objects (a stimulus wedge with two wide red stripes painted across it vs. a similar wedge with just one wide red stripe). A series of problems was provided, with each problem being presented until the animal attained 20 correct responses out of 25 trials or until 100 trials had been run. Findings revealed that three times as many errors were made when two-dimensional stimuli were used rather than three-dimensional stimuli.

A study by Hara and Warren (1961) is of particular significance, since it reflects a more analytic approach to the problem of salience. These investigators examined how increasing the number of cues in the discriminanda affected discrimination learning in cats. The stimulus objects they used varied with regard to visual form, size, or brightness. The authors found that if the two stimuli making up the discrimination task differed on all three dimensions—for instance, if one stimulus was a large, bright square and the other stimulus was a small, dark circle—the cats' performance level reached 99 percent correct during the training trials provided. On the other hand, if the stimuli differed on just two dimensions (large, dark triangle vs. large, bright circle) or on just one dimension (large, dark triangle vs. large, dark circle), performance declined to 90 and 82 percent, respectively.

Hara and Warren's (1961) findings are noteworthy, since they demonstrate that the ease of learning a discrimination problem is related to the number of stimulus elements or to the different attributes of the discriminanda. But it should be pointed out that in some studies the role of the varying stimulus elements that comprise the discriminanda is far more complex. For example, in an experiment discussed later in this chapter, Reynolds (1961) found that pigeons learning a discrimination appeared to ignore certain prominent stimulus elements that were a part of the discriminanda and instead selected other attributes to cue their response.

**The Role of the S—** It has been assumed that in the learning of a discrimination task, it is important for the subject to learn *not* to respond to the S—, in addition to learning *to* respond to the S+. Investigators have demonstrated that the organism's response to the negative stimulus in the simple discrimination learning task plays an important role in the learning of the correct response. A good example of this finding is in a study by Harlow and Hicks (1957). Their procedure consisted of having monkeys learn a series of discrimination problems using the Wisconsin General Test Apparatus. On the first training trial, only a simple stimulus object was presented. With Group 1, the stimulus object was always rewarded on Trial 1; with Group 2, the stimulus object was never rewarded on this trial. On Trials 2 through 6 (only six trials were provided on each problem), the object presented on the first trial was paired with a new stimulus object to form the discrimination problem. If the original object had been the S+ on Trial 1, it continued to be positive on the following five trials; if it was negative on Trial 1, it continued to serve as the S—. See Table 5-1 for an outline of this procedure. Figure 5-3 presents the percentage of correct responses on Trial 2 over the 90 problems provided the animals. Note that the presentation of the S— on the first trial, in contrast to the presentation of the S+, resulted in superior learning.

Responding to the S— appears to help the organism in learning a discrimination task. One might ask—is there any specific

TABLE 5-1. Procedure used in Harlow and Hicks's (1957) discrimination study in which a single object was presented on Trial 1, with or without reward, followed by five discrimination trials in which the object used on the first trial was a part of the discrimination task.

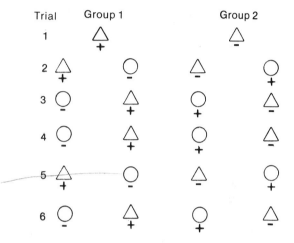

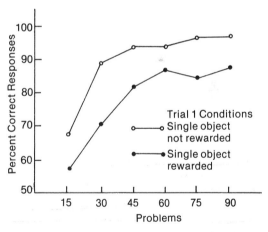

FIGURE 5-3. Discrimination learning set curves based on Trial 2 responses following rewarded and unrewarded Trial 1 responses. Adapted from H. F. Harlow and L. H. Hicks, "Discrimination learning theory: Uniprocess vs. duo-process. *Psychological Review*, 1957, 64, 104–109. Copyright © 1957 by the American Psychological Association. Reprinted by permission.

ratio or percentage of responses made to the positive and negative stimulus presentations that will lead to optimal learning? The answer appears to be a resounding "no." Different investigators have found differing ratios of nonreinforced to reinforced trials yielding optimal learning; Fitzwater (1952), Birch (1955), Lachman (1961). For example, Birch (1955) noted that a 1:1 ratio yielded better discrimination task learning than a ratio of either 1:3 or 3:1. But Lachman (1961) found that a 3:1 ratio was superior to a 1:1, which in turn was superior to a 1:3. The necessity of providing nonreinforced trials in order to achieve optimal discrimination learning has been demonstrated—but the specific ratio of nonreinforced to reinforced trials is undoubtedly dependent on a variety of conditions that have yet to be identified.

## Errorless Discrimination Learning

The organism's response to the S— has been found to be of considerable value in the learning of a discrimination problem. However, some investigators have shown that it is possible for a subject to learn a discrimination task without ever responding to the S—. This effect has been demonstrated in three operant studies conducted by Terrace (1963a, 1963b), teaching pigeons to discriminate between different colored plastic keys. Terrace's procedure consisted of presenting his subjects with a single stimulus, S+, for a fixed amount of time, followed by the presentation of the S—. Two basic conditions were manipulated in his first study. The first of these was the way in which the S— was presented. A *constant* procedure consisted of presenting the S— (green key) for the same length of time that the S+ (red key) was presented, with the brightness of the two keys being the same; in contrast, a *progressive* procedure consisted of gradually changing the S— from a nonilluminated key of five seconds' duration to a bright green key of three minutes' duration. These changes in duration and intensity were made in progressive stages.

The second condition examined was whether the S— should be introduced early or late in the training trials. For the early condition, the S— was introduced during the first conditioning session, while for the late condition, several weeks of training on the S+ alone preceded the introduction of the S—. The two basic training conditions provided four experimental groups: (1) constant-early, (2) constant-late, (3) progressive-early, and (4) progressive-late. Twenty-eight discrimination training sessions were provided. As Figure 5-4 indicates, the subjects in the progressive-early group acquired the discrimination with virtually no responses to the S—, their range of errors being 5 to 9.

In contrast, the range of errors for the progressive-late group was 35 to 760. For the constant-early group, the range of errors was 191 to 210; for the constant-late group, it was 1922 to 4153. A second experiment, in which Terrace (1963a) made a few modifications in the procedure, produced similar findings, while a third study (Terrace, 1963b) revealed that a more difficult discrimination task could also be learned without errors using the early-progressive introduction of the S—.

In summary, there appear to be two necessary conditions for the acquisition of a discrimination without the subject responding to the S—: (1) the introduction of the S— immediately after conditioning of the response to the stimulus correlated with reinforcement, and (2) provision of an initially large difference between the S+ and S—, which is progressively reduced to a smaller and constant difference.

The second condition used by Terrace (1963a)—in which the difference between the S+ and S— was gradually reduced by increasing the brightness of the S— key—has been termed **fading;** it represents an important procedure in obtaining errorless discrimination performance. Moore and Goldiamond (1964) have confirmed the importance of fading by examining discrimination learning with children. In their study, six nursery school children were given a matching to sample task in which a triangle was projected on a milk glass window for four seconds using full (110 v) intensity. The children were asked to "look at the picture in the top window." This picture

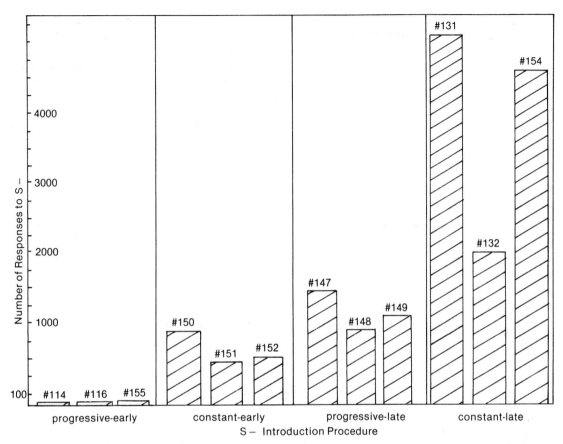

FIGURE 5-4. The number of responses to S− made by each bird during all 28 S+ and S−
sessions. Adapted from H. S. Terrace, "Errorless transfer of a discrimination across two
continua." *Journal of the Experimental Analysis of Behavior*, 1963, 6, 223–232. Copyright © 1963
by the Society for the Experimental Analysis of Behavior, Inc. Reprinted by permission.

was then turned off, and three triangles were
presented in three windows located below the
first window. The children were asked to
point to the triangle that was the same as the
first one they had viewed.

Two experimental conditions were examined. In one, the illumination of all of the test
triangles was the same as that of the originally
presented triangle. The second condition,
which examined the contribution of fading,
consisted of presenting the correct test triangle
at the same intensity as the originally presented triangle; the other two were presented
at a lower intensity. Throughout the trials, the
illumination was increased, beginning with 0

volts increasing through 16 steps until all the
test triangles had the same intensity as the
sample. Results from all six subjects indicated
that the fading procedure aided discrimination
performance. Other investigators working in
school situations have demonstrated the role
of fading in errorless discrimination learning.
See Box 5-1.

What is the value of demonstrating that a
discrimination task can be learned without the
subject making errors? First, errorless discrimination findings contrast markedly with the
findings of some other investigators, who indicate that the organism's response to the S−
is necessary for the discrimination task to be

**BOX 5-1**

An interesting application of errorless discrimination training and the use of the fading procedure—to teach children to discriminate letters of the alphabet—was reported by Egeland (1975).

In his study, the subjects were children, aged 4 to 5 years, enrolled in a pre-kindergarten program and unfamiliar with letters. A matching to sample format was employed in which the child was required to discriminate between two similar letters by selecting the letter that matched the sample previously presented. The pairs of letters used were R-P, Y-V, G-C, Q-O, M-N, and K-X.

The procedure used with the errorless training group on early trials was to highlight in red the cue that differentiated one letter from the other. Thus, the stem of the R in the R-P discrimination was colored red, while the rest of the letter was black. During the course of training trials, the red highlighting was gradually faded until the stem of the R was black. A second group of subjects learned to discriminate between the letters using a traditional discrimination procedure; here, subjects were informed after making a choice whether their response was correct or incorrect. Egeland provided 10 training trials, followed immediately by 5 posttest trials, with 5 additional test trials given one week later. Egeland found that the errorless training group made significantly fewer errors than the traditional discrimination learning group on both the immediate and the delayed posttest trials. He reported that many of the children in the traditional discrimination group had considerable difficulty in understanding why an incorrect choice was wrong. Egeland has indicated the educational value of errorless discrimination training as a technique for dealing with many of the problems young children have in learning to discriminate letters or words.

learned with optimum efficiency. It is obvious that the differences between the two procedures should be further investigated to determine under what circumstances each method will result in superior performance. Second, there has been some evidence to indicate that the responses that are not followed by reward may result in the subject becoming frustrated and experiencing decreased motivation to continue to learn. The use of the errorless discrimination procedure may be of value in minimizing such effects. Finally, the finding that it is possible to learn a discrimination problem without making errors has some implication for those theoretical analyses of discrimination learning positing that discrimination performance is related to the development of inhibition produced by the subject responding to the S—.[1]

## Motivational Variables

Motivational variables have been extensively investigated with signaled and unsignaled learning tasks, so it is not surprising that experimenters have also been interested in the contribution of these variables to discrimination learning. The reinforcement and aversive parameters that have been investigated have included (1) frequency, (2) amount or intensity, and (3) temporal delay between the response and the presentation of the aversive stimulus or reward.

**Frequency**    An examination of the learning curves obtained for discrimination tasks almost always reveals increased discriminability as a function of increasing the frequency of reinforcement to the S+. There is little doubt that such learning is a function of the number of rewards to the S+, although, as was noted earlier, the number of nonrewarded trials may also make a contribution.

**Amount of Reward**    Much of the experimental evidence reveals discrimination learning to be an increasing function of the amount of reward provided. Cowles and Nissen (1937), using small and large pieces of banana and orange as rewards for chimpanzees learning a discrimination task, found that learning took place more rapidly when large rewards were used. Subsequent experiments have confirmed the findings of Cowles and Nissen (1937); Greene (1953), Schrier and Harlow (1956), Leary (1958), and Davenport (1970). However, some investigators have been unable to demonstrate this effect; Reynolds (1949), Maher and Wickens (1954), and Fehrer (1956).

Can these findings be generalized to human subjects? We would assume so, since our everyday experiences frequently suggest that individuals learn more rapidly if large rewards are provided rather than small. But surprisingly, the experimental evidence does not support our assumption. Miller and Estes (1961) used as a reward (a) knowledge of results, (b) 1 cent, or (c) 50 cents; while Estes, Miller, and Curtin (1962) used as a reward (a) knowledge of results, (b) 1 cent, or (c) 25 cents. They found that these differing rewards did not influence discrimination task learning for either 9-year-olds or college students. But one must be cautious when considering findings obtained from reward studies using students as subjects. For many students, pleasing the instructor or "doing well" in a school-related task is an intangible but potent reward. As a result, the influence of the small and tangible rewards provided by the experimenter may be obscured.

**Motivational Intensity and Task Difficulty: The Yerkes-Dodson Law** One procedure used to manipulate the motivational variable of reward is varying the amount of food, as noted in the previous section. When one is using an aversive stimulus, it is assumed that the termination of this stimulus, following a correct response, serves as reinforcement. It is thus possible to vary motivation by providing subjects with different intensities of shock, followed by shock termination.

When shock intensity has been varied with discrimination tasks, some experimenters have found an interaction between shock intensity and task difficulty. More specifically, they have noted that although very intense shock results in the most rapid learning of an easy discrimination, an intermediate level of shock provides optimal learning when the dis-

crimination is more difficult. This relationship between level of motivation and task difficulty was first noted by Yerkes and Dodson (1908).

These investigators had mice learn three visual discrimination tasks of increasing difficulty. In addition, three different levels of shock intensity were used to motivate the animals. The authors found that with the easiest task—that is, when there was a large difference between the brightnesses of the two gray papers that were the discriminanda—increasing the intensity of shock resulted in increasing performance. But when the discrimination became more difficult, optimal learning took place with lower shock intensities. Yerkes and Dodson concluded, "An easily acquired habit . . . may be readily formed under strong stimulation, whereas a difficult habit may be acquired readily only under relatively weak stimulation" (p. 482).

Subsequent studies using rats by Hammes (1956), Broadhurst (1957), and Dennenberg and Karas (1960), which varied the intensity of the aversive stimulus as well as the difficulty of the discrimination task, confirmed Yerkes and Dodson's findings.

The deleterious effect of an aversive stimulus on the *maintenance* of a reasonably complex task by human subjects has been reported in a study by Patrick (1934). In this study, college students were placed in a room that had four doors, only one of which was unlocked. It was only through this unlocked door that the subject could leave the room. Which door was unlocked varied, but the subject could learn that the door that was open on any given trial would be locked on the next. It was thus possible to increase the probability of finding the unlocked door on the first "guess" from 25 to 33 percent. Subjects were given 10 trials a day for 10 days in order to obtain a "control" measure of performance. Following these trials, the subjects were again placed in this problem situation, but this time a specific type of aversive stimulation was provided during each trial—namely, shock, a cold shower of water, or a blast of a klaxon horn. Patrick found that when the subjects were performing under the aversive stimulus conditions, in contrast to their control performance, the probability of their responding correctly decreased significantly. It was also observed that a great deal of emotional responding appeared to be in evidence; the subjects would repeatedly pull on locked doors, dash frantically from one door to another, etc.

One explanation for the findings would be that the organism's emotionality increases with the onset of aversive stimulation. These strong emotional responses, elicited by intense stimulation, are more likely to interfere with the learning of difficult tasks or their maintenance than with the learning or maintenance of easy ones.

If such an explanation is correct, it would be expected that the Yerkes-Dodson law would not be operable when motivation was manipulated by varying the amount of reward or level of deprivation. Increases in these motivational conditions would not be accompanied by the strong emotional responses that can interfere with the learning of a complex task. Neither Fantino, Kasdon, and Stringer (1970) nor Hochhauser and Fowler (1975) were able to obtain experimental findings supporting the Yerkes-Dodson law when manipulating such conditions. Fantino et al. (1970) varied the level of food deprivation of pigeons while requiring these subjects to learn detour problems of varied complexity. Hochhauser and Fowler (1975) placed rats on moderate or high levels of food deprivation, provided rewards of 1, 2, or 4 pellets of food, and had the animals learn discrimination tasks that varied in difficulty. Both studies revealed that as task complexity increased, increasing the level of motivation resulted in superior learning.

**Delay of Reward and Acquisition Training**
The effects of delaying reward, found with nonsignaled and signaled tasks, are also observed with discrimination tasks. In a classic study by Grice (1948), groups of rats were given training on a black-white discrimination problem, with a delay of either 0, .5, 1.2, 2.0, 5.0, or 10 seconds introduced between the animal's correct response and its reward of food. The criterion of learning was 18 correct responses out of 20 trials. Performance for the

varying groups, as indicated in Figure 5-5, reveals that the 0 delay group learned most rapidly, followed by the .5, 1.2, and 2.0 second delay groups. When a delay of 5 seconds was introduced, the animals in this group experienced considerable difficulty in learning. The animals provided with a delay of 10 seconds were unable to learn the discrimination, even though in some cases they were given as many as 1400 trials.

Subsequent studies by Keesey (1964), Topping and Parker (1970), and Culbertson (1970) were interesting confirmations of Grice's (1948) findings. In these studies, brain stimulation was used as the reward. The use of this type of reinforcement permits the experimenter to exercise more precise control over the length of the delay interval than when traditional rewards such as food or water are employed. In Culbertson's (1970) study, rats learned a discrimination problem in which their receiving brain stimulation for making a correct response was delayed for either 0, .5, 1.0, 2.0, 3.0, or 5.0 seconds. Five

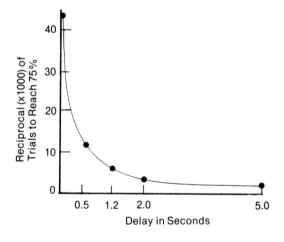

FIGURE 5-5.    Rate of learning as a function of delay of reward. The experimental values are represented by black dots, and the smooth curve is fitted to these data. Adapted from G. R. Grice, "The relation of secondary reinforcement to delayed reward in visual discrimination learning." *Journal of Experimental Psychology*, 1948, 38, 1–16. Copyright © 1948 by the American Psychological Association. Reprinted by permission.

hundred acquisition trials were provided. Figure 5-6 illustrates the experimental findings, with the 0 and .5 second delay groups being clearly superior to all of the other experimental groups. It is not clear, however, why the 3.0 second delay group should have learned the discrimination more rapidly than the 2.0 second delay group.

The delay of reward variable has stimulated a great deal of research using children. In a study by Terrell and Ware (1961), kindergarteners and first graders were asked to solve concurrently two easy discrimination prob-

lems. With one problem, there was an immediate reward (light flash) after the correct response; with the second problem, the reward was delayed for seven seconds. Training trials were provided until the subject reached a criterion of six consecutive correct responses. In a second experiment, more difficult discrimination tasks were provided, although the same immediate and delayed reward conditions were examined. Results from both experiments indicated that the subjects learned significantly more rapidly when rewarded immediately than when given the de-

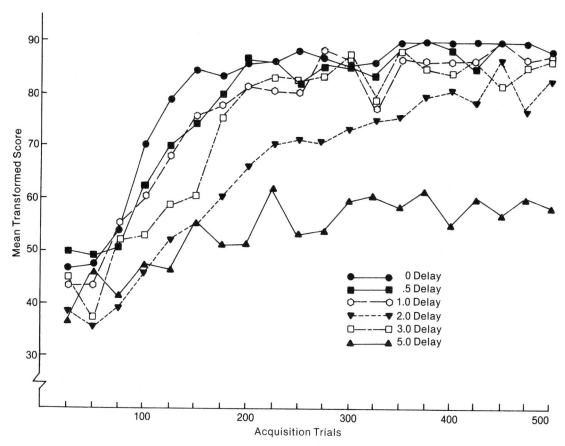

FIGURE 5-6.    Mean discrimination acquisition scores following arc-sine transformation. (An arc-sine score of 45 corresponds to 50 percent, while an arc-sine score of 90 corresponds to 100 percent.) Adapted from J. L. Culbertson, "Effects of brief reinforcement delays on acquisition and extinction of brightness discrimination in rats." *Journal of Comparative and Physiological Psychology*, 1970, 70, 317–325. Copyright © 1970 by the American Psychological Association. Reprinted by permission.

layed reward. In Experiment 1, the mean number of trials to learn was 6.6 and 16.6 for the immediate and delayed conditions respectively, whereas in Experiment 2, the means were 16.6 and 22.7.

The effect of the delay of reward variable on performance appears to decline for older children, particularly when easy tasks are used. Perhaps this is because the children are better able to use the delay period to rehearse the correct response. Hockman and Lipsitt (1961) used fourth-grade children as subjects in learning an easy (two stimulus) and a difficult (three stimulus) discrimination problem. Correct responding was rewarded by the presentation of a red light, while an incorrect response was accompanied by a buzzer. The time interval between the subject's response and the presentation of the red light or buzzer varied —either 0, 10, or 30 seconds. The criterion was 12 correct responses or a maximum of 36 trials. Results indicated that the learning of the easy discrimination task was not influenced by the delay interval; however, the learning of the difficult task was affected by delay.

**Delay of Reward and Maintenance Responding** Much of the experimental interest in delay of reward has centered around how this variable influences acquisition, but Cox and D'Amato (1977) have demonstrated that reinforcement delay can also disrupt the maintenance of discrimination responding. In their study, monkeys were first given extensive training on a simple two-choice discrimination problem. The procedure consisted of having the animals learn to push a microswitch 15 times, with the last response causing a projector to produce two discriminative stimuli on a screen. Pressing a key below the S+ resulted in the immediate presentation of a pellet of food, whereas pressing the S— key produced dimming of the illumination in the experimental chamber for 1 minute.

After extensive training resulting in the animals responding to the S+ at a high level of accuracy, a delay of reinforcement procedure was instituted. After the animal had made a discriminative response, delay periods of 2, 4, 8, 16, and 32 seconds were provided,

in increasing order. Twenty-four trial sessions were provided utilizing these varying intervals of delay of reinforcement. A high level of maintenance responding was noted when 2, 4, and 8 second delay intervals were used, but as the interval was increased from 8 to 16 seconds, a decrement in correct responding gradually appeared. With a 32 second delay interval, correct responding declined to below 70 percent.

### Cognitive Variables

**Awareness** It has already been shown that by providing specific types of instructions to experimental subjects, one can facilitate or inhibit conditioned response learning. In this section we will examine the contribution of instructions to the learning of conditioned discrimination tasks. Particular interest will be paid to the way instructions affect the subject's awareness of the CS-US contingency. Many studies have used a task in which the CS-US contingency is "masked." Some subjects are given instructions that mislead them about the purpose of the study. Other subjects, given the same task, are informed about the CS-US contingency. Dawson and his associates have conducted a series of experiments of this type; Dawson's (1970) study illustrates the method and experimental findings. In Dawson's Experiment 2, subjects were given 60 trials, with six tones presented on each trial. The first tone was either 950, 1000, or 1050 Hz. The other five tones were 800, 950, 1000, 1050, and 1200 Hz, presented in random order. Subjects were instructed to perform three tasks following the presentation of the last tone: (1) determine which of the last five tones had the same pitch as the first tone, (2) determine which of the last five tones had the highest pitch, and (3) determine which of the last five tones had the lowest pitch. The 1200 and 800 Hz tones served as CS+ and CS—, with the CS+ followed by the US (shock) 75 percent of the time. The conditioned response was the galvanic skin response. An "aware" group was instructed that the shock would usually but not always follow the highest (or the lowest) tone, but would never follow any other tone. An "unaware" group was told that shock would be presented periodically, since the experimenter was interested in determining whether such stimulation would facilitate the subject's ability to respond correctly. At the end of 60 trials, all subjects were administered a questionnaire which included the multiple choice item "shock usually followed (a) the highest tone, (b) the middle tone, (c) the lowest tone, (d) it was not systematic, (e) I couldn't tell."

The findings obtained from this study, as revealed by the mean GSR discrimination scores for the aware and unaware groups, are presented in Figure 5-7. The unaware group failed to condition, while conditioning was observed with the group made aware of the CS-US contingency. These findings confirm the results of earlier experiments conducted by Dawson and Grings (1968) and Dawson and Satterfield (1969), and are in keeping with a subsequent study by Dawson and Biferno (1973). All of these studies have indicated that for unaware subjects, CS-US pairings that were embedded in a masking task were not sufficient to establish GSR conditioning. When an identical number of CS-US pairings was provided on the same task and the subject was told of the nature of the CS-US contingency, a conditioned response was readily established.

These findings have been used by Dawson to support the position that awareness of the CS-US contingency should not be considered as another variable contributing to the strength of a conditioned discrimination, but rather, awareness should be considered a basic condition that must be present if a CR is to be established in the human subject.

There has not been complete agreement with Dawson's view. Some investigators, such as Maltzman (1971, 1977) and Pendry and Maltzman (1977, 1979), have held that conditioned discrimination GSR experiments are not true conditioning studies; rather, they view the GSR as only an orienting response to the varying stimuli provided by the experimenter. Maltzman has argued that in the conditioned discrimination study, the subject dis-

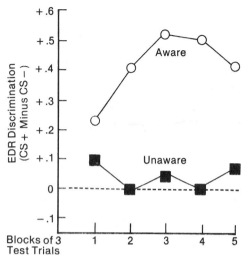

FIGURE 5-7.  Mean discrimination scores on blocks of test trials. Adapted from M. E. Dawson, "Cognition and conditioning: Effects of masking the CS-UCS contingency on human GSR classical conditioning." *Journal of Experimental Psychology*, 1970, 85, 389–396. Copyright © 1970 by the American Psychological Association. Reprinted by permission.

covers the significance of the CS that serves as a signal for the subsequent presentation of the US. This type of stimulus change (in contrast to the presentation of the CS−) arouses a different and larger GSR response in the subject, which is mistakenly identified as a "conditioned" response.

The possibility that the GSR obtained in conditioned discrimination experiments may not be "learned" suggests that experiments should be conducted to examine other kinds of conditioned responses. Nelson and Ross (1974) have examined the differential conditioning of the eyeblink using (1) a masking task, (2) a modified masking task, or (3) no masking task, combined with the subjects either (a) looking or (b) not looking at a silent movie. An awareness of the tone-airpuff (CS-US) contingency was not manipulated as in Dawson's study but was assessed using a post-experimental questionnaire.

In the masking task used by Nelson and Ross, subjects were required to estimate the length of 2 and 5 second intervals of time, with the explanation that the purpose of the study was to examine time estimation during distraction. The subjects not given the masking task were informed that the experimenters were interested in measuring their reactions to "certain events." During this time, subjects were (or were not) looking at a film. One hundred conditioning trials were provided, with conditioned responding measured by a CS+/CS− difference score. The postexperimental questionnaire identified those subjects who became aware of the CS-US contingency during the experiment and those who did not. Results indicated that engaging in the masking task or viewing the film resulted in much poorer differential conditioning than if no masking task or film viewing was provided. In keeping with Dawson's (1970) earlier findings, unaware subjects (as measured by the questionnaire) performed more poorly than aware subjects across all conditions. But contrary to Dawson's finding, Nelson and Ross (1974) found that some unaware subjects did reveal conditioning. Moreover, subjects who were aware of the CS-US contingency but did not view the film performed better than aware subjects who did view the film. As Nelson and Ross point out, some factor other than the knowledge of the relationship among the stimuli, at least as defined by the postexperimental interviews, would appear to operate to reduce differential responding in such instances.

Finally, it is appropriate to call attention to the results of a classical conditioning study conducted by Campbell, Sanderson, and Laverty (1964). These investigators, unlike Dawson, did not use a conditioned discrimination task, but their findings do have relevance. In their experiment, a conditioned GSR was established in five subjects. A tone served as the CS, and the administration of the drug succinylcholine chloride dihydrate (Scoline) was the US. The effects of this drug, which produces respiratory paralysis (total paralysis of all muscular activity), lasted for about 100 seconds in the experiment cited. The sudden termination of respiration was terrifying—the subjects later expressed the belief that they thought they were going to die.[2] Only a single CS-US trial was presented, followed by 30 extinction trials. One week and three weeks later, 30 and 40 additional extinction trials were provided. Findings indicated that the GSR during these extinction trials did not extinguish but appeared to become stronger. And yet, all subjects were aware that after the first conditioning trial they would never again receive the US. The experimental evidence seems reasonably clear that awareness of the CS-US contingency does contribute to the strength of a conditioned response, but whether or not the subject must be aware of the contingency before conditioning can take place needs to be studied further.

**Learning to Learn**  A second cognitive process to be discussed in this section can be inferred from the concept of a learning set. The term **learning set** was chosen by Harlow (1949) to describe his finding that monkeys were able to solve object discrimination problems with increasing efficiency as a function of their previous experience with this type of task. In the task Harlow used, the monkey had to choose one of two objects—such as a small funnel vs. a wooden cube—both of which covered food wells in the Wisconsin General Test Apparatus. The position of the objects was shifted from left to right in a balanced and predetermined order; the subjects had to learn to choose one of the objects consistently in order to obtain the raisin or peanut placed in the food well.

In Harlow's (1949) study, 344 discrimination problems were provided to a group of eight monkeys, with a different pair of discriminanda being used with each problem. Each of the first 32 problems was run for 50 trials, but only 6 trials were provided for each of the next 200 problems. For the last 112 problems, an average of just 9 trials was provided. Figure 5-8 shows the learning curves indicating the percentage of correct responses on the first 6 trials of the discrimination tasks, while Figure 5-9 plots the percentage of correct responses on Trials 2 to 6 as a function of the number of problems previously presented. It may be observed that both figures indicate an increase in learning efficiency as more and more problems are provided for the monkey to solve.

Many subsequent studies have demonstrated that organisms other than primates, such as rats, cats, pigeons, and dolphins, can learn successive discrimination problems with increasing efficiency. But there appear to be substantial performance differences between primates and these other organisms. Sutherland and Mackintosh (1971) have indicated that primates seem to develop rules for the solution of discrimination problems that are beyond the capacity of most of these other animals. Herman and Arbeit (1973) found

that the bottlenose dolphin is capable of learning set performance comparable to that obtained by monkeys.

It has been generally accepted that the most likely explanation for how primates acquire a learning set with object discrimination problems is that they adopt a simple strategy (a cognitive process) consisting of "win-stay, lose-shift." That is, if the stimulus object that has been chosen results in reward, the subject should stay with that choice. If, however, the object chosen does not result in reward, there should be a shift to the other object on the next trial. Support for this position is found in a study by Schusterman (1962). Chimpanzees were first trained on an object-alternation discrimination task. With this task, the same stimulus object is rewarded on alternate trials, thus demanding a win-shift,

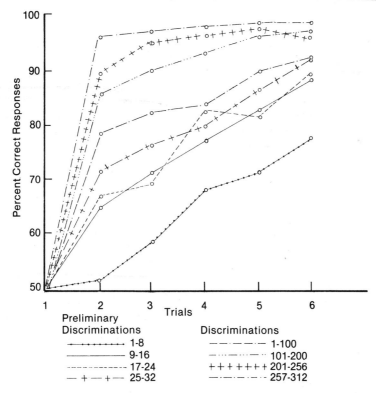

FIGURE 5-8.   Discrimination learning curves obtained from successive blocks of problems. Adapted from H. F. Harlow, "The formation of learning sets." *Psychological Review,* 1949, 56, 51–65. Copyright © 1949 by the American Psychological Association. Reprinted by permission.

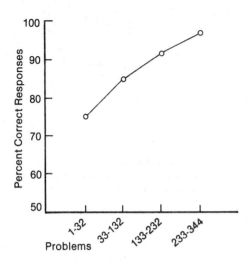

FIGURE 5-9. Discrimination learning set curve based on responses for Trials 2-6. Adapted from H. F. Harlow, "The formation of learning sets." *Psychological Review*, 1949, 56, 51–65. Copyright © 1949 by the American Psychological Association. Reprinted by permission.

lose-stay strategy. When these animals were switched to an object discrimination task demanding a win-stay, lose-shift strategy for optimal performance, poorer performance was obtained.

We have surveyed several experiments examining the contribution of cognitive variables to discrimination learning. Additional studies in which investigators have posited the operation of other cognitive variables could be cited. For example, D'Amato (1973) has posited the presence of a short-term memory process in monkeys learning a matching to sample task. Church and his associates—Church, Getty, and Lerner (1976), Church (1978)—have argued for the existence of an internal clock that rats use to make temporal discriminations. But at this stage in our science, we have little more than a listing of a number of different concepts that experimenters have identified as cognitive and have assumed to be contributors to discrimination learning. The task remains for some investigator to provide an overview integrating these diverse concepts.

## THE NATURE OF DISCRIMINATION LEARNING

How does discrimination learning take place? This section will discuss briefly some of the theoretical positions proposed to answer this question.

Pavlov (1927) examined discrimination learning using the successive presentation of stimuli, in which a CS+ and a CS− were presented on randomly determined trials. Pavlov hypothesized that such learning arose from the operation of two processes—the development of excitatory strength to the CS+ and the development of inhibitory strength to the CS−.

Some years later, Hull (1929) and Spence (1936, 1937a, 1937b) proposed a theory of discrimination learning based on Pavlov's analysis. In addition to the basic assumption made by Pavlov that excitatory and inhibitory strength develop to the CS+ and CS−, Hull and Spence proposed that (1) both excitatory and inhibitory tendencies generalize to other stimuli on the same stimulus continuum as the CS+ and the CS−; (2) the excitatory and inhibitory tendencies interact algebraically; and (3) discrimination responding is determined by the product of this algebraic interaction. Figure 5-10 presents Spence's (1937b) analysis of the discrimination learning process in which the CS+ was hypothesized to be a 256 sq cm stimulus, the CS− hypothesized to be 160 sq cm. Excitatory and inhibitory generalization gradients have been postulated, with the net excitatory strength accrued for each stimulus indicated.

Pavlov, Hull, and Spence all assumed that excitatory and inhibitory strength developed between the organism's response and each stimulus element of the discriminanda perceived by the subject. For example, if a pigeon had to discriminate between a white triangle placed on a red background (S+) and a white square placed on a green background (S−), reinforcing the S+ would result in excitatory strength being established between the instrumental response and (a) the white triangle and (b) the red background; nonreinforcement of the S− would result in inhibi-

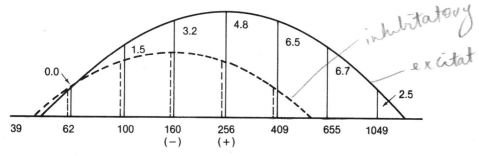

FIGURE 5-10.    Spence's theoretical representation of discrimination learning. Continuous line indicates the generalization of excitatory strength; dotted line reveals the generalization of inhibitory strength. Numerical values, such as 1.5, 3.2, etc., represent the net excitatory strength accruing to each stimulus value. Adapted from K. W. Spence, "The differential response in animals to stimuli varying within a single dimension." *Psychological Review*, 1937, 44, 430–444. Copyright © 1937 by the American Psychological Association. Reprinted by permission.

tory strength developing between nonresponding and (a) the white square and (b) the green background.

The theoretical position of Pavlov, Hull, and Spence has been challenged on several counts. Köhler (1955) disputed Pavlov's assumption that subjects responded to the absolute and specific characteristics of the discriminanda. He argued that subjects responded to relationships or configurations of stimuli. One way to settle this controversy was to use a transposition test.

**Transposition Testing**

In a study in 1918 examining the nature of the stimulus perceived by the subject, Köhler (1955) trained chickens to peck for grain placed on the darker side of two gray papers. Following such training, the birds were then tested on a new pair of stimuli: (a) the original gray paper to which they had been previously trained to respond and (b) a still darker paper. (The provision of different stimuli or the transposing of stimuli constitutes the transposition task.) Köhler found that the birds pecked at the darker paper. From this result, he argued that his subjects had learned during the original training to respond to the relationship between the stimuli—the differences in color—since during the transposition test they responded to the darker of the stimuli, rather than to the stimulus to which they had been originally trained.

Spence's (1937b) rejoinder to Köhler was that a transposed response did not necessarily require a relational explanation, and, in fact, he was able to use his model to predict Köhler's results. Note from Figure 5-10 that if, following discrimination training on the 256 sq cm (S+) and 160 sq cm (S−), the experimental subject is provided with test stimuli of 256 sq cm and 409 sq cm, Spence's model predicts that the subject should respond to the larger stimulus since it has greater net excitatory strength. On the other hand, if the test discriminanda consisted of the 256 sq cm and 1049 sq cm stimuli, the model would predict responding to the smaller of the two stimuli. Spence (1937b), using chimpanzees as subjects, experimentally tested these predictions and obtained findings in accord with his model.

Investigators soon became aware that Spence's theoretical analysis of discrimination learning was dependent on the characteristics of the excitatory and inhibitory stimulus generalization gradients that he had posited to arise from training on the S+ and S−. As shall be shown in Chapter 7, experimental work has suggested that stimulus generalization gradients do not typically have the shape and symmetry that Spence depicted in his discrimination model. Difficulties in determining the shape of the excitatory and inhibitory generalization gradients hamper experimenters attempting to use Spence's model to make predictions about responses to test stimuli following discrimination training.

In addition, several experiments have provided convincing evidence for relational responding. One of these was a study by Lawrence and DeRivera (1954) using the Lashley jumping apparatus described earlier. Each stimulus card used by these experimenters was divided in half, with one shade of gray being placed on the top half and another shade of gray on the bottom half. Seven different shades of gray ranging from very light gray (1) to very dark gray (7) were used. The stimulus cards used in the training trials all had the middle gray (4) on the bottom half. This middle gray was combined with three lighter grays, 1/4, 2/4, 3/4, and three darker grays, 5/4, 6/4, 7/4. These six different patterns were used randomly throughout the training trials. Two identical cards were used on each trial, one in each window of the apparatus. The subjects had to learn to jump to the right window when the top half of the stimulus card was lighter than the bottom half (stimulus cards 1/4, 2/4, 3/4) and to jump to the left window when the top half of the stimulus card was darker than the bottom half (stimulus cards 5/4, 6/4, 7/4). This task has been identified as a successive discrimination task—in contrast to the simultaneous discrimination task in which different stimuli are presented to the experimental subject.

The Spence-Hull position, which assumed that subjects respond to the specific characteristics of stimuli, would predict that the shades 1, 2, and 3 would become associated with the response of jumping to the right, and that the shades 5, 6, and 7 would be associated with the response of jumping to the left. A relational position, however, would hold that the specific shades of gray found on the stimulus cards would be of minor importance, and that responding would be to the relationship noted between the top and bottom half of the cards. Stimulus cards darker on the top than on the bottom would be associated with jumping to the left; stimulus cards lighter on the top than on the bottom would be associated with jumping to the right. Table 5-2 illustrates the experimental arrangements and predictions made by each theoretical position.

By changing the values of the gray placed on the bottom half of the card, it was possible to provide a test of the two theoretical positions. For example, if shade 2 was placed on the bottom and shade 3 on top, the top stimulus would be darker than the bottom, which would result in the relational position predicting that the animal should jump to the left. The specificity position, however, would predict that the animal would jump to the right, since the shade 3 stimulus had been associated with that response during training. On the other hand, if shade 6 was placed on top and a shade 7 gray on the bottom, the specific stimulus position would predict that the animal would jump left, while the relational position would predict that the animal should jump right.

Similar test trials were provided after training, with results of 264 trials indicating that approximately 80 percent of the responses were in keeping with the relational position and just 20 percent with the Spence-Hull position.

Most current investigators have taken the position, in keeping with Lawrence and DeRivera's (1954) findings, that both absolute and relational responding can be found in discrimination learning; which type predominates in a given task will depend on a number of experimental conditions.

Although a number of these conditions have been delineated, we will cite only two to support this position. Relational responding to test stimuli is enhanced if the stimuli presented during the original training can be perceived together, perhaps as a single configuration, as found in Lawrence and DeRivera's (1954) study. In contrast, absolute responding to test stimuli is obtained if presentations of the training stimuli are separated in time and space. This type of presentation minimizes the possibility of the subject perceiving any relationship between the stimuli, and places emphasis on the subject perceiving the absolute characteristics of the discriminanda.

TABLE 5-2.    Experimental arrangements and predictions provided by the specific stimulus and relational models of discrimination learning

*Training:*

| 1 | 2 | 3 |
|---|---|---|
| 4 | 4 | 4 |

Animal jumps to right window

| 5 | 6 | 7 |
|---|---|---|
| 4 | 4 | 4 |

Animal jumps to left window

*Specific Stimulus Assumptions:*

Subject learns to associate grays 1, 2, and 3 with right window, and grays 5, 6, and 7 with left window.

*Relational Position Assumptions:*

S learns to jump right when the top half of the card is lighter than the bottom half; S learns to jump left when the top half of the card is darker than the bottom half.

*Example of Test Trials and Prediction:*

| 3 |
|---|
| 2 |

Specific Stimulus: Animal should jump right
Relational: Animal should jump left

Absolute

| 6 |
|---|
| 7 |

Specific Stimulus: Animal should jump left
Relational: Animal should jump right

A second condition has to do with the characteristics of the stimuli used. Relationships between some training stimuli are difficult to perceive. For example, if two quite different stimuli are used, such as a circle and a square, it is very difficult for the experimental subject to conceptualize these stimuli in terms of some relationship, so the subject responds to the absolute characteristics of the stimuli. The experimental findings of Jackson and Jerome (1940), Baker and Lawrence (1951), and Rudel (1957) have confirmed the role of these conditions in determining whether transposition testing will reveal absolute or relational responding.

## The Continuity versus Noncontinuity Controversy

A second challenge to the Hull-Spence theory of discrimination learning arose from the work of Lashley (1929) and Krechevsky (1932a, 1932b, 1938), who held that animals learning a discrimination task attempted various solutions before arriving at the correct one. These presolution responses were designated by Krechevsky as hypotheses that the animal adopted and abandoned until it found one leading to the solution of the problem. (Krechevsky's position marks an early attempt to identify a cognitive process operating in animals.)

Since animals were responding on the basis of an hypothesis, it was assumed that they selected only a single cue or stimulus element of the discriminanda to which to respond. While responding to that cue, the animal learned nothing about the correctness (or incorrectness) of other cues that were part of the task. In addition, it was assumed that when learning did take place, the associative relationship between the appropriate stimulus elements and the response took place very rapidly.

We can note that Lashley-Krechevsky and Hull-Spence were in disagreement on two basic issues. First, did the subject associate with its response all the stimuli it perceived at the time the correct response was made? Or, were only certain elements of the discriminanda perceived by the animal, while others were ignored? Second, did learning take place gradually and continuously over trials? Or, did learning take place rapidly, with the animal's earlier performance making little or no contribution to the solution? These two issues coalesced into the continuity-noncontinuity controversy, a dispute that has extended over a period of three decades.

Most of the experiments conducted to answer the two questions employed a stimulus reversal task. The specific procedure was as follows. The experimental group was provided with a small number of trials on a discrimination task in which two stimuli—such as black and white cards—were presented, with one of these being consistently reinforced. For the control group, each stimulus was reinforced on half of the trials; thus the number of reinforced trials was the same for both groups. This early training has been referred to as the **presolution period.** Following such training, the discrimination task for the experimental group was reversed, with the previously designated negative cue becoming positive and the positive cue becoming negative. For the control group, one stimulus was consistently reinforced. Learning trials were provided until both groups of subjects reached a criterion.

Continuity theorists predicted that the experimental group should learn the reversal problem more slowly than the control group. Their reasoning was that the early training trials in which the experimental group was consistently reinforced for responding to the positive stimulus should interfere with their reversal learning, since the positive stimulus was switched to negative. The control group should not have this difficulty, since neither stimulus was consistently reinforced during the early training trials.

Noncontinuity advocates predicted that the reinforced presolution trials for the experimental group should not result in negative transfer, since the animals during these trials were not responding to the relevant stimulus elements—they had not "hit" upon the correct hypothesis. Thus, practice prior to the time the actual learning took place would be of no value in the subsequent solving of the problem.

Most of the experiments that were conducted using the stimulus reversal task supported the continuity position; see Spence (1945), Ehrenfreund (1948), Ritchie, Ebeling, and Roth (1950), Gatling (1951). As Riley (1968) has written, "It is probably fair to say that in 1950 most psychologists in the field of learning, regardless of their particular sympathies, were convinced that the continuity position was essentially correct . . ." (pp. 128–129).

## Current Theorizing—The Problem of Selective Attention

About the time that most investigators were convinced of the correctness of the continuity position, a number of experimental findings emerged that posed problems for the continuity position and necessitated a reexamination of the discrimination learning process. Lawrence (1949) and Reynolds (1961) were two of a number of experimenters who found that not all of the stimulus elements used in a discrimination experiment were perceived by their experimental subjects. Reynolds's (1961) study illustrates this type of finding. Two pigeons were given successive discrimination training in which the positive stimulus was a white triangle placed on a red background (S+), whereas the negative stimulus was a white circle on a green background (S−). Following training in which the pigeons learned to peck at the S+ but not the S−, test trials consisting of one-minute presentations of only the (1) triangle, (2) circle, (3) red background, and (4) green background were provided. Several test trial sessions were used, with a different order of stimulus presentations in each session. One subject responded very frequently to the triangle but made very few responses to the red background, even though both of these stimulus elements made up the S+. As would be expected, little responding was noted to the circle and the green background, the stimulus elements that comprised the S−. A second subject, however, responded primarily to the red background and little to the white circle. One interpretation of these findings is that the stimulus elements that made up the S+ did not control responding equally well.[3]

Reynolds's finding that a subject may respond to one positive stimulus element but not to another raises the question of why certain attributes should be able to exert control over responding. Johnson and Cumming (1968) have demonstrated that the previous training of an experimental subject may play an important role in determining this effect.

In their Experiment 1, pigeons were given a compound discrimination task. They were trained to respond to a key displaying a vertical line placed on a green background (S+); a horizontal line on a red background served as the S−. After five sessions of training, single stimulus test presentations revealed findings similar to those obtained by Reynolds (1961) in that the birds responded almost exclusively to the presentation of the green background and did not respond to the other part of the compound stimulus, the vertical line.

Experiment 2 attempted to determine if such test responding could be changed by first giving the subjects training on the vertical line. The procedure consisted of providing discrimination training in which the vertical line served as the S+, while either a horizontal line or a red background was used as the S−. Following these preliminary sessions, training and testing using a compound stimulus (vertical line and green background vs. horizontal line and red background) was conducted as in Experiment 1. The experimenters discovered that responding during the test sessions was predominantly to the vertical line, indicating that the kind of preliminary training experienced by the birds made a significant contribution to what stimulus element was selected during the compound stimulus training.

This finding—that the perceptual effectiveness of a specific stimulus element can be changed as a function of the organism's experience—has been identified as blocking. Another example of blocking is found in a later study by vom Saal and Jenkins (1970). These investigators trained pigeons in a successive discrimination task. First the pigeons learned to respond when the stimulus key was red and not to respond when it was green. A second training session consisted of reinforcing the response to the red key accompanied by a 1000 Hz tone, whereas the presentation of the green key accompanied by noise was not reinforced. Following training on this discrimination task, test trials were provided in which the nine combinations of auditory (tone, noise, silence) and visual (red, green, white) stimuli were used. Results revealed that the auditory stimulus exercised much less control over the experimental group than over the control group, which never received the original red-green training. Thus, the original color discrimination training given to the experimental group appeared to block responding to the subsequently presented auditory stimulus. This phenomenon of blocking has been frequently reported; see Chase (1968), Miles (1970), and Mackintosh and Honig (1970).

These findings have resulted in new theories of discrimination learning being proposed; see Zeaman and House (1963), Lovejoy (1968), Sutherland and Mackintosh (1971). All of these theories propose that discrimination learning involves the operation of two learning processes. One of these is the familiar associative process found in signaled tasks, in which a response becomes associated with a specific stimulus and reinforcement is associated with a specific response. The second process has been identified by some as a selective process; see Sutherland and Mackintosh (1971). Here, the subject learns to attend to certain stimulus dimensions of the discriminanda and not to others. Thus, the selective perception of the stimuli that make up the discriminanda constitutes a learning process in addition to the associative one.

## SUMMARY

Discrimination tasks are considered apart from the nonsignaled and signaled tasks discussed in earlier chapters because some variables that contribute to discrimination learning do not operate with these other types of tasks. Several theoretical explanations have been proposed for discrimination learning.

Stimulus salience, or the characteristics of the discriminanda, represents the most important stimulus variable that has been investigated with discrimination learning tasks. Not surprisingly, virtually all researchers have found that as the discriminanda become more salient, discrimination learning takes place more rapidly.

A second stimulus variable investigated has been the contribution of responding to the S−. It has been assumed that in the learning of a discrimination task, it is important for the subject to learn not to respond to the S−, in addition, of course, to learning to respond to the S+. Several studies have demonstrated such to be the case. Experience with the S− results in learning taking place more rapidly than if the experimental subject did not have experience with the S−. However, there is little likelihood of finding any fixed percentage or programming of S− trials that will result in optimal learning, since this is undoubtedly a function of the experimental conditions used.

It is possible for a subject to learn a discrimination task without responding to the S−. Terrace (1963a) has demonstrated that if the S+ is presented only on early trials and then the S− is made gradually more perceptible, it is possible for the organism to learn the discrimination without ever responding to the S−. This process has been identified as errorless discrimination learning.

Three motivational variables have been investigated: (1) frequency, (2) amount or intensity, and (3) temporal delay between the response and the presentation of the aversive stimulus. Virtually all investigators have found that discrimination learning is a function of the frequency with which reward is provided, the S+. Most of the experimental evidence indicates that such learning is also related to the amount of reward employed. As the amount of food or time during which the animal is permitted to eat is increased, discrimination learning takes place more rapidly.

In studies of the motivational variable of shock (and the termination of shock), an interaction between shock intensity and task difficulty has been discovered. That is, increasing the intensity of shock when an easy discrimination task is used results in learning taking place more rapidly; however, an intermediate level of shock provides optimal learn-

ing if the discrimination task is more difficult to learn. This relationship between level of motivation and task difficulty has been described as the Yerkes-Dodson law.

Delay of reinforcement has also interested experimenters. They have found that as the time interval between the making of the response and the securing of reward is increased, discrimination learning becomes poorer.

The contribution of cognitive variables to discrimination learning has also been examined. Harlow (1949) discovered that monkeys were able to solve object discrimination problems with increasing efficiency as a function of their previous experience with this type of task. The cognitive variable would appear to operate in the animals' adoption of the strategy "win-stay, lose-shift."

A second major area of experimenter interest has been the determination of the nature of discrimination learning. Hull and Spence were advocates of the position that excitatory and inhibitory strength accrued to the S+ and S−, with the discriminatory response learned being related to the algebraic summation of these two values. An objection to this position was raised by Köhler, who posited that subjects in discrimination learning tasks responded to the relationship that existed between the stimuli. Thus, subjects learned to respond to a stimulus that was larger, darker, rounder, etc., than another stimulus, rather than to its absolute characteristics. The absolute versus the relational point of view was tested with the transposition test. In this test, the training stimuli are transposed during a test series in order to determine if the subject will respond relationally or absolutely. Experimental findings have indicated both types of responding.

Other issues that arose in the analysis of discrimination learning included: (1) did the subject associate with the response all the stimuli it perceived at the time the correct response was made? and (2) did discrimination learning take place gradually, with an accumulation of excitatory strength occurring over trials, or did such learning take place very rapidly, with the animal testing varying hypotheses until one of them resulted in the solution of the problem? These issues have coalesced into the continuity-noncontinuity controversy. Early tests of the two rival positions favored the continuity position, but more recent studies have supported a modified noncontinuity position.

## NOTES

1. Terrace (1972) has argued that errorless discrimination learning is a process fundamentally different from learning with errors. Rilling (1977) has taken issue with this position. His research has indicated that the behavior of subjects who make no errors (or very few) in learning a discrimination task is not fundamentally different from the behavior of subjects who make many errors except, of course, for differences in error production. The research of Rilling and his associates suggests that it is the procedure used in errorless discrimination training rather than the making (or not making) of errors that is responsible for apparent behavior differences found be-

tween the two conditions. See Rilling and Caplan (1973), Rilling, Caplan, Howard, and Brown (1975), Rilling, Richards, and Kramer (1973).

2. The five experimental subjects were male alcoholic patients who volunteered for the experiment. All of them had a long history of drinking and had been in the hospital for several weeks. The use of such a procedure without informing the subjects about the action of the drug prior to conducting the experiment poses a serious ethical problem.

3. Wilkie and Masson (1976) replicated Reynolds's (1961) study and obtained similar findings, although during test trials their birds responded almost exclusively to color and not to the shape that had been previously associated with reward. However, when they provided their subjects with a second discrimination task consisting of the shape previously associated with reward and a shape never experienced before, the birds rapidly learned to respond to the shape previously associated with reward. Presumably, their birds had learned to attend to a particular shape and associate it with reward during the original learning task but the test trial performance did not measure such learning.

# CHAPTER SIX

# Experimental Extinction

The presentation of the US, or reinforcement, is undoubtedly the most important operation in the establishment of a classically or instrumentally conditioned response. But what if, following the acquisition of a response, the US is no longer presented, or the instrumental response is no longer followed by reinforcement? Under such circumstances, there is a gradual cessation of responding. The operation of omitting the US or withholding reinforcement and the ensuing decrement in responding has been defined as **experimental extinction.**

Extinction can often be observed in everyday activities. The pet dog, when no longer rewarded for sitting up or rolling over, will eventually stop responding to the verbal command; the child, after finding that the cookie jar no longer contains cookies, will eventually stop searching. The adaptive significance of the extinction process is evident; it ensures that an organism's response does not persist when reinforcement no longer occurs.

The cessation of responding arising from an extinction operation should not be confused with a loss of responding due to forgetting. The basic experimental operation for defining forgetting is to place a time interval between the original learning and the test for retention. Within this time interval, some type of intervening event is usually presented to the subject, in order to determine how this event influences the forgetting of the original learning. Chapter 10 will examine the forgetting process.

## EXTINCTION OPERATIONS

The extinction operation used with classical conditioning is straightforward—the CS continues to be presented but the US is omitted. To extinguish a conditioned salivary response or a conditioned eyeblink in which a tone serves as the CS and meat powder or an airpuff as the US, only the tone is presented, resulting in a gradual decline and eventual cessation of the conditioned response.

When an appetitive instrumental conditioning task is used, removing the reward also serves to extinguish the response. But several problems arise when the instrumental task utilizes an aversive stimulus such as shock, thus involving escape or avoidance responses.

The removal or elimination of shock results in a loss of the reinforcing function since shock reduction does not take place. But there is also a loss of the eliciting function. That is, there is no shock presentation to "motivate" responding. As a result, many experimenters have followed the procedure suggested by Church (1971). For the extinction operation in an escape task, Church presented the aversive stimulus in the goal box, in addition to presenting it in those parts of the apparatus where it had been provided during acquisition. Just as the extinction operation in experiments utilizing reward consists of removing reinforcement, the presentation of the aversive stimulus in the goal box also removes reinforcement, since shock termination does not take place. An example of this procedure is found in a study by Bower (1960), who trained rats to escape from a 250 v shock by running to a safe goal box. Extinction trials following such training were conducted by presenting the same intensity of shock in the goal box, in addition to continuing to present it in the start box and runway. Extinction took place quite rapidly.

The problem of providing an appropriate extinction operation for instrumental avoidance tasks has been much more difficult to solve. The traditional procedure has been for the experimenter to omit the presentation of the aversive stimulus. However, since the subject has learned to avoid the aversive stimulus, functionally the aversive stimulus is also omitted on acquisition trials. Thus, there is no opportunity for the experimental subject to become aware that the aversive stimulus is no longer being presented. In assessing the traditional procedure, Davenport and Olson (1968) have pointed out that this method ". . . is no more extinction of the instrumental avoidance response than the decreased tendency for Ss to respond when satiated for food is extinction in the positive reinforcement situation" (p. 5).

Since the appropriateness of the omission procedure has been questioned, investigators have been unsure of what method to use to extinguish an instrumental avoidance response. The operations utilized during extinction trials have taken the form of either (1) presenting the aversive stimulus at random intervals and independent of the response made by the organism or (2) presenting the aversive stimulus only when the subject makes the previously learned avoidance response. Because of the different extinction operations used, the extinction of avoidance responding will be considered separately in a subsequent section.

## WHAT DOES EXTINCTION PERFORMANCE MEASURE?

Prior to 1940 a common practice among investigators was to infer from an extinction measure the amount or degree of learning that had taken place during acquisition. In *Principles of Behavior,* Hull (1943) lent support to this practice by considering experimental extinction to be one of the four response measures from which the strength of the learning process could be inferred. But as was pointed out in Chapter 2, experimenters are now recognizing that using extinction to measure the strength of a previously learned response is undoubtedly an error.

Although investigators are sure that experimental extinction does not measure previously learned responding, they do not know what it does measure. Continued responding despite nonreward suggests the operation of persistence; in fact, some current investigators have conceptualized extinction as a measure of persistence; see Amsel (1972), Banks (1973), Chapin and Dyck (1976), Dyck, Mellgren, and Nation (1974), Nation and Massad (1978), and Nation and Woods (1980). But many other experimenters consider extinction to be only a particular kind of behavior arising from the operation of withholding reward; their major objective has been to determine how stimulus and motivational variables influence such behavior.

## STIMULUS VARIABLES

Early classical conditioning investigators were interested in examining resistance to extinction as a function of the number of CS alone trials. Data obtained from Pavlov (1927) and presented in Figure 2-4 illustrate the typical finding that responding decreases as the number of CS presentations increases.

Experimenters have also been interested in how resistance to extinction is influenced when the stimulus conditions present during acquisition are changed during extinction. In conditioning the eyeblink, Grant, Schipper, and Ross (1952) found that changing the intertrial interval from the value provided during acquisition to another during extinction resulted in more rapid extinction than when the same intertrial interval was used during both acquisition and extinction trials. This finding is in keeping with a general assumption made by some investigators that the greater the change of stimulus conditions from acquisition to extinction, the more rapidly extinction will take place.

An organism's responding is not controlled by all of the stimuli present in the learning task. If a salient cue present during acquisition were altered during extinction, responding would undoubtedly be influenced to a much greater extent than if a less salient cue were changed. Such an explanation seems reasonable in accounting for the findings of Brown and Bass (1958) and Marx (1958), who have been unable to support the findings of Grant, Schipper, and Ross (1952).

## MOTIVATIONAL VARIABLES

Motivational variables have generated the most interest among experimenters examining extinction, since it is the removal of reward that defines the extinction operation. The reward conditions manipulated during training trials include amount, delay, and frequency. Partial reinforcement is also a motivational variable, but it has been examined so extensively that it will be discussed in a separate section.

### Amount of Reward

Studies examining the effect of increasing the amount of reward on lever pressing or runway performance have yielded similar findings—increasing the amount of reinforcement during acquisition trials (by varying the size or number of food pellets) decreases resistance to extinction; see Hulse (1958), Wagner (1961), Ison and Cook (1964), Marx (1967), Roberts (1969), and Campbell, Batsche, and Batsche (1972). An extensive study by Roberts (1969) illustrates this finding. Rats, provided with 48 trials to learn to traverse a runway, received 1, 2, 5, 10, or 25 pellets of food. This was followed by 31 extinction trials. All animals received one trial a day. The animals' starting times most clearly reveal the nature of the relationship between the amount of reward obtained during acquisition and performance during extinction. Those animals who had received the largest number of food pellets during acquisition trials extinguished most rapidly, whereas those receiving the smallest

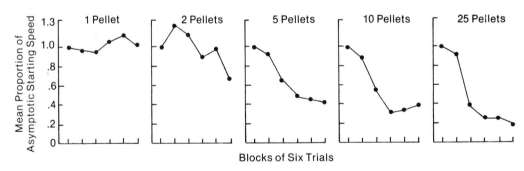

FIGURE 6-1.   Extinction curves as measured by starting times for each amount of reward used during acquisition. Adapted from W. A. Roberts, "Resistance to extinction following partial and consistent reinforcement with varying magnitudes of reward." *Journal of Comparative and Physiological Psychology*, 1969, 67, 395–400. Copyright © 1969 by the American Psychological Association. Reprinted by permission.

number of pellets extinguished least rapidly. See Figure 6-1.

## Delay of Reward

Investigators have found that delaying reward for a constant length of time after the subject makes an instrumental response during acquisition trials increases resistance to extinction; the control group, of course, receives reward immediately. See Fehrer (1956), Tombaugh (1966), Wike and McWilliams (1967), and Tombaugh (1970).

In Fehrer's (1956) study, rats traversing a runway were provided 37 acquisition trials spaced over five days. One group of animals was delayed 20 seconds prior to receiving 10 seconds of drinking time, whereas a second group was provided 10 seconds of drinking time followed by 20 seconds of detention in the goal box. Two other groups had immediate access to water and were permitted to drink for either 10 or 30 seconds. Twelve extinction trials followed acquisition. Fehrer found that the two delay groups extinguished less rapidly than either of the immediate reinforcement groups. A lever pressing study by Tombaugh (1970), which examined constant delay conditions of 15, 30, and 45 seconds, produced similar findings. The group with a 45 second delay took longest to extinguish, followed by the groups with 30 and 15 second delays.

The increased resistance to extinction caused by delay of reinforcement is also found when the delay period is provided on some trials but not on others. In a study by Knouse and Campbell (1971), groups of rats traversing a runway were provided different delays of reinforcement on half of their 50 acquisition trials; no delay of reinforcement was given on the other half. Delay periods of either 0, 8, 16, 24, 32, 40, 48, or 56 seconds were examined. Reward consisted of 15 seconds of eating wet mash. Forty extinction trials were provided after acquisition training, with increasing resistance to extinction being related to the length of the delay provided during acquisition. Figure 6-2 reveals these findings.

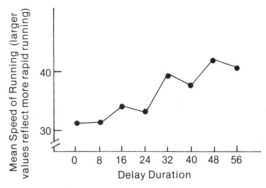

FIGURE 6-2.   Mean running speeds for each delay duration during extinction. Adapted from S. B. Knouse and P. E. Campbell, "Partially delayed reward in the rat: A parametric study of delay duration." *Journal of Comparative and Physiological Psychology*, 1971, 75, 116–119. Copyright © 1971 by the American Psychological Association. Reprinted by permission.

## Frequency of Continuously Rewarded Trials

When extinction has been examined as a function of the frequency of continuously rewarded trials, the experimental findings have been contradictory. The results are related to the kind of task employed. When the Skinner box was used, most investigators found that the extinction of the bar pressing response related positively to the number of reinforced responses provided during acquisition; see Williams (1938), Perin (1942), Harris and Nygaard (1961), Dyal and Holland (1963), Uhl and Young (1967). In the Uhl and Young (1967) experiment, 180, 360, and 730 bar pressing responses, each reinforced with a sucrose solution, were followed by extinction trials. As Figure 6-3 indicates, resistance to extinction was positively related to the number of reinforced responses the animal made.

However, when the learning task was having the rat traverse an alley, a different finding has been obtained. Experimenters have found that increasing the number of reinforced trials results in more rapid extinction, a result referred to as the **overlearning extinction effect (OEE)**. This finding was originally

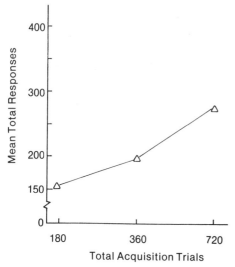

FIGURE 6-3. Mean total extinction responses as a function of total number of acquisition trials. Adapted from C. N. Uhl and A. G. Young, "Resistance to extinction as a function of incentive, percentage of reinforcement, and number of nonreinforced trials." *Journal of Experimental Psychology*, 1967, 73, 556–564. Copyright © 1967 by the American Psychological Association. Reprinted by permission.

reported by North and Stimmel (1960). They found that rats receiving 45 acquisition trials extinguished less rapidly than subjects receiving 90 or 135 trials. Many subsequent runway studies have confirmed this result; see Ison (1962), Siegel and Wagner (1963), Clifford (1964, 1968).

At this time, it is difficult to reconcile the disparate findings of the bar pressing and runway studies, although it can be suggested that two variables need further examination. First, investigators using a Skinner box and the bar pressing response typically use a small amount of reward; in contrast, large amounts are often used in runway studies. It may be that a large amount of reward produces intense frustration during extinction, which contributes in some way to the overlearning effect found in runway studies. Ison and Cook (1964) have provided some support for this position. In their study, groups of rats were provided with either 30 or 75 training trials on

the runway, with half of each group receiving 1 pellet of food (small reward) and the other half receiving 10 pellets (large reward). Fifteen trials a day were provided for either two or five days, following which the animals received 30 extinction trials. Results indicated that the animals that received 75 trials with 10 pellets of food extinguished most rapidly; animals receiving 75 trials with just 1 pellet of food, however, revealed the greatest resistance to extinction.

A second variable, perhaps interacting with the amount of reward, is the difference in effort between bar pressing and traversing the runway, and the difference in timing between programming extinction trials over a single session and distributing them over several sessions. Using a lever pressing task, Senkowski (1978) was unable to obtain the overlearning extinction effect in one experiment (Experiment 1), thus confirming the findings of many other investigators, but was able to demonstrate this effect in a second experiment (Experiment 2). Both experiments were conducted under identical conditions except that extinction trials in the first study (which did not demonstrate OEE) were distributed over seven sessions whereas extinction trials in Experiment 2 were provided in a single session. Such findings suggested to Senkowski that "session-related variables . . . may be important determinants of extinction performance" (p. 140).

## PARTIAL REINFORCEMENT

### Varying Partial Reinforcement Schedules

The effects of partial reinforcement on experimental extinction have been extensively examined. Humphreys's (1939a) classically conditioned eyeblink study, described in Chapter 3, obtained a most unusual extinction effect (or so it was regarded at that time) with a partial reinforcement schedule. Three groups of college students were given one of the following training schedules: (1) 96 CS-US trials; (2) 48 CS-US trials and 48 CS alone trials (the partial reinforcement group); and (3) 48 CS-US trials. Humphreys reported that the group given 96 trials with 50 percent reinforcement took significantly longer to reach extinction than either of the two continuously reinforced groups. See Figure 6-4 for these results. The superiority of a partial reinforcement schedule in producing resistance to extinction has been designated a **partial reinforcement effect** (PRE).

When animals have been used as experimental subjects in classical conditioning experiments, the partial reinforcement effect has not been always obtained; see Wagner, Siegel, Thomas, and Ellison (1964), Berger, Yarczower, and Bitterman (1965), Wagner, Siegel, and Fein (1967). Mackintosh's (1974) careful examination of these animal studies has led him

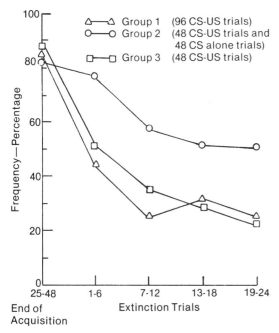

FIGURE 6-4.   Course of extinction frequency. The 24 extinction trials are divided into four groups of 6 trials each. An average for the preceding 24 acquisition trials (labeled 25–48) is plotted to serve as a reference point for the extinction results. Adapted from L. G. Humphreys, "The effect of random alternation of reinforcement on the acquisition and extinction of conditioned eyelid reactions." *Journal of Experimental Psychology*, 1939, 25, 141–158. Copyright © 1939 by the American Psychological Association. Reprinted by permission.

to conclude that "although it is clear that partial reinforcement *may* increase resistance to extinction of a classically conditioned response, the generality of the effect leaves much to be desired and even when an effect does occur, it is often relatively small" (p. 74).

However, in the study of instrumental conditioning tasks, literally hundreds of experiments have demonstrated that, regardless of the kind of experimental subject, an intermittent schedule of reward invariably results in the PRE; see Weinstock (1958), Bacon (1962), Coughin (1970).

An obvious next step, after Humphreys (1939a) found that a 50 percent reinforcement schedule increased resistance to extinction, was to vary the percentage of trials reinforced during the acquisition series. In their examination of the classically conditioned eyelid response, Grant and Schipper (1952) varied the percentage of US presentations. The US was programmed to follow the CS on 0, 25, 50, 75, or 100 percent of 60 training trials provided on Day 1 and of 32 trials on Day 2. Performance on the 25 extinction trials, which immediately followed Day 2's training trials, revealed a U-shaped function, with the 0, 25, and 100 percent reinforcement groups showing the least resistance to extinction and the 50 and 75 percent groups indicating the greatest.

It is important to examine these findings somewhat more analytically. At the end of the acquisition trials, there were substantial differences among the varying groups in the percentage of conditioned responses; the 75 and 100 percent groups had the largest number of CRs, while the 0 and 25 percent groups had the fewest. Grant and Schipper (1952) hypothesized that two factors appeared to be responsible for the U-shaped function they obtained: (1) the organism's terminal level of acquisition performance, resulting from differing numbers of reinforcements or CS-US trials, and (2) the organism's ease of discriminating the acquisition trials from extinction trials. Gibbs, Latham, and Gormezano (1978) obtained a similar functional relationship between extinction performance and the percentage of CS-US trials. In their study examining the classically conditioned nictitating membrane response of the rabbit, 600 acquisition trials were provided, with reinforcement schedules of either 0, 5, 15, 25, 50, or 100 percent. Three hundred extinction trials were provided after acquisition. Figure 6-5 presents the percent of conditioned responses made during the extinction trials for each of these reinforcement schedules.

Grant and Schipper's examination of differing percentages of reinforcement was followed by a host of investigations using instrumental tasks to examine this variable. Lewis (1960), after reviewing many of these experiments, concluded that the relationship between resistance to extinction and percentage of US presentations or reinforced trials could best be described as U-shaped, a conclusion echoed by many subsequent writers. It must be kept in mind that this conclusion seems to hold only when the groups receiving a small percentage of reinforced trials during acquisition reveal little learning at the end of training. When terminal acquisition performance level is fairly high for these groups, the percentage of US presentations–extinction function changes. Consider a study by Bacon (1962) in which 16 groups of rats were trained to traverse a runway, with 10, 30, 100, or 300

acquisition trials, and with either 30, 50, 70, or 100 percent of these trials reinforced. Following such training, 30 extinction trials were provided. Figure 6-6 plots speed of running during extinction trials as a function of the two manipulated variables, the number of acquisition trials and the percentage of reinforced trials.

Bacon (1962) has written that the data clearly support the two-process position proposed by Grant and Schipper (1952). After just 10 acquisition trials, only the reinforcement process is operating, so resistance to extinction is directly related to the percentage or number of reinforcements received. After 30 trials, both the reinforcement and the discrimination process appear to be operating, so the U-shaped function is obtained on extinction trials. Finally, with 100 and 300 acquisition trials, the response has been well learned by all groups, regardless of the percentage of reinforced trials, so only the discrimination process appears to operate during extinction. See Box 6-1.

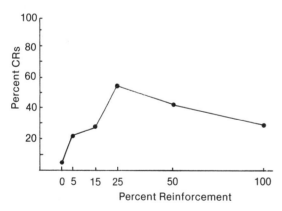

FIGURE 6-5.   Percentage of CRs made during 300 extinction trials for each of the varying reinforcement schedules provided during acquisition. Adapted from C. M. Gibbs, S. B. Latham, and I. Gormezano, "Classical conditioning of the rabbit membrane response." *Animal Learning and Behavior*, 1978, 6, 209–215. Reprinted by permission of the Psychonomic Society.

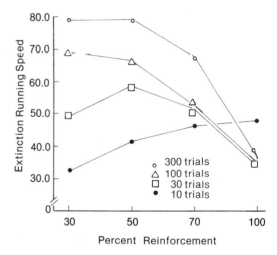

FIGURE 6-6.   The effect of different numbers of acquisition trials on mean extinction running speed as a function of percentage of reinforcement. Adapted from W. E. Bacon, "Partial-reinforcement extinction following different amounts of training." *Journal of Comparative and Physiological Psychology*, 1962, 55, 998–1003. Copyright © 1962 by the American Psychological Association. Reprinted by permission.

■■■ BOX 6-1 ■■■■■■■■■■■■■■■■■■■■■■■■■■■■■■■■■■■■■■■■

The playing of a slot machine, which provides intermittent reinforcement, has been a frequently cited example of how partial reinforcement influences responding.

Lewis and Duncan (1956) have used the slot machine to experimentally study the effects of partial reinforcement. Seven groups of college students served as subjects. They were provided with an unlimited number of disks with which to play the machine, and told that it would be possible to win tokens that could be cashed in for five cents apiece after they decided to stop playing. Each group was given eight acquisition trials and provided a different percentage of reinforcement on these trials—namely, 100, 75, 50, 37$\frac{1}{2}$, 25, 12$\frac{1}{2}$, and 0 percent. Except for the 0 percent group, all subjects received a token on the eighth trial, in addition to any tokens they received on other trials, the number depending on the percentage of reinforcement they were programmed to receive. Extinction trials immediately followed the acquisition trials, with the subjects being encouraged to play as long as they wanted.

Results indicated that the percentage of reinforcement provided the varying groups had a significant effect on the total number of plays, as shown in the figure below. It will be recalled that Bacon (1962), using rats, observed that when a well-learned response was extinguished, the percentage of reinforced trials provided during acquisition was inversely related to the animal's resistance to extinction. Lever pulling was a well-learned response among the college students, so Lewis and Duncan's finding that their subjects' resistance to extinction was inversely related to the number of reinforced responses provided during the eight acquisition trials is in keeping with Bacon's point of view.

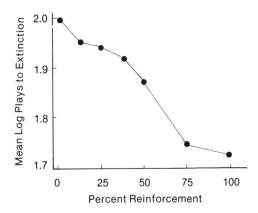

BOX FIGURE 6-1.   Mean log trials to extinction as a function of the percentage of trials reinforced during acquisition. Adapted from D. J. Lewis and C. P. Duncan, "Effect of different percentages of money reward on extinction of a lever pulling response." *Journal of Experimental Psychology*, 1956, 52, 23–27. Copyright © 1956 by the American Psychological Association. Reprinted by permission.

■■■■■■■■■■■■■■■■■■■■■■■■■■■■■■■■■■■■■■■■■■■■■■■■■■■■

## Patterns of Partial Reinforcement

It is possible to vary the patterning or sequencing of the reinforced and nonreinforced trials as well as the percentage. Some investigators have demonstrated that such patterns play an important role in determining extinction performance. In an early runway study, using a pattern of either random or alternating reinforced and nonreinforced trials, Tyler, Wortz, and Bitterman (1953) found that those rats provided alternating trials extinguished more rapidly than the group provided the random sequence. This finding has been confirmed by other experimenters; see Capaldi (1958), Campbell, Knouse, and Wroten (1970).

The patterning variable, in acquisition trials in the form of reinforced-nonreinforced (RN) or nonreinforced-reinforced (NR) sequences, has also been examined. Grosslight's expectation was that the NR pattern should result in superior resistance to extinction. He reasoned that subjects receiving the NR pattern, in contrast to the RN, should learn that reinforced trials always followed nonreinforced—learning that would support superior resistance to extinction when carried over into extinction trials. Studies by Grosslight, Hall, and Murnin (1953) and Grosslight and Radlow (1956, 1957), which examined the contribution of RN and NR patterns on extinction, have supported Grosslight's position. Capaldi (1966, 1967, 1971) has provided a sequential theory of partial reinforcement based on this type of reinforcement-nonreinforcement patterning. His position will be considered later in this chapter.

## THEORIES OF EXTINCTION

Why does responding decline with the presentation of only the CS? One explanation might be that nonreinforcement "erases" the association previously established by reward. Such an explanation assumes that the organism's response to the CS after extinction trials will be the same as the response made to the CS prior to acquisition trials, but we know that such is not the case. After extinction the CR may reappear, as in the case of spontaneous recovery; moreover, the number of acquisition trials needed to reestablish to CR after extinction is smaller than that required to establish the CR originally.

What other explanations have been proposed for experimental extinction? Pavlov's (1927) experiments led him to hypothesize that in addition to the excitation arising from CS-US pairings, a second central nervous system process, inhibition, arose from the presentation of the CS. The function of the US with which the CS was paired on conditioning trials was to retard the development of this inhibitory process. The removal of the US during extinction trials thus led to a more rapid development of the inhibitory process, until inhibition eventually masked the excitatory effect produced by CS-US trials. Thus, Pavlov (1927) wrote:

> The cortical cells under the influence of the conditioned stimulus always tend to pass, though sometimes very slowly, into a state of inhibition. The function performed by the unconditioned reflex after the conditioned reflex has become established is merely to retard the development of inhibition. (p. 234)

Pavlov also assumed that the inhibitory effect was temporary and fragile. Thus, the reappearance of the CR, as noted in spontaneous recovery, lent support to the transitory nature of inhibition. The finding that the presentation of a novel stimulus would elicit an extinguished CR, the phenomenon of disinhibition, indicated its fragility.

A second explanation of extinction, often identified as interference theory, was proposed by Guthrie (1935) and Wendt (1936). They hypothesized that the removal of reinforcement resulted in the organism learning to make other responses that were incompatible with the making of the conditioned or instrumental response. These interfering responses, learned during extinction trials, eventually precluded the appearance of the conditioned (or instrumental) response. The interference theory was supported by detailed observations of extinction behavior that revealed an increase in other kinds of responses, as the previously learned response declined in strength. Wendt (1936), for example, observed that after monkeys had learned to open a drawer to a cue in order to obtain food, the removal of reward resulted in an increase of a variety of activities other than drawer pulling, such as biting, vocalizing, running about in the cage, etc.

Neither an inhibition nor an interference theory was able to account for all of the findings noted in extinction experiments. Inhibition theory had difficulty in accounting for the varying kinds of behavior that frequently took place during extinction trials, while interference theory suffered from the fact that proponents were unable to specify the motivational stimulus that elicited the interfering response or the nature of the reinforcement that presumably strengthened such responding.

## Hullian Theory

Hull (1943), in his *Principles of Behavior*, provided a theory of extinction that incorporated both inhibitory and interfering response constructs. Briefly, Hull hypothesized that an inhibitory state, called **reactive inhibition** (RI), developed whenever any response was made by the organism. He considered reactive inhibition to be a primary motivational state which, if sufficiently strong, had the capacity to produce a cessation of the response that produced the state. Inasmuch as reactive inhibition was hypothesized to dissipate over time and with rest, it could be likened to Pavlov's concept of inhibition.

Thus, he hypothesized that the rat's response of traversing a runway or a pigeon's pecking at an illuminated key would generate a motivational state, which he called reactive inhibition. If the response continued for a sufficiently long time, reactive inhibition was hypothesized to accumulate so that it eventually prevented the response from being made. Not making the response, or rest, was assumed to result in the dissipation of reactive inhibition, thus permitting the response to again be made. Hull acknowledged that reactive inhibition bore a striking resemblance to fatigue but preferred to consider reactive inhibition to be only an intervening variable. This position gave him considerable latitude in his postulation of how reactive inhibition was presumed to operate.

Hull (1943) also posited a second inhibition process, identified as learned or **conditioned inhibition.** When the subject rested, the cessation of responding was reinforced by the dissipation of reactive inhibition. This conditioned resting response, or not responding,

the strength of which did not dissipate with time, could be considered a learned response that interfered with the making of the conditioned (or instrumental) response. In summary, reactive inhibition was hypothesized to summate with conditioned inhibition to form an inhibitory state that eventually would become strong enough to prevent the organism from responding, thus producing experimental extinction.

Unfortunately, Hull's theoretical account of experimental extinction based on the constructs of reactive and conditioned inhibition fared no better than the inhibition and interference explanations. It would serve no useful purpose to delineate all of the conceptual and experimental problems with Hull's theory. However, the findings from two experimental paradigms illustrate some of the difficulties with Hull's proposed operation of reactive inhibition. One paradigm has been identified as silent extinction, the other as latent inhibition.

**Silent Extinction** Hull (1943) had posited that a basic condition for the occurrence and development of reactive inhibition was the necessity for the organism to make a response. However, it has been demonstrated that when a conditioned response has been extinguished, further presentations of the CS will continue to strengthen the extinction process. This phenomenon, called **silent extinction,** was evidenced by reduced amounts of spontaneous recovery and/or increased difficulty in reconditioning the conditioned response. Brogden, Lipman, and Culler (1938) demonstrated this phenomenon in an early experiment. In their study, four dogs were conditioned to flex their right forelimb when a 1000 Hz tone (CS) was presented. Shock was used as the US. Following acquisition trials, extinction trials were provided until the conditioned response could no longer be elicited by the CS. Two dogs were then reconditioned, while the other two animals received 400 additional CS presentations prior to being reconditioned. Spontaneous recovery was greater and reconditioning was much more readily obtained with the two animals that had not received the additional 400 CS presentations.

**Latent Inhibition** A second paradigm that challenges Hull's concept of reactive inhibition has been identified as **latent inhibition.** It is illustrated in an experiment by Lubow and Moore (1959).

Both sheep and goats served as subjects and received 10 nonreinforced presentations of either a flashing light or a turning rotor. Following these pretest trials, the animals were presented with either the light or the rotor as the CS on their first conditioning trial. A shock to the foreleg, which elicited leg flexion, served as the US. On the second trial, each subject received the other CS (either the light or rotor); on subsequent trials, the CSs were alternated until a learning criterion of 10 CRs to each CS had been reached. Preexposing the animals to a specific stimulus prior to using it as the CS inhibited the formation of the conditioned response to that stimulus. Note, however, that the preexposure of the CS did not produce any identifiable response—which should have resulted in the development of reactive inhibition.

In the two decades since Lubow and Moore's (1959) discovery, a host of experimenters have demonstrated the phenomenon using a variety of organisms, such as goldfish (Braud, 1971), rabbits (Lubow, Markham, and Allen, 1968), rats (Ackill and Mellgren, 1968), and humans (Schnur and Ksir, 1969). In addition, several parameters of latent inhibition have been identified, including the effects of the number of nonreinforced preexposures of the CS (Ackill and Mellgren, 1968), the intensity of the preexposed CS (Schnur and Lubow, 1976), and the length of the interval between the last CS preexposure and the beginning of acquisition trials (James, 1971). The interested reader can consult Lubow (1973), Mackintosh (1974), or Hall (1976) for an extended discussion of the concept.

### Generalization Decrement Theory

Explanations for extinction proposed since Hull's (1943) have been limited in scope. Generalization decrement theory is one example. It proposes that during training an organism learns to respond to a complex of stimuli, including the reinforcing agent. A change in any aspect of the stimulating conditions during extinction trials will result in a response decrement, and such decremental responding may be used to infer the operation of the extinction process. (This effect was noted in our earlier discussion on the effect of changed stimulus conditions on extinction.)

The removal of reward is an alteration of the stimulus conditions. But this change in reinforcement provides a motivational change as well, eliminating the incentive and reinforcing function, which in turn results in response variability. These variable responses are likely to interfere with the making of the previously learned response, thus hastening extinction.

### Cognitive Explanations: The Role of Instructions

No completely comprehensive explanation for extinction has been developed by cognitive theorists, but they have noted that cognitive variables (such as awareness, expectancies, etc.) can play an important role in accounting for the response decrement that is found when reinforcement is removed.

With classical conditioning tasks using humans, many experimenters have found they can facilitate extinction by telling their subjects that the US will no longer be presented; see Cook and Harris (1937), Lindley and Moyer (1961), Wickens, Allen, and Hill (1963), Grings and Lockhart (1963). The Grings and Lockhart (1963) study illustrates the procedure and general findings. Colored geometrical forms, such as red triangles, blue squares, or yellow circles, were used as individual CSs, paired with shock (US) which elicited the galvanic skin response. After receiving a number of CS-US pairings, half of the subjects were told that there would be no more shock, while the other half of the subjects were not given these instructions. Three extinction trials were then provided, with results, as indicated in Figure 6-7, clearly revealing the effect of instructions. The increase in responding for the instructed subjects was not statistically significant.

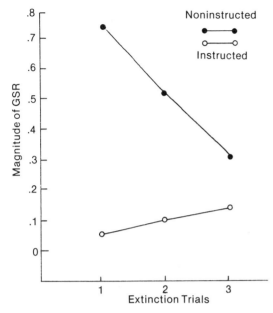

FIGURE 6-7. Magnitude of the conditioned GSR during extinction for the instructed and noninstructed groups. Adapted from W. W. Grings and R. A. Lockhart, "Effects of 'anxiety-lessening' instructions and differential set development on the extinction of GSR." *Journal of Experimental Psychology*, 1963, 66, 292–299. Copyright © 1963 by the American Psychological Association. Reprinted by permission.

## A Descriptive Account of Experimental Extinction

Another approach to the study of experimental extinction has been to provide a descriptive account of the experimental subject's behavior during extinction trials. Such an approach is illustrated by Wong's (1978) analysis of the rat's extinction behavior in the runway. In order to provide his animals with the opportunity to engage in a variety of responses during extinction trials, Wong drastically modified the traditional straight nonobstructed runway with simple starting and goal boxes. Animals were placed in an entry box from which they could jump a hurdle leading into a starting box. The starting box contained a drinking tube, a model animal, and a sand

digging apparatus. A runway adjoined the starting box. Small strips of pressboard divided the runway into 9 (Experiments 1 and 2) or 12 (Experiment 3) equal segments. All segments were numerically coded so that the animal's route in traversing the runway could be recorded. A small opening in the runway led to an exploration box. The goal box contained a sand digging apparatus, a model animal, a can lid which the animal could bite, a door which led to a small escape box, and the food cup.

This apparatus permitted Wong to record the animal's behavior in considerable detail. Wong was able to obtain measures of sniffing, grooming, immobility, and most of the instrumental activities that brought the animal into direct contact with various parts of the apparatus. These included drinking, biting, sand digging, and exploring, in addition to running the habitual and alternate routes through the runway and to the goal box.

By analyzing these varying kinds of behavior throughout extinction trials, Wong came to the conclusion that extinction involves an orderly succession of three qualitatively different stages of behavior. In the first of these, identified as a habit stage, the predominant behavior of the animal is the repetition of the response acquired during the learning trials. However, these responses are performed more vigorously than before. The second stage is characterized by investigatory behavior. Here, there is considerable variation in the route taken to the goal box, coupled with exploratory behavior. Finally, the last stage consists of the animal abandoning second-stage behavior and engaging in sub-goal behavior characterized by drinking, sand digging, etc. In an apt summary of these stages, Wong (1978) has noted that in case of repeated failure to secure reward it is only natural for the subject to first repeat the same response that has been successful (Stage 1) and then to try alternative responses (Stage 2) before switching to alternative goals (Stage 3). Responses that compete with the previously acquired running response are seldom found in Stage 1 but do play a major role in extinction behavior during Stages 2 and 3.

An important contribution of Wong's (1978) descriptive analysis is that it recognized that specific learning variables, such as the amount of reward, will influence each of the three stages of extinction behavior differently. Wong's work has also indicated that extinction is even more complex than previously believed, and that the different theoretical positions might all have validity, depending on the stage of extinction examined. As he has indicated, the new task that faces extinction theorists is to determine how a specific theoretical position is related to these different stages of extinction. It will be interesting to note whether or not his challenge is responded to.

### The Extinction of Avoidance Responding

There has been no operation generally agreed upon for use in extinguishing an avoidance response. Traditionally, extinction has called for the omission of the US, but as noted earlier in the chapter, the omission of the aversive stimulus in avoidance conditioning is inappropriate. As a result, alternative methods of extinguishing the avoidance response have been to present the US randomly during extinction trials or to present the US whenever the subject makes the avoidance response.

When these latter two procedures are contrasted with the traditional method of omitting the US, substantial differences in extinction performance can be noted. In a study by Bolles, Moot, and Grossen (1971), rats were provided with 100 training trials in which they learned to avoid shock by running to an adjacent compartment in a shuttle box. A buzzer served as the CS, and the interstimulus interval was 10 seconds. The making of an avoidance response resulted in three conditions: (1) avoidance of the shock, (2) termination of the CS (buzzer), and (3) a 10 second period of lights-out in the "safe" compartment; thus, the animals were given feedback concerning the correctness of their response. One hundred extinction trials were then provided in which one or more of the three basic conditions were changed. These changes were as follows: (1) the CS continued to be

presented after the avoidance response had been made, (2) the light in the safe compartment was not extinguished, and (3) shock was presented after 10 second CS presentations regardless of the subject's response.

In a second experiment, the shock presentation condition was further examined by (a) shocking all responses, (b) providing traditional extinction operations in which shock was not presented, or (c) shocking only avoidance response if it occurred.

Results from both experiments revealed that changing those stimulus conditions involving continued presentation of the buzzer and light had little influence on extinction. In Experiment 1, continuing to present the buzzer or the light in the safe compartment after the avoidance response had been made had little influence on the rate of extinction—responding continued at a relatively high level throughout the extinction trials.

However, manipulating the shock contingency had different results. Punishing all responses decreased resistance to extinction, but responding during these trials continued to be superior to responding when only the avoidance response was punished. The translation of such performance into number of avoidance responses produced during extinction indicated that the punishment of all behavior conditions resulted in 25 responses, while the punishment of only the avoidance response condition resulted in just 4. This demonstrates the effectiveness of this method in extinguishing responding.

### Solomon, Kamin, and Wynne's Theory of Extinction

Solomin, Kamin, and Wynne (1953), in conducting active avoidance learning experiments with dogs, noted that when the traditional method of extinguishing the avoidance response was used (omitting the US), their experimental animals would make hundreds of responses without any decrement in responding. How could such prolonged responding be explained? They provided an explanation based on two principles, the conservation of anxiety and partial irreversibility. But before we look at these, it is necessary to describe Mowrer's (1947) two-factor theory of avoidance learning, which provided the foundation for Solomon, Kamin, and Wynne's (1953) position.

Mowrer (1947) proposed that avoidance learning consisted first of classically conditioning a fear response to the CS, with the aversive stimulus serving as the US. Fear, having stimulus characteristics, then elicited the instrumental avoidance response, which in turn was strengthened by fear reduction. Let us illustrate the specific operation of Mowrer's two-factor theory with the example of a rat learning to avoid shock by running from one compartment to another in a shuttle box. The animal is placed in one compartment, where he is presented with a 10 second tone which is followed by a shock. After a few trials, the animal learns to avoid the shock by running into the adjacent compartment during the 10 second presentation of tone and before the onset of shock. Mowrer assumed that as a result of the tone and shock being presented together, the tone, through a classical conditioning process, becomes capable of eliciting fear, a part of the unconditioned response to pain. Such fear elicits the instrumental response of the animal—running to the adjacent compartment. This avoidance response is reinforced by the reduction in fear that takes place after the avoidance response has been made and the subject is secure in the safe compartment.

Solomon, Kamin, and Wynne reasoned that in order to extinguish the instrumental avoidance response, it would first be necessary to extinguish the fear response that elicited the avoidance response. But they pointed out that during extinction trials the subject removed itself from the presence of the CS so rapidly that the CS appeared to be almost ineffective in arousing fear. Since the instrumental response was not followed by fear reduction, the instrumental response started to weaken, as revealed by the animal taking a longer time to respond when the CS was presented. But the delay in responding once again allowed the CS sufficient time to elicit the fear response, so that the instrumental avoidance response was again followed by fear reduction and decreased latency in responding. The authors posited that this state of affairs could

result in the experimental subject making avoidance responses for thousands of trials.

Solomon, Kamin, and Wynne (1953) were unable to see how such prolonged responding could be successfully integrated with the findings obtained from appetitive tasks, in which extinction takes place much more rapidly. As a result, they posited two principles to account for their unusual findings. The first principle was the "conservation of anxiety," which arises when the instrumental response to the CS is made too rapidly to permit the CS to elicit fear (or anxiety). In brief, the conditioned fear response is "conserved" by the rapidity with which the instrumental response is made. The second principle was identified as the principle of "partial irreversibility," which states that the fear or anxiety conditioned under such circumstances is so strong that it can never be extinguished. Such being the case, the instrumental response elicited by the emotional state will continue to be made.

What is the present status of Solomon, Kamin, and Wynne's (1953) position? A basic problem has been in demonstrating the pivotal role that fear is presumed to play in eliciting the avoidance response. Black (1959), using dogs as his experimental subjects, conditioned the heart rate response, a presumed indicator of fear, in addition to having his animals learn to make a panel pushing response in order to avoid intense shock. Black was able to condition both responses, but during extinction trials found that the heart rate response extinguished before the avoidance response. The correlation between speed of extinction of the avoidance and cardiac CRs was not significant.

Kamin, Brimer, and Black (1963), using rats as their experimental subjects, examined the extinction of a shuttle box avoidance response. They related such responding to the amount of fear present on each trial. In Experiment 1, three groups of subjects were run, with an extinction criterion of either 0, 5, or 20 consecutive failures to respond to the CS. With each group, the intensity of fear to the CS was independently measured by using a conditioned emotional response task. Although fear declined as the extinction criterion grew more stringent, nonetheless substantial amounts of fear were exhibited by all groups of animals. Subjects that met the five failure criterion were nearly as fearful, as measured by the CER task, as animals that had not received any extinction trials. This indicated a disparity between strength of avoidance responding and the amount of fear. This finding, along with acquisition data that also indicated little relationship between successful avoidance of the instrumental response and amount of fear, led the authors to conclude that "the data on the whole reveal a considerable lack of parallelism between fear and instrumental behavior, and thus encourage speculation that variables other than fear of the CS are largely responsible for the maintenance behavior" (p. 501).

Almost two decades later, Mineka (1979) has echoed the conclusion of Kamin et al. that the presence (or absence) of fear does not appear to play any basic role in the acquisition and extinction of avoidance responding.

**Response Prevention or the Phenomenon of Flooding** Investigators have frequently pointed to an apparent similarity between (1) the persistence of responding in laboratory avoidance learning tasks using animals and (2) some specific human behaviors motivated by anxiety, phobias, etc. However, the laboratory procedures for extinguishing learned avoidance responses would be difficult to use in modifying human behavior. One method that has shown some promise for dealing with the problem of speeding up the extinction of avoidance responding has been called **response prevention** or **flooding.**

As originally employed by Solomon et al. (1953) and Page and Hall (1953), the flooding procedure consists of preventing the organism from making the avoidance response when the CS is presented, thus indicating that the aversive stimulus is no longer associated with the CS. In both of these shuttle box avoidance experiments, a barrier was placed between the compartments to stop the subject from making the instrumental response during extinction trials. Both experiments revealed that extinction of the avoidance response took place much more quickly with this method than with the traditional method of omitting the US.

Both Marks (1972, 1975) and Kazdin (1978) have reported that variations of the flooding procedure have clinical applications. Many investigators have reported that this procedure has been successful in reducing fear and anxiety elicited by snakes, spiders, test-taking situations, etc. A detailed examination of this topic can be found in Baum (1970) and Mineka (1979).

### Extinction Theories of Partial Reinforcement

We have noted that investigators have been unable to provide a general theory of extinction that can account for the variety of experimental findings obtained. One alternative has been for experimenters to develop mini-theories—theories that attempt to account for why extinction takes place with a specific type of learning task or with the operation of a particular experimental condition. We have noted the postulation of one such mini-theory in our examination of the principles of conservation of anxiety and partial irreversibility proposed by Solomon et al. (1953).

The finding that partial reinforcement, in contrast to continuous, leads to greater resistance to extinction has been identified as the **partial reinforcement effect** (PRE). A number of mini-theories have been proposed to account for this effect. We shall examine the most promising of these.

**The Discrimination Hypothesis** An early theoretical explanation for the partial reinforcement effect (PRE), identified as the discrimination hypothesis, was provided by Mowrer and Jones (1945). These investigators conducted a study in which four groups of rats were trained in a Skinner box on a FR 1, 2, 3, or 4 schedule. A fifth group was placed on a VR 2.5 schedule. After extensive acquisition training, several extinction sessions were provided. It was found that the total number of bar presses made during extinction was a function of the reinforcement schedule; animals provided the FR 4 schedule extinguished least rapidly, followed by the FR 3, VR 2.5, and FR 2. The continuously reinforced group (FR 1) extinguished most rapidly.

Mowrer and Jones posited that when the change in stimulus conditions (from acquisition trials to extinction trials) was difficult to discriminate, greater resistance to extinction occurred than when such a discrimination was easy. They reasoned that providing a partial reinforcement schedule during acquisition trials made it more difficult for the organism to discriminate between acquisition and extinction trials than when acquisition trials were continuously reinforced. Hence, there was greater resistance to extinction in partially reinforced subjects.

One positive attribute of the discrimination hypothesis is that it can be applied to classical as well as instrumental learning tasks, using either appetitive or aversive motivation. Earlier we noted that the experimental findings obtained in the classically conditioned eyeblink study of Grant and Schipper (1952) could be explained, at least in part, by a discrimination hypothesis. Similarly, this hypothesis has been used to explain the findings of Tyler, Wortz, and Bitterman (1953). They observed that a group of rats provided with alternating reinforced and nonreinforced acquisition trials extinguished more rapidly than a group provided with randomly reinforced trials. However, one problem with this theory is that its proponents have not specified the conditions that determine whether discrimination between acquisition and extinction will be easy or difficult.

Some experimenters have argued that if partially reinforced trials are provided and then followed by a series of continuously reinforced trials, the discrimination hypothesis should predict no PRE. This follows, since the subject should be able to discriminate easily between the last of the continuously rewarded acquisition trials and the first of the extinction trials. But the finding of Theios (1962), Perry and Moore (1965), and Gibbs, Latham, and Gormezano (1978), who used this kind of experimental design, have indicated that the PRE continues to be found.

In Theios's (1962) study, three groups of rats were each provided with a block of 70 trials with 40 percent random reinforcement, followed by either 0, 25, or 70 continuously reinforced trials. Two control groups received 70 or 140 continuously reinforced trials. Forty extinction trials were provided after the acquisition training. Theios found that the PRE continued to be manifested even though as many as 70 continuously reinforced trials immediately preceded extinction trials.

The challenge to the discrimination hypothesis rests on the position that only those acquisition trials immediately preceding the extinction trials are critical in any discrimination made between acquisition and extinction. And yet, there is no reason to assume that such must be the case. It could be argued that the conditions found in all of the trials in an acquisition series contribute to the discriminative response made by the organism, although acquisition trial conditions closest to extinction trials should be most important.

**Generalization Decrement Theory**   The generalization decrement theory, briefly described under general theories of extinction, has played a prominent role in explaining PRE. An early advocate of this position was Sheffield (1949). She proposed that the reward presented in a continuously reinforced series of trials resulted in specific stimulus aftereffects that became part of the stimulus pattern on every trial after the first. That is, chewing movements, food in the mouth, etc. (stimulus effects present during eating in the goal box), became a part of the stimulus situation for the animals when placed in the starting box for the next trial. The instrumental response acquired was attached to all of these cues. When extinction trials were provided, stimulus aftereffects associated with reward were no longer present in the starting box. The changed stimulus conditions thus contributed to the decline of instrumental responding. With a partial reinforcement regimen, the cues arising from nonreinforced acquisition trials also become a part of the stimulus pattern to which the animal learned to respond. Since these cues were also present during extinction, the acquisition-extinction change was minimized, resulting in greater instrumental response strength.

Sheffield (1949) assumed that the aftereffects generated by reward should dissipate with time. In an experiment designed to test this assumption, she placed groups of rats on either a 50 or 100 percent reinforcement schedule, with the animals receiving an interval of either 15 seconds or 15 minutes between trials of traversing a runway for food. Thirty acquisition trials were followed by thirty extinction trials. Results indicated that the PRE was obtained when the 50 and 100 percent reinforced groups were provided an intertrial interval of 15 seconds but *not* when an intertrial interval of 15 minutes was used. These findings were in keeping with Sheffield's assumptions concerning the role of stimulus aftereffects in the PRE. Unfortunately, most subsequent investigators were not able to replicate her findings. Weinstock (1958), for example, still found the PRE when he provided his partially reinforced rats with a 24-hour intertrial interval.

**Sequential Aftereffects**   Capaldi (1966, 1967, 1971) has also proposed an aftereffect theory. Unlike Sheffield, he did not conceptualize stimulus aftereffects as specific physical events whose influence dissipated within a short period of time. He hypothesized that stimuli arising from nonrewarded trials form a long-lasting memory trace, which becomes a part of the stimulus pattern on rewarded trials. If on a rewarded Trial 2, for example, the animal remembers receiving nonreward on the previous trial, the memory of nonreward becomes a part of the total stimulus pattern that is conditioned to and acquires control over the organism's instrumental response. The organism's resistance to extinction is determined by a comparison of the memory trace formed during the acquisition trials with the memory trace generated during extinction.

Operationally, Capaldi's theory rests on the sequence or patterning of reinforced and nonreinforced trials that forms the partial reinforcement regimen. His theory has led him to identify several partial reinforcement conditions that play a role in determining the organism's resistance to extinction. One of these is the number of nonreward-reward (N-R) transitions experienced. This condition, however, assumes importance only if a small number of acquisition trials are provided in a session.

In a study by Capaldi and Hart (1962) examining the number of N-R transitions, two experiments were conducted. Rats were trained to traverse a runway under either continuous, random, or single alternations of reward. In the first experiment, nine training trials per day were provided for three days. A basic difference between the two partial reinforcement groups was in the number of nonreward-reward (N-R) transitions each day. The single alternation group received four N-R transitions each, while the random group received just one, although the percentage of reinforcement was the same for both groups. In the second experiment, similar conditions were examined but just two days of training (nine trials per day) was provided. Results from both studies indicated that the single alternation group had the greatest resistance to extinction, thus supporting the position that the number of N-R transitions contributed to the partial reinforcement effect.[1]

A second condition of importance to Capaldi's theory is the number of nonreinforced trials preceding a reinforced trial, or what has been identified as N length (such as N-R, N-N-R, N-N-N-R, etc.). To examine this variable, Capaldi and Kassover (1970) trained rats to run an alley, giving either one, two, or three consecutive nonrewarded trials which were both preceded and followed by rewarded trials. The 10 days of training was followed by 7 days of extinction (six trials per day). Results revealed that resistance to extinction was positively related to the number of consecutive nonrewarded trials provided. It has been hypothesized that the memory trace arising from three consecutive nonrewarded trials became a part of the memory trace arising from the rewarded fourth trial. Capaldi and Kassover accounted for the group's greater resistance to extinction by assuming that the memory trace arising from the three nonrewarded trials was most similar to the memory trace arising from extinction trials.

**Frustration Theory**   Another explanation of the partial reinforcement effect has been proposed by Amsel (1958). Amsel used rats traversing a runway as his basic experimental paradigm. He assumed that some nominal number of reinforcements was responsible for the animal establishing an expectancy of reward. After the rat established an expectancy of reward, not finding reward on a given trial elicited a primary motivational (or emotional) response, frustration, in the rat. Amsel identified this as Rf. When a number of nonrewarded trials were provided as a part of a partial reinforcement regimen, a conditioned form of this primary emotional response (rf) was acquired. The conditioned frustration response (rf) and its sensory consequences (sf) became conditioned through stimulus generalization to other parts of the apparatus—the runway and starting box. This conditioning supported the animal's running response.

The association between the rf-sf mechanism (elicited by the starting box and runway) and the running response was strengthened by reinforcement. Partially reinforced animals thus learned to make the instrumental response in the presence of a conditioned emotional response, frustration. Animals given continuous reinforcement were not frustrated, so they had no opportunity to learn to respond in the presence of the conditioned emotional response. When these continuously reinforced animals were given extinction trials, the frustration generated by nonreward elicited overt responses that interfered with the instrumental response of running, thus facilitating extinction. Since partially reinforced animals had learned to make the running response in the presence of the conditioned emotional response, they were not as profoundly influenced by extinction trials and thus continued to respond.

**Test of Capaldi's and Amsel's Positions**
Considerable experimental interest has been generated by the theoretical positions of Capaldi and Amsel; perhaps most interest has been directed toward an examination of the PRE that can be obtained when only a few acquisition trials are provided. Frustration theory originally demanded that the experimental subject receive some critical number of training trials, since it was necessary not only to generate an expectancy of reward, but also

to provide the partially reinforced subjects with the opportunity to learn to respond in the presence of frustration. Quite early, Amsel (1958) acknowledged such to be the case, writing that "PRE will be evident only after some critical number of training trials . . ." (p. 114).

However, a number of investigators were able to demonstrate the PRE with only two to five training trials, fewer than Amsel had originally anticipated would be necessary; see McCain (1966, 1968), Godbout, Ziff, and Capaldi (1968), Capaldi, Lanier, and Godbout (1968). In addition, Capaldi and Waters (1970) demonstrated that the PRE could be obtained when animals were given a series of nonrewarded trials followed by continuously rewarded trials. The extinction performance of rats given either 5 or 10 continuously reinforced trials of traversing a runway was compared with the performance of a partially reinforced group that received 5 nonrewarded trials followed by 5 rewarded trials. Capaldi and Waters found that the partially reinforced animals were more resistant to extinction. Since all of the nonrewarded trials preceded the rewarded trials, it was difficult to see how frustration could develop and thus account for the PRE.

Several explanations for these experimental findings have been provided. Amsel revised his earlier position to incorporate the fact that an expectancy for reward could increase much more rapidly than he had previously assumed. Amsel, Hug, and Surridge (1968) noted that the PRE could be obtained with just five acquisition trials (three reinforced, two nonreinforced) if a number of food pellets (10 or 24) were presented on each of the three reinforced trials. These experimenters observed that when a large number of pellets were provided, the animals made multiple approaches to the food cup, with such responding resulting in an appropriate increase in reward expectancy.

A somewhat different explanation for the partial reinforcement effect obtained with small numbers of acquisition trials has been provided by Brooks (1969, 1971, 1980). Brooks assumed that the expectancy for reward at the end of the training trials is greater for the continuously reinforced animals than for those that are partially reinforced. As a result, extinction trials produce greater amounts of primary frustration for the continuously reinforced subjects, which in turn leads to more rapid extinction.

Brooks's (1969) experimental procedure is illustrated in his first study. Acquisition training consisted of placing each rat in a goal box for six trials, using either a continuous or partial (three rewarded, three nonrewarded) schedule and either a large or small reward. Four groups of subjects were thus formed: (a) continuous, small reward; (b) continuous, large reward; (c) partial, small reward; and (d) partial, large reward. Following the six goal box placements, the animals were given 25 extinction trials. During each of these trials, a door that rested on a hurdle (the hurdle and door formed one wall of the goal box) was raised, permitting the animal to jump the hurdle and enter an adjoining compartment. After jumping, the animal remained there for 10 seconds and then was placed in a retaining cage to await the next trial. If the animal did not jump out of the goal box within 60 seconds, it was removed and placed in a retaining cage to await the next trial.

Findings indicated that only the continuously reinforced group given the large reward acquired the hurdle jumping response. Since Daly (1969) had earlier shown that the speed of hurdle jumping out of nonrewarded situations could be used to measure frustration intensity, Brooks assumed that the greatest frustration was present in his continuously reinforced, large reward group. Brooks, in generalizing his findings to traditional runway studies, reasoned that extinction trials generated a large amount of frustration in continuously reinforced animals. Such heightened emotional responding was likely to result in responses that competed with the running response, thus leading to rapid extinction.

Brooks (1980) used differences in the amount of frustration present at the end of acquisition training to explain the findings obtained by Capaldi and Waters (1970). These investigators, it will be recalled, found that

nonrewarded trials given prior to a block of rewarded trials will also result in the PRE. Brooks assumed that these early nonreinforced trials would retard the growth of reward expectancy. In contrast, animals that did not receive nonrewarded trials would have greater amounts of reward expectancy at the end of the acquisition trials. When extinction trials were provided, larger amounts of frustration would be generated for these animals, resulting in more rapid extinction.

Brooks demonstrated this in a series of experiments. He concluded that his results

> show that nonrewarded experience given prior to reward experience increases persistence of responding in extinction in brief acquisition situations. . . . it appears that this increased persistence results from a lowering of incentive [reward expectancy] during acquisition in groups receiving the initial nonrewards. This statement is based on the findings that subjects given the initial nonrewards followed by continuous reward do not show learning of hurdle jumping to escape nonreward. Subjects not receiving the initial nonrewards, however, do show such learning. (pp. 149–150)

At present, there appears to be little difference between Amsel's frustration theory and Capaldi's sequential aftereffect position in the adequacy with which they explain the PRE findings. Critical experiments to differentiate between these two theoretical positions have yet to be performed. One problem has been that both Amsel's and Capaldi's theories have usually been examined with rats learning a simple task—the traversing of a runway. Relatively few investigators have attempted to examine these theories with other kinds of subjects learning different types of tasks.

## SUMMARY

Experimental extinction has been defined as the operation of omitting the US or withholding reinforcement and the resulting decrement in responding that arises from this operation. Early investigators assumed that extinction could be used to infer the amount or degree of learning that had taken place during acquisition. Although most current investigators reject this position, there has not been any agreement as to what extinction does measure. Many investigators have regarded extinction as only one of many behavioral measures of interest.

Stimulus, motivational, and cognitive variables have been manipulated in the examination of extinction. Probably the most frequently investigated stimulus variable has been stimulus change—the general findings indicate that resistance to extinction is related to the amount of stimulus change taking place between the acquisition and the extinction trials.

Motivational variables have generated considerable interest. The reward conditions manipulated during training trials include amount, delay, frequency, and intermittency. When amount is manipulated, most studies indicate that an increase in the amount of reinforcement provided during acquisition trials decreases resistance to extinction. When delay of reinforcement is manipulated, experimental findings have indicated that a delay between the making of the response and the securing of the reward increases resistance to extinction.

Studies of the frequency of continuously rewarded trials have provided unusual findings. Some investigators have found that resistance to extinction was positively related to the number of reinforced responses; other investigators have found that increasing the number of reinforced trials resulted in more rapid extinction, a result referred to as the overlearning extinction effect (OEE). When partial reinforcement schedules are used, the most typical finding has been that an intermittent schedule of reinforcement results in increasing resistance to extinction, an effect identified as the partial reinforcement effect (PRE).

One theory of extinction has emphasized the concept of inhibition, first proposed by Pavlov. He assumed that neural inhibition arose from the presentation of the CS; when sufficient inhibition accumulated, it masked the excitatory process produced by the CS-US trials and produced a cessation of responding. A second explanation has been identified as

interference theory. This theory hypothesizes that the removal of reward results in the subject learning to make other responses that eventually interfere with the previously learned response, thus leading to extinction. Hull proposed a third theory of extinction utilizing the concepts of inhibition and interference. Hull's theory has not stood the test of time, so no current theory can adequately explain all of the experimental findings.

In Wong's account of extinction, he describes this behavior as being composed of three stages: (1) repeating the same response as previously made, (2) trying alternative responses, and (3) switching to alternative goals that demand new responses.

Providing an appropriate operation for extinguishing an avoidance response has been a problem for many experimenters. An animal that has learned to make an avoidance response does not have the opportunity to learn that the aversive stimulus is no longer presented. Several alternative operations for extinguishing the avoidance response have been proposed, with perhaps the most frequently used being to present the aversive stimulus after the avoidance response has been made. Another operation, called flooding, physically prevents the experimental subject from making the avoidance response. Some clinicians have reported success in using this procedure to reduce fear and anxiety in humans.

The failure to find a viable general theory of extinction has resulted in many investigators attempting to explain extinction in cases where only a single variable has been manipulated. Frequently, this variable has been partial reinforcement. The problem has been to account for why partial reinforcement, in contrast to continuous, leads to greater resistance to extinction.

Theoretical accounts for the partial reinforcement effect have centered around three explanations: the discrimination hypothesis, sequential aftereffects, and the effects of frustration. The discrimination hypothesis states that resistance to extinction is a function of the ease or difficulty with which the experimental subject discriminates the acquisition trials from the extinction trials. Subjects placed on a continuous reinforcement schedule, for example, find it easier to discriminate these trials from extinction trials than do subjects who have been partially reinforced. As a result of the easier discrimination, extinction takes place more rapidly.

The sequential aftereffects theory posits that stimuli arising from nonrewarded trials form a long-lasting memory trace which becomes a part of the stimulus pattern learned on rewarded trials. The organism's resistance to extinction is determined by a comparison of the memory trace formed during these acquisition trials with the memory trace generated during extinction trials.

Frustration theory assumes that during acquisition trials animals establish an expectancy for reward. When reward is not forthcoming during extinction trials, frustration is generated. Frustration elicits responses that interfere with the previously learned instrumental response. Animals placed on a partial reinforcement schedule learn, in effect, to respond to frustration during acquisition trials, thus delaying extinction.

### NOTE

1. This study is not in keeping with the findings of Tyler, Wortz, and Bitterman (1953), who have reported rapid extinction for an alternating reward group. Capaldi and Hart (1962) suggested that the Tyler et al. findings may have been related to their animals actually learning the alternation pattern, with such learning confounding the experimental findings.

# CHAPTER SEVEN

# Stimulus Generalization

In Chapter 2, we discussed Watson and Rayner's (1920) study of conditioning Albert, an 11-month-old child, to be afraid of a white rat. In a second part of this study, Watson and Rayner found that five days after such conditioning had taken place, a rabbit, a dog, a fur coat, cotton wool, and a Santa Claus mask were also capable of eliciting the conditioned fear response. Thirty days later, the presentation of these stimuli continued to elicit fear. This finding, that a classical (or instrumental) conditioned response can be elicited by stimuli other than the conditioned stimulus, has been defined as **stimulus generalization.**

The fact that Albert was afraid of a variety of objects or stimuli to which he had not been originally conditioned is not surprising. We are all aware that behavior may be controlled by stimuli that differ from those originally encountered. Such a process makes good adaptive sense, since it is obvious that the stimulus found in one situation is never precisely duplicated in a second, yet survival may depend on appropriate responding. This point was recognized by Pavlov (1927), who wrote:

> natural stimuli are in most cases not rigidly constant but range around a particular strength and quality of stimulus in a common group. For example, the hostile sound of any

beast of prey serves as a conditioned stimulus to a defence reflex in the animals which it hunts. The defence reflex is brought about independently of variations in pitch, strength and timbre of the sound produced by the animal according to its distance, the tension of its vocal cords and similar factors. (p. 113)

The importance of generalization in contemporary society is recognized in many ways. Our educational system is predicated on the assumption that knowledge and skills acquired in school will generalize to environmental settings outside the institution; parents teach their children good manners at home, hoping that such behavior will generalize outside the home; therapists aim to have their patients' responses change in the clinical setting and then generalize to outside the office.

## EXPERIMENTAL INVESTIGATIONS OF STIMULUS GENERALIZATION

The first experimental demonstration of stimulus generalization was conducted in Pavlov's laboratory. One of Pavlov's associates, Petrova, conditioned a dog to salivate whenever tactile stimulation, which had been used as the CS, was applied to a point on one of its hind paws. The US was an acid solution placed in the mouth. Four other points were plotted equal distances apart and up from the paw along the hind leg. When these points were stimulated, Petrova found that such stimulation also elicited salivation.

In the United States, early stimulus generalization studies using classical conditioning operations were performed by Bass and Hull (1934) and Hovland (1937a, 1937b, 1937c, 1937d). The work of Hovland has long been regarded as a model, not only for its basic experimental design, but also for its demonstration of typical findings.

Hovland planned to condition the galvanic skin response to one tone and then use other tones to test for generalization. But how was he to select the tones to be used? His decision was to use tones that were equally discriminable from one another. That way he would not be subject to the criticism that the test stimuli he used were not discriminable from the conditioned stimulus or from one another.

In order to obtain equally discriminable tones, he used a psychophysical procedure which scales or arrays tones along the dimension of a just noticeable difference (jnd). This procedure resulted in his selection of four tones—namely, 153, 468, 1000, and 1967 Hz—each of which was 25 jnds from the next. Hovland's scale was thus based not on physical differences among tones (frequency), but on the psychological dimension of discriminability.

Hovland's GSR conditioning experiment consisted of conditioning one group of subjects to the highest tone (1967 Hz) and a second group to the lowest (153 Hz). Following 16 conditioning trials, extinction trials were provided. Each subject was presented with the original CS and the three test tones on each of four separate occasions, thus providing 16 extinction trials in all. The extinction data were combined for both groups of subjects to form the generalization curve in Figure 7-1.

Investigators in the United States at first assumed that it was necessary to follow Hovland's procedure of using a jnd scale to ex-

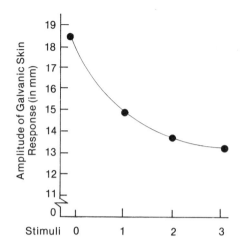

FIGURE 7-1. Composite curve showing responses to the CS (Stimulus 0) and to the three test tones (Stimuli 1, 2, and 3), which were 25, 50, and 75 jnds removed from the CS. Adapted from C. I. Hovland, "The generalization of conditioned responses: I. The sensory generalization of conditioned responses with varying frequencies of tone." *Journal of General Psychology*, 1937, 17, 125–148. Reprinted by permission.

amine generalization. This assumption resulted in virtually no animal studies being conducted during the decade following Hovland's work, since establishing a jnd scale with animals was an extremely difficult task. But Grice and Saltz (1950) rejected the necessity of using a jnd scale with animals and proceeded to examine generalization using test stimuli that were physically similar to the training stimulus. Their apparatus was a runway ending at a white disk placed on a door leading to food. The disk served as the discriminative stimulus. One group of rats was trained to run to a 20 sq cm disk, while a second group was trained to run to a 79 sq cm disk. The test for stimulus generalization used disks of different sizes. For these test trials, the group that had trained on the 79 sq cm disk was divided into five subgroups; each group was given test trials using a disk of either 79, 63, 50, 32, or 20 sq cm. The group trained on the 20 sq cm disk was divided into four subgroups; each of these subgroups was tested with a disk of either 20, 32, 50, or 79 sq cm. The stimulus generalization curves obtained from these groups are shown in Figure 7-2.

The Grice and Saltz (1950) study was important for several reasons. Many psychologists had assumed that the "true" shape of the generalization curve was concave, as Hovland (1937a) had previously found. Grice and Saltz's findings indicated that the form of the generalization curve was not constant but was a function of the experimental conditions employed. Their study also demonstrated the feasibility of examining generalization using

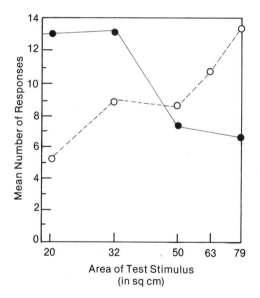

FIGURE 7-2. Generalization functions showing mean number of extinction responses for each test group. The solid line indicates the group trained on the 20 sq cm disk; the dotted line indicates the group trained on the 79 sq cm disk. Adapted from G. R. Grice and E. Saltz, "The generalization of an instrumental response to stimuli varying in the size dimension." *Journal of Experimental Psychology*, 1950, 40, 702–708. Copyright © 1950 by the American Psychological Association. Reprinted by permission.

animals and scaling the test stimuli along a physical dimension.

But Grice and Saltz's study did raise one methodological problem. Since 25 nonrewarded trials were used in their test for generalization, it was likely that the extinction process was contributing to the test performance of the experimental animals, but there was no way of assessing such influence. How best to overcome this difficulty? One answer was provided by operant investigators. By placing animals on some type of interval or ratio reinforcement schedule during acquisition, one can obtain a large number of generalization test responses that are relatively uninfluenced by the extinction process.

One of the early studies of this type was conducted by Guttman and Kalish (1956), who trained pigeons to peck at an illuminated key in order to receive food. Different groups of subjects were trained under a variable interval schedule. The training stimulus was presented for 60 seconds, followed by 10 seconds when the experimental lights were turned off (blackout), followed by 60 seconds of stimulus presentation, etc. Four groups of birds were trained to respond to one of the key colors, measured in nanometers as 530 nm, 550 nm, 580 nm, or 600 nm. After stable responding or maintenance behavior had been established, generalization testing consisted of randomly presenting 11 different wavelengths on a key, with each wavelength appearing for 30 seconds. Twelve of these sessions were provided. The findings obtained with each training stimulus are presented in Figure 7-3. When all of these values are combined, the resultant gradient is as shown in Figure 7-4. This gradient, although concave, differs markedly from Hovland's (1937a) "classic" curve and thus confirms the results of Grice and Saltz (1950), whose findings indicated that generalization is a function of the experimental conditions that are employed.

Guttman and Kalish's (1956) study was of major methodological significance, since their findings demonstrated the feasibility of using an operant procedure and a VI reinforcement schedule to investigate stimulus generalization.

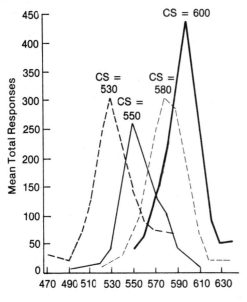

FIGURE 7-3. Mean total responses on the generalization test as a function of the wavelength of the stimuli for four groups for whom the original CS was either 530, 550, 580, or 600 nm. Adapted from N. Guttman and H. I. Kalish, "Discriminability and stimulus generalization." *Journal of Experimental Psychology*, 1956, 51, 79–88. Copyright © 1956 by the American Psychological Association. Reprinted by permission.

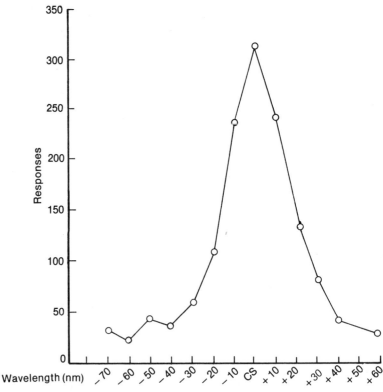

FIGURE 7-4. The mean generalization gradient for all CS groups combined. Adapted from N. Guttman and H. I. Kalish, "Discriminability and stimulus generalization." *Journal of Experimental Psychology*, 1956, 51, 79–88. Copyright © 1956 by the American Psychological Association. Reprinted by permission.

## Generalization of Inhibition

Earlier we discussed Pavlov's assumption regarding the existence of the neural correlates of conditioned responding—namely, excitation and inhibition. Since Petrova's experiment indicated that the excitatory process could generalize, Pavlov assumed that the inhibitory process could also generalize. Krasnogorsky, another of Pavlov's associates, provided an empirical demonstration of this phenomenon. A conditioned salivary response was established to each of four stimulation points located along the hind leg of a dog. Following such training, conditioned responding to one of these points was extinguished. Krasnogorsky then noted that when stimulation was provided to the other locations, conditioned responding was considerably reduced. Presumably, the inhibitory tendencies generated by extinction had generalized to the other locations, resulting in the response decrement.

In contrast to the large number of experiments examining the generalization of excitatory tendencies, the amount of work investigating generalization of inhibition (or generalization of extinction, as it has sometimes been referred to) is sparse. Hovland (1937a) conducted one generalization of inhibition study, examining the classically conditioned GSR, but it was not until the early fifties that experimenters using instrumental and operant conditioning tasks again became interested in demonstrating its operation; see Kling (1952), Honig (1961), Dubin and Levis (1973).

Honig's (1961) study, which mirrored the method pioneered by Guttman and Kalish, illustrates the experimental findings. Pigeons were placed on a VI schedule and trained to peck at a key in which 13 different colored stimuli ranging from 510 nm to 630 nm were presented and equally reinforced. Two experimental groups then had their responses to the 570 nm stimulus extinguished; one group was given just one extinction session, the other group two such sessions. A control group was not given any extinction trials. Generalization testing was then instituted; each of the 13 colored stimuli was presented without reinforce-

ment. Results for the control group and the two experimental groups are shown in Figure 7-5. It may be noted that for the two experimental groups an orderly gradient was obtained; the smallest number of responses was made to the 570 nm stimulus which received extinction training. Dubin and Levis's (1973) study, using tones rather than color as the discriminative and test stimuli, has confirmed the findings of Honig (1961).

## STIMULUS VARIABLES INFLUENCING THE GENERALIZATION PROCESS

After the operation of stimulus generalization was demonstrated, it is not surprising that investigators became interested in examining a number of the conditions that contribute to this process. One thread which ties many of these studies together is how these varying conditions influence the discriminability of the stimuli. Intuitively, it would seem that any variable that made it easier for the experimental subject to discriminate between the original training stimulus and the test stimuli should produce a steeper generalization gradient; conversely, if the experimental variable resulted in discrimination becoming more difficult, the generalization gradient would become flatter.

### Time of Testing

If the test for generalization is provided sometime after the original training has been completed, is there a greater generalization than if such testing is provided immediately following the acquisition trials? The studies of Perkins and Weyant (1958), Thomas and Lopez (1962), and McAllister and McAllister (1963) have all demonstrated a flatter generalization gradient when the testing period is delayed, suggesting that delay enhances the possibility of the subject confusing the original stimulus with the test stimulus.

In Perkins and Weyant's (1958) study, four groups of rats were trained to traverse a black (or white) alley in order to obtain food

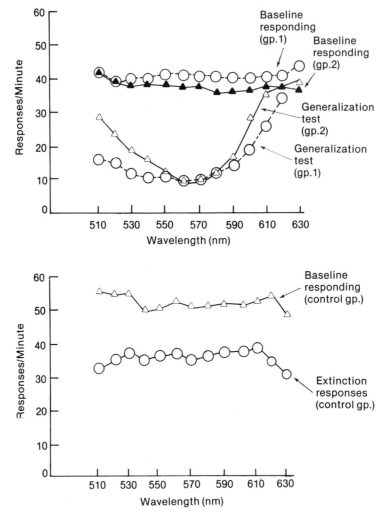

FIGURE 7-5. Response rates for the two experimental and one control group at the end of training and for generalization of extinction. Adapted from Figures 1, 2, and 3, by W. K. Honig, "Generalization of extinction on the spectral continuum." *The Psychological Record*, 1961, 11, 269–278.

in a goal box. Animals then received generalization test trials either immediately following the training or seven days later. Half of each group was provided trials on the same black (or white) runway as was used during training; the other half was given trials on a differ-

ent runway. Running speed was used as the response measure. The findings (see Figure 7-6) show that the groups not tested until seven days after the original training produced a much flatter generalization gradient than the group tested immediately after training.

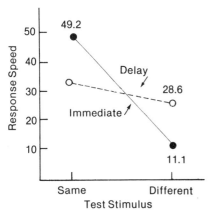

FIGURE 7-6. Median response speed (100/response time in seconds) for the two test conditions. Adapted from C. C. Perkins Jr. and R. G. Weyant, "The interval between training and test trials as a determiner of the slope of generalization gradients." *Journal of Comparative and Physiological Psychology*, 1958, 51, 596–600. Copyright © 1958 by the American Psychological Association. Reprinted by permission.

## Amount of Training

Several experimental studies have demonstrated that the possibility of confusion of the training stimulus and test stimuli may be reduced by giving the subject more training with the original stimulus. In Hearst and Koresko's (1968) study, pigeons were placed on a VI schedule and trained to peck at a vertical line (0°) which was projected on a response key. Training sessions (50 min./session) were provided each day for either 2, 4, 7, or 14 days. Following such training, generalization tests were given. Each of the eight orientations of the stimulus line—0° (the training stimulus), 22.5°, 45°, 67°, 90°, 112.5°, 135°, or 157° —was presented in random order a single time, thus forming a test series. Ten such series were provided. Two experiments were conducted, one utilizing White Carneux birds, the other White King. Figure 7-7 presents the findings. It may be noted that as the number of days of training increased, the generalization gradient became steeper, thus supporting the position that more training results in in-

creased discriminability between the training stimulus and each of the test stimuli.

## The Discriminability of Stimuli

The results of the studies mentioned may be explained by hypothesizing that the experimental conditions manipulated served to increase or decrease the subject's ability to discriminate the stimulus used in the original training from the test stimuli. In fact, many consider generalization and discrimination to be different ways of explaining the same behavior. Brown (1965) has written that "generalization and discrimination turn out to be nothing more than two different ways of reporting the same experimental results" (p. 11).

If such is the case, then greater amounts of generalization should be obtained when it is difficult to discriminate the training and test stimuli from one another than when such stimuli are easy to discriminate. The findings obtained in an experiment conducted by Kalish (1958) confirm this. Kalish's procedure consisted of presenting a specific visual stimulus as a training stimulus or standard and instructing the college student subjects to try to remember it. Hues of 500, 530, 560, and 580 nm were used as standards, while the test stimuli presented were four hues above and four hues below the standard, with each test hue separated by 10 nm. Subjects responded by lifting their hand from a telegraph key if the test stimulus was the same as the standard. Findings indicated that the shape of the stimulus generalization gradient obtained with each standard hue conformed to the discriminability curve obtained for human subjects.[1] Kalish concluded from these findings that there is "striking evidence for the supposition that the processes of generalization and discrimination, as generally defined, bear an inverse relationship to each other and that they are fundamentally dependent upon the characteristics of the underlying stimulus continuum" (p. 642). Thomas and Mitchell (1962), in a later study, obtained results confirming Kalish's findings.

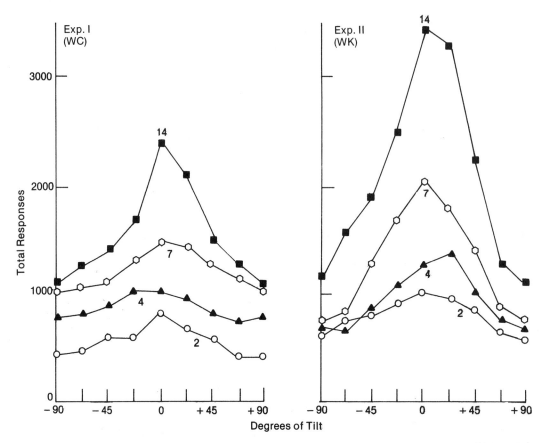

FIGURE 7-7.   Gradients of generalization for groups receiving 2, 4, 7, or 14 days of VI training. The training stimulus for all Ss was a vertical line (0°) on the response key. White Carneaux (WC) birds are shown on the left, White King (WK) on the right. Adapted from E. Hearst and M. B. Koresko, "Stimulus generalization and amount of prior training on variable interval reinforcement." *Journal of Comparative and Physiological Psychology*, 1968, 66, 133–138. Copyright © 1968 by the American Psychological Association. Reprinted by permission.

### Previous Discrimination Training

Discrimination has been assumed to play an important role in the stimulus generalization process, and yet, for more than two decades after Hovland's (1937a) early studies, discrimination tasks were never used in generalization experiments. But just how does the learning of a discrimination during training trials influence the generalization process?

Hanson (1959) used an operant task to answer this question. Four groups of pigeons were provided discrimination training in which the S+ was a 550 nm hue and the S− was either 555, 560, 570, or 590 nm. A control group was trained to respond only to the presentation of a 550 nm hue. Following VI training, the subjects were given tests for generalization with 13 hues ranging from 480 nm to 620 nm. The generalization gradients for the groups are shown in Figure 7-8.

Several findings should be noted. First, the control group, which did not have the benefit of discrimination training, produced a much flatter gradient than that of the groups provided discrimination training. Second, dis-

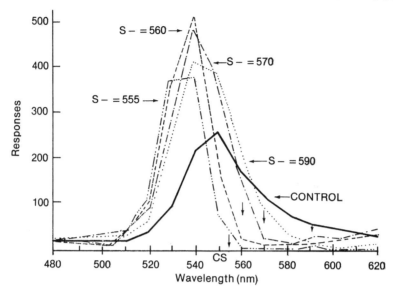

FIGURE 7-8. Mean generalization gradients for the control and four discrimination groups, identified by the values of the negative stimulus. Arrows indicate the positions of the negative stimuli. Adapted from H. M. Hanson, "Effects of discrimination on stimulus generalization." *Journal of Experimental Psychology*, 1959, 58, 321–334. Copyright © 1959 by the American Psychological Association. Reprinted by permission.

crimination training resulted in a much steeper generalization gradient being obtained on the S− side; as the S− grew more distant from the S+, the gradient became less steep. The presentation of a 560 nm test stimulus, for example, resulted in the group with an S− of 590 nm producing the largest number of responses, followed by those groups trained with S−s of 570, 560, and 555 nm. Finally, it should be noted that the presentation of the discriminative stimulus (S+) did not elicit maximum responding during the test for generalization. Instead, there was a shift of maximum responding from the S+ in a direction away from the S−. Thus, more responses were made to the 540 nm test stimulus than to the 550 nm hue which served as the S+. Such displaced responding to the S+ during generalization tests has been identified as **peak shift.** This phenomenon has been of theoretical interest, since it suggests that responding to the S− during training trials has produced an inhibitory state that has generalized to adjacent stimuli, resulting in a shifting of maximum responding away from the S+. Purtle

(1973) has provided an extensive review of the peak shift phenomenon.

It is obvious from Hanson's (1959) findings that discrimination training resulted in a steepening or sharpening of the generalization gradient, with the steepening confined primarily to the side of the S−. Subsequent studies by Hanson (1961) and by Thomas and Williams (1963) have demonstrated that such steepening can be obtained on both sides of the S+ if two S−s are used. In Hanson's study, one group of pigeons was given discrimination training in which responses to a 550 nm hue were rewarded but responses to the 540 and 560 nm hues were not reinforced. A control group was trained to respond only to the 550 hue. Following training, there were 12 generalization test sessions consisting of random presentations of stimuli ranging from 490 to 610 nm. The findings, as Figure 7-9 indicates, show a relatively symmetrical gradient for both groups of subjects, although responding by the experimental group was restricted to those stimuli bounded by the two nonreinforced stimuli.

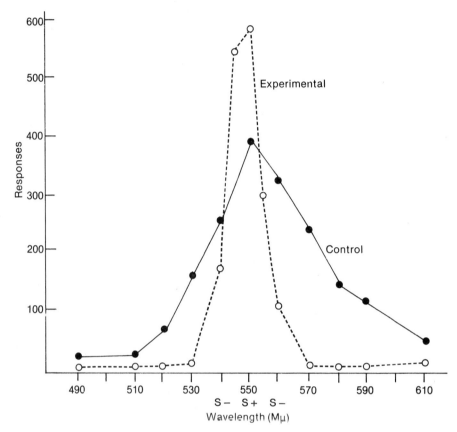

FIGURE 7-9.    Mean generalization for a control group not given discrimination training and an experimental group trained on a discrimination with the 550 nm stimulus reinforced and the 540 and 560 nm stimuli not reinforced. Adapted from H. M. Hanson, "Stimulus generalization following three-stimulus discrimination training." *Journal of Comparative and Physiological Psychology*, 1961, 54, 86–90. Copyright © 1961 by the American Psychological Association. Reprinted by permission.

## GENERALIZATION OF HUMAN INSTRUMENTAL RESPONDING

The capacity of the pigeon to perceive color, coupled with the simplicity of the pecking response, has resulted in many investigators using these subjects and this type of task to examine the nature of stimulus generalization. But findings obtained with animals invariably raise the question of whether or not these findings can be generalized to humans.

An early human generalization study was conducted by Brown, Bilodeau, and Baron (1951), who told their subjects that the task was a reaction time experiment. The appara-

tus consisted of seven lamps placed in a row and uniformly spaced at 8° intervals. The subjects were instructed to lift their finger from a response key as quickly as possible after the lighting of only the middle lamp. Subjects were informed that the other lamps would occasionally be turned on; if they should respond by mistake, they should not be unduly concerned about it. Each of the six peripheral lamps was lit 4 times, the lightings being interspersed among 104 illuminations of the middle lamp. Two experiments using this same task and procedure were conducted. Results, found in Figure 7-10, show that the generalization curve obtained by these experimenters is

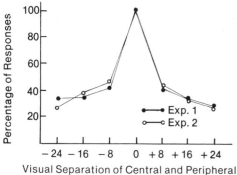

FIGURE 7-10.    Responses to lights in Experiments 1 and 2. Adapted from J. S. Brown, E. A. Bilodeau, and M. R. Baron, "Bidirectional gradients in the strength of a generalized voluntary response to stimuli on a visual-spatial dimension." *Journal of Experimental Psychology*, 1951, 41, 52–61. Copyright © 1951 by the American Psychological Association. Reprinted by permission.

quite similar to the gradient obtained when pigeons were used as subjects.

### The Central Tendency Effect

Maximum responding is invariably to the S+ when a signaled learning task is used and the test stimuli are distributed symmetrically around the S+. The study by Brown, Bilodeau, and Baron (1951) illustrated this pattern of responding. But is such symmetrical responding always found, even when the test stimuli are not evenly distributed around the S+? Thomas and Jones (1962) attempted to answer this question. In their study, identified to the subjects as an experiment in color perception, subjects were first presented with the standard or training stimulus, a hue of 525 nm (middle green), and asked to remember it. The subjects were then randomly divided into five groups and tested with different sets of generalized stimuli in order to determine how the relation of the S+ (525 nm) to the test stimuli would influence generalization. The test stimulus presentations (which included the standard) for the varying groups were as follows: Group 1: 485, 495, 505, 515, *525* nm; Group 2: 495, 505, 515, *525*, 535 nm; Group 3: 505,

515, *525*, 535, 545 nm; Group 4: 515, *525*, 535, 545, 555 nm; Group 5: *525*, 535, 545, 555, 565 nm. The testing procedure consisted of presenting the five visual stimuli that made up each set in random order; 12 different sets of presentations were provided.

The number of responses made to the different test stimuli for each group was used to construct generalization gradients, presented in Figure 7-11. When the standard 525 nm stimulus was placed in the middle of the range, a symmetrical gradient was obtained. For the other groups, there was a tendency for subjects to respond more frequently to stimuli closer to the center of the test series, so the peak of the generalization gradient was displaced away from the value of the standard stimulus. The authors identified this finding as a **central tendency effect**.

### The Role of Labels

It might be assumed that when experimental subjects are presented with a specific visual stimulus to remember, they attach a verbal label to the color. If such is the case, can the labeling procedure influence the generalization process? Thomas and DeCapito (1966) sought to answer this question. Using a procedure similar to that employed by Thomas and Jones (1962), Thomas and DeCapito asked their experimental subjects, when presented with the standard stimulus, to label the color using only a single word. The training or standard stimulus used in the experiment could be described as *blue-green*; some subjects labeled this stimulus as *blue*, whereas others identified it as *green*. In a second part of the study, the standard stimulus used was *yellow-orange*; some subjects labeled it *yellow*, while others designated it as *orange*. The generalization gradients obtained reflected the kind of labeling provided. Subjects who had labeled the training stimulus as *green* responded more frequently to test stimuli on the green side and less to stimuli on the blue side than the subjects who had labeled the standard stimulus as *blue*. A similar effect was noted when the standard stimulus was labeled *orange* or *yellow*.

Responses

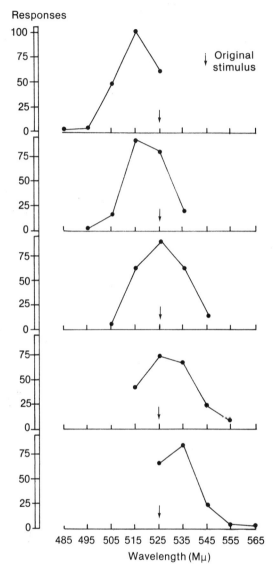

FIGURE 7-11. Generalization gradients of the five experimental groups. The gradient of Group 1 is at the top of the figure, with that of Group 2 directly below it, etc. Note that the value of the original stimulus is the same for all groups. Adapted from D. R. Thomas and C. G. Jones, "Stimulus generalization as a function of the frame of reference." *Journal of Experimental Psychology*, 1962, 64, 77–80. Copyright © 1962 by the American Psychological Association. Reprinted by permission.

## Secondary or Learned Stimulus Generalization

In many of the studies reviewed in this chapter, experimenters have used auditory stimuli varying in pitch or loudness, or visual stimuli varying in hue or brightness, to examine the generalization process. When such sensory stimuli are used, it has been often assumed that the connection existing between the stimulus used in training and the test stimulus has been innately determined. These innately determined connections, presumed to exist among sensory stimuli and hypothesized to play an important role in generalization findings, have been the defining characteristic in the concept of **primary** stimulus generalization.

It is possible, however, that the connections existing among the stimuli used in a generalization experiment have been established through learning; when such stimuli are used, the generalization process has been designated as **secondary** or **learned**. For example, when an experimental subject has been conditioned to respond to the word "frigid," using the word "cold" as a test stimulus may also elicit a response. Presumably, the synonymous relationship between the two words has been established through learning.

An early study by Razran (1939) utilizing synonyms and homophones as test stimuli illustrates this concept. A salivary CR was established by using words such as "style" or "urn" as conditioned stimuli, and pretzels or candy as the US to elicit the salivary response. This response was measured by placing a roll of dental cotton under the tongue of the subject and removing it after a specified length of time—usually a minute. The amount of salivation was measured by comparing the weight of the cotton before and after it was placed in the subject's mouth. After the CR had been established, test stimuli consisting of synonyms such as "fashion" or "vase," and homophones such as "stile" or "earn," were presented. Razran's findings indicated that it was possible to obtain conditioned responses to both synonyms and homophones, with the synonyms providing the greater response strength. Secondary stimulus generalization experiments such as this one, using verbal stimuli or units of language as the conditioned and test stimuli, have been identified as **semantic generalization** studies.

Another example of semantic generalization is illustrated in an experiment by Riess (1946), who conditioned the galvanic skin response to adjectives, and then tested for generalization using synonyms, antonyms, and homophones. A loud buzzer served as the US. Riess's experimental subjects differed in chronological age: Group 1 had a mean age of 7 years, 9 months; Group 2 had a mean age of 10 years, 8 months; Group 3 had a mean age of 14 years; Group 4 had a mean age of 18 years, 6 months. The interesting feature of Riess's findings was that generalization effects for Groups 3 and 4, the oldest groups, were similar to the results obtained by Razran (1939); synonyms provided the greatest amount of generalization and homophones the least. In contrast, the youngest group of subjects showed just the reverse—homophones provided the greatest amount of generalization and synonyms the least.

Intuitively, it would appear that stimulus generalization operating in everyday situations is more likely to be secondary than primary. And yet, in spite of its much greater frequency of occurrence, secondary stimulus generalization has been only infrequently studied.

## INTERPRETATIONS OF STIMULUS GENERALIZATION

How can the phenomenon of stimulus generalization be explained? Current explanations have their antecedents in the work of early theorists, beginning with Pavlov.

### Early Theoretical Accounts

Pavlov assumed that stimulus generalization was due to a fading wave of excitation irradiating from the point on the cortex that was stimulated by the presentation of the CS. Test stimuli whose cortical representations were contiguous to the CS could elicit the conditioned response. But Pavlov also assumed that the wave of excitation produced by the CS grew progressively weaker as a function of its distance from the cortical representation of the CS; thus, the excitation arising from the test stimuli and coming in contact with these weak excitatory representations of the CS would elicit only a weak response.

Physiologists have found no evidence of neural excitation spreading in this fashion, so Pavlov's neurological explanation of stimulus generalization is no longer accepted. Thompson (1965) has written that Pavlov's "concepts of spreading cortical waves of excitation and inhibition become difficult to interpret with the advent of the neuron doctrine in neurophysiology" (p. 154).

Hull and Spence, working in the tradition of Pavlov, did not make any neurological assumptions about the stimulus generalization process. They did assume, however, that as a result of conditioning trials, the conditioned response became associated with a zone of stimuli, adjacent to the CS. The development of this zone of stimuli—or afferent continuum, as Hull phrased it—arose as an innate characteristic of the organism, so the process responsible for the organism responding to a stimulus located within this zone was identified as primary stimulus generalization.

Several assumptions were important to the Hull-Spence explanation of stimulus generalization. First, it was assumed that subjects responded to test stimuli not because they were unable to discriminate such stimuli from the CS, but because of the excitatory tendencies that had been established between the test stimuli and the response during training. Second, inhibition was also assumed to generalize, with the shape of the generalization gradient being similar to that produced by excitation. Finally, the process of secondary stimulus generalization was posited, which accounted for responding when the connections among stimuli located along the afferent continuum had been learned rather than produced by the innate characteristics of the organism. We noted in the previous section the work of Razran (1939) and Riess (1964) in demonstrating secondary stimulus generalization.

Some experimental findings were in keeping with the Hull-Spence model of stimulus generalization. It will be recalled from the discussion of discrimination learning in Chapter 5 that Spence (1937a) posited excitatory and inhibitory generalization gradients, which were assumed to arise when a discrimination task was learned. From the interaction of these gradients, Spence was able to make some specific predictions in transposition responding.

The Hull-Spence position was challenged by Lashley and Wade (1946), who wrote that "stimulus generalization is generalization only in the sense of failure to note distinguishing characteristics of the stimulus or to associate them with the conditioned reaction" (p. 81). From this point of view, stimulus generalization was nothing more than a failure on the part of the subject to differentiate the conditioned stimulus from the generalized stimulus presented during the test period. These authors further argued that the generalization gradients obtained were only products of the testing procedure. That is, test trials should direct the subject's attention to the relevant stimulus attributes that differentiate the conditioned stimulus from the test stimulus. When this difference between the training stimulus and test stimulus was noted by the subject, there would be a decline in responding (or weaker responses) that characterizes generalization gradients.

Neither theoretical position remained unscathed from the findings of experiments designed to examine their adequacy. Chapter 5 noted that the results of several transposition experiments were not in accord with Spence's predictions. Perhaps most damaging to the Hull-Spence position was the fact that many investigators rejected their premise that learning consisted of the establishment of specific stimulus-response relationships, a premise that was fundamental to their explanation of stimulus generalization.

Lashley and Wade's position has not fared any better. These authors emphasized the necessity for the subject to be aware of the stimulus dimension that differentiated the CS from the generalized test stimulus in order for a decremental generalization gradient to be demonstrated. This position suggested an interesting experimental test—raising experimental subjects under conditions in which the subjects would never have the opportunity to be aware of the relevant stimulus attribute or dimension, which would subsequently be changed in a test for stimulus generalization. The Lashley and Wade position would predict that, since these organisms had never experienced changes in this attribute, a flat generalization gradient would be obtained from the findings.

A study by Peterson (1962) provided support for the Lashley and Wade position. Ducklings were raised from birth in cages illuminated only by a monochromatic light of 589 nm and were subsequently trained to peck at a 589 nm illuminated key. Following training, they were tested for stimulus generalization using keys illuminated with eight different wavelengths ranging from 480 to 650 nm. The obtained generalization gradient was flat; the birds responded with equal frequency to all of the stimuli used. The results for the control birds, which had been raised normally, showed the decremental stimulus generalization gradient generally obtained by investigators.

Unfortunately, Peterson's (1962) findings have not stood the test of time; many later experimenters have been unable to replicate his findings. Mountjoy and Malott (1968) and Riley and Leuin (1971) using chicks, Rudolph, Honig, and Gerry (1969) using quail and chicks, and Tracy (1970) using ducklings have all found decremental stimulus generalization gradients after raising their birds in an environment in which exposure to visual stimuli was carefully controlled.

The Riley and Leuin (1971) study illustrates the nature of these results. After hatching, White Leghorn chickens were maintained in a light-tight brooder illuminated by a monochromatic light of 589 nm. Beginning at

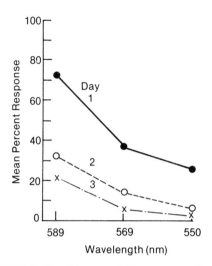

FIGURE 7-12. Mean relative generalization gradient for chicks tested with all three wavelength values. Adapted from D. A. Riley and T. C. Levin, "Stimulus-generalization gradients in chickens reared in monochromatic light and tested with a single wavelength value." *Journal of Comparative and Physiological Psychology*, 1971, 75, 399–402. Copyright © 1971 by the American Psychological Association. Reprinted by permission.

10 days of age, the birds were trained over a four day period to peck at a translucent key illuminated with a 589 nm light. A VI 1 minute schedule was used. After training, three days of testing were provided. Each day 21 extinction trials were presented in which the key was illuminated by test stimuli of 589 nm, 569 nm, and 550 nm. One group of subjects which was tested with all three wavelengths produced generalization curves, as indicated in Figure 7-12. The curves are not flat, as had been predicted by Lashley and Wade's hypothesis.

## Current Considerations

The theoretical positions of Hull and Spence and Lashley and Wade have undergone considerable modification over the years. These revised positions have not provided a complete explanation of the stimulus generalization process, but they have contributed to a better understanding of the phenomenon. At present, there is no single explanation of stimulus generalization that will adequately account for the myriad of findings. Since stimulus generalization has been demonstrated with almost every type of organism, using both very simple and complex stimuli and a variety of learning tasks, a single adequate explanation cannot be provided. But let us consider the thrust of some of the explanations that have been proposed.

If the training and test stimuli used in the stimulus generalization experiment can be placed along some basic sensory continuum, such as hue or brightness for visual stimuli, the presentation of a specific stimulus value during training trials will elicit a cortical response to the training stimulus and to other stimulus values that lie on the same sensory continuum. After the organism has learned to respond to the training stimulus, responding will also be elicited by these other stimulus values, thus providing a generalization gradient. This explanation was proposed by Thompson (1965), who suggested that "the amount of behavioral stimulus generalization given by an organism to a test stimulus is a monotonic increasing function of the degree of overlap of excitation in the cerebral cortex resulting from a training and test stimulus" (p. 159). Some physiological evidence has supported such an explanation. For example, if a green hue strikes the retina of the eye, retinal elements that are maximally sensitive to that cue will fire, but other hues similar to green may also fire the elements; the probability that a hue will fire the retinal elements is a function of its distance from the original hue. Presumably, training trials have produced differential associative strength between the response and a range of stimuli, so the presentation of a test stimulus may elicit a response, but one reduced in strength.

If the learning task utilizes a more complex discriminative stimulus, consisting of several relatively discrete stimulus elements (for instance, a white circle on a red background), these varying stimulus elements will provide differential control over the response. Subjects tested for generalization will respond to the test stimulus to the extent that the stimulus elements contained in it overlap with those stimulus elements that comprise the training stimulus. The smaller the overlap of the stimulus elements is, the weaker the generalized response. For example, when a pigeon is reinforced for pecking at a red disk on which a white circle has been placed, it has been assumed that the organism's response is associated with both stimulus elements, the redness and the circularity. The presentation of a generalized stimulus, such as just one of these elements, will elicit a response that will be weaker than the one made to the presentation of both stimulus elements. The explanation for this is that smaller amounts of associative strength exist between the single element and the response.

These explanations have their antecedents in the Hull-Spence position, since the explanations assume that during training trials associative strength is established between a stimulus and a response. The strength of the response elicited by the test stimulus during the stimulus generalization test is related to the strength of the original S-R relationship.

A more cognitively oriented explanation has been proposed by Riley and Lamb (1979). They suggested that during training the experimental subject classifies or identifies the stimulus along some dimension, and then responds in keeping with the payoff that has accompanied such responding. One examination of this position was provided by Cumming and Eckerman (1965), who had pigeons learn a discrimination task. Responding to the keys on the extreme right side of a brightly illuminated (1.1 log foot-lamberts), 10 inch stimulus strip of 20 response keys would result in food; responding to the keys on the extreme left side of the strip when it was dimly illuminated (.1 log foot-lamberts) would also result in food. Following such training, generalization testing was provided in which four brightness values, .1, .6, .8, and 1.1 foot-lamberts, were presented. An examination of where the pigeons pecked along the strip of response keys when the generalized test stimuli (.6 and .8 log foot-lamberts) were presented disclosed that the birds distributed their pecks

to these two brightnesses at the two ends of the strip. Such responding suggested that they classified each generalized stimulus in terms of bright or dim and responded appropriately.

This stimulus classification position would appear to be compatible with the findings of Thomas and his associates, who examined the influence of labeling or classifying the training stimulus on stimulus generalization. It will be recalled that such responding appeared to be dependent on the nature of the label rather than on associative strength that had been established between the training stimulus and the response on a single training trial.

Finally, an explanation for many examples of stimulus generalization found in human behavior may be related to Riley and Lamb's (1979) classification hypothesis and what Bruner, Goodnow, and Austin (1960) termed categorizing behavior. Bruner, Goodnow, and Austin wrote that "to categorize is to render discriminably different things equivalent, to group the objects and events and people around us into classes, and to respond to them in terms of their class membership rather than their uniqueness" (p. 1). Thus, the training stimulus and test stimulus would be classified by the subject as equivalent because of identical class membership, resulting in the subject responding to the test stimulus. Such responding could not be attributed to the stimulus generalization process, since the training and test stimuli were regarded by the subject as identical.

## SUMMARY

Stimulus generalization, as originally discovered by Pavlov in his classical conditioning studies, refers to the capacity of a stimulus other than the CS to elicit the conditioned response. Hovland (1932a) was an early investigator to examine this process. His experimental procedure was to first condition the GSR to one tone (CS), then test for generalization with three other tones, each removed from the CS by either 25, 50, or 75 just noticeable differences. A concave gradient was obtained, with test stimuli closest to the CS eliciting the largest GSR.

A stimulus generalization experiment conducted by Grice and Saltz (1950) in the fifties was important because it demonstrated that this process could operate with animals learning an instrumental task. In this study, the relationship between the discriminative stimulus and the test stimuli was based on the physical similarity of the stimuli rather than psychological similarity (as with the jnds).

Guttman and Kalish (1953) examined stimulus generalization using an operant procedure. Pigeons placed on an interval or ratio reinforcement schedule were trained to peck at an illuminated disk. The color of the disk served as the discriminative and test stimuli. Their procedure has been extensively used in generalization studies.

Pavlov was an early investigator to demonstrate the generalization of inhibitory tendencies. The method used was to condition a response to several CSs. One CS was then extinguished; the other CSs served as test stimuli. Results showed that the capacity of these other CSs to elicit the CR was diminished as a result of the one CS undergoing extinction.

Stimulus generalization has generated a great deal of interest among current investigators. Many studies have been designed to examine how selected conditions influence the generalization process. Time of testing, amount of training, and the discriminability of the stimuli have been three variables found to influence generalization. Discrimination training provided prior to the generalization test has also been of experimental interest; findings indicate that such training produces a much steeper gradient than that of control groups not provided discrimination training.

Several theoretical explanations for stimulus generalization have been provided. Pavlov believed that generalization was due to a fading wave of excitation that irradiated from the point on the cortex stimulated by the presentation of the CS; however, physiologists have found no evidence for neural excitation spreading in this fashion. Hull (1943) assumed that as a result of conditioning trials, the conditioned response became associated with a zone of stimuli, making up an afferent stimulus continuum. Presentation of a test stimulus that was located along this continuum elicited generalized responding. Lashley and Wade (1946) posited that stimulus generalization resulted from a failure on the part of the subject to differentiate the conditioned stimulus from the test stimulus presented during the test period.

Current research findings suggest that stimulus generalization is a complex phenomenon for which there may be several explanations. When basic sensory stimuli are used, there may be a physiological base for responses to test stimuli. In other instances, the response may arise from learning, the subject having learned to categorize different stimuli as equivalent.

## NOTE

1. It has been well established that human subjects cannot discriminate among the varying hues in the visual spectrum with equal accuracy. It is more difficult, for example, to discriminate among some of the yellow-orange hues (e.g., 590–600 nm) than it is to discriminate among some of the greens (530–540 nm).

# CHAPTER EIGHT

# The Generalization and Application of Basic Learning Principles

The kinds of responses examined in the past seven chapters were quite simple—for instance, a rat traversing a runway or a pigeon pecking at an illuminated key. These responses were all in the repertoire of the experimental subject. The relationships that were established among the stimuli, responses, and reinforcements can best be described as representing simple associative learning. But laboratory investigations utilizing very basic kinds of learning tasks with animals as the experimental subjects raise two questions. (1) Can these experimental results be generalized to human beings? (2) Can laboratory findings be generalized to applied or nonlaboratory settings?

Although these issues have been mentioned previously, this chapter will deal with them more extensively.

## THE USE OF ANIMALS AND HUMAN BEINGS AS EXPERIMENTAL SUBJECTS

Any discussion of a learning principle generated from a rat or pigeon experiment often results in a student asking, "Sure, it works with rats or pigeons, but what about humans?" This problem has not been of great

concern to those investigators who deal with the structure and function of human physiology. The findings of many studies investigating biological functions in animals are applicable to human beings. The respiratory properties of hemoglobin are similar in mice, whales, and humans; a basic knowledge of human nerve physiology was obtained from the frog and squid. The use of mice and monkeys in attempts to find cures for polio, cancer, and a host of other diseases is well accepted. It is when animals are used to learn something about human behavior that skepticism arises.

The proposed applicability of behavioral principles generated from experiments conducted with animals to human behavior was discussed by Pavlov (1927), who wrote that since "the higher nervous activity exhibited by the cortex rests, undoubtedly, on the same foundation in man as in the higher animals, some very general and tentative inferences can even now be drawn from the latter to the former" (p. 395). His research findings led him to conclude that "in the dog two conditions were found to produce pathological disturbances . . . namely, an unusually acute clashing of the excitatory and inhibitory processes, and the influence of strong and extraordinary stimuli. In man precisely similar conditions constitute the usual causes of nervous and psychic disturbances" (p. 397).

It was Thorndike (1911), however, who exercised the most influence on psychologists in the United States. He assumed that all animals were "systems of connections subject to change by the law of exercise and effect and they differ only in the particular connections formed as well as in the efficiency of the connections" (p. 280). Since Darwin's evolutionary principles had been accepted, and since there was an obvious relationship between the organism's structure and its function, it is not surprising that Thorndike's working assumption eventually became a basic operating principle for many investigators, coming to full flower in Hull's (1943) *Principles of Behavior* and in the operant conditioning movement of Skinner.

Hull proposed a series of learning principles that, although generated primarily from experiments with animals, were purported to be basic behavioral laws having **generality** for all organisms. Some years later, Skinner (1959) wrote:

> Pigeon, rat, monkey, which is which? It doesn't matter. Of course, these three species have behavioral repertoires which are as different as their anatomies. But once you have allowed for differences in the ways they make contact with the environment, and in the ways they act upon the environment, what remains of their behavior shows astonishingly similar properties. (pp. 374–375)

Many current investigators are in accord with this general position. Dinsmoor (1970), for example, has written:

> the question remains, of course, whether experimental findings obtained with rats, pigeons, and monkeys can be applied to human beings. The similarities in anatomical structure and biological functioning would suggest that the fundamental principles should be much the same. The pigeon, to be sure, is not a mammal, and his physiology is somewhat different from that of man, but the correspondence between the behavioral processes observed with birds and with mammalian species adds to our confidence in the degree of

biological continuity that prevails. The rat and the monkey might also be considered to be smaller humans with fur and tails. (p. 3)

Estes (1975) has taken a similar position, writing, ". . . again and again aspects of learning formerly assumed to be reserved for the higher positions on the scale of intellect turn out to be demonstrable at progressively lower levels" (p. 5). He has pointed out that some experimenters have been able to make a case for a rehearsal-like process operating with animals, a process that some individuals have attributed only to humans.

Other investigators have been skeptical that the learning principles discovered with animals have generality to humans. Finkelman (1978) wrote that studying rat behavior in mazes provides much information about rat behavior in mazes and not much else. In a more formal attack on this issue, Lockard (1971) argued that the laboratory comparison of two animal species unrelated by descent and ecologically dissimilar is of limited scientific utility. It has been his position that white rats are not simple versions of human beings, and that the place of rats in psychology is primarily limited to the study of rat behavior and not human behavior.

Uncertainty concerning the acceptability of the generality position is found among the European ethologists, whose approach to the study of behavior differs markedly from that of investigators in the United States.

### The Ethological Approach

**Ethology,** the comparative study of behavior, was brought to the attention of contemporary psychologists with the publication of Tinbergen's (1951) book *The Study of Instinct.* This volume, along with the writing of another European, Lorenz (1935, 1950, 1958), provided a different way of analyzing behavior; it also indicated the shortcomings of the point of view that had been adopted by psychologists in the United States. Ethologists stressed the **adaptive** significance of an animal's behavior, an emphasis similar to the emphasis physiologists had placed on the adaptive significance of structure. Ethologists assumed that a genetic factor, passed from generation to generation, is responsible for the transmission of behavior patterns needed for the organism's survival. Evolution selects those anatomical features that lead to survival, and behavior patterns are selected in much the same way.

Ethologists have traditionally observed the animal in its natural setting in order to obtain an **ethogram,** a description and catalog of the varying behavior patterns observed. Goodall's (1963) widely publicized description of the behavior of wild chimpanzees is one example. Once the animal's behavior has been catalogued, there follows a detailed examination of the animal's specific responses, as well as a description of the characteristics of the stimuli that appear to elicit them. Many of these responses have been identified as fixed-action patterns, and can be described as innate or instinctive movements. These patterns are assumed to be inborn—they are an internally coordinated sequence of movements which require only a releasing stimulus to be put into action.

The fixed-action pattern may take place without any apparent awareness by the animals of the particular function that the act is presumed to play. A simple example is found in a dog hiding a bone in the livingroom of a home—the animal attempts to cover it as if it were burying it in the ground. But much more elaborate illustrations can be provided. When the female spider (*Cupiennius salei*) spins a cocoon, she first produces a base plate, then a raised rim which provides the opening into which she deposits her eggs, and finally closes the opening. If she is disrupted after the base plate has been completed and moved to another location, she will not produce a base plate but instead will spin only a few threads before continuing with the construction of the rim, leaving the bottom of the cocoon open. Thus, when she lays her eggs, they fall to the ground.

A second contribution of the ethological approach has been the emphasis placed on sign or key stimuli. It is a **key stimulus** that is responsible for instigating or eliciting the fixed-action pattern. Eibl-Eibesfeldt (1970) has written:

In analogy to a key that opens a lock, the key stimuli act upon a mechanism . . . that normally prevents the release of central impulses when it is not appropriate and will open the way to the musculature when the appropriate key stimuli are received. Each functional cycle has its own key stimuli, and the animal reacts to correspondingly different key stimuli. (pp. 67–68)

Ethological research has indicated that a variety of key stimuli release many different fixed-action patterns in a host of species. For instance, the movement of small insects appears to be a key for the toad's prey catching response—if the insect remains motionless, the toad will fixate on the spot where the insect was last moving but will rarely snap at the motionless prey. In sharks, the odor of blood releases the search-for-prey pattern; for the mosquito and bedbug, the key stimulus is the heat radiated from warm-blooded animals. The list is virtually endless. See Box 8-1.

Ethologists have hypothesized that there is an **innate releasing mechanism** (IRM)—a central nervous system process that permits nerve impulses to proceed to the effectors only when certain stimuli are encountered. The IRM can be conceptualized as a stimulus filter, with the source and characteristics of the filtering action largely, though not totally, unknown. Maturana, Lettvin, McCulloch, and Pitts (1960) examined the visual system of the leopard frog and identified five types of ganglion cells in the frog's retina, each of which responds to different stimuli. For instance, one group of cells responds with vigorous discharges when a small object that is darker than its background passes over the receptive field. The authors have called these cells "beetle detectors," since they play an important role in the frog's response to prey.

An important contribution of ethologists has been their identification of specific behaviors (or assumed processes) of which most psychologists in the United States had not been aware. Imprinting is one example.

**Imprinting**   The origins of **imprinting** theory are found in the early observations of Spalding (1873), who found that as soon as a chick

■■■ BOX 8-1 ■■■

Ethologists have been especially interested in identifying the stimuli that elicit instinctive responses found in animals. Their position has been that many of these responses appear to be elicited or released by specific attributes of a complex stimulus—stimuli which they have identified as **sign stimuli.**

Tinbergen's (1951) examination of the fighting behavior in the male stickleback fish is a classic example of this type of work. The fighting of male sticklebacks in the spring is directed especially against other male sticklebacks. Tinbergen was interested in determining what stimulus characteristics of the male were responsible for eliciting the fighting behavior. His procedure was to construct a number of models, some of which are illustrated in the figure below. The model identified as N was an accurate imitation of the fish except that it lacked the red throat and belly found in the male. The other models, labeled R, are very crude imitations lacking many of the characteristics of the species, but all possessing a red belly. When these models were placed in the water, Tinbergen found that the sticklebacks reacted vigorously only to the red models, although the fish were perfectly able to see the other details of these crude imitations. Redness in the male was thus identified as a sign stimulus that elicited fighting behavior.

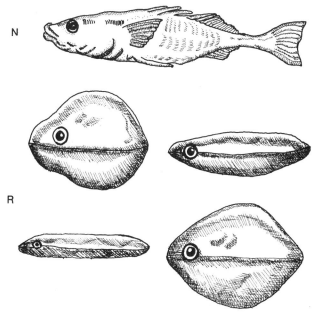

BOX FIGURE 8-1.   Models used in eliciting fighting behavior in the male stickleback. The top model, N, is an accurate reproduction of the male fish except that it lacks a red throat and belly. The four lower models, R, are crude imitations but all have the appropriate color. Adapted from N. Tinbergen, *The Study of Instinct*, published by Oxford University Press, 1951.

could walk, it would follow any moving object, whether it was the hen that hatched it, a duck, or even a human. Lorenz (1935), who won the Nobel prize in 1973 for his contribution to ethology, drew attention to the behavior of young ducklings or goslings who ex-

hibited the same type of following behavior. Lorenz noted that such behavior was observed even if the young bird was exposed to a parent of another species, the result being a durable bond established with the foster species that excluded members of the bird's own kind.

Lorenz identified a number of attributes that he believed differentiated the imprinting process from learning. First, imprinting appeared to operate at only a certain stage or particular time in the bird's development, a time that has been called the **critical period.** For instance, following behavior would not be found in a bird that had been kept in darkness since hatching and thus not exposed to a moving stimulus during the critical period. Second, the external stimulus that elicited the behavior had to possess certain well-defined characteristics. Finally, the imprinting process was irreversible. The effects of imprinting could not be reversed by subsequent learning.

Lorenz further noted that the bird's behavior arising from the imprinting process consisted of (a) first perceiving the object and following it, (b) a tendency to approach the object in preference to other objects, and (c) the uttering of cries of distress as the object escaped perceptual contact, coupled with sounds of contentment when contact was reestablished.

Most current investigators would agree that imprinting is responsible for a young organism's filial attachments becoming increasingly restricted to a given object or class of objects. But the position that imprinting is a basically different process from learning has not been accepted. Lorenz's observations that imprinting behavior is acquired within a brief period of time without obvious reinforcement and that it is irreversible have generated considerable laboratory interest in the phenomenon.

An experiment by Ramsay and Hess (1954) and a subsequent one by Hoffman, Searle, Toffey, and Kozma (1966) illustrate the nature of these investigations. The Ramsay and Hess study examined following behavior, using ducklings as the experimental subjects. After hatching, the birds were confined in light-tight boxes for varying periods of time, either 1–4, 5–8, 9–12, 13–16, 17–20, 21–24, 25–28, or 29–32 hours. After this time, the imprinting object was presented. This object was a decoy male Mallard duck, which moved down a 12 foot runway for either 10 or 30 minutes. During the imprinting period, the ducklings could follow the model. The findings were somewhat variable, but the results from this early study did indicate that 50 percent of the ducklings who had been confined for 13–16 hours followed the male model. When the confinement period lasted for 29–32 hours, however, following behavior was not observed, thus suggesting that the critical period for imprinting following behavior had passed.

The methodology employed by Hoffman et al., which he also used in many subsequent experiments (see Hoffman, 1978), differs from that in the preceding study. These investigators used the distress call of the duckling as an indicator of the bird's reactions to the imprinting stimulus. (Recall that Lorenz observed that the distress cries of the bird when separated from the critical stimulus arose from the imprinting process.) In contrast to following behavior, this response has the advantage of being fully developed when the bird is first hatched. It can be examined not only when the imprinted stimulus is present, but also when it is absent.

The apparatus used by these investigators consisted of a large wooden box divided by a fine-mesh stainless-steel screen into two equally sized compartments. One compartment housed the duckling; the other, called the stimulus compartment, housed the imprinting object. For an imprinting stimulus, the experimenters used a rectangular block of foam rubber mounted over an electric train engine so it could move back and forth along the length of the stimulus compartment. The stainless-steel screen separating the two compartments permitted one-way vision; thus, the imprinting object in the stimulus compartment was visible only when the lamps in the compartment were illuminated. The train moved only when power was provided. With this arrangement, the investigator could present or withdraw the imprinting stimulus rapidly, with movement controlled as the situation demanded. Figure 8-1 illustrates the apparatus.

In the Hoffman et al. (1966) study, three ducklings together received six 20 minute imprinting sessions during the first 48 hours

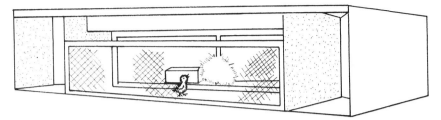

FIGURE 8-1.   Apparatus used to study imprinting. The imprinting stimulus (visible behind the rear screen) consists of a block of foam rubber mounted over the cab of a model train engine. With this apparatus, stimulus presentation is produced by illuminating the stimulus compartment and moving the engine back and forth. When its compartment is darkened, the stimulus is not visible. Adapted from L. A. Eiserer and H. S. Hoffman, "Priming of duckling's response by presenting an imprinted stimulus." *Journal of Comparative and Physiological Psychology*, 1973, 83, 345–359. Copyright © 1973 by the American Psychological Association. Reprinted by permission.

after hatching. For the entire 20 minutes the stimulus compartment was illuminated and the train moved back and forth. Three days later, when the ducklings were five days old, they were exposed individually to a short test period in the apparatus. During this time, the imprinting stimulus was repeatedly presented and withdrawn. During stimulus withdrawal, examiners made the train disappear by stopping it and extinguishing the lights in the stimulus compartment. Hoffman et al. found that within a few seconds of stimulus withdrawal, each duckling began to emit distress calls which persisted more or less continuously until the stimulus was presented again. When the moving train reappeared, distress calling lessened almost immediately.

During the past decade, the imprinting process, particularly as it relates to the filial attachment of birds to varying stimulus objects, has been extensively investigated. Experimenters in the United States have become most interested in examining how such behavior is related to a variety of experimental conditions, including characteristics of the stimulus object and the length of the critical period; see Hess (1973) or Hoffman (1978).

However, this book's objective is not to systematically review these experimental findings, but to provide the reader with some appreciation for the traditional ethologist's approach to the study of behavior. What is fundamental is that ethologists never considered learning to be a general process that differed only in degree among species; rather, they considered learning to be a much more specific process that interacted with the animal's innate response capacities in order to enable each species to survive in its particular environment.

An earlier chapter noted the psychologist's surprise at the findings that the delay of reinforcement gradient for rats learning to avoid a toxic substance could be measured in hours, rather than in seconds, as a number of earlier studies had found. But such a finding would cause no consternation among ethologists, because they would never assume that a learning principle that had been found to operate in one task would necessarily generalize to another.

However, the ethological position has not been free of criticism. In an early critique, Lehrman (1953) called attention to a number of problems found in Lorenz's ethological theory of innate or instinctive behavior. Perhaps the most basic problem Lehrman cited was the difficulty of determining precisely what constitutes "innate" behavior. Lehrman also noted that the use of this concept adds little to one's understanding of the origins of behavior. Nonetheless, the contribution of the ethologist's position to psychology in the United States has been salutary, not because it revived instinct theory but because it called attention to a number of empirical areas of study that had been largely ignored by investigators in the United States.

### The "Misbehavior" of Organisms

There has been another source of skepticism about the generality of learning principles; some individuals have observed that learning principles that operate in the laboratory do not always seem to work in other situations. Breland and Breland (1961) have made a business of teaching a wide variety of "tricks" to animals who then are exhibited at zoos, department stores, fairs, trade conventions, and even on television shows. The training procedures used by the Brelands have been quite successful, but there have been some unusual failures.

One failure occurred when they attempted to teach a pig to pick up a large wooden coin and deposit it in a piggy bank. Coins were placed a few feet from the "bank," and the pig was required to carry each coin to the bank and deposit it, receiving a reward for every four or five coins deposited. Inasmuch as pigs learn quite rapidly and are very tractable animals, difficulties were not anticipated. The pig would learn the task quite rapidly, but over a period of weeks the pig would deposit the coins in the bank at a progressively slower pace. The animal might run eagerly to get the coin, but on its way to deposit it, it would repeatedly drop it, root it, drop it again, pick it up, toss it in the air, drop it, and root it.

This type of behavior, the authors have written, is not what would normally be expected on the basis of the operation of learning principles generated in the laboratory. Breland and Breland observed that their animals, after having learned a specific behavior pattern, gradually *drifted* into behaviors that were entirely different from those learned. They called this phenomenon **instinctive drift.** The general principle states that whenever an animal has strong instinctive behavior that bears some similarity to the learned response, the animal's learned responding will drift toward the instinctive behavior. Such drifting will take place even though it may delay or preclude the receiving of reinforcement. Thus, the pig's rooting behavior with the wooden coin was similar to what the pig would have

done with a piece of food. Powell and Curley (1976) have noted a similar drifting effect when working with Mongolian gerbils and cotton rats, thus indicating that the phenomenon has some generality.

A second failure of laboratory learning principles in nonlaboratory situations occurred when the Brelands attempted to train a chicken to play a modified baseball game. The game was arranged so that a ball would roll toward home plate and the chicken would pull a chain to swing a bat (a small metal bar). If the ball was hit, a bell would ring and the chicken would run to first base, receiving food at that location. Preliminary work in teaching the bird to pull the chain and run to the sound of the bell went well, but when a ball was introduced, there was chaos. If the ball was hit, the chicken would not run to the base to get food but would chase the ball around the field.

The "misbehavior" of animals is not limited to the kinds of situations described by the Brelands; it may also be noted in the laboratory. When using an avoidance task with rats or pigeons, many investigators have experienced great difficulty in getting these animals to respond appropriately in order to avoid shock. Meyer, Cho, and Wesemann (1960) have reported that their rats had great difficulty learning to depress a lever in order to avoid shock. Their animals failed to show reliable avoidance *after several thousand trials* although there was never any problem in training these animals to make escape responses. These findings were confirmed by Smith, McFarland, and Taylor (1961) and D'Amato and Schiff (1964), whose rats also had trouble learning to press a bar in order to avoid shock.

Hoffman and Fleshler (1959) and Smith and Keller (1970) have had problems in getting pigeons to avoid shock by pecking at a key. Smith and Keller have reported that although some avoidance pecking was noted, this response rapidly dropped out and was replaced by wing flapping and jumping against the panel containing the key.

Other investigators have found their subjects to be capable of learning certain tasks very rapidly, the acquiring of taste aversion responses being one example. The disparity in number of trials required to get an animal to learn one response in contrast to another has been a problem for those investigators who have assumed that the *kind* of response to be acquired should not play any role in the rapidity with which it is learned. Rozin and Kalat (1971) have argued that such an assumption is false—that the wild rat's aversion to poisoned food, for example, is governed by learning principles different from those generated in the laboratory. These differences in learning, they have argued, are in keeping with evolutionary adaptation; there is no reason to assume that generally applicable laws of learning exist independently of the situation in which they are manifested. The ethologists, it will be recalled, made a similar argument.

Seligman (1970) has attempted to provide some integration of the findings of rapid and slow rates of learning by assuming that a continuum of preparedness is found with all organisms. The organism may be prepared to associate certain events, unprepared to associate some, and countraprepared to associate others. This continuum, he has indicated, stems from the specialized sets of sensory and receptor apparatus that have arisen from the organism's long evolutionary history. Seligman has analyzed numerous learning studies to support his premise. The taste aversion studies, for example, deal with a task for which the organism is prepared to associate the appropriate events, and as a result, learning takes place rapidly. In contrast, many avoidance learning tasks require the experimental subject to associate events that are contrary to its evolutionary history, so learning takes place very slowly, if at all.

## The Other Side of the Coin

The evidence just presented suggests that psychologists have been naive in their search for learning principles that have some generality beyond the specific type of task and species of experimental subject that is being used. But as in most issues, there is another side of the coin.

The "misbehaviors" by Breland and Breland's (1961) animals have been noted, but what has been conveniently forgotten is the *successful* application of learning principles with more than 6000 animals, representing more than three dozen different species learning many difficult tasks.

It is likely that those experimenters who have found their animals incapable of acquiring certain avoidance responses have failed to take into consideration the contribution of innate behavior. Bolles (1970), in accounting for these avoidance learning failures, has posited that animals come into the world with defensive reactions already a prominent part of their response repertoire. Thus, the gazelle does not flee from an approaching lion because it has been previously bitten by a lion —it runs away from any large object that approaches it because such responding is innate, one of its **species-specific defense reactions** (SSDR). Bolles (1970) has indicated that the organism's SSDR generally takes one of three forms: (1) running or flying away, (2) freezing, or (3) adopting some type of pseudoaggressive response. If the avoidance response demanded by the experimenter in the laboratory is not one of these, the animal experiences great difficulty in learning, as indicated by the work of Meyer, Cho, and Wesemann (1960), D'Amato and Schiff (1964), etc.

The ethologists' objection that the learned response required by laboratory tasks was artificial and unrelated to the kind of behavior observed in the animal's natural environment has led Schwartz (1974) to make an interesting counterargument. Schwartz has readily accepted the position that the learning of animals in their natural environment is greatly influenced by their genetic makeup; thus, laboratory findings, which minimize the genetic contribution, may bear little relationship to the learning principles that operate when the animal is in its natural habitat. But, he has argued, much of human behavior can be characterized as attaching arbitrary responses to unusual stimulus situations. Learning to speak a second language, drive a car, play bridge, or use statistics is only distantly related to genetically determined behaviors. It is these arbitrary types of learning tasks that hold the most interest for psychologists.

The result, Schwartz has speculated, may be that principles generated from laboratory studies do not apply to the species in their normal environment, but since much of human behavior may be described as arbitrary learning, such learning principles may well apply to human beings. As the author has written, "It is odd, but perhaps reassuring to think that by studying the behavior of pigeons, in arbitrary situations, one learns nothing about the principles that govern the behavior of pigeons in nature, but a good deal about the principles that govern the behavior of people" (p. 196).

### Can the Generality Question Be Resolved?

Most contemporary investigators, such as Harlow, Gluck, and Suomi (1972) or Logan and Ferraro (1978), see an empirical answer to the problem of assessing the generality of learning principles. That is, any generalization that is extended to include a new species or a different environment remains a hypothesis to be tested, and is subject equally to disconfirmation and confirmation. Confirmation presumably indicates the existence of generality, while disconfirmation, although suggesting that a generalization of findings cannot be made, may reflect nothing more than the limitation of the method used.

Consider those studies attempting to determine whether human language data can generalize to the chimpanzee. The experimental evidence indicates that chimpanzees cannot acquire vocal language. The reason is that their mouth and throat were not designed to permit human-like vocalizations. Can it be concluded, then, that the chimpanzee cannot acquire language? Such a conclusion would be premature, since, as discussed in Chapter 4, many investigators are convinced that these animals can communicate with words and word combinations transmitted by means other than vocalization.

Must empirical tests, experiments, always be conducted in order to determine whether or not a learning principle will gener-

alize to another species? Probably, although two other criteria might be used to provide a tentative answer to the question. One criterion suggested by Harlow et al. (1972) is anatomical similarity between species, although all analogous brain structures should not be given equal consideration. Probably the most sophisticated criterion for assessing the capacity of an organism to learn complex tasks is the cytoarchitectonic structure of the neocortex—not the mass of the brain but the delicate organization of cells in or near the cortical outer fringe. There is, however, one anomaly—birds have little or no cortex and yet are successful in solving problems at a level of complexity equal to or beyond that achieved by rats, cats, and dogs.

A second criterion may be related to what Warren and Kolb (1978) have called class-common behaviors. Many species share common behaviors as well as common structures. An examination and comparison of an animal's natural behaviors should help identify class-common behaviors, which in turn would provide a base for generalizing experimental findings from one species to another.

### THE APPLICATION OF LEARNING PRINCIPLES IN NONLABORATORY SITUATIONS

The second question posed at the beginning of this chapter asked whether learning principles generated from laboratory tasks could be generalized to nonlaboratory situations. The work of the Brelands touched on this question, but there are also many other interesting and diverse examples.

### Conditioning Operations

One early example of the application of conditioning operations is found in the treatment of enuresis first proposed in the United States by Mowrer and Mowrer (1938). They believed that a classical conditioning procedure could be used to prevent children from bedwetting. An apparatus was devised to detect the presence of urine through a sensing mechanism contained in a pad on which the child slept. When the child urinated, a bell or buzzer went off to awaken the child, who would then stop voiding and go to the toilet to complete the act. Viewing the process as a classical conditioning procedure, the Mowrers paired the conditioned stimulus of the child's bladder distension with the unconditioned stimulus of the alarm, which produced an unconditioned response of awakening. After an appropriate number of pairings, the bladder distension (CS) should result in a conditioned response of awakening, which in turn would be followed by subsequent urination in the toilet rather than the bed.[1] Figure 8-2 illustrates the procedure.

Some investigators have questioned whether the treatment illustrates a classical conditioning procedure. For instance, Lovibond (1963) considered it to be an example of passive instrumental avoidance. The child learns to not urinate in bed in order to avoid the presentation of the aversive stimulus—the alarm. However, it does not matter, for this book's purposes, which classification best describes the treatment conditions but only that this procedure has been successful in treating a behavior problem. A recent review by Doleys (1977) has indicated that, in a dozen studies conducted using such a conditioning operation between 1965 and 1975, bedwetting was arrested in 75 percent of the experimental subjects.

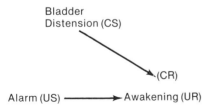

FIGURE 8-2. Classical conditioning procedure used to eliminate bedwetting.

The use of conditioning procedures to eliminate undesirable behavior and to foster appropriate responding has grown tremendously since the Mowrers first became interested in treating enuresis. Three general procedures have been used to modify undesirable behavior. A relatively infrequent method has been to use experimental extinction. A second has been to punish the inappropriate response, generally by presenting some type of aversive stimulus when the objectionable response is made. This procedure has been identified as **aversion therapy**. The third procedure has been to have individuals learn new responses to the old stimulus situations, using some type of reward or reinforcement to strengthen such behavior.

### Experimental Extinction and Desensitization

Experimental extinction involves presenting the CS without the US (classical conditioning) or not providing reward after an instrumental response has been made (instrumental conditioning). One nonlaboratory example of extinction is found in a study by Williams (1959). He reported that the parents of a 21-month-old child would become quite distressed when their child threw tantrums if they left the room before he was asleep. The parents were requested to attempt to extinguish the response by putting the child to bed and leaving the room, not to return when the child cried. On the first occasion, the tantrum lasted for 45 minutes before the child went to sleep. The next night no tantrum ensued, and for the next six nights there was a gradual cessation of crying until it completely stopped. However, the next evening the child became agitated when put to bed by his aunt, who then stayed in the room until he went to sleep. The following evening the tantrum returned, but this behavior was again extinguished by the parents refusing to enter the room. Figure 8-3 reveals the amount of crying for the two series of extinction trials.

The extinction procedure, as utilized by Williams (1959), has not been particularly effective in eliminating fear or anxiety, since an

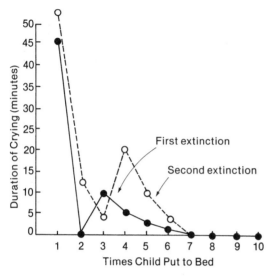

FIGURE 8-3. Duration of crying as a function of the number of times the child was put to bed. Adapted from C. D. Williams, "The elimination of tantrum behavior by extinction procedures." *Journal of Abnormal and Social Psychology*, 1959, 59, 269. Copyright © 1959 by the American Psychological Association. Reprinted by permission.

avoidance response does not provide the subject with the opportunity to learn that the aversive stimulus is no longer presented. As a result, Wolpe (1958) used counterconditioning or desensitization to help eliminate these undesirable responses.

It is interesting that Wolpe's discovery of his technique resulted from his work with cats. Severe trauma was first produced in these animals by depriving them of food and then shocking them when they began to eat. This resulted in emotional responses being made in the presence of the environmental stimuli that had been associated with shock. Wolpe then began to feed his cats in an environmental situation distinctly dissimilar from the original environment where they had received shock. By gradually moving toward situations that approximated the environment where the animals had been fed originally, Wolpe found that he was able to overcome the animals' neurotic responses and restore them to apparent normality. Conceptually, he had

retrained or counterconditioned the emotional response, replacing it with the positive affective state that generally accompanies eating.

It was obvious that feeding responses could not be used when trying this procedure with humans. Wolpe's search for a response that would be antagonistic to anxiety and fear led him to the work of Jacobson (1938), who had recommended the use of relaxation as a treatment for the emotionally disturbed. Briefly, Wolpe's desensitization procedure consists of having the subject learn to relax deeply and then imagine, rather than actually experience, a series of anxiety-evoking stimuli. Prior to having the subject actually begin therapy, the therapist develops a collection of a number of anxiety-evoking events, hierarchically arranged from those eliciting very weak emotional responses to those eliciting strong responses. The therapeutic procedure then consists of the therapist asking the subject to imagine the weakest event in the hierarchy repeatedly until no more anxiety is elicited by that event. The next item in the hierarchy is then presented, etc., until after a number of sessions, even the strongest anxiety-evoking stimulus fails to elicit any anxiety.

Wolpe used the following situations, hierarchically arranged from weak to strong, to treat a housewife suffering from claustrophobia: (1) reading about miners trapped underground; (2) being told of somebody in jail; (3) going on a journey by train; (4) traveling in an elevator alone; (5) being locked in a small room; (6) being stuck in an elevator.

Wolpe (1961) has analyzed the effectiveness of his procedure, reporting success with 35 of 39 patients. A follow-up covering from six months to four years indicated that 20 of these subjects did not experience any relapse or emergence of new symptoms. Subsequent evaluative reviews by Rachman (1967), Bandura (1969), and Paul (1969) have indicated that desensitization appears to be an effective treatment for adults with a variety of anxiety-based problems. Hatzenbuehler and Schroeder (1978) examined this procedure with children and came to the same conclusion. Snakes, rats, spiders, mice, loud noises, darkness, reading, and test taking are some of the fear-provoking stimulus situations that have yielded to the desensitization procedure.

## Aversion Therapy

The use of aversive stimuli in controlling undesirable behavior, or aversion therapy, has taken a variety of forms in attempts to eliminate such habits as cigarette smoking, compulsive eating, and alcoholism. The aversion therapy procedure is similar to the operations used in the laboratory for passive avoidance learning. The aversive stimulus, usually shock, is presented after an undesirable response is made, with such presentation being provided for a series of trials. Rachman and Teasdale's (1969) volume, devoted solely to an examination of the varieties of aversion therapy, illustrates the popularity of this procedure.

An unusual example of aversion therapy is found in a study by Lang and Melamed (1969). A 9-month-old infant was plagued with chronic vomiting, which had persisted for more than four months. The infant was actually starving to death in spite of a variety of methods being used to attempt to alleviate the condition. The experimenter's first task was to distinguish initial chewing, sucking, and swallowing responses from the first weak sign of reverse peristalsis, which preceded the vomiting reflex. Once this sign or cue was identified, the treatment was deceptively simple; it consisted of a brief but intense electric shock applied to the child's leg at the first sign of regurgitation, and repeated at intervals of one second until the vomiting had stopped. According to the authors, success was achieved with the first treatment, although five additional treatments were subsequently administered. Over the next two weeks body weight increased by 20 percent, and follow-up examinations after one and two years revealed that the child's weight was normal.

Alcoholism has been treated frequently with aversion therapy. Here, the aversive stimulus generally consists of the injection of a drug such as emetine or apomorphine. In this procedure, the subject ingests the drug (or is injected with it) and then drinks alcohol. The drug alone, or in combination with alcohol, produces severe physical discomfort accompanied by retching and vomiting. After several pairings of the drug and alcohol, the subject develops a negative affective state at the sight and smell of alcohol, resulting in avoidance of its use.

## Covert Sensitization

When using aversion therapy procedures, some therapists have had difficulty in handling and controlling the presentation of the physical stimuli (US) used to elicit the avoidance response. Drugs must be administered by a physician, while using an electric shock involves a relatively elaborate apparatus. Moreover, it is difficult to provide a drug dosage or intensity of shock that is effective as an aversive stimulus and yet does not harm the patient.

An alternative to the employment of such physical stimulation has been the use of covert stimuli. Cautela (1966) has called this procedure **covert sensitization.** Briefly, this technique consists of having a subject *imagine* that the appetitive stimulus eliciting the undesirable response has become aversive, and that it is now accompanied by a feeling of revulsion. When the appetitive stimulus is avoided the subject is instructed to feel calm and relaxed. These trials of imagining the appetitive stimulus becoming aversive are alternated with feelings of calm and relaxation that accompany the making of the avoidance response.

Cautela's (1966) early report illustrated how this procedure was used in treating obesity. A 200 pound school teacher was interested in losing weight. First, she was taught to relax in a training session. Then:

[she was asked to visualize that] while she was preparing the supper she started to reach for a piece of bread to make a peanut butter sandwich. Just as she reached the bread she would begin to feel sick to her stomach. She could feel the vomit come up to her mouth and then she would vomit all over the supper she was preparing. She then would have to clean it all up. When she could visualize the complete scene and feel a little sick to her stomach she was to signal with her finger. This was repeated three or more times using cake, cookies, and pie as the tempting foods. On the next trial she was asked to visualize that when she was tempted to eat a piece of cake she felt a little sick but this time she would say to herself, "Oh, I don't want that food." She would then feel immediately calm and relaxed. Ten additional trials (scenes) were presented. On every other trial she would resist the temptation and feel calm and relaxed. She was asked to repeat this procedure at home, every day until the next therapy session. (p. 39)

Cautela reported that the subject's imagined aversion to eating when preparing food was subsequently coupled with an imagined aversion to eating snacks. At the end of therapy, the subject had reduced her weight to 134 pounds.

Cautela's (1966) description of the covert sensitization procedure coupled with its successful application in treating obesity (a successful case of treating alcoholism was also reported) was followed by a host of experimenters using this technique to treat a variety of behavioral disorders. Many of the published findings were case studies and lacked appropriate control groups. But a study by Janda and Rimm (1972) using covert sensitization to treat obesity did not have this methodological difficulty.

Janda and Rimm's (1972) subject population consisted of 18 overweight subjects who were divided into one experimental and two control groups. One control group (nontreated) was told that they had been placed on a waiting list for therapy and so would not receive any treatment. It was necessary, however, for them to report for weekly weigh-ins. A second control group, designated as "realistic attention," attended the same number of therapy sessions (six) as the experimental group but only received relaxation therapy coupled with a general discussion of personal problems. The experimental group, following relaxation training on the first session, was given covert sensitization treatment during the next five sessions. During these sessions

they were asked to vividly imagine approaching the specific foods that contributed to their obesity, to imagine the subsequent aversive consequences, and to feel calm and relaxed when the avoidance response was made.

Results indicated that by the end of the six therapy sessions, the experimental group lost 9.5 pounds, in contrast to a 4.5 pound loss by the controls and a .7 pound gain for the "realistic attention" group. A follow-up over six weeks indicated that the experimental group had a mean loss of 11.7 pounds, the "realistic attention" group a gain of 2.3 pounds, and the nontreated control a loss of .9 pounds.

Little and Curran's (1978) careful examination of many of the covert sensitization studies conducted over the past decade has indicated that, in spite of occasional successes, it remains to be demonstrated that this procedure provides a consistently successful method of treating obesity, alcoholism, and smoking; the procedure has been shown to have promise, however, in treating sexual deviance.

### Reinforcement Procedures

Undoubtedly the widest application of learning principles is in situations in which the experimenter views the organism's behavior as an operant that can be modified by the provision of an appropriate response-reinforcement contingency. One of the earliest experiments of this variety was conducted by Ayllon and Azrin (1964, 1965). They had their experimental subjects, patients in a mental hospital, perform a variety of activities that were necessary and/or useful in the institution, such as serving meals, washing dishes, cleaning floors, etc. Reinforcement for such activity was provided in the form of tokens, which could be subsequently exchanged for rewards. Rewards included consumable goods such as candy or milk at a cost of from 1 to 5 tokens, a choice of television programs for 3 tokens, a private audience with the ward psychologist at 20 tokens, or even a trip to town for 100 tokens. Eight experiments conducted in two studies (Ayllon and Azrin, 1964, 1965) all demonstrated that the reinforcement procedure was effective in maintaining desired performance. The effect of the rewards was clearly demonstrated, since the patients' performance in formerly rewarded tasks deteriorated markedly when they were discontinued. See Box 8-2.

The use of a reinforcement procedure with a specific clinical disorder is found in Brady and Rieger's (1975) study of patients having anorexia nervosa. This disorder, found most frequently with females, is characterized by profound weight loss due to self-imposed restriction of food intake, and often aggravated by excessive exercise and self-induced vomiting. Sixteen hospitalized patients, ages 15 to 35 years, served as subjects. Reinforcement was provided if the patient's morning weight was at least half a pound more than her weight the previous morning. Reinforcement in most cases was a pass permitting the patient to leave the hospital for six hours. Results indicated that a mean gain of approximately 4 pounds per week was achieved, with an overall mean gain of 17 pounds when the patients were discharged from the hospital.

### Other Applications of Response-Reward Contingencies

The successful establishment of response-reward contingencies in institutional, industrial, and educational settings is illustrated in the following experimental studies. Stephens

and Burroughs (1978) reduced absenteeism among hospital personnel by permitting employees to become eligible for a drawing in a lottery if they were not absent during a three week period. Each lottery prize was twenty dollars, with the number of prizes in any one lottery determined by the number of people participating. The experimental design called for two treatment groups. Subjects in the first group were told that they would become eligible for a prize if they were not absent over a three week period, whereas subjects in the second group were told that they would become eligible for a prize if, over the same three week period, they were not absent during all of eight randomly selected dates. Findings indicated that both reward systems resulted in a significant decrease in absenteeism, with no differences noted between the two kinds of experimental treatment.

Tardiness, like absenteeism, is a management problem. Hermann, deMontes, Dominguez, Montes, and Hopkins (1973) have demonstrated the effectiveness of a reinforcement contingency in dealing with this difficulty. In a Mexican manufacturing company, 131 workers had accumulated 750 instances of tardiness throughout the year, in spite of an annual bonus given for punctuality and attendance. Twelve male workers who had chronic problems with tardiness participated in the study, with six of them serving as experimental subjects and six as controls. Experimental subjects were provided a series of treatment and

---

**BOX 8-2**

An interesting and early use of the operant procedure is illustrated in a story about Benjamin Franklin, as related by Knapp and Shodahl (1974). While Franklin was on a fort-building expedition, the chaplain complained to him of low attendance at prayer meetings. Franklin knew that when the men enlisted they had been promised, in addition to pay and provisions, a gill of rum a day, half of which was regularly served to them in the morning and half in the evening. Since the men were most punctual in receiving it, Franklin suggested to the chaplain, "It is, perhaps, below the dignity of your profession to act as steward of the rum, but if you were to deal it out and only just after prayers, you would have them all about you" (p. 656). The chaplain liked the idea, and, with the help of a few men to measure out the liquor, the procedure was implemented. Never were prayer meetings more generally and more punctually attended.

no treatment conditions. On treatment days, coming to work on time was reinforced by giving the subjects a bonus voucher worth 20 cents, which could be cashed in at the end of the week. (The average daily pay was $4.00.) On nontreatment days (or baseline condition), these subjects were told that the payment for daily punctuality was going to be suspended, but they would be told if and when such payment was to be reinstated.

Control subjects were not told about the experiment.

Results of the study are found in Figure 8-4. Control subjects had a fairly high and steady level of tardiness. In contrast, whenever bonus vouchers were used, tardiness was reduced in the experimental subjects.

The excessive activity level of some children in school is quite disruptive to other members of the class. Schulman, Suran,

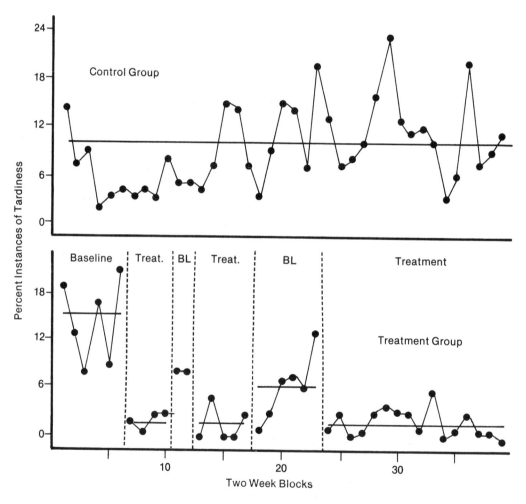

FIGURE 8-4.   The upper graph presents the instances of tardiness of the control group; the lower graph provides this information for the experimental group. The horizontal lines represent the means for each of the conditions. Adapted from J. A. Hermann, A. I. deMontes, B. Dominguez, F. Montes, and B. L. Hopkins, "Effects of bonuses for punctuality on the tardiness of industrial workers." *Journal of Applied Behavior Analysis*, 1973, 6, 563–570. Copyright © 1973 by the Society for the Experimental Analysis of Behavior, Inc.

Stevens, and Kupst (1979) have demonstrated the effectiveness of reinforcement in reducing this type of behavior. Their subjects were 11 children, ages 9 to 13, who were enrolled in a day hospital program for emotionally disturbed children. Classroom sessions conducted at the hospital were used to examine the efficacy of their reinforcement procedure. During the entire period of the experiment, all of the children wore a biomotometer, an electronic device that measured their general motor activity. When the child's movements exceeded a certain level of activity over a designated period of time, feedback was provided in the form of an auditory signal (beep) transmitted through an earphone which the child wore.

Following the establishment of a baseline activity level over five sessions, the children were informed that they could earn a reward if they would slow down whenever they heard a beep. They were not told, however, what level of activity would result in reinforcement, only that the fewer signals they heard the better chance they would have to earn the reward. If during the hour-long classroom ses-

sion the children's activity level was below 80 percent of their baseline activity level, the children were rewarded by being given a choice of candy or a toy. Following five periods in which the experimenters provided reward for appropriate behavior, there were five additional sessions in which reward was not contingent upon activity. During these sessions, the children wore the apparatus without the earphone, and they were told that they would earn a reward just for wearing it. Rewards were provided after each session. Figure 8-5 summarizes the mean activity of the subjects for the baseline, contingent reward, and noncontingent reward sessions. Providing a reward significantly reduced activity, but when the response-reward contingency was removed, increased activity similar to baseline responding was obtained.

Summing up, the use of learning principles to change behavior outside the laboratory has not been totally successful. Aversion therapy, for example, has rarely had success rates beyond 50 percent, particularly when the results from long-term, follow-up investigations are included. But such limited success

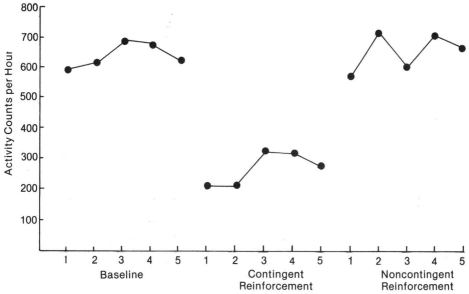

FIGURE 8-5.    Summary of mean activity for all children across baseline, contingent reinforcement, and noncontingent reinforcement trials. Adapted from J. L. Schulman, B. G. Suran, T. M. Stevens, and M. J. Kupst, "Instructions, feedback, and reinforcement in reducing activity levels in the classroom." *Journal of Applied Behavior Analysis*, 1979, 12, 441–447. Copyright © 1979 by the Society for the Experimental Analysis of Behavior, Inc.

does not necessarily say anything about the validity of the learning principles. In nonlaboratory situations, it is very difficult to control the many variables that can contribute to the success or failure of the program. The limited success of some programs in changing behavior might be a result of these noncontrolled variables, rather than a reflection on the validity of the learning principle.

## SUMMARY

Experimental studies of learning using laboratory tasks frequently raise two questions. (1) Can results using animals as subjects be generalized to human beings? (2) Can laboratory findings be generalized to nonlaboratory settings?

Many psychologists, beginning with Pavlov (1927), have assumed that behavioral principles generated from animal learning studies apply to human behavior. But other investigators have been quite skeptical, pointing to a number of failures of such generality. European ethologists, in examining animal behavior, have stressed the adaptive significance of animal behavior. They have considered learning to be a specific process that interacts with the animal's innate response capacities, enabling each species to survive in its particular environment. The ethological position has called attention to a number of areas that investigators in the United States had previously ignored, such as the role of key stimuli, imprinting, etc.

Many believe that the generality question has an empirical answer. That is, any generalization that is extended to include a new species or a different environment remains a hypothesis to be tested—equally subject to disconfirmation and confirmation.

Laboratory findings have frequently been applied to nonlaboratory situations. Classical conditioning operations have been used to treat enuresis and a variety of other behavioral problems. More often, however, instrumental conditioning operations have been used in these nonlaboratory situations.

In the desensitization procedure, an instrumental procedure designed to eliminate phobic and anxiety responses, the patient first imagines a situation that only elicits a weak anxiety response. After the anxiety response to this situation has been extinguished, a slightly stronger anxiety-producing situation is imagined, and then also extinguished. Stronger and stronger anxiety-producing situations are systematically presented, with the anxiety response in each instance extinguished, until such time that the subject is able to imagine the strongest anxiety-producing situation without feeling anxiety.

A second treatment method is covert sensitization. Here the subject learns to avoid making a response by imagining an aversive event taking place when such a response is made. Thus, the overweight subject who desires to reduce imagines getting sick when eating a snack. These trials are alternated with the imagined rejection of such foods, followed by relaxation.

Probably the most frequently used instrumental learning procedure has been to establish response-reinforcement contingencies. Here, when the subject makes an appropriate response, it is followed by reinforcement, which increases the probability of that response. Response-reward contingencies have been used to modify the behavior of individuals in various institutional, industrial, and educational settings.

## NOTE

1. Mowrer (1980) has provided an interesting historical account of the development of the apparatus and the beginnings of the work described in Mowrer and Mowrer (1938). The originality of the apparatus and treatment is in some dispute, since Mowrer acknowledged that Morgan and Witmer (1939) had been working on a similar apparatus since 1932. Kazdin (1978) has written that such an apparatus and treatment had also been used in Germany, France, and Russia in the early 1900s.

# CHAPTER NINE

# Verbal Learning:
# The Traditional Approach

The landmark experiments of Ebbinghaus (1913) demonstrated that it was possible to use the scientific method to examine a higher mental process, thus changing the study of memory from an art to a science. Although he entitled his monograph *Memory*, he used the term *learning* for the process in which a list of nonsense syllables, or consonant-vowel-consonant units, was acquired through repetitive reading and recitation. When he placed varying time intervals—20 minutes, 24 hours, 31 days, etc.—between such learning and the relearning of these lists, the relearning scores were identified as measuring retention.

The approach of investigators who have been guided first by Ebbinghaus and then by John B. Watson, the founder of Behaviorism, has been called traditional, since the learning of lists has been the basic experimental task, and the learning of such tasks has frequently been analyzed in terms of stimulus and response relationships. In addition, traditional investigators have accepted the distinction between learning and retention made by Ebbinghaus. Here, learning is inferred from changes in the subject's performance over varying numbers of trials or presentations of the material, whereas retention refers to the persistence of such behavior over a period of time. The retention of material has usually been measured after hours or days; the subject does not practice the previously learned material during this interval.

## MATERIALS, TASKS, AND RESPONSE MEASURES

The first concern is to find out what kinds of material, tasks, and response measures the experimenters have used in their examination of list learning.

### Materials

Ebbinghaus, aware that words differed in their capacity to arouse associations, invented the nonsense syllable in order to eliminate this problem. Such syllables, currently identified as CVCs, consisted of two consonants separated by a vowel—REV, for example. Subjects were generally required to spell the syllable rather than attempt to pronounce it. Ebbinghaus's materials have since been expanded to include the use of single letters, bigrams (two letters), consonant syllables (three consonants), digits, and isolated words.

## Types of Tasks

List-learning tasks have been enlarged from the **serial-learning** task utilized by Ebbinghaus; they now include free-recall, paired-associate, and verbal-discrimination tasks.

In **serial-learning** tasks, the subject must learn the items in the order in which they were presented. When the **anticipation procedure** is used, each item on the list is assumed to serve as a stimulus or cue which the subject uses to anticipate the next item and respond with it. When this next item is presented, it indicates to the subject the correctness of the response as well as serving as a stimulus for the next item. The first item on the list is cued by an asterisk or some other arbitrary visual stimulus. Items, generally presented with a memory drum or slide projector, are exposed for a fixed period of time, usually 1, 2, 3, or 4 seconds. In a second serial-learning procedure, the list is presented either in an item by item fashion or by showing the complete list of items at once, following which the subject is instructed to write down or verbally report the items in the same order in which they were presented. This is known as the **study-test procedure.**

If the experimenter does not require the subject to recall the items on the list in the order in which they were presented, the list-learning task is called **free learning** or **free recall.**

The **paired-associate** (PA) task is made up of a list of pairs of items, usually CVCs or words, such as XED-TIV, MUL-HEV, JOX-FUP. The subject is asked to recall the second item after the first item of the pair is presented. The list frequently consists of 10 to 15 pairs of items, with the position of each pair in the list being changed from trial to trial. This procedure requires the subject to learn to associate the first item of the pair with the second; it prevents the subject from learning the responses in serial order, as might be done if each pair remained in the same position from one trial to the next. Anticipation and study-test procedures have been used with paired-associate tasks, as well as with the serial-learning tasks.

The PA task was first used by Calkins (1894, 1896) shortly after Ebbinghaus's experiments employing serial learning, but it was not used extensively until the early 1950s. The task can be conceptualized as a series of stimulus and response relationships, since the first item of the pair can be considered as a stimulus used to cue the subject's response (represented by the second item).

The last type of list task is **verbal discrimination.** The list consists of a number of pairs of verbal items, frequently 40 or more. The subject has to learn which item of each pair was designated by the experimenter as correct. This task is similar to the discrimination learning task discussed in Chapter 5, except that the stimuli are words or verbal symbols.

Illustrations of the varying tasks using CVCs, CCCs, or words as the materials to be learned are provided in Table 9-1. In all of the learning tasks, the experimenter can provide the subject with a predetermined number of presentations of the material (or trials), or continue trials until the subject reaches some arbitrary criterion, such as one errorless trial.

## Response Measures

The response measures in verbal learning experiments are (1) relearning or savings, (2) recall, and (3) recognition. The **relearning measure** is generally converted into a savings score by computing the difference between the number of trials originally required to learn the material and the number of trials required to relearn it to the same criterion. The **savings score formula** is

$$\text{Savings} =$$

$$\frac{\text{No. trials required for} \_ \text{No. trials required to}}{\text{original learning} \quad \text{relearn the material}}$$

$$\overline{\text{No. of trials required for original learning}}$$

Although originally employed by Ebbinghaus (1913), the savings method has been infrequently used. One reason is that it takes much more time to obtain this measure than any of the others. However, some interest in the savings method has recently been expressed by

TABLE 9-1.   Types of tasks, materials, and requirements used in list-learning experiments

| Type of Task | Material | List | | Requirement |
|---|---|---|---|---|
| Serial Learning | CVCs | ZUH CEJ GEC KOJ QEM VEH | | Subject must learn the items in the order in which they were presented. |
| Free Recall | Words | viand torque pinnace excise despot | | Subject is not required to learn the items in any particular order. |
| Paired Associate | CCCs | ZGF-DNT FJH-PNK BFM-HZL TZL-LRD | | Subject must learn to associate the second item of the pair with the presentation of the first item. |
| Verbal Discrimination | Words | pencil sheath *careen* inure | *patrol* levee beguile *recoil* | Subject must learn to choose the item which the experimenter has arbitrarily designated as correct. |

Nelson and his associates; see Nelson (1971, 1978), Nelson and Rothbart (1972), Nelson, Fehling, and Moore-Glascock (1979).

The recall method requires the subject to reproduce or generate the materials or target items that have been presented. The number or percentage of correct responses is typically used as the performance measure. For example, the presentation of a list of 50 words might be followed with instructions to the subject to recall as many as possible. The number of words correctly recalled would be used as the recall measure.

Recognition means knowing that a particular event has been experienced on an earlier occasion. In everyday situations, individuals experiencing a given stimulus situation will state that they do (or do not) recognize the situation. It is possible in such instances for "dishonest" individuals to indicate that they have recognized the situation when actually they have not. In verbal learning tasks, experimenters have assumed it necessary to keep their subjects "honest"—to have them refrain from claiming to recognize an item when they have not. This has been accomplished by combining the target item with a number of distractors to form a recognition test. Here, the subject is instructed to recognize or choose the previously experienced item from among the alternatives provided. Wallace (1980) has recently defined such measures as **recognition-discrimination measures,** to distinguish them from measures of recognition memory in which distractors are not used.[1]

The sensitivity of recognition memory for verbal material, as measured by a recognition-discrimination test, has been demonstrated by Shepard (1967). In one part of his study, 540 common nouns and adjectives were presented (such as *child, office*) and also 612 sentences (such as *A dead dog is no use for hunting ducks*). Following the presentation of such material, a recognition test consisting of 68 pairs of an original item and a distractor was administered. The mean percentage of correct answers was 88.4 for the words and 89.0 for sentences.

Many studies, beginning with Luh's (1922) very early investigation which was replicated by Postman and Rau (1957), have indicated that recognition memory, as measured by the discrimination task, is superior to recall memory. But investigators today are aware that any comparison between these response measures is tenuous at best, since all performance measures are dependent on the experimental procedures employed. In the case of recognition-discrimination memory, it is obvious that this measure is related to the characteristics of the distractors used in the discrimination test.

This problem can be illustrated by conducting the following hypothetical experiment. Two groups of subjects are presented with identical lists of CVCs, following which each group is given a different recognition test. Group 1 is given a test in which the distractors are other CVCs, whereas Group 2 is given a test in which common words are the distractors. All would agree that recognition performance for Group 2 should be superior to that for Group 1.

The role of distractors on recognition-discrimination memory has been experimentally demonstrated by many investigators. McNulty (1965) has shown that recognition memory declines when the distractors are orthographically (physically) similar to the target words (for instance, plunger–plunder). Underwood (1965) and Anisfeld and Knapp (1968) have shown that recognition test performance is adversely influenced when the distractors are related associatively to the target items (for example, rough–smooth) or are synonyms (such as girl–female). Since the characteristics of the distractors used in the recognition-discrimination test play such an important role in determining the performance level, any comparison of performance on this task with recall performance should be recognized as being specific to that particular experiment.

## ATTRIBUTES OF
## VERBAL MATERIALS

It will be recalled that Ebbinghaus assumed that all nonsense syllables had a similar capacity to elicit associations, but Glaze (1928) has demonstrated that Ebbinghaus's assumption was in error. When association values were obtained for some 2000 CVCs, Glaze found large differences among them; investigators have used Glaze's CVC association values in their experiments for more than three decades. Archer (1960) and Noble (1961) have provided more current association measures of CVCs. See Box 9-1 for a description of Glaze's (1928) study.

### Meaningfulness

Guided by Glaze's (1928) work with nonsense syllables, Noble (1952b) obtained an association measure of *words* that he defined as meaningfulness (*m*). Noble had his subjects write as many free associations as they could generate in 60 seconds to each of 96 words. He found that the number of associations elicited by these words varied, thus suggesting that a word, like a nonsense syllable, has an association value. Noble found that words such as *money*, *army*, and *kitchen* elicited a large number of associations, whereas other words, such as *bodkin* and *ulna*, elicited very few. Table 9-2 provides a sample of the meaningfulness values for words that Noble (1952b) used. Later, Noble, Stockwell, and Pryer (1957) found that it was not necessary for subjects to actually write out or produce the associations; reliable association values could be obtained by having subjects rate each word on a rating scale as to the number of associations it elicited.

TABLE 9-2.    Meaningfulness (*m*) values for a sampling of verbal items obtained from Noble (1952b)

| | | | |
|---|---|---|---|
| gojey | .99 | kennel | 5.52 |
| attar | 1.71 | insect | 7.39 |
| femur | 2.09 | money | 8.89 |
| rostrum | 2.73 | kitchen | 9.61 |
| argon | 3.34 | | |

BOX 9-1

Early investigators of verbal learning assumed that at least some of the nonsense syllables they used in their experiments were meaningful in that they elicited associations of one type or another. Cason (1926) and Glaze (1928) experimentally demonstrated the validity of this assumption. Glaze's study was more extensive, and his calibration of the meaningfulness of more than 2000 syllables served as a standard of reference for the next 25 years. His population of 2019 syllables included all of the nonsense syllables that could be constructed from the English alphabet, with the letter Y serving as both a consonant and a vowel. Words were eliminated from the population.

Fifteen college students served as subjects. A tachistoscope was used to present 252 syllables to each subject in one sitting; a number of sittings were required for presentation of all the syllables. Subjects were instructed that when the syllable appeared they should indicate with one or two words what the syllable meant. If the syllable meant something that could not be expressed, they were to respond with the word "yes." If the syllable meant nothing, the subject was instructed not to say anything.

An association value for each nonsense syllable was obtained and expressed as a percentage of the number of subjects who had indicated that the syllable elicited an association. Below is a sampling of the association values obtained by Glaze for a number of the nonsense syllables.

| 100% | 73% | 53% | 33% | 20% | 0% |
|------|-----|-----|-----|-----|-----|
| BAL | BOV | CAZ | DAH | BEJ | GUQ |
| DEP | HEV | KOB | JOD | FUP | QIJ |
| ROV | MUL | SUB | VUP | SAJ | XUK |
| WIL | VAM | WEM | ZON | WEQ | ZIW |

## Other Attributes

There is little doubt that Noble's (1952b) identification of meaningfulness led investigators to search for other characteristics of isolated words. These attributes include the following.

*Familiarity.* Noble (1953) measured the familiarity of a word by asking subjects to rate how often they had come in contact with it, using the terms *never, rarely, sometimes, often,* and *very often* to describe the extent of their contact.

*Pronounceableness.* Underwood and Schulz (1960) measured pronounceableness by instructing subjects to rate verbal items on the relative ease or difficulty of pronouncing each item.

*Vividness and Imagery.* Tulving, McNulty, and Ozier (1965) and Paivio (1965) had subjects rate nouns as to the ease with which they produced a picture or a visual image. Subsequently, Paivio, Yuille, and Madigan (1968) had subjects provide imagery ratings for 926 nouns. Table 9-3 illustrates some of the ratings that were obtained.

*Pleasantness.* In an early study by Noble (1958), subjects were asked to rate 96 items, which he had originally scaled for meaningfulness, as to whether they were *neutral, pleasant, unpleasant,* or *mixed.* Silverstein and Dienstbier (1968) also had subjects rate two syllable nouns on a pleasantness scale.

TABLE 9-3.   Imagery values for a sampling of words obtained from Paivio, Yuille, and Madigan (1968)

| | | | |
|---|---|---|---|
| interim | 1.97 | fatigue | 5.05 |
| context | 2.13 | paper | 6.30 |
| virtue | 3.33 | orchestra | 6.77 |
| profession | 3.83 | grass | 6.96 |
| salary | 4.70 | | |

*Objective Word Frequency.* The objective word frequency measure was not developed by using a rating scale but obtained from either the Thorndike and Lorge (1944) or Kučera and Francis (1967) frequency counts. These counts indicate the frequency with which a word appears in print. Kučera and Francis examined 500 samples of words, with approximately 2000 words/sample, covering a variety of topics. Their count is based on the tabulated frequencies of all the words in all of their samples.

This list covers what we consider to be the most important of the word attributes, but it is not exhaustive. Other characteristics studied include the number of dictionary meanings (Saltz and Modigliani, 1967), concreteness (Gorman, 1961), ease of defining the word, and animateness (Berrian, Metzler, Kroll, and Clark-Meyers, 1979).

## Interrelatedness of Word Attributes

Since words can be classified by a variety of attributes, one may ask, "Are these attributes measuring unique characteristics, or do they all appear to be measuring a similar component?" Unfortunately, there has not been one comprehensive study that systematically examined the relationship existing among all of the attributes enumerated. But there is a suggestion from the experimental studies of Noble (1953), Hall (1967), Paivio, Yuille, and Madigan (1968), and Paivio (1968) that meaningfulness ($m$), familiarity, objective frequency, and pronounceableness are all reflections of the operation of the attribute **meaningful-**ness, and that imagery or vividness represents a second unique attribute, **imagery.** Frincke's (1968) factor analytic study is in keeping with this point of view, since he found that many of these word attributes could be grouped into two conceptual categories. One he identified as meaningfulness–familiarity; the second as imagery–concreteness. The recent work of Toglia and Battig (1978) has suggested that the attribute of **pleasantness** is different from these other two basic attributes. In summary, it would appear that meaningfulness, imagery, and pleasantness represent three basic attributes of words.

## TASK VARIABLES

The general approach of many experimenters has been to determine how different conditions or variables contribute to verbal learning. Traditional investigators have been reluctant to search for conditions "inside the subject's head," feeling more comfortable examining variables associated with the characteristics of the task. The work of Glaze (1928) indicated that one such task variable was association value, and as noted in the previous section, Glaze's work was followed by the identification of a variety of other verbal attributes.

## Attributes of Verbal Stimuli

McGeoch's (1930) study indicated that the number of CVCs recalled in a free-recall learning task was a function of the association value of the nonsense syllables that comprised the list. This work was followed by a multitude of investigations examining how meaningfulness, objective frequency, familiarity, pronounceableness, vividness, imagery, etc., contributed to the acquisition of serial-, free-recall, and paired-associate learning tasks. The literature is far too extensive for any systematic review of these findings, but most experimenters have found that the learning of each of these tasks is positively related to the attributes delineated. In brief, as meaningfulness, objective frequency, familiarity, imagery, etc., of the verbal material increases, acquisition takes place more rapidly.

To illustrate, Noble (1952a) constructed three serial lists of 12 words/list. The words making up each list differed in meaningfulness (or their *m* value). Noble required his subjects to learn each list until a criterion of one perfect trial was reached. Significant differences were obtained in the number of trials needed to reach the criterion for each list, as shown in Figure 9-1.

Kimble and Dufort (1955) and Noble and McNeely (1957), using lists of paired associates which varied as to meaningfulness (*m*), have also found *m* to be a variable that influences acquisition. Using the Thorndike-Lorge frequency count as a measure, investigators have found that differences in the objective frequency of words on the experimental list influenced both free-recall learning [see Hall

(1954), Underwood, Ekstrand, and Keppel (1965)] and paired-associate learning [see Postman (1962a), Martin (1964)].

Finally, vividness or imagery has also been demonstrated to be a significant variable. Tulving, McNulty, and Ozier (1965) constructed three lists (16 words per list) that differed in vividness; meaningfulness of the words was held constant. The words used in each list are found in Table 9-4. Each subject learned all three lists using free recall. On each of eight trials, the material was presented at a rate of one word per second. The subject was then given 60 seconds to recall as many of the words as possible. Significant differences in recall scores were obtained, with the material rated highest in imagery or vividness being the easiest to learn. Figure 9-2 illustrates these findings. Paivio (1965) and Yarmey and Paivio (1965) have confirmed the importance of imagery in the learning of paired associates.

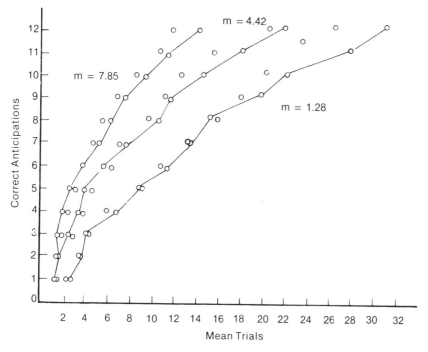

FIGURE 9-1.    Mean number of trials required to anticipate correctly 12 successive items. The (*m*) parameters denote average meaningfulness of the lists. Adapted from C. E. Noble, "The role of stimulus learning (*m*) in serial verbal learning." *Journal of Experimental Psychology*, 1952, 43, 437–446. Copyright © 1952 by the American Psychological Association. Reprinted by permission.

TABLE 9-4.   Experimental lists differing in vividness or imagery

| High | Medium | Low |
|------|--------|------|
| apron | abode | buyer |
| balloon | bucket | crisis |
| bunny | builder | entry |
| butler | cargo | founder |
| cabbage | fiber | output |
| camel | hamlet | patron |
| chorus | handful | renown |
| cigar | madame | routine |
| circus | pebble | rover |
| comet | porter | rumour |
| granny | pudding | session |
| jungle | summit | surplus |
| lantern | thicket | tariff |
| rainbow | trainer | topic |
| runner | veteran | treason |
| satin | voter | vigour |

Adapted from Tulving, McNulty, and Ozier (1965). Copyright (1965) Canadian Psychological Association, reprinted by permission.

## Abstractness of Stimuli

A stimulus attribute that seems qualitatively different from the characteristics previously described is **abstractness**. The use of a real object in an experiment is less abstract than a picture of that object, whereas a picture is less abstract than a word describing the object. One might expect to find that the abstractness of stimuli would result in recall differences. Bevan and Steger (1971) have demonstrated this. In their study, 21 small common objects, such as an apple, book, bottle, cup, eraser, key, match, pencil, etc., served as the objects, while photographs of these objects or their names were used as more abstract stimuli. A number of counterbalanced sequences were used; each sequence consisted of 7 objects, 7 pictures, and 7 object names. Following a single presentation of the stimulus material, the subjects, either fourth graders or college students, were asked to recall as many of the objects as possible. The findings for both groups of subjects (see Figure 9-3) reveal a

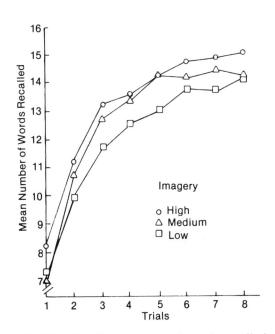

FIGURE 9-2.   Mean number of words recalled as a function of trials for three lists differing in imagery of words listed. Adapted from Tulving, McNulty, and Ozier (1965). Copyright (1965) Canadian Psychological Association, reprinted by permission.

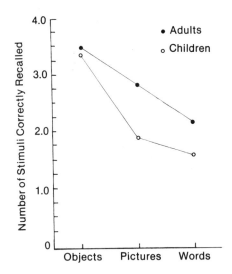

FIGURE 9-3.   Free recall as a function of level of abstractness of stimuli in fourth graders and college students. Adapted from W. Bevan and J. A. Steger, "Free Recall and Abstractness of Stimuli." *Science,* 1971, 172, 597–599. Copyright © 1971 by the American Association for the Advancement of Science.

very orderly progression of recall, with real objects being recalled the best and object names the worst. Gardiner and Watkins (1979) have confirmed Bevan and Steger's (1971) findings.

## Stimulus Position

The serial-learning task demands that the subject recall the items in the same order in which they were presented. It has been found that errors (or correct responses) are not equally distributed over all of the positions in the list. Rather, a bow-shaped curve is obtained: items located at a position just beyond the middle of the list are subject to the most errors, while items at the end of the list are subject to more

errors than those items at the beginning of the list.

Ward (1937) and Hovland (1938) demonstrated this serial position effect using CVCs. A later study by McCrary and Hunter (1953) is noteworthy, since they examined the serial position effect with both meaningful (common names) and nonmeaningful (CVCs) material. In their procedure, subjects were provided with a list of 14 items, with learning being carried out until a criterion of one errorless trial was reached. Figure 9-4 provides the serial position curves for both kinds of material. The curve is much flatter when names are used as the experimental material. However, if the data are plotted using percentage of total errors made at each serial position, little dif-

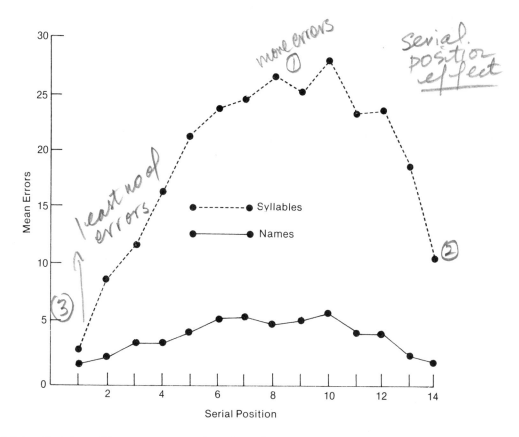

FIGURE 9-4.   Serial position curves as a function of the characteristics of the material used. Adapted from J. W. McCrary and W. S. Hunter, "Serial Curves in Verbal Learning." *Science*, 1953, 117, 131–134.

ference can be noted between the two types of material (see Figure 9-5). The fewest number of errors was recorded for items at the beginning of the list, next fewest errors for items located at the end of the list, and the largest number of errors was recorded for items positioned just past the middle of the list.

The serial position effect can be readily obtained and has been replicated both within and outside the laboratory. The effect can be noted in the learning of a poem, a speech, or even motor skills tasks. Jensen (1962) has shown that misspellings are much more frequently found in the middle of a word than at the beginning or the end. Gymnasts and other competitors whose serially presented activities are recalled and graded by judges would be wise to place their most difficult and spectacular feats at the beginning or at the end of their

routine, thus increasing the probability that the judges will remember them.

It has also been found that there are more errors for items in the middle of the list than for those at the beginning or at the end when the free-recall task is employed. But unlike the findings obtained with serial-learning tasks, the free-recall findings reveal fewer errors for items located at the end of the list than for items located at the beginning.

Murdock's (1962) findings are typical of the results obtained with free-recall tasks. In this most comprehensive study, the serial position effect was examined as a function of the length of the list as well as the presentation time. Lists of 10, 15, and 20 words were presented at a rate of 2 seconds per item, while other lists of 20, 30, and 40 items were presented at a rate of 1 second per item. A 1.5

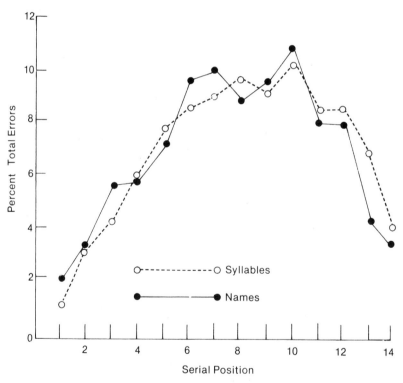

FIGURE 9-5.  Serial position curves as a function of the characteristics of the material used. Note that the ordinate expresses performance in terms of percentage of total errors. Adapted from J. W. McCrary and W. S. Hunter, "Serial Curves in Verbal Learning." *Science*, 1953, 117, 131–134.

minute recall period followed the presentation of a list, during which time the six groups of subjects were requested to write down as many of the words as they could remember, without regard to the order of presentation. The serial position curves, shown in Figure 9-6, all have the same general form. The items located at the end of the list were recalled best (the recency effect); items located at the beginning of the list were learned next best (the primacy effect); and items located in the middle of the list were the most difficult to learn.

How can we account for the unusual distribution of errors that is found with serial and free-recall list-learning tasks? Several explanations for this effect were proposed more than forty years ago by Lepley (1934) and Hull (1935). Although an evaluation of these

theoretical positions would be too lengthy for inclusion here, careful scrutiny of these theories has revealed serious deficiencies. Theoretical explanations for the position effect obtained with free-recall tasks have been provided by a few recent investigators, such as Glanzer and Cunitz (1966), but problems with these explanations have also been noted.

Most investigators have eschewed making theoretical explanations for the position effect, preferring to devote their attention to an examination of experimental variables. One such variable deals with the distinctiveness or isolation of the first and last item on the list, brought about by the temporal interval placed between trials. The contribution of the intertrial interval is indicated in a study by Glanzer and Peters (1962), who had their sub-

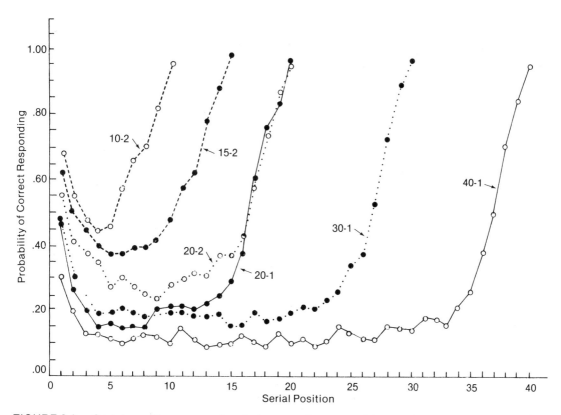

FIGURE 9-6. Serial position curves for six free-recall groups. Adapted from B. B. Murdock, "The serial position effect of free recall." *Journal of Experimental Psychology*, 1962, 64, 482–486. Copyright © 1962 by the American Psychological Association. Reprinted by permission.

jects learn a serial list of 10 items using either a 0, 2, 4, 8, or 16 second intertrial interval. They found that as the time between trials decreased, the distribution of errors approached linearity, with the traditional bow-shaped curve virtually disappearing when the 0 second intertrial interval was used.

If, however, the serial list contains some distinctive cue when the 0 second intertrial interval is examined, the bow-shaped curve reappears. Coppage and Harcum's (1967) study illustrates this finding. Subjects serially learned a list of 10 CVCs with no intertrial interval provided. However, one syllable was typed in red while all others were in black. The red syllable was located in either the first, third, fifth, seventh, or ninth position. The learning criterion was 20 successive correct responses. An analysis of the errors made by each of the five experimental groups revealed typical bow-shaped curves, with the red syllable appearing to serve as the first item on the list and yielding the fewest number of errors.

The lesson to be learned is that even a learning phenomenon as apparently simple as the serial position effect is quite complex; the unequal distribution of errors, as a function of the position of the item in the list, appears to arise from the operation of a number of conditions. The identification of these conditions and their relative contribution to the composite curve continues to be a problem for investigators.

### The Isolation Effect

The last stimulus condition to be discussed is called the **isolation effect.** Von Restorff (1933) demonstrated that a two digit number was more easily learned if it was placed among a list of CVCs than if it was placed among a list of other two digit numbers. Von Restorff attributed her findings to the "isolation" of the digit among the CVCs, which provided a homogeneous background. This isolation effect has also been called the **von Restorff phenomenon.**

The isolation of an item can be carried out using a variety of procedures. One method

is to make the physical presentation of the isolated item different from that of the other list items. Jones and Jones (1942), for example, examined the isolation effect by having one item in their experimental list printed in red, with the remaining items printed in black. A second procedure has been to provide semantic isolation. Kimble and Dufort (1955) produced an isolation effect by using an item low in meaningfulness (Noble's m), while the remaining list items had high meaningfulness values. A third procedure required that subjects in the experimental condition perform a different mental operation on the to-be-isolated item than control subjects. For example, it is possible to "isolate" the word *Lincoln* by instructing the experimental group to look for a president's name among the list of items presented and remember it. This procedure is of interest today, since it places emphasis on what operations the subject performs during learning, in contrast to manipulations of the external stimulus event.

Research has revealed that the learning of the isolated item is a function of the amount or degree of its isolation. Gumenik and Levitt (1968) provided subjects with a serial-learning task consisting of nine CVCs projected on a screen. For one condition, the size of each control item was small (2.3×4.5 inches), whereas the size of the isolated item was much larger—either (a) 3.3×6.4, (b) 4.7×9.1, or (c) 6.7×13.0 inches. For a second condition, the size of each control item was represented by the largest projection (6.7×13.0 inches), with the isolated item being smaller—namely, (a) 4.7×9.1, (b) 3.3×6.4, or (c) 2.3×4.5 inches. The results, as indicated by the mean number of errors in noting the isolated item over 30 learning trials, are presented in Table 9-5. As the difference between the isolated item and the control item increased, the number of errors made on the isolated item decreased.

A question arose almost immediately after the isolation effect had been discovered: How does the learning of the isolated item influence the learning of the remaining items on the list? In an early serial-learning study by Jones and Jones (1942), two lists of 10 CVCs were used. All of the items on the control list

TABLE 9-5.    Number of errors as a function of the size of the isolated item

| Size of Unisolated CVCs in Inches | Number of Errors by Size of Isolated CVCs in Inches | | | |
|---|---|---|---|---|
| | 2.3 × 4.5 | 3.3 × 6.4 | 4.7 × 9.1 | 6.7 × 13.0 |
| Small (2.3 × 4.5) | 15.5 | 13.2 | 11.0 | 7.8 |
| Large (6.7 × 13.0) | 11.9 | 15.5 | 14.4 | 21.2 |

Adapted from W. E. Gumenik and J. Levitt, "The von Restorff effect as a function of difference in the isolated item." *American Journal of Psychology*, 1968, 81, 247–252. Copyright © 1968 by the University of Illinois Press.

*2nd year English B*

were printed in black, while on the experimental list the seventh CVC was printed in red, but all of the other CVCs were in black. Subjects were required to learn the material to a criterion of one errorless trial. A week later they were asked to relearn the material to the same criterion. Findings indicated that although the red CVC was more rapidly learned and better retained than its control, thus confirming the isolation effect, no difference was obtained between the experimental and control list when overall learning or retention was examined. Subsequent studies conducted by Newman and Saltz (1958), Jensen (1962), Roberts (1962), and Lippman and Lippman (1978) have confirmed this finding.

Isolation effects have also been demonstrated with paired-associate learning tasks. An interesting problem has been to determine if paired-associate learning is facilitated more by the isolation of the stimulus or of the response item of the pair. Research conducted by Kimble and Dufort (1955), Nachmias, Gleitman, and McKenna (1961), and Newman (1962) produced equivocal findings, but a later study by Erickson (1965) demonstrated that, although isolating either the stimulus item alone or the response item alone facilitated the learning of the pair, the isolation of the stimulus item produced the greater facilitation.

Wallace's (1965) review and evaluation of the varying explanations for the isolation effect have revealed inadequacies in all of them. As Lippman and Lippman (1978) recently acknowledged, "an adequate theory of the isolation effect has yet to be offered" (p. 49).

## MOTIVATION

The examination of motivational variables has generated little interest among most verbal learning investigators.[2] This does not mean that motivation is believed to play an unimportant role in verbal learning. This neglect stems from the assumption that the motivation of the college student, who usually serves as an experimental subject in such studies, is sufficiently high that further increases can have only a minimal effect on performance.

Verbal learning experimenters have been interested by intention, a concept often related to motivation. Sometimes people learn without trying or intending to do so. Experimenters brought this problem into the laboratory in order to examine learning under "incidental" and "intentional" conditions.

But how can these conditions be differentiated? Operationally, experimenters have accomplished this by using different types of instructions. For intentional learning, the subjects are provided with instructions indicating that they should learn the material since there will be a subsequent testing session; for incidental learning, the instructions do not indicate that such learning should take place. Two different types of incidental procedures have been used. One has been to expose the material to the subject with no instructions to learn. For example, Biel and Force (1943) used CVCs with six different types of print (Bodoni, Caslon, etc.). With a tachistoscope, subjects were presented with 12 different CVCs, and they were asked to indicate the kind of print they found most legible. At the end of the session, the subjects were asked to recall as many of the CVCs as possible.

A second "incidental" procedure has been to have the subject learn a task, but during the learning period the subject is shown material not covered by the learning instructions. When the task has been learned, the subject is asked to recall the material not covered by the instructions. In a study by Bahrick (1954), 14 geometric forms, filled in with 7 colors, served as the experimental material. The subjects were instructed to learn the forms using a serial anticipation procedure, but the role of color was not mentioned. After the subjects had reached a criterion of one perfect trial, they were asked to indicate which color was associated with which form.

Investigators have found that subjects can learn without intent to do so—that is, under incidental learning conditions. However, intentional learning results in superior performance. One study illustrating this result was conducted by Postman, Adams, and Phillips (1955), who had two groups of subjects rate 30 adjectives with respect to their frequency of use in the subject's daily speech. An intentional learning group was asked to remember as many of the items as possible, whereas the incidental group was not given these instructions. After the adjectives had been rated, the subjects were given five minutes to recall as many as possible. Results indicated that the intentional group recalled 12.62 items and the incidental group 9.41, thus demonstrating superior recall for the intentional group, but also revealing that the incidental group had learned more than 30 percent of the items presented.

Unlike Postman et al. (1955), some experimenters have been unable to find that intentional learning instructions result in superior recall. In one part of an extensive study conducted by Hyde and Jenkins (1973), five groups of subjects were each given different orienting tasks to perform on 24 unrelated words, which served as the experimental material. These tasks were to: (1) rate the words as to their pleasantness or unpleasantness; (2) estimate their frequency of usage; (3)

detect the occurrence of the letters "e" and "g" in each of the words; (4) determine whether the words were nouns, verbs, adjectives, or "some other" part of speech; or (5) determine whether each word would result in an intelligible sentence when appropriately placed among a sequence of words. Half the members of each group were informed that they would be asked to recall the words when the orienting task had been completed, whereas the other half were not so informed. The authors found that although recall scores differed depending on the type of orienting task the subjects were asked to do, no significant differences in recall were obtained between the intentional and incidental learning groups.

Can these differences be reconciled? Postman (1964) has concluded that intent per se is not a significant variable in learning, a conclusion accepted by most current investigators. Rather, differences in recall between intentional and incidental learners can be explained by the different kinds of cognitive activity or strategies adopted by each group while learning the material. For example, given a list of words to rate for frequency of usage and instructions to remember the words, the "intent to learn" subject may attempt to devise some story that incorporates each of the words on the list into a coherent whole. The subject not given instructions to remember would be unlikely to construct such a narrative. The difference in recall between the two subjects would reflect a difference in cognitive activity rather than a difference between incidental and intentional learning. It is possible, of course, that the incidental learner may engage in an activity that also contributes to subsequent recall. When such is the case, the incidental learner's recall performance on the learning task would be similar to that obtained by the intentional learning group. Thus, the nature of the orienting task plays an important role in determining the amount of learning that takes place with incidental learners. As a result, current experimenters have shifted their interest from an examination of the intentionality of the subject to examining the kind of cognitive activity or processing that is demanded by the orienting task.

## COGNITIVE VARIABLES

Early experimenters, working in the tradition of a strict behavioristic psychology, were reluctant to extend their search to include processes inside the organism's head and to posit such constructs as ideas, strategies, or plans which the experimental subject might adopt in a list-learning task. The early emphasis on stimulus or task variables, as reflected in the search for word attributes, was in keeping with this point of view.

But it became apparent that the divergent findings obtained in some studies could not be accounted for just by reference to the operation of stimulus or task variables. It seemed necessary to determine the nature of the experimental subject's strategies or covert activities in order to account for the results. Some investigators have considered the subject's plans or strategies as covert responses, thus preserving the stimulus-response framework; however, many experimenters today simply consider these concepts as cognitive variables, with terms such as stimulus selection, mediation, and organization being used to describe an organism's cognitive activity.

### Stimulus Selection

In Chapter 5's examination of discrimination learning it was noted that many investigators hypothesized that animals learning a discrimination task engaged in selective perception. The animal does not respond to all of the stimulus elements that make up the discriminanda; some elements are ignored, while others are used to cue the response.

A similar effect is observed in verbal learning tasks, but this process has been called **stimulus selection**. An excellent demonstration of the stimulus selection process can be found in one part of the paired-associate study by Underwood, Ham, and Ekstrand (1962). Each paired-associate item consisted of a trigram placed on a colored background, paired with a single digit that served as the response. The stimulus components can be seen in Table 9-6. Learning trials were provided until each subject reached a criterion of one perfect trial.

TABLE 9-6. Stimulus components used in the paired-associate task

| Trigrams | Colors |
| --- | --- |
| GWS | Red |
| DWK | Brown |
| NXQ | Yellow |
| DHX | Blue |
| BWD | Orange |
| GVS | Black |
| BXD | Green |

Ten transfer trials were then provided in order to determine what stimulus element the subjects had used in their learning trials to cue their responses. For one transfer group, only the background colors were presented as stimuli; whereas for a second group, the trigrams were presented without their distinctive background colors. A control group was used in which the transfer task involved presenting each trigram with its appropriately colored background. Figure 9-7, which indicates acquisition curves for the three experimental groups, clearly reveals the operation of the stimulus selection process. When the colors were presented alone, virtually complete transfer resulted, but when the trigrams were presented, there was a marked decline in performance. Quite obviously, most subjects had selected the background colors as the stimuli to cue their responses.

### Mediation

A second cognitive process is **mediation**, a concept used by early associationists. They assumed that an association between two noncontiguous events took place only because of the role of a mediator. Thus, an association between events A and C could be established by associating A with B and B with C, with event B serving to mediate the A-C association. For example, a subject learning to associate the stimulus word *dog* with the response *nine* might use the word *cat* as a mediator. When *dog* was presented, the subject would think *cat*, which in turn would elicit *nine*. Since there were previous associations between *dog* and *cat* and *cat* and *nine*, the learn-

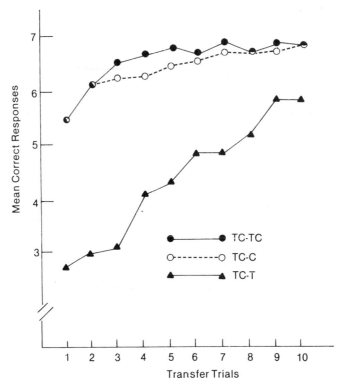

FIGURE 9-7.   Acquisition curves on the ten transfer trials. Adapted from B. J. Underwood, M. Ham, and B. R. Ekstrand, "Cue selection in paired-associate learning." *Journal of Experimental Psychology*, 1962, 64, 405–409. Copyright © 1962 by the American Psychological Association. Reprinted by permission.

ing of the *dog–nine* association should take place quite rapidly.

Underwood and Schulz (1960) have examined mediation in paired-associate learning. These experimenters asked their subjects how they went about associating specific stimulus and response pairs. They found that almost 75 percent of such associations were reported to have been acquired by means of a mediated association. Moreover, these investigators found that learning took place more rapidly for those pairs of items for which their subjects had reported the use of mediators, in contrast to those pairs of items for which mediators were not required.

A study by Wood and Bolt (1968) has demonstrated the facilitative effect of mediators. In their experiment, subjects learned a paired-associate task in which the stimuli were single letters and the responses were high-frequency words. An experimental group of subjects were told that they would be given a mediator in order to help them associate each letter with its appropriate response. The mediator was written out and placed in parentheses between the stimulus and the response on each of the study trials. Each mediating response started with the same letter as the stimulus and was a strong associate of the response. For example, the stimulus-response pairs T-chair, K-queen, and M-lamb had the mediating responses *table*, *king*, and *mutton*, with the presentation of the paired associates appearing as: T(table)–chair; K(king)–queen; M(mutton)–lamb. A control group was not provided with mediators. Subjects received

TABLE 9-7. Mean number of correct responses

| | Trials | | | |
|---|---|---|---|---|
| | 1 | 2 | 3 | 4 |
| Control | 3.25 | 6.25 | 8.42 | 10.17 |
| Experimental (mediating) | 5.92 | 9.50 | 12.08 | 13.17 |

Adapted from data by Wood and Bolt (1968).

four alternating study and test trials. The test trials consisted of presenting only the stimulus letters, with the subject required to call out the appropriate response. Table 9-7, which presents recall scores for the experimental and control groups for the four test trials, clearly indicates the facilitative effect of the use of mediators.

Most frequently, subjects make up their own mediators. When this is done, they are called **natural language mediators** (NLM). The facilitative effect of natural language mediators has been demonstrated in a study conducted by Adams, McIntyre, and Thorsheim (1969). In this study, subjects learned a list of 10 paired associates. After each pair had been presented, the subjects were asked to report the mediator they had used to associate the items. If they did not use any, they were to report "Rote." Eight trials were provided. The percentage of correct responses for mediated and rote responses is shown in Figure 9-8. Obviously, the use of natural language mediators facilitated the learning process.

**Organized Mediation—Mnemonics** A formal, well-organized system of mediators is an example of a mnemonic, a technique or strategy used by individuals as a memory aid. Their operation can be seen in the stage performances of professional mnemonists who demonstrate extraordinary acts of memory. These performers can go through a deck of cards, pausing only long enough to see each one briefly, and then name the cards in the precise order in which they were presented. Or they can meet 100 people, associate each face with a different name, and shortly thereafter proceed to correctly identify each person

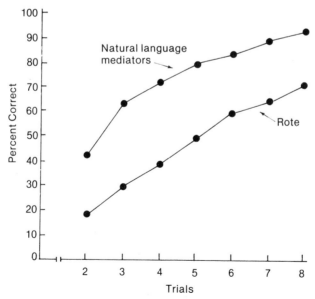

FIGURE 9-8. A comparison of mediated and rote verbal learning. Adapted from J. A. Adams, J. S. McIntyre, and H. I. Thorsheim, "Natural language mediation and interitem interference in paired-associate learning." *Psychonomic Science*, 1969, 16, 63–64. Reprinted by permission of the Psychonomic Society.

in the group. The secret of their success is in the use of an elaborate mnemonic system.

Yates (1966) traced the history of these techniques and found that they were invented by the ancient Greeks. In an age before printing, mnemonics were invaluable aids for orators who had to talk for hours without recourse to notes. Even today, many people still use these techniques. We remember the number of days in each month by recalling the familiar "Thirty days hath Septembe . . . ," or we remember the notes on the line of the treble clef by reciting "Every good boy does fine" (EGBDF). More elaborate systems have been provided, for instance, in the best seller *Memory Book* by Lorayne and Lucas (1974).

The foundation for any mnemonic system is the learning of a sequential series of words that may be visualized and firmly fixed in the individual's memory. Once these images have been established, new items to be remembered are associated with each of the original images. When it becomes necessary to recall these new items, the previously visualized items are recalled as cues for those items that were more recently acquired.

One technique, mentioned earlier in this book, is the method of loci. Here the sequential series of items are familiar geographic locations that permit the individual to figuratively "walk" from one place to another in a fixed order. In learning a list of words, for example, a learner would associate each word with a different location. The individual then "walks" through the varying places in order to recall the word associated with each location.

A second technique has been described as the "peg-word" system. It is illustrated by the following rhyme: "One is a bun, two is a shoe, three is a tree, four is a door, five is a hive, six are sticks, seven is heaven, eight is a gate, nine is a line, and ten is a hen." More elaborate peg-word systems have been devised in which the peg-words have been associated with the first 100 digits. The general procedure is similar to that employed with the method of loci. Each word on a list of words to be remembered is associated with a peg-word. When the words must be recalled, the well-learned peg-words serve as cues for the list words.

The study of mnemonics was disdained by early psychologists. In fact, as recently as 1960, Miller, Galanter, and Pribram (1960) wrote that experimental psychologists believed that mnemonic devices were immoral tricks suitable only for stage magicians. But as Hoffman and Senter's (1978) review of mnemonic techniques has indicated, experimental interest in mnemonics began in the mid to late 1960s with the studies of Bugelski, Kidd, and Segmen (1968), Bugelski (1968), and Ross and Lawrence (1968), all demonstrating the superiority of recall when mnemonic techniques were used.

In an extensive study by Bugelski (1968), experimental subjects learned the rhyme presented earlier ("one is a bun," etc.) and were then given six different paired-associate lists to learn. Each list had the same stimulus numbers, 1 through 10, while the responses were 10 concrete nouns. Different nouns were used with each list. Subjects were instructed to learn each list by forming a visual image linking each noun to the peg-word associated with each number. Control subjects were not taught the rhyme, nor were they told anything about using images to help them learn the list of words. All subjects studied the first list and were then given an immediate recall test. The second list was then studied and followed by an immediate recall test, and so on until all six lists had been learned and recalled. A final recall test was provided in which the subjects were asked to provide the words from all lists associated with "number 1," all "number 2 words," etc. The results of Bugelski's (1968) study are in Figure 9-9. Recall performance for the experimental group on the six lists was statistically superior to that for the control; on the final recall test, the number of words correctly recalled by the experimental group was almost twice that of the control.

Ross and Lawrence (1968) have reported similar findings using the method of loci. In one experiment (Study 2), subjects learned 52 sequential locations following a walk through the grounds of a university campus. Subjects were then required to learn a list of 40 words on each of four consecutive days, with the words on each list being presented only once.

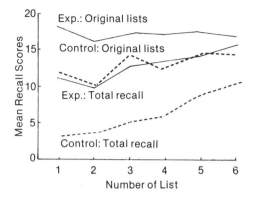

FIGURE 9-9. Learning scores for original learning of each of the six lists and total recall scores for experimental and control groups. Adapted from B. R. Bugelski, "Images as mediators in one-trial paired-associate learning. II. Self-timing in successive lists." *Journal of Experimental Psychology*, 1968, 77, 328–334. Copyright © 1968 by the American Psychological Association. Reprinted by permission.

With each trial, each word was to be associated with a specific location. At the beginning of the second, third, and fourth sessions, subject were asked to recall the words from the previous day's list before learning a new list. Results indicated that the mean number of words recalled for the four sessions ranged from 35.8 to 38.4. The 24 hour delay in recall produced some decrement, with the mean number of words recalled for each of the four sessions ranging from 30.2 to 38.4 words. Although the experiment lacked a control group, these recall scores are considerably higher than those obtained by subjects participating in similar experiments who did not use mnemonic techniques.

**Visual Imagery in the Mnemonic System**
The importance of using visual imagery in the mnemonic system has been readily acknowledged. Professional mnemonists have added the "principle" that when the subject forms a visual image of the peg-word with the item to be learned, the resultant image should have the two items interacting and should be quite bizarre.

Wollen, Weber, and Lowry (1972) have experimentally examined the role of interaction and bizarreness. They found that interaction did indeed contribute to recall, but bizarreness did not. In their study, 18 high-imagery nouns were used to form 9 paired associates. For each pair, line drawings were made depicting the objects in four different ways: (1) noninteracting–bizarre; (2) interacting–bizarre; (3) interacting–nonbizarre; (4) noninteracting–nonbizarre. Below each drawing, the words corresponding to the objects were printed. An example of the piano–cigar pair is presented in Figure 9-10. These four different types of drawings were made into slides and presented to four experimental groups of subjects. A control group saw only the word pairs without the pictures. All subjects were given one study trial, two seconds long, followed by a test trial in which the stimulus word was presented along with instructions that the subject should recall the appropriate response. Results are presented in Table 9-8. Those subjects who had seen pictures with interaction recalled a significantly greater number of responses than those who saw pairs of pictures with no interaction. The bizarreness of the picture, however, did not enhance recall. An interesting finding was that the control group, which had been presented with only pairs of words without pictures, recalled a larger number of correct responses than either of the groups with noninteracting conditions. It is possible, as the authors suggest, that the presentation of noninteracting pictures inhibited subjects from using mediators, which in turn contributed to the poorer recall scores.

Senter and Hoffman (1976) were able to replicate Wollen, Weber, and Lowry's (1972) findings that interactiveness was an important variable in recall. But Webber and Marshall (1978) have shown that bizarreness can make a contribution when relatively long retention intervals are used. In their study, bizarreness did not result in superior retention when immediate recall was demanded; however, when a retention interval of seven days was utilized, the bizarreness of the picture did contribute to superior recall.

Noninteracting, nonbizarre

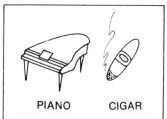

Noninteracting, bizarre

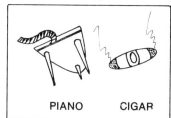

Interacting, nonbizarre

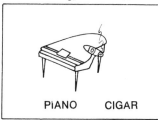

Interacting, bizarre

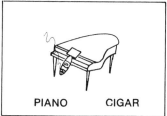

FIGURE 9-10. Adapted from K. A. Wollen, A. Weber, and D. H. Lowry, "Bizarreness versus interaction of mental images as determinants of learning." *Cognitive Psychology*, 1972, 3, 518–523. Reprinted by permission of the Academic Press.

TABLE 9-8. Mean number of correct responses for each condition

|  |  | Bizarreness | |
|---|---|---|---|
|  |  | Present | Absent |
| Interaction | Present | 6.67 | 6.60 |
|  | Absent | 3.05 | 3.50 |
|  | Control | 5.50 | |

Adapted from K. A. Wollen, A. Weber, and D. H. Lowry, "Bizarreness versus interaction of mental images as determinants of learning." *Cognitive Psychology*, 1972, 3, 518–523. Reprinted by permission of the Academic Press.

An interesting replication of the role of interaction on memory has been provided by Lutz and Lutz (1977) using brand names and their products. After using the Yellow Pages of a telephone directory to obtain the names of 48 companies and their products, the experimenters made up interactive and noninteractive pictures of each word pair to serve as the experimental material. Subjects looking at the interactive pictures were able to recall significantly more brand names than a group viewing the noninteractive pictures.

**A Case History of a Professional Mnemonist —Mr. S** Performers who exhibit unusual memories on stage usually employ extensive mnemonic systems that were developed through many hours of study. But from time to time, individuals have been found who have an apparently innate ability to remember extraordinary amounts of material. One such man, S, is described in *The Mind of a Mnemonist*, written by the Russian psychologist A. R. Luria (1968), who observed and tested S for almost 30 years. S was able to remember long lists of words, nonsense material, tables of numbers, mathematical formulas, etc., after only a single reading and for very long periods of time. See Box 9-2.

An unusual aspect of S's mental operations was that the remembering of material was generally accompanied by a marked degree of synesthesia, a condition in which a sensation obtained from one modality will elicit a sensation in another modality. Some synesthetic experience is found with most individuals. The hearing of a high tone, for example, may be accompanied by "seeing" bright red and yellow colors. But for S, the

An interesting example of how S was able to remember material is described by Luria (1968) in the following example. A "mathematical" formula that had no meaning was presented for study:

$$N \cdot \sqrt{d^2 \times \frac{85}{vx}} \cdot \sqrt{\frac{276^2 \cdot 86x}{n^2v \cdot \pi 264}} \; n^2b = sv \frac{1624}{32^2} \cdot r^2s$$

Luria reports that S examined the formula closely, lifting the paper up several times to get a closer look at it. Then he put it down, shut his eyes, and after seven minutes came through with an exact reproduction of the formula.

The following is an account of S's procedure in recalling the first part of the formula:

> Neiman (N) came out and jabbed at the ground with his cane (.). He looked up at a tall tree which resembled the square root sign ($\sqrt{\phantom{x}}$), and thought to himself: "No wonder the tree has withered and begun to expose its roots. After all, it was here when I built these two houses" ($d^2$). Once again he poked with his cane (.). Then he said: "The houses are old, I'll have to get rid of them ( $\times$ ); the sale will bring in far more money." He had originally invested 85,000 in them (85). Then I see the roof of the house detached (____), while down below on the street I see a man playing the Termenvox (vx). He's standing near a mailbox, and on the corner there's a large stone (.) which has been put there to keep carts from crashing up against the houses. (pp. 49–50)

Fifteen years later, S was still able to trace his pattern of recall in precise detail, even though he had been given no previous indication that he would be tested on this material.

▄▄▄▄▄▄▄▄▄▄▄▄▄▄▄▄▄▄▄▄▄▄▄▄▄▄▄▄▄▄▄▄▄▄▄▄▄▄▄▄▄▄▄▄▄▄▄▄▄▄▄▄▄▄▄▄▄▄▄▄▄▄▄▄▄▄▄▄▄▄▄▄▄▄

synesthetic response was much more elaborate. If he was asked to listen to a 30 Hz tone, he reported that at first he saw a strip 12–15 cm wide in the color of old tarnished silver. Gradually, this strip narrowed and was converted into an object that glistened like steel. The presentation of a 50 Hz tone, on the other hand, resulted in S "seeing" a brown strip against a dark background that had red tongue-like edges. Accompanying this tone was a sense of a taste like that of sweet and sour borscht, a sensation he described as gripping his entire tongue.

These added sensory components seemed to play an important role in S's recall, since he reported that he recognized words not only by the images they evoked but by the whole complex of sensations that were present. S reports:

> usually I experience a word's taste and weight, and I don't have to make an effort to remember it—the word seems to recall itself.

But it's difficult to describe. What I sense is something oily slipping through my hand . . . or I'm aware of a slight tickling in my left hand caused by a mass of tiny, lightweight points. When that happens I simply remember, without having to make the attempt. (p. 28)

In spite of his unusual ability to remember verbal materials, S had a poor memory for faces because he said that they were so changeable. Unlike most individuals, who tend to single out certain features by which to remember faces, S saw faces as changing patterns of light and shade, which varied as the individual's face changed with his or her mood. S also had difficulty grasping entire passages of prose, since each word would call up a different image, and working out some order for these images was frequently a difficult and exhausting job. Moreover, if the material was read to him at a fairly rapid pace, the images would collide, with the result that his face would register confusion and finally utter bewilderment.[3]

## Organization

The last cognitive variable to be discussed in this chapter is **organization**, a construct that refers to the tendency on the part of the individual to integrate or arrange the stimulus material so as to provide the material with greater coherence, unity, and/or understanding.

**Chunking**  In a paper describing one such organizational process, **chunking**, Miller (1956) posited that an individual's immediate memory span was quite limited and could hold only about seven items. But the memory span could be increased or expanded, Miller pointed out, not by increasing the number of items that could be retained but by increasing the size of the unit. By organizing the material and combining smaller units into larger ones or chunks, as Miller termed them, an individual could retain larger and larger amounts of material.

An example that Miller used to illustrate the chunking operation involved an individual just beginning to learn telegraphic code. At first, the telegrapher hears each dit and dah as a separate chunk. Soon, he is able to organize these sounds into letters so that he deals with letters as chunks; after some practice, the letters are organized into words that represent larger chunks. Finally, the telegrapher begins to hear whole phrases. Larger and larger chunks thus emerge as the telegrapher learns the code. Some investigators consider this process of chunking, in which items are combined or organized to form still larger units, to be a basic cognitive process operating in many learning tasks.

In verbal learning tasks, Bower (1969) considered a chunk of verbal material to be a highly integrated or coherent group of words, indexed by a strong tendency of the subject to recall the words together as a unit. Miller's chunking hypothesis would predict that the number of chunks and not the number of words would be critical in a free-recall task. In a study by Bower (1969) examining this hypothesis, subjects were provided one trial in which they were presented and asked to recall (a) 12 unrelated nouns, presented singly, such as flag, sun, couch; (b) 12 triplets—combinations of 3 unrelated nouns, such as baby, cabin, fur; and (c) 12 familiar clichés of 3 words, such as ball point pen, mail order catalogue, Rose bowl parade. Results were in keeping with the chunking hypothesis; there was no difference in the number recalled between the singly presented nouns and the 3 word clichés, which were always remembered as a unit. The number of triplets recalled, however, was significantly lower. Bower (1969) has concluded, "In almost every aspect, pre-established word groups (clichés) behave like single words in recall. . . . Recall limits are expressible in chunks, not words" (pp. 612–613).

**Clustering**  A second organizational process, somewhat related to chunking and observed in free-recall tasks, is **clustering**. In a study by Bousfield (1953) in which clustering was first noted, subjects were first presented with a randomized list of 60 words consisting of 15 items obtained from each of four different categories—namely, animals, vegetables, names, and professions. Immediately following the presentation of items, subjects were given 10 minutes to write down all of the words they could recall. Bousfield found that the subject revealed a greater than chance tendency to place items in clusters or groups that contained members of the same category. Thus, a subject's written recall might be dog, cat, cow, bean, pea, John, Bob, Joe, doctor, dentist, etc. Since the varying words forming a cluster can be described in terms of their membership in a general class or category, the name **category clustering** has been given to this type of organizational activity.

The phenomenon of clustering has been extensively studied, with many more conditions than can be presented in this introduction. Two examples, however, will illustrate the general nature of these studies. Mathews (1954) and Tulving and Pearlstone (1966) examined clustering as a function of the number of categories that comprised the word list. These experimenters found that as the number of categories increased, at least up to six, recall also increased. The kind of categories used was a second topic of interest. Bousfield and Wicklund (1969) and Fagan (1969) have found that when subjects are presented with sets of words that rhyme, such as dead, led, wed, head, they will tend to group them in their recall protocols, thus revealing **acoustical clustering**. Similarly, Freund and Underwood (1969) have reported that subjects will cluster their recall if alphabetical categories—sets of words all beginning with the same letter—are employed. But not all experimenter-identified categories have resulted in clustering, as Cofer and Bruce (1965) found when using clusters of words based on grammatical form class, such as nouns, verbs, and adjectives. In this study, subjects did not cluster these sets of words any more than would have been expected by chance.

**Subjective Organization**   In clustering experiments, the organization of the subjects' recall protocols is related to the categories of items provided by the experimenter. The material in most learning tasks, however, is not so organized; in fact, the experimenter attempts to use words that are quite unrelated. Nonetheless, as noted in the examination of natural language mediators (NLM), subjects will frequently attempt to generate some natural or subjective kind of organization for the material they are asked to learn.

Tulving (1962) has found evidence of this type of organization in his examination of free recall learning. His experimental procedure consisted of selecting 16 unrelated words and arranging them in 16 different trial orders so that each word appeared just once in each position. Sixteen trials were provided, with the words presented at intervals of 1 second. Following each trial, the subjects were given 90 seconds to write down in any order as many words from the list as they could remember.

In Tulving's analysis, a subject's subjective organization (SO) score was a measure of

the actual organization obtained compared to the maximum that could be achieved. Maximum organization was indicated by a score of 1.00, a value obtained by a subject who recalled all of the words on all trials in the same order. In contrast, a score of 0 would be obtained if the subject recalled each word in a different position on each trial. As can be noted from Figure 9-11, subjective organization, as indicated by the subject recalling words in the same order, increased over successive blocks of trials. Tulving's (1962) study demonstrates that subjects do organize their recall sequentially, even in the absence of any kind of organization that is provided by the list itself.

Many other studies have investigated the contribution of varying types of organization, or what some investigators have described as **retrieval schemes**. When an experimenter describes the organizational principle of an experiment to the subject, or when the subject discovers it, recall is enhanced. But even in cases where no obvious organizational scheme exists, subjects almost invariably provide their own in order to aid recall.

## SUMMARY

Traditional investigators, following the lead of Ebbinghaus, have examined the verbal learning process using list-learning tasks, with nonsense syllables (CVCs) or words serving as the material to be learned. The list-learning tasks can be described as: (1) serial learning, (2) free recall, (3) paired associates, and (4) verbal discrimination. The response measures used to infer the learning process have been (a) relearning or savings, (b) recall, and (c) recognition, with this last measure also being called recognition-discrimination, since experimenters have typically required the subject to recognize (discriminate) the correct response from several distractors. Some experimenters were interested in comparing recall and recognition-discrimination measures in an effort to determine which measure is more sensitive. It is now apparent that any measure of recognition-discrimination is related to the

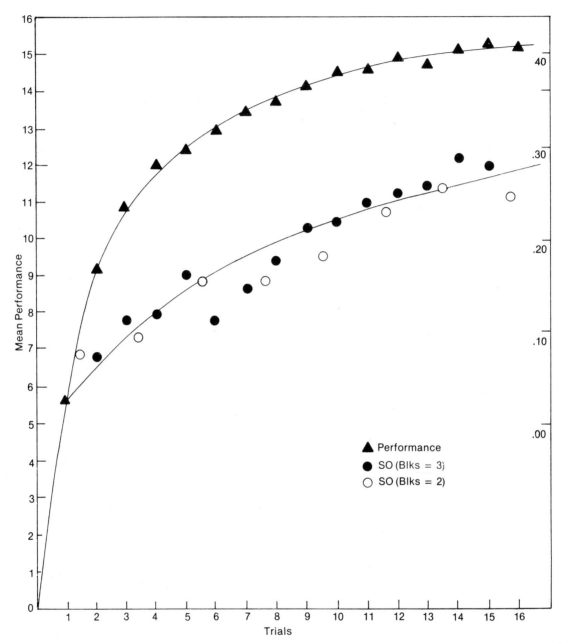

FIGURE 9-11. Mean performance (upper curve) and mean subjective organization (SO) (lower curve) as a function of trials. (Values of performance are to be read from the left ordinate, SO from the right ordinate.) Adapted from E. Tulving, "Subjective organization in free recall of 'unrelated' words." *Psychological Review*, 1962, 69, 344–354. Copyright © 1962 by the American Psychological Association. Reprinted by permission.

kinds of distractors used. Thus, any particular experimental finding indicating the superiority of one of these measures is specific to the experimental conditions used; any general conclusion is obviously inappropriate.

For some time, traditional investigators were primarily concerned with how list learning was influenced by stimulus or task variables; more recently there has been interest in the contribution of motivational and cognitive variables to list learning.

Most interest in task variables centered around (a) the characteristics of the material to be learned, (b) the position of the stimulus item in the list, and (c) the isolation of items in the list. Ebbinghaus assumed that nonsense syllables were homogeneous in their ability to elicit associations, and thus equally difficult to learn. Some years later, Glaze (1928) demonstrated that this was not the case. Glaze examined more than 2000 syllables and found large differences in their capacities to evoke associative responses. The association values that he established for the syllables have been used by learning psychologists for a very long time.

Investigators after Glaze became interested in determining how words differed along a variety of dimensions. Meaningfulness or association value, familiarity, pronounceableness, imagery, vividness, and pleasantness were some of the attributes studied, although all of these attributes may not be totally different from one another. Some evidence suggests that only three truly different or unique attributes have been identified: meaningfulness, imagery, and pleasantness.

Most experimenters have found that these attributes relate to the ease with which list-learning tasks are acquired. Thus, as the items in the list become more meaningful, easier to pronounce, or more vivid image-producers, the task becomes easier to learn.

A second task variable is stimulus position. When serial-learning and free-recall tasks are used, it is generally found that a bow-shaped curve describes the distribution of errors in the learning of these tasks. Most errors are found in the middle of the list, with fewer errors being found at the end positions.

A third task variable is an isolation effect. Items that appear to be isolated or different from the rest of the items on a list are more easily learned. For instance, if a single CVC is printed in red and placed among black CVCs, it will be learned more readily than if that CVC had the same color as all of the other CVCs on the list.

A general variable that has interested a few traditional investigators has been motivation. Although motivation has generated much experimental interest in the area of animal learning, the same has not been true for verbal learning. Most investigators believe that their human subjects are already so highly motivated that any attempt to increase their motivation would contribute little to influencing performance. One motivational topic has been the differences between incidental learning—learning without intent to learn—and intentional learning. The experimental evidence indicates that intent to learn has not been a significant variable in list-learning studies. When differences between incidental and intentional learning groups are found, they are generally attributed to the different types of cognitive activity engaged in by each group.

Traditional experimenters have only recently become interested in investigating cognitive variables, since there was a general reluctance on their part to examine variables that appeared to operate "inside the organism's head." Nonetheless, such an approach seemed necessary if a better understanding of the learning process was to be achieved. One cognitive variable that was posited was stimulus selection, a process whereby experimental subjects select and respond to only some of the stimulus elements that make up the discriminanda. The operation of the stimulus selection process has thus become an important consideration in any analysis of how learning takes place.

A second cognitive variable, mediation, refers to the subject's use of ideas, thoughts, or covert responses as aids in learning to associate one item with another. In the learning of paired associates, for example, most subjects use mediators in order to more readily associate one item with another. In some experiments, the subjects have been provided with already identified mediators. Experimental findings indicate that when mediators are used, list learning takes place more rapidly. Other experiments have shown that subjects provide their own mediators, which have been identified as natural language mediators (NLM). Professional mnemonists generally use an elaborate system of mediators in order to help them remember extraordinary amounts of material.

A third cognitive variable has been identified as an organizational process; it refers to the general tendency on the part of the subject to integrate or arrange the material to be learned in order to facilitate such learning. One specific organizational process is chunking—the subject organizes items into larger and larger units. It has been found, for example, that lists of three word clichés such as ball point pen, Rose bowl parade, and good old days are no more difficult to learn than lists of single unrelated words, and much easier to acquire than lists of three unrelated word units.

Another organizational process is clustering, the tendency on the part of the subject to group similar items together in recall, although the items were not originally presented in groups.

Finally, the last type of organizational process is subjective organization. In the absence of some type of experimenter-provided organization of the material, the experimental subjects will provide their own organization, just as they provide their own natural language mediators.

## NOTES

1. It is possible that experimenters have erred in assuming that subjects will invariably claim to recognize many more items than they actually do. Wallace (1978) has found that, in recognizing target words without distractors, his subjects provided a level of performance only slightly higher than that obtained when distractors were used.

2. Several exceptions can be noted. In an extensive series of studies, Taylor and Spence (1952) and their associates examined the contribution of anxiety on serial- and paired-associate learning tasks, whereas Walker (1958) and his associates investigated the role of arousal on paired-associate learning. Neither of these efforts has generated any continuing interest among current experimenters.

3. Hunt and Love (1972) report the case history of VP, who appears to have a memory capacity rivaling that of Luria's S. Hunt and Love have not had the opportunity to study VP for as long a period as Luria has studied S, so it is not possible to report VP's memor when retention intervals are measured in years. One interesting difference between VP and S is that with VP, visual imagery does not appear to play an important role in his memory ability.

# CHAPTER TEN

# Retention and Forgetting: The Traditional Approach

Traditional investigators have been interested not only in examining how learning takes place, but also in following the lead of Ebbinghaus to determine the course of retention and forgetting. Retention and forgetting represent two sides of the same coin, since material that has not been retained is forgotten. Nonetheless, these constructs have given rise to separate areas of investigation and can be considered to have separate identities.

In keeping with the traditional approach, experiments examining retention and forgetting have continued to use list-learning tasks, with the basic experimental material being CVCs and words. But there are also a few investigators working within the traditional position who have examined the retention and forgetting of connected discourse or prose.

## RETENTION

### The Length of the Retention Interval

For most experimenters, **retention** is the persistence of previously acquired material over time. A first step in studying retention has been to describe how the amount of material that is retained changes as varying time or retention intervals are placed between the original learning and the test for retention. In-

tuitively, one realizes that, at least for most material learned, as the length of the retention interval increases, the amount retained decreases.

The earliest experimental demonstration of this relationship was provided by Ebbinghaus (1913). In his study, lists of nonsense syllables (13 per list) were learned until a criterion of two errorless recitations was reached. Following an interval of either 1/3 of an hour, 1 hour, 9 hours, 1 day, 2 days, or 31 days, each list was relearned to the original learning criterion. Different lists were learned and retained for each of the retention intervals examined.

Figure 10-1 shows a retention curve in which Ebbinghaus's saving scores have been plotted as a function of the varying retention intervals. It may be noted that after a rather precipitous drop in performance for the retention intervals up to nine hours, the subsequent decline in performance was quite small over the remaining time periods.

Early investigators assumed that Ebbinghaus's findings indicated the general nature of retention (or forgetting). However, psychologists today know that the slope of any retention curve, like the slope of any learning curve, is related to the experimental materials and conditions. This is illustrated by the find-

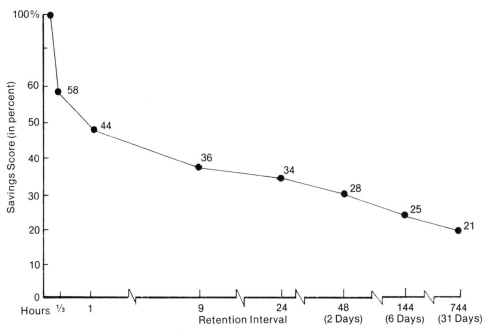

FIGURE 10-1.  Retention as a function of the amount of time elapsing between learning and the test for retention. Based on data from Ebbinghaus (1913).

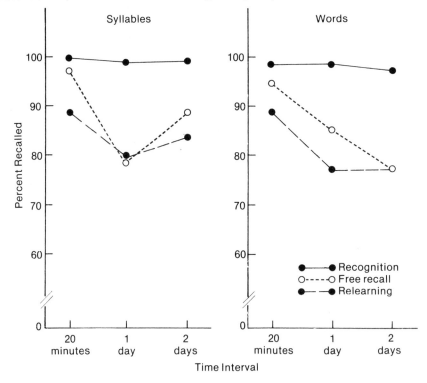

FIGURE 10-2.  Retention curves for nonsense syllables and words as a function of the method of measurement. Adapted from L. Postman and L. Rau, "Retention as a function of the method of measurement." *University of California Publications in Psychology,* 1957, 8, 217–270.

ings of Postman and Rau (1957), ~~who had their subjects learn lists (12 items each) of~~ CVCs and words to a criterion of one perfect recitation, with retention of this material measured either 20 minutes, 24 hours, or 48 hours later. Figure 10-2 presents retention curves using recognition, free-recall, and relearning measures as a function of the kind of experimental material utilized.

It is readily apparent that different curve slopes were obtained by these experimenters as a function of the kind of experimental material used and how retention was measured. But contrary to the conclusions arrived at by some experimenters, no general statement can be made about the sensitivity of the varying retention measures that Postman and Rau (1957) employed. As mentioned in Chapter 9,

---

**BOX 10-1**

If you read material to your infant son or daughter, would you expect to find any retention of that material 5, 10, or 15 years later? We would not expect to discover any remembering, but such a result is possible, according the findings obtained in a study by Burtt (1932, 1937, 1941). The materials he used consisted of varying selections from Sophocles' *Oedipus Tyrannus* in the original Greek, with each selection consisting of approximately 20 lines or about 240 syllables. When his son Benjamin was 15 months of age, Burtt read to him 3 of these selections once daily for a period of three months—a total of 90 repetitions of each passage. These selections were then replaced with 3 other passages that were read to him each day for the next three months. This procedure of reading 3 selections/day for a three month period, followed by a different set of selections, etc., was continued until the child was 3 years old, and 21 different selections had been presented. At this point the readings were discontinued.

When Benjamin was 8½ years old, 7 selections, one from each three month period, were selected and, along with 3 new selections, were used to measure retention using a relearning method. Another one-third of the original passages plus 3 control passages were used to measure retention when the subject was 14 years old, and finally the remaining one-third of the selections plus 3 control passages were used to measure retention when Benjamin was 18½ years old. Each retention period consisted of first reading all 10 passages—seven old and three new—for 18 trials. (The reading of all 10 passages constituted one trial.) Beginning with the nineteenth trial, every third trial employed a prompting method in which the experimenter read each section slowly, with the subject attempting to anticipate the next syllable in the passage. The number of trials required by the subject to recite the entire selection verbatim and without prompting served as the measure of retention.

Burtt's findings were as follows: at age 8½ years, Benjamin required a mean of 317 trials to recite the previously presented selections of material, whereas for control materials he required a mean of 435 trials. At 14 years of age, the mean was 149 trials for the previously presented material and 162 trials for the new material. At age 18½ years, the mean number of trials for relearning and learning the experimental and control passages was 189 and 191 respectively. It may then be noted that a savings score of 27 percent was obtained when the retention interval was over 5 years in length. Savings declined to just 8 percent when the retention interval approximated 10 years. Finally, a retention interval of about 15 years resulted in no savings, and Burtt (1941) concluded that the last retention interval was "sufficient to eradicate completely any trace of the original stimulation in infancy" (p. 437).

comparisons between different response measures are tenuous at best, since performance level must be always related to the specific experimental conditions employed. There is little doubt that Postman and Rau's (1957) recognition measure could have been changed by using different types of distractors.

The retention intervals examined by most investigators have been quite short. Although a general interest has been expressed in determining the course of retention over longer intervals of time, such as years, few investigators have conducted such experiments because of the problem of subject availability. Rarely are the subjects who originally learned the experimental material available to be tested for retention years later. A study by Burtt (1941) represents an exception. See Box 10-1.

### Current Long-Term Retention Studies—the Cross-Sectional Approach

Long-term retention studies are difficult to conduct because of the difficulty of keeping subjects available for very long retention intervals. The recent studies of Squire and Slater (1975) and Bahrick, Bahrick, and Wittlinger (1975) are noteworthy because these experimenters have solved the problem of subject availability by using a cross-sectional approach. This procedure employs only a single retention test which is given at approximately the same time to all subjects. Variations in the time that the material was originally learned, however, provide different retention intervals.

In one part of the Squire and Slater (1975) study, the materials to be recalled were television programs presented between 1957 and 1972. The "amount of original learning" was controlled by using those shows that had been on the air for only a single season. In addition, Neilson ratings indicated equivalent audience popularity. Experimental subjects were 17 adults and 16 high school students (17 years old), with the retention test consisting of recognition-discrimination items. Following is an example of the type of test used:

*Year 1962:* Which of the following was a TV show?
(a) Bloody Noon (b) Latest Thing
(c) Fair Exchange (d) Red River Road

(Answer: Fair Exchange)

Figure 10-3 provides the retention curves for the two groups of subjects as a function of the year that the TV show was presented. Typical decremental performance curves were obtained for both groups of subjects. High school students recognized 1967–72 shows slightly better than adults, but for programs appearing before 1965–66, the students per-

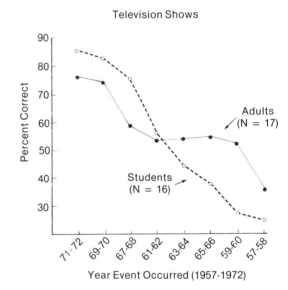

FIGURE 10-3.   Recognition of the names of television programs that aired for only one season between 1957 and 1972. Adult subjects (aged 26–71 yr, *M* = 51 yr) were compared with high school students (aged 17 yr). Adapted from L. R. Squire and P. C. Slater, "Forgetting in very long-term memory as assessed by an improved questionnaire technique." *Journal of Experimental Psychology: Human Learning and Memory*, 1975, 1, 50–54. Copyright © 1975 by the American Psychological Association. Reprinted by permission.

formed more poorly than the adults. This general finding is reasonable, since the students were all younger than 9 years of age when these early programs were presented and it is likely that they never saw some of them.

These findings, combined with those of the second part of the study which measured the subject's recall of horses that had won important races, have demonstrated the value and usefulness of the cross-sectional approach in the study of retention.

Bahrick, Bahrick, and Wittlinger's (1975) study was much more extensive than Squire and Slater's (1975) study and can serve as a model for experimenters desiring to use the cross-sectional approach. Almost 400 subjects, ranging in age from 17 to 74, were used, with the data collection period extending over a period of 40 months. Retention of the names and faces of classmates with whom the experimental subjects graduated was examined, with graduation yearbooks serving as the source material. The retention interval was measured from the time a subject graduated from high school until the retention tests were administered. Nine retention intervals were examined: 1/3, 3/4, 2, 4, 8, 15, 26, 34, and 48 years. (All retention intervals have been rounded to the closest year.)

In order to use the cross-sectional procedure, the experimenters had to solve a number of problems. For example, the pictures to be used differed depending on when they were taken, and so had to be made homogeneous with respect to size, hairstyle, etc. And inasmuch as the graduating classes differed in size, appropriate sampling procedures of the experimental materials had to be devised.

Six retention tests were administered, but since no useful purpose would be served by describing all of them, we shall mention just three. (1) Free recall—subjects were asked to list all of the names that they could remember (both first and last) of members of their graduating class. (2) Picture recognition—subjects had to recognize the face of a graduating class member placed among four distractors. Ten such items comprised the test. (3) Name recognition—the subject had to recognize the name of a graduating class member placed among four distractors. Ten such items comprised the test.

Figure 10-4 presents retention curves for the free recall of names and for recognition of

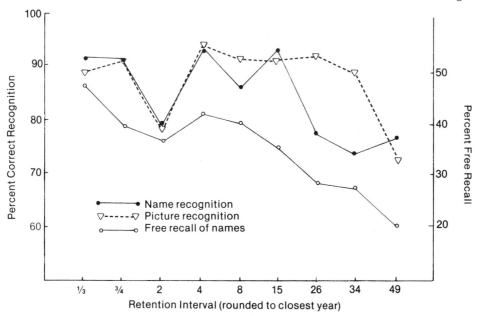

FIGURE 10-4.   Retention curves for name recognition, picture recognition, and free recall of names. Adapted from data provided by Bahrick, Bahrick, and Wittlinger (1975).

names and faces. It is remarkable that recognition for faces remains quite high over a very long period of time. Although name recognition is poorer, it is still substantial. It is only when the retention interval is lengthened beyond 30 years or so that recognition memory appears to decline. On the other hand, free recall of names systematically declines over the retention interval, a finding that is in keeping with the results of other free-recall studies.

From a methodological point of view, the cross-sectional approach does not provide the control of extraneous variables that can be provided by laboratory investigations of memory. For example, as Bahrick, Bahrick, and Wittlinger (1975) have acknowledged, laboratory control over the conditions of original learning is sacrificed. But the cross-sectional method does permit investigations of retention that cannot be adequately or conveniently conducted in the confines of the laboratory. This approach is not a substitute for laboratory investigations of retention but is an addition that investigators will surely find valuable in the future. See Box 10-2.

---

**BOX 10-2**

Can retention performance *increase* over time? In view of the preponderance of studies that find performance to decline as a function of the length of the retention interval, the results of a series of experiments conducted by Erdelyi and his associates, which indicate a performance *increment* over the retention interval, are most puzzling. This phenomenon of increasing retention performance has been termed **hypermnesia.**

In one study demonstrating this effect, Erdelyi and Kleinbard (1978) presented 60 slides containing either (a) simply sketched pictures of objects, such as a fish or phone, or (b) names of these same objects to two groups of subjects at the rate of one slide/five seconds. After the slides had been presented, subjects were given seven minutes to recall as many of the items as they could. Following this recall period, subjects were requested to relax and think about the items for seven minutes, following which another seven minute recall period was provided. This was followed by a third seven minute relaxation/seven minute recall period. Subjects were then given 37 recall sheets, each containing space for 60 items, with instructions to attempt to recall the experimental items three or more times each day so as to provide 37 additional recall protocols. These recall periods were conducted outside the laboratory, but subjects were asked to scrupulously limit them to seven minutes. (It should be pointed out that the individuals who comprised the experimental subjects were acquaintances of the experimenter and judged to be highly reliable and honest.) About a week later, when the subjects returned to the laboratory to hand in the completed recall forms, three more recall sessions were provided, interspersed with "relax and think" intervals. All subjects were required to write the names of 60 nonrepeating items on all recall sheets, guessing if necessary in order to complete the protocol.

The figure opposite presents the retention curves of the picture and word groups across some 164 hours. It may be observed that the recall of pictures systematically increased over time, increasing from 26.7 items on the first recall trial to 38.3 items some 164 hours later, an increase of 44 percent. There was no recall growth beyond the first take-home recall trial for words, although there is some indication of recall increasing within the first 10 hour period.

**cont**

cont

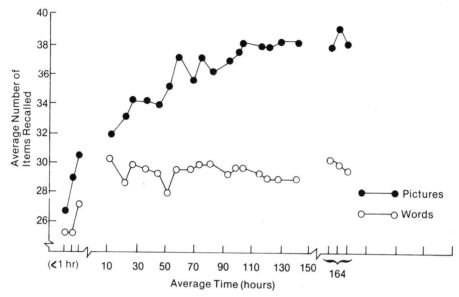

BOX FIGURE 10-1.   Average "forgetting" curves for picture and word lists. Adapted from M. H. Erdelyi and J. Kleinbard, "Has Ebbinghaus decayed with time? The growth of recall (Hypermnesia) over days." *Journal of Experimental Psychology: Human Learning and Memory*, 1978, 4, 275–289. Copyright © 1978 by the American Psychological Association. Reprinted by permission.

The authors see no contradiction between their findings and the results of Ebbinghaus and traditional investigators, since they have viewed Ebbinghaus's findings as being "based on very special procedures and very artificial stimuli." Rather, the authors "suggest that retention over time is a fan-shaped family of curves which, depending on a variety of factors, may increase, decrease, or remain the same" (p. 286).

But contrary to these statements, retention experiments utilizing pictures, faces, and meaningful material have been conducted, all with the same general finding—performance declines as the retention interval increases. Erdelyi and Kleinbard's (1978) results are most provocative and suggest the necessity of conducting additional studies to confirm their findings as well as to delineate the specific conditions that contribute to increased recall over time.

## Variables Contributing to Retention

An examination of retention curves reveals a decline in performance as the retention interval increases. The slope of the curve or the nature of the decrement depends on the kind of material to be remembered as well as the type of performance measure used. But in addition to these factors, investigators have been interested in how certain experimental conditions can influence retention. Although all of the variables that have been examined cannot be discussed, we will examine the three that have been generally regarded as most significant.

**Strength of the Original Learning** One would expect to find that the amount of retention is related to how well the material was originally learned, and the experimental evidence supports this expectation. An early study demonstrating this effect was conducted by Underwood (1954), who had subjects learn a serial list of 14 CVCs to a criterion of either 7 or 13 correct responses on a single trial. In a second study, subjects learned a paired-associate list of adjectives (10 pairs) to a criterion of either 5 or 10 correct responses on a single trial. Retention scores obtained 24 hours later revealed that those groups that learned the list to the more rigorous criteria recalled the greater number of items.

What has not been recognized as frequently, however, is that continued practice beyond the criterion of one perfect trial will have an effect on subsequent retention. Such continued practice past the point of complete mastery has been defined as **overlearning.** The classic overlearning study was performed by Krueger (1929) more than fifty years ago. Lists of nouns (12 nouns/list) were learned by subjects to either (1) a criterion of one perfect trial, (2) a criterion of one perfect trial plus 50 percent additional (overlearning) trials, or (3) a criterion of one perfect trial plus 100 percent additional (overlearning) trials. The lists were then relearned 1, 2, 4, 7, 14, or 28 days later, with the first trial providing a recall score. Table 10-1 indicates these recall scores obtained as a function of the degree of learning and the retention interval. It may be observed that overlearning trials significantly aided retention, although the increase in recall scores

was less when overlearning trials were increased from 50 to 100 percent than when they were increased from 0 to 50 percent.

The overlearning effect would appear to have considerable practical value, since continued practice on material already learned to a point of mastery can take place with a minimum of effort and yet will prevent significant losses in retention. Few investigators have attempted to replicate Krueger's results or extend his findings to other types of material or different tasks. A study by Postman (1962b) is an exception. In his study, high- and low-frequency nouns were used to construct two serial lists (12 items/list) which subjects learned by the anticipation method. Following Krueger's procedure, groups of subjects learned these lists to a criterion of one perfect trial (0 percent overlearning), or 50 or 100 percent overlearning. Seven days after the original learning had taken place, groups relearned the original list to a criterion of one perfect trial.

Postman, like Krueger, found that overlearning significantly influenced retention of both types of materials as measured by the mean number of trials required to relearn the material. For the high-frequency words, the mean number of trials to relearn the list was, respectively, 6.12, 4.69, and 3.69 after 0, 50, and 100 percent overlearning trials. The corresponding mean number of trials required to relearn the low-frequency list words was 7.31, 5.44, and 3.75. Postman's findings, which confirm Krueger's results, point to the value of practicing beyond the point of complete mastery in order to increase retention.

TABLE 10-1. Recall scores as a function of degree of learning and retention interval

| Retention Interval (days) | Mean Words Recalled Degree of Learning | | |
|---|---|---|---|
| | 0% | 50% | 100% |
| 1 | 3.10 | 4.60 | 5.83 |
| 2 | 1.80 | 3.60 | 4.65 |
| 4 | .50 | 2.05 | 3.30 |
| 7 | .20 | 1.30 | 1.65 |
| 14 | .15 | .65 | .90 |
| 28 | .00 | .25 | .40 |

Adapted from Krueger (1929).

**The Role of Contextual Stimuli**   Material is always learned and remembered within an environmental context. A list of words or CVCs to be learned is only a part of the experimental environment. The time of day, the kind of equipment, the nature of the laboratory room, the characteristics of the experimenter, and the method of presentation all provide a context or background for the specific material that is to be learned and/or recalled.

Many investigators have demonstrated that retention is maximized when the environment or context during recall is the same as it was during learning. Thus, the reinstatement of the learning environment at recall produces optimal performance.

A study by Smith, Glenberg, and Bjork (1978) illustrates this type of experiment. In one experiment (Experiment 2), subjects learned two lists of paired associates. List 1 was learned on Day 1 in one environment (Location A), while List 2 was learned the next day in a different environment (Location B). Location A was a small windowless room, containing a large blackboard and glass cabinets and located in an old building off the main campus. Here, the list of paired associates was presented using a slide projector. Location B was a small room containing windows and a mirror and located in a large modern central campus building; the experimental material was presented with a tape recorder. On Day 3, subjects were asked to recall words from both lists; however, some subjects recalled these items in Location A, the others in Location B. Results indicated that more words were recalled from List 1 than from List 2 when recall took place in Location A (where List 1 words had been originally learned), whereas more words were recalled from List 2 than from List 1 when recall took place in Location B (where List 2 words had been originally learned). Godden and Baddeley (1975) have reported similar findings in their examination of changes in natural environments. See Box 10-3.

Investigators have provided several explanations for the effects of a changed context on retention. A performance explanation assumes that when subjects attempt to recall material in an unfamiliar context, they attend to their changed surroundings with anxiety or suspicion, which in turn depresses performance. A second explanation, based on associative relationships, assumes that an association is established between the material that is learned and the context in which such learning takes place. When the learning and recall contexts are the same, the subject is able to use those associations that had been established between the learned items and the location to aid in the recall of those items. The changed context does not make such associations available, thus depressing performance.

The results obtained from most investigators cannot be used to distinguish between these explanations, but a series of experiments by Smith (1979) does support the associative position. Smith found that when subjects were placed in a changed environment for the recall test but were asked to remember the characteristics of the room in which the original learning had taken place, or were shown slides of the original learning room, thus reinstating contextual associations, their performance was similar to that of subjects who learned and recalled the items in the same environment.

**State-Dependent Effects** The last variable to be discussed in the context of retention is state-dependent effects, which bear a striking similarity to context effects. Specifically, a state-dependent effect refers to the phenomenon whereby material that has been learned under the influence of one physiological or emotional state is best remembered when the subject is again in that same state. Anecdotes testifying to the existence of this phenomenon abound. Goodwin, Powell, Bremer, Hoine, and Stern (1969) have reported clinical evidence that alcoholics, when sober, were not able to find money or alcohol that they had hidden when they were drunk, but they did remember the hiding places when they were again intoxicated.

In an experiment designed to examine state-dependent effects produced by the ingestion of alcohol, Weingartner, Adefris, Eich, and Murphy (1976) had 11 female subjects participate in each of four experimental conditions: (a) learn and recall while sober; (b) learn and recall when intoxicated; (c) learn while sober, recall while intoxicated; (d) learn while intoxicated, recall when sober. The experimental lists were composed of high-and low-imagery words. Following a single presentation and immediate recall of the items, the

BOX 10-3

Most learning and retention experiments are conducted in unimaginative environmental locations, generally a college classroom or research cubicle. But the environmental settings of an experiment conducted by Godden and Baddeley (1975) examining context effects were a far cry from the college campus. In this study, members of a university diving club learned lists of 36 unrelated words on shore (dry environment) and also underwater (wet environment), and were then asked to recall these words either in the same environment in which the words were learned or in the other environment. In summary, the 16 students who participated performed under each of four experimental conditions: (1) learn dry, recall dry; (2) learn dry, recall wet; (3) learn wet, recall wet; and (4) learn wet, recall dry; with 24 hours separating each experimental session. The words in each list were auditorily presented twice, with 10 seconds between presentations. After the last word in the second presentation had been given, subjects were asked to copy digits for 30 seconds. Four minutes later, remaining in either the same environment or having moved to the other, they were given 2 minutes to write down as many words as they could recall.

When subjects were in the dry environment, they sat by the edge of the water, with their masks tipped back, breathing tubes removed, listening to the words over their underwater-communication earphone. When in the wet environment, subjects dove to approximately 20 feet, taking with them a formica board on which the words could be written and two pencils. Heavy weighting enabled them to sit on the bottom of the open water site to participate in the experiment.

Results clearly revealed that superior recall took place when subjects learned and recalled the words in the same environment. See Box Table 10-1.

But could the decrease in performance be attributed to the disruption produced by a diver moving from a wet environment to dry, or vice versa? Such a possibility exists, and it was investigated in another experiment conducted by Godden and Baddeley. In their second study, in which the word lists and conditions were similar to the first, subjects were required to learn and recall in the dry environment. In one condition they rested between the learning and recall conditions, while in the second they first learned the words but were then asked to enter the water and dive to a depth of 20 feet before recalling them. Results indicated that this disruption had no effect on their subsequent recall.

BOX TABLE 10-1.    Recall of words by divers as a function of learning and recall environment

| Learning Environment | Recall Environment | | |
|---|---|---|---|
| | Dry | Wet | Total |
| Dry | 13.5 | 8.6 | 22.1 |
| Wet | 8.4 | 11.4 | 19.8 |
| Total | 21.9 | 20.0 | |

Adapted from D. R. Godden and A. D. Baddeley, "Context-dependent memory in two natural environments: On land and underwater." *British Journal of Psychology,* 1975, 66, 325–331.

subjects were asked to recall the words four hours later. Intoxication, as indicated by blood alcohol levels of .060–.095, was produced by having the subjects drink vodka and fruit juice a half-hour prior to the learning and/or recall of the word lists. State-dependent effects were obtained; the subjects recalled a significantly greater number of words when the learning and recall took place under the same condition—either sober or intoxicated—than when the learning took place under one condition and recall under the other. As might be anticipated, greater amounts of recall were found for high-imagery words than for low-imagery words. See Figure 10-5.

Bower, Monteiro, and Gilligan (1978) have obtained state-dependent effects by manipulating the emotionality of their subjects. Their general procedure was to use hypnosis to induce the emotional moods of happiness and sadness in subjects while they were learning and recalling word lists. Although unsuccessful in their first two experiments to demonstrate the state-dependent effect, the investigators were able to obtain positive findings in Experiment 3, using an experimental design where their subjects learned one list of words while happy and a second list while sad. After reading and summarizing a chapter from a book, which was a distractor task, the subjects re-entered the hypnotic state, reacquired either the happy or sad emotional state, and then were asked to recall the items from both lists. In keeping with the theory of state-dependent effects, maximum recall was obtained when the learning and recall of the material took place under the same emotional state.

## FORGETTING

Although retention and forgetting are two sides of the same coin, traditional investigators have maintained the identity of each of these concepts. The retention of verbal material has been examined, as noted earlier, as a function of the length of the retention interval, the kind of experimental material utilized, the strength of the original learning, etc. But most experimenters have been more concerned with forgetting than retention, asking the very basic question, "Why do we forget?"

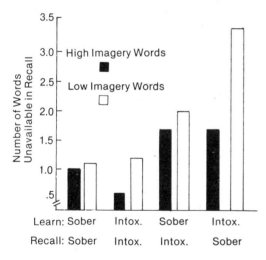

FIGURE 10-5.   Number of words *not* recalled, in relation to whether the subject's recall state was the same as or different from the learning state. Adapted from H. Weingartner, W. Adefris, J. E. Eich, and D. L. Murphy, "Encoding-imagery specificity in alcohol state-dependent learning." *Journal of Experimental Psychology*, 1976, 2, 83–87. Copyright © 1976 by the American Psychological Association. Reprinted by permission.

### Time and Disuse versus Interference as Explanations for Forgetting

Many early psychologists believed that forgetting arose from two interrelated conditions—disuse and time. Forgetting occurred because the previously learned material was not used. The neural trace that had been laid down during the learning of the material decayed or deteriorated with time and disuse, so eventually the previously learned material was lost or forgotten.

Some investigators objected to this explanation. Their position was that forgetting took place because specific activities that were learned by the subject during the retention interval interfered with the material to be recalled. One examination of this hypothesis was undertaken by Jenkins and Dallenbach (1924), who assumed that if the disuse theory was correct, it should make no difference what kind of activity the subject engaged in during the retention interval. On the other hand, an interference position would predict that an activity such as sleep should provide less interference (and greater recall) for earlier learned material than a waking activity. In Jenkins and Dallenbach's experiment, subjects first learned a list of 10 CVCs to a criterion of one perfect trial. After 1, 2, 4, or 8 hours of either (a) normal waking activity or (b) sleeping, the subjects were asked to recall the material. Results, as Figure 10-6 indicates, show that the CVCs were better retained after inter-

vals of sleeping than after corresponding periods of wakefulness. Since the same amount of time had elapsed between the original learning and the test for recall for both groups, the disuse theory was unable to account for the differential forgetting that took place. Jenkins and Dallenbach concluded that forgetting is "a matter of the interference, inhibition, or obliteration of the old by the new" (p. 612), with sleep insulating the newly learned material from the interfering activities. Later experimenters confirmed these findings; see Van Ormer (1932), Newman (1939), Lovatt and Warr (1968).

Several years after Jenkins and Dallenbach's (1924) experimental findings were published, McGeoch (1932) attacked disuse theory in a classic paper by arguing that it was the characteristics of the events taking place during the retention interval that determined the amount of forgetting that would occur. The passage of time, he wrote, was not an explanation for forgetting but rather a condition within which causative events took place. The iron bar rusts not because of time, but because the iron combines with oxygen. McGeoch's paper not only appeared to silence those theorists who assumed that forgetting could be attributed to disuse or decay of the neural trace but provided the foundation for what current investigators have designated as an **interference theory** of forgetting. It must be acknowledged, however, that the decay theory did not die; it reappeared several decades later when the concept of short-term memory was posited to play an important role in human remembering and forgetting.

An interfering event is the learning of other material that competes with the material to be recalled. If the interfering material is learned prior to the learning and recall of the experimental material, the operation is identified as **proactive inhibition** (PI). If the interfering material is learned between the last learning trial of the experimental material and its subsequent recall, the operation is designated as **retroactive inhibition** (RI). Two experimental designs describing these paradigms are found in Table 10-2.

Two aspects of these experimental designs should be noted. The first is that the

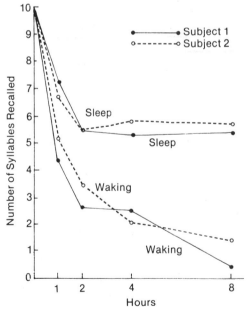

FIGURE 10-6. Mean number of syllables recalled after intervals of sleeping and waking. Adapted from Jenkins and Dallenbach (1924).

TABLE 10-2.   Experimental designs for proactive and retroactive inhibition.

| Experimental Group | Proactive Inhibition | | | Retroactive Inhibition | | |
|---|---|---|---|---|---|---|
| | Learn Task 1 | Learn Task 2 | Recall Task 2 | Learn Task 1 | Learn Task 2 | Recall Task 1 |
| Control Group | Rest | Learn Task 2 | Recall Task 2 | Learn Task 1 | Rest | Recall Task 1 |

"rest" condition does not mean that control subjects really rest. In most instances they are given some task to perform in order to prevent the rehearsal of the previously learned material. For instance, the rapid naming of colors, repeating of digits, etc., has often been used as a "rest" task. In other instances, control subjects have been asked to learn a second task, but one that has been judged to be irrelevant to the originally learned task.

Second, in keeping with the Ebbinghaus tradition, list-learning tasks have been used. Most investigators have employed lists of paired associates. When these tasks are used, a specific notation denotes the stimuli and responses that comprise the pairs. The notation A-B is used to indicate the stimulus and response items employed in the original learning task, while the notation used to denote the interfering task will vary, depending on the kind of stimuli and responses provided by the experimenter. If the stimuli in the interfering list are identical to those in the original but the responses are different, an A-B, A-C notation is

used. If the responses in the interfering list are identical to those in the original list but the stimuli are different, an A-B, C-B notation would be used. In some instances, the stimuli and responses in the original list may be re-paired to provide different paired associates in the interfering task. In such instances, the notation used is A-Br. Finally, an A-B, C-D notation indicates that the stimuli and responses on the interfering list are completely different from those used in the original learning. Table 10-3 illustrates the varying notations.

It should be noted that "intervening" activities in proactive or retroactive paradigms do not necessarily result in inhibition and forgetting. In some instances, the learning of such intervening material facilitates retention. It has been generally found that the A-B, C-B, and A-B, A-Br paradigms result in inhibition, and they have been used almost exclusively in proactive and retroactive inhibition studies. The A-B, C-B paradigm, on the other hand, facilitates retention. Theoretically, the A-B, C-D paradigm, which has been used by many experimenters as a control condition, should result in neither inhibition nor facilitation, but as shall be noted later, Newton and Wickens (1956) observed that, at least in their study, the A-B, C-D paradigm produced inhibition.

TABLE 10-3.   Notation and examples used to indicate varying stimulus-response relationships in proactive and retroactive inhibition experiments

| Original Task | | Interfering Task | |
|---|---|---|---|
| Stimulus | Response | Stimulus | Response |
| A Active | B Pencil | A Active | C Sugar |
| A Active | B Pencil | C Bright | B Pencil |
| A Active Engine | B Pencil Lower | A Active Engine | Br Lower Pencil |
| A Active | B Pencil | C Bright | D Sugar |

### An Analysis of Retroactive Inhibition

Most early psychologists, following the lead of McGeoch (1932), believed that forgetting could be attributed to retroactive inhibition. Proactive inhibition was given little consideration. Moreover, it was assumed that the basic source of interference with the RI paradigm arose from the two sets of responses competing during the recall of the original list. For example, if an originally learned paired-associate item was *active-pencil*, while an interpolated pair was *active-sugar*, it was assumed that the responses of *pencil* and *sugar* would compete with each other when the stimulus *active* was presented during the recall test. If the originally learned response, *pencil*, was forgotten in such circumstances, it was attributed solely to the action of the competing response, *sugar*. Thus, the A-B, A-C paradigm became an important one for investigating the contribution of RI to forgetting.

Melton and Irwin (1940) made an interesting discovery regarding the contribution of response competition to retroactive inhibition. In their RI study, 18 CVCs were presented in serial order to the subjects for 5 trials, following which a second list was presented for either 5, 10, 20, or 40 trials. These second-list learning trials were followed by relearning trials of the first list to a criterion of two perfect recitations. In an examination of their subjects' performance during these relearning trials, the experimenters made special note of the number of overt responses that belonged to the second list. Melton and Irwin (1940) believed that the overt responses or intrusions would provide an index of the amount of response competition between the original and interpolated responses. Admittedly, the number of overt intrusions would not reflect the total amount of forgetting, since it was as-

sumed that forgetting could also be attributed to covert response competition. Nonetheless, it was believed that there should be a positive relationship between the total amount of retroactive inhibition observed and the number of overt intrusions. As retroactive inhibition increased, so should the number of overt intrusions.

When Melton and Irwin compared the total amount of RI with the number of intrusions, they were surprised to find that no consistent relationship could be noted between these measures. Figure 10-7 presents their results. The total amount of RI increased to an asymptote at approximately the level of 20 trials of second-list learning, while the amount of RI attributed to overt competition declined after 10 trials of interpolated learning and was virtually nonexistent at 40. Melton and Irwin reasoned that some process other than response competition must contribute to forgetting. They identified this process as Factor X. Later, it was called an **unlearning process.** When first-list responses intruded during the learning of second-list responses, these first-list responses were not "reinforced" and were thus unlearned or extinguished.

The result was that these first-list responses were not available when first-list relearning or recall trials were provided. A two-factor theory of RI thus emerged; competition taking place between responses dur-

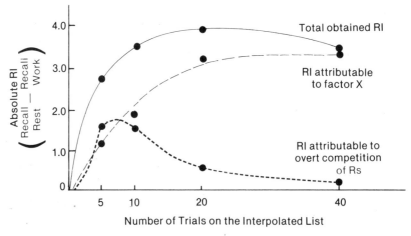

FIGURE 10-7.   Relationship between the amount of retroactive inhibition and the degree of learning of the interpolated material. Adapted from Melton and Irwin (1940).

ing relearning or recall was one factor, and the unlearning of first-list responses during second-list learning was the second. Note that the unlearning process should not operate with proactive inhibition, since this paradigm does not provide the opportunity for second-list responses to be unlearned. Moreover, since two factors contribute to RI and only a single factor to PI, this supported the position emphasizing the greater contribution of retroactive inhibition to the process of forgetting.

Experiments by Underwood (1948a, 1948b) contributed to a further understanding of the operation of the unlearning factor. In one study, Underwood (1948a) had subjects learn two lists of paired adjectives (A-B, A-C), each to a criterion of one perfect trial. Recall of either the first or second list took place under the following conditions: (1) List 1 recalled after 5 hours (RI); (2) List 2 recalled after 5 hours (PI); (3) List 1 recalled after 48 hours (RI); and (4) List 2 recalled after 48 hours (PI).

Underwood found that after 5 hours the recall of first-list responses (RI paradigm) was

significantly less than the recall of second-list responses (PI paradigm), a finding in keeping with the two-factor theory that posited RI to be more important to forgetting than PI. A surprising finding, however, was that after 48 hours there was no difference in the recall of the two lists. As can be noted from Figure 10-8, an increase in the recall score for the RI condition from 5 to 48 hours was accompanied by a decline in the recall score for the PI condition. Underwood suggested that if the concept of unlearning was enlarged to include spontaneous recovery of associations that had been unlearned during the presentation of the second list, the increased recall for the RI condition could be adequately explained. Later experimental evidence suggested that such **spontaneous recovery**, as inferred from increases in recall of first-list responses over time, could be obtained with intervals as short as a half-hour; see Abra (1969) and Kamman and Melton (1967).

### A Further Examination of Two-Factor Theory

During the past several decades, considerable interest has been generated in further examining unlearning, spontaneous recovery, and response competition processes.

**Unlearning and Spontaneous Recovery**  In a study by Underwood (1948b), subjects learned two lists of 10 paired associates (A-B, A-C paradigm), each to a criterion of one perfect trial. Following the learning of the second list, and after an interval of either 1 minute or 5, 24, or 48 hours, Underwood made an unusual request of his subjects. He presented them with the common stimulus words (the same stimulus words were used in both lists) and asked them to report the first response word that came to mind. If no response was provided within 10 seconds, the subject was asked to respond with any word that came to mind. This operation was subsequently designated as the **modified free recall (MFR) procedure.** Figure 10-9 presents the frequency with which first- and second-list responses were made as a function of the time since second-list learning.

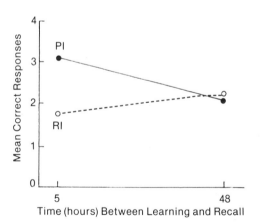

FIGURE 10-8.   Mean number of correct anticipations on the first relearning trial after 5 and 48 hours. RI refers to the recall of the first list, PI to the recall of the second. Adapted from B. J. Underwood "Retroactive and proactive inhibition after five and forty-eight hours." *Journal of Experimental Psychology*, 1948, 38, 29–38. Copyright © 1948 by the American Psychological Association. Reprinted by permission.

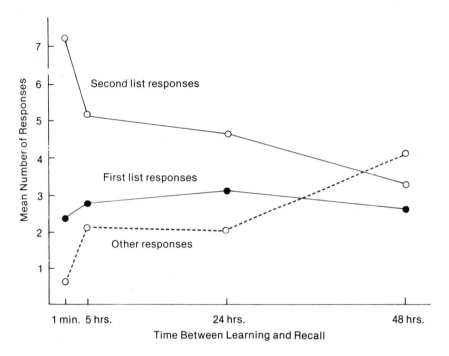

FIGURE 10-9.    Mean frequency of response on the free-recall trial for the four different time intervals. Adapted from B. J. Underwood, " 'Spontaneous recovery' of verbal associations." *Journal of Experimental Psychology*, 1948, 38, 429–439. Copyright © 1948 by the American Psychological Association. Reprinted by permission.

It may be noted that 1 minute after the second-list learning task had been completed, the subjects responded with many second-list responses; but as the retention interval increased to 48 hours, these responses declined in frequency of occurrence. Underwood attributed this decline to the forgetting of these responses. On the other hand, the frequency of first-list responses remained almost constant over the entire 48 hours. There was no "forgetting" of these responses. Underwood assumed that there was some process operating with first-list responses that ran counter to normal forgetting, a process that he believed was spontaneous recovery.

The modified free-recall procedure devised by Underwood provided information about the strongest responses that the subject would make (or had available) to the stimulus words on the list. But there continued to be a problem about the "fate" of first-list responses. In the RI experiment, did subjects fail to respond with first-list responses during the final recall period because they thought that first-list responses were inappropriate in that setting, or because such responses were actually unavailable? It will be recalled that the basic tenet of the unlearning hypothesis was that first-list responses were unavailable, since they had been unlearned during the subject's learning of the second list.

One answer to this problem was provided by Barnes and Underwood (1959), who modified the MFR procedure to create a procedure designated as **modified modified free recall** (MMFR). Here, experimental subjects were asked, after having learned different list responses to a common stimulus, to respond from both lists, if possible.

In a retroactive inhibition experiment conducted by Barnes and Underwood (1959) using the MMFR procedure, subjects learned two paired-associate lists in which CVCs served as stimuli and two syllable adjectives

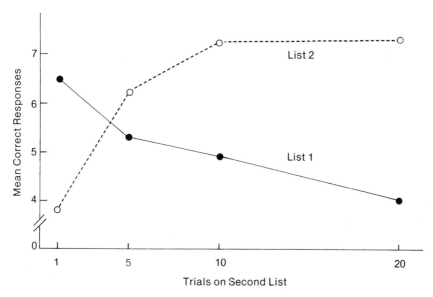

FIGURE 10-10.   Mean number of responses correctly recalled in the A-B, A-C paradigm. Adapted from J. M. Barnes and B. J. Underwood, " 'Fate' of first-list associations in transfer theory." *Journal of Experimental Psychology*, 1959, 58, 97–105. Copyright © 1959 by the American Psychological Association. Reprinted by permission.

as responses. An A-B, A-C design was used. Following the learning of the A-B list, the A-C list was presented for either 1, 5, 10, or 20 trials. Following the appropriate number of A-C trials, each subject was provided with a piece of paper on which each stimulus CVC was printed and asked to write down the two responses that had been associated with it. Results are presented in Figure 10-10. As the number of trials of the A-C list increased, the number of correct responses from this second list also increased, but the number of correct responses appropriate for the A-B list showed a gradual decline. Since the subjects were instructed to recall the adjectives from both lists if at all possible and not pressed to respond rapidly during this recall period, any competition between responses should have been eliminated. The decline of the first-list responses was attributed to the unlearning of these responses during second-list learning. Barnes and Underwood's (1959) experiment thus provided important support for the existence of an unlearning process operating in retroactive inhibition studies.

**Generalized Response Competition**   It was noted that when an A-B, A-C relationship existed between stimuli and responses on the first and second lists, substantial amounts of proactive or retroactive inhibition were obtained. In contrast, most investigators have found that the use of the A-B, C-D design generally minimizes inhibition effects. An exception to this finding was noted by Newton and Wickens (1956), who observed a substantial amount of forgetting in an RI experiment even though an A-B, C-D paradigm was used. The authors suggested that during recall of the original-list responses there was a tendency on the part of the subjects to restrict their responses to those which had been learned on the interpolated list, a phenomenon that they called **generalized response competition**. Subsequently, Postman, Stark, and Fraser (1968) identified this tendency as **response-set interference**. They believed that this developed not during the recall of the original responses, as Newton and Wickens had suggested, but during the learning of second-list responses.

Postman and Underwood (1973) have written that subjects establish a set for giving responses from a particular list during a particular learning session—this makes it difficult for the subject to switch almost instantaneously to provide responses from another list. Thus, there is a tendency for the subject in the RI experiment to respond with second-list responses during the recall period designed to elicit first-list responses.

One might assume that if the original-list responses were made available to the subject during or prior to the recall period, the interference arising from an inappropriate set to recall second-list responses might be minimized.

Several procedures have been used to make the originally learned responses available during the test period. One has been to use a recognition test—the appropriate responses are provided along with distractors. Postman's (1976) examination of RI studies that used a recognition measure rather than recall supports the availability assumption. Only small amounts of RI are obtained when a recognition test is used.

In a second availability procedure, prior to the recall period the subjects are provided with another task that utilizes the to-be-recalled response terms. It would be assumed that making the responses available in this way would reduce or change the subject's set to recall second-list responses. The experiments of Cofer, Failie, and Horton (1971) and Postman and Gray (1978) have noted reductions in inhibition with such a procedure.

In the Postman and Gray (1978) study, two successive lists of 12 paired associates were learned by three experimental and three control groups. The task used the A-B, A-C paradigm, which maximizes forgetting. Following the learning of the A-C list, the first experimental group was given a series of arithmetic problems to do prior to the recall of first-list responses. Subjects in the second experimental group were shown first-list responses and asked to provide two ratings for each response; these ratings were the subject's estimates of the speed in learning the responses during the original learning period. Subjects in the third experimental group were asked to provide similar ratings and then were asked to recall all of the responses they could.

The three control groups did not learn the second list of paired associates; their treatment prior to the recall of first-list responses paralleled that of the experimental group (arithmetic problems, ratings, or ratings and recall). Table 10-4 indicates retention scores for the three experimental groups and three control groups. The learning of the second list of paired associates significantly interfered with the retention of first-list responses, as revealed by the performance scores of the experimental groups. However, comparison of the retention scores for the three experimental groups shows that the reinstatement of the response by the rating procedure significantly improved performance. Thus, Experimental Groups 2 and 3 each recalled more items than Experimental Group 1. But a comparision between the performance of the two response–reinstatement experimental groups (Groups 2 and 3) and their appropriate controls indicates that the reinstatement procedure did not eliminate inhibition effects completely. Other processes such as unlearning and response competition undoubtedly make a contribution.

## The Role of Proactive Inhibition in Forgetting

The last topic in our discussion of interference theory is the contribution of proactive inhibition to forgetting. Of the varying processes hypothesized to operate with retroactive inhibition, only response competition has been

TABLE 10-4.   Mean scores on the first-list retention test

|  | Arithmetic Problems | Rating Procedure | Rating Procedure and Free Recall |
|---|---|---|---|
| Control | 9.81 | 9.00 | 9.25 |
| Experimental Groups | (1)4.38 | (2)5.81 | (3)5.63 |

Adapted from Postman and Gray (1978).

assumed to also operate with proactive inhibition. It is not surprising, therefore, that most psychologists, at least until the late 1950s, assumed that PI was less important than RI because it had only a single inhibitory process.

In a most important paper, Underwood (1957) suggested that this position was incorrect and that PI made a much greater contribution to forgetting than had been previously assumed. Underwood noted that if a subject learned a list of CVCs and then was asked to recall them after an interval of 24 hours, a substantial amount of forgetting was observed. Traditionally, such forgetting had been attributed to RI, with the interfering activities being assumed to take place between the original learning and the subsequent test for recall. But Underwood reasoned that this was an incredible stretching of interference theory to believe that such forgetting was produced by the learning of material that subjects had learned outside the laboratory.

Underwood believed that it made more sense to assume that the interference arose from proactive inhibition—responses that the subject had learned prior to learning the experimental material. But a basic problem was to identify the nature of these responses. Underwood and Postman (1960) reasoned that such responses had to be acquired outside the laboratory and that they consisted of (1) letter-sequence habits and (2) word-sequence habits. Letter-sequence habits were defined as habits that developed through the normal course of learning a language. For example, if a two letter combination, QJ, was used as a response term in a paired-associate task, the subject's previously learned letter-sequence habit, QU, should make the learning of QJ difficult. Moreover, after QJ had been acquired, the older QU habit would recover in strength with the passage of time and interfere with any subsequent recall of QJ.

Word-sequence habits were defined as the learning of sequences of words that frequently occur in the language. If the sequence "black-rubber" was to be learned and subsequently recalled, the previously learned word-sequence habit "black-white" would have to first be unlearned; moreover, the subsequent recovery of the "black-white" sequence would interfere with the recall of the "black-rubber" sequence.

Some investigators have attempted to obtain experimental support for the contribution of extra-experimental interference in the recall of list-learning material, but their findings have been quite discouraging; see Underwood and Postman (1960), Postman (1962a), Ekstrand and Underwood (1965), Underwood and Ekstrand (1966, 1968).

An experiment conducted by Underwood and Ekstrand (1968) demonstrates the kinds of studies that have been conducted and typical experimental findings. An experimental list of 15 paired associates was constructed using "high-crossed associates." In this list, 15 highly associated stimulus-response pairs of words were used, such as *table-chair, hammer-nail*, etc. The pairings used in the list, however, were crossed or scrambled so that the stimulus word *table* might be paired with the response *nail* whereas the stimulus word *hammer* might be associated with the response word *chair*. A control list of paired associates consisted of the same stimulus words paired with neutral responses. These response words had the same first letter and number of syllables as the response words used in the experimental list, but previously established associations did not exist between the stimuli and responses. Twenty-four hours after both lists had been learned to a criterion of 12 out of 15 responses correctly anticipated, a retention test was provided.

The extra-experimental hypothesis would predict greater forgetting of the experimental list, since the pairs of words learned in natural language—e.g., *table-chair, hammer-nail*—should interfere with the recall of the laboratory-learned pairs of items. But the findings were directly opposite to the prediction—the experimental list was better recalled than the control list!

### The Status of Interference Theory

During the past decade, interference theory has been under attack; in fact, some investigators have expressed doubt that this theory of forgetting will survive. Although this is probably an exaggeration, there is no doubt that some very legitimate problems exist.

When the subject learns only a single list of words or CVCs in the laboratory and the experimenter examines the retention of these items (interfering lists are not provided), forgetting appears to take place at a relatively uniform rate, regardless of the characteristics of the material learned. For example, after a subject learns lists of high- or low-frequency words or high- or low-association CVCs to the same criterion, a recall test provided 24 hours later will reveal that these lists have been forgotten at about the same rate. If interfering materials, presumably arising from an extra-experimental source such as natural language habits, are held accountable for the forgetting that has been observed over the 24 hour period, it is necessary to assume that the interference provided by natural language habits is the same regardless of the kind of material learned.

Interference theorists have assumed that such competition must be of a very general nature, but its identification has remained elusive. In summary, one inadequacy of interference theory has been that it cannot account for the uniformity of the forgetting process regardless of the kind of material learned.

A second inadequacy was found through the puzzling experimental findings of Ekstrand and his associates, who have resumed the work of Jenkins and Dallenbach (1924) in examining the role of sleep on retention. Since there is now much more information about the characteristics of sleep, Ekstrand was interested in how such information might add to a better understanding of the effects of sleep on recall.

Five different stages of sleep have been identified through the use of electroencephalographic features. Stages 1 through 4, collectively known as non-REM, are each indicated by specific EEG features and the absence of rapid eye movements (REM) on the part of the sleeping subject. The fifth stage, the REM stage, is similar to Stage 1 except that there are periodic bursts of rapid eye movements. Typically, REM sleep occupies about 20 percent of a normal night's sleep, with most of REM sleep taking place in the second half of the typical 8 hour sleep period.

Yaroush, Sullivan, and Ekstrand (1971) examined how recall was affected by the first four hours of sleep (small amounts of REM) versus the second four hours (large amounts of REM). The first group of subjects learned a list of 15 paired associates to a criterion of 10 out of 15 correct responses just before retiring. Four hours later, they were awakened and provided several recall tests. The second group of subjects went to bed shortly after appearing at the laboratory, but four hours later they were awakened, learned the experimental material to the same criterion, returned to bed, and then four hours later were awakened and tested for recall. See Table 10-5 for this design. Results, which were confirmed in a subsequent study by Barrett and Ekstrand (1972), indicated that performance was superior for the group that recalled the material after the first four hours of sleep. Thus, the first group revealed an absolute recall decrement of 1.50 items in contrast to a decrement of 3.50 items for the second group.

Ekstrand (1972) has acknowledged that it is difficult to reconcile these findings with an interference theory of forgetting, since it is necessary to assume that the second four

TABLE 10-5.   Experimental design examining first 4 hours of sleep versus second 4 hours on recall

| | | 8 hours of sleep | | | |
|---|---|---|---|---|---|
| Experimental Group     A | Learn PA list | Sleep 4 hours | Recall PA list | Sleep 4 hours | |
| Experimental Group     B | | Sleep 4 hours | Learn PA list | Sleep 4 hours | Recall PA list |

hours of sleep creates greater interference than the first four hours. Such greater interference effects would appear to be attributed to differential neural activities that are found in the varying stages of sleep. This explanation stresses that physiological conditions must at least partly account for the forgetting process.

A third inadequacy has been the inability to obtain interference effects when recognition rather than recall measures are employed. Retroactive inhibition studies by Garskof and Sandak (1964) and Postman, Stark, and Fraser (1968) have revealed that massive amounts of interpolated learning, which produce substantial amounts of forgetting when recall measures are used, produce only very small amounts of forgetting when measured by recognition tests.

## The Forgetting of Prose and Connected Discourse

Many psychologists believe that a basic difficulty with an interference theory of forgetting is its limited generality. Many experimenters have been unable to find PI and RI effects when prose or meaningful material has been used as the experimental material; see McGeoch and McKinney (1934), Deese and Hardman (1954), Hall (1955), Ausubel, Robbins, and Blake (1957).

However, a substantial number of experiments conducted more recently have demonstrated that PI and RI effects can be obtained with prose. Studies by Anderson and Myrow (1971), Myrow and Anderson (1972), Anderson and Carter (1972), and Bower (1978) are representative of these experiments.

Bower's (1978) experimental material consisted of a series of simple declarative sentences, such as "The fireman watered his plants." The subject of the sentence, "fireman," was designated as the stimulus, while the predicate, "watered his plants," was viewed as the response. Twenty unrelated sentences, all utilizing a profession name as the subject ("a teacher," "a carpenter," etc.) and a simple verb phrase as the predicate ("shot a deer," "sold his house," etc.), served as the original material to be learned.

An anticipatory procedure was used; the professional name was presented to the subject, who then had to respond with the verb phrase. After subjects had correctly anticipated each verb phrase of the original material, a second list of sentences was used as interfering material. One experimental group learned entirely different sentences, whereas a second experimental group learned sentences in which the same professional names were used but paired with different verb phrases. A third experimental group had the professional names and verb phrases used in the original material re-paired. For example, the sentences "The fireman watered his plants" and "The teacher sold his house" might be re-paired to form "The teacher watered his plants" and "The fireman sold his house." The three notations used by interference theorists to describe these three experimental groups' second-list learning are (1) C-D, (2) A-C, and (3) A-Br. A group that was not provided a second list of sentences served as a control.

Bower's findings shall not be detailed other than to point out that the amount of recall for each group was in keeping with the predictions made by interference theory. Recall was the best among the control subjects, followed by groups (1) C-D, (2) A-C, and (3) A-Br. Bower has concluded that interference theory applies as much to meaningful propositional learning as it does to verbatim memorizing in standard, rote, verbal-learning tasks. He has acknowledged that critics might complain that he has done nothing more than demonstrate the interference phenomenon in sentences by the simple device of forcing the subject to treat meaningful learning as rote-learning. But as he has pointed out, there are some basic dissimilarities between his procedures and those used in list-learning tasks. For example, his subjects did not have to respond verbatim, and they were told to use whatever meaningful elaboration of the material they desired in an effort to learn the verb phrases. Moreover, the response (predicate) contained a meaningful combination of words, unlike the responses in typical paired-associate tasks.

Perhaps a closer approximation of the kind of meaningful material that is encountered in nonlaboratory situations is found in three experiments conducted by Anderson and Myrow (Experiments I and III, 1971) and Myrow and Anderson (Experiment II, 1972).

In these studies, all utilizing the same general procedure, high school students learned textbook type prose consisting of (a) an anthropological discussion of fictitious primitive tribes (Experiments I and III) or (b) the history, doctrine, and teachings of Zen Buddhism and Buddhism (Experiment II). These experiments are most interesting, since Anderson and Myrow used an interference position to guide them in devising the sentences that served as the interpolated learning material. These sentences were designed to inhibit retention of some parts of the original prose passage (which would reflect retroactive inhibition) or to facilitate the retention of other parts. Neutral sentences were also used which were anticipated to have no influence on retention. Illustrative sentences of the type used in the interpolated prose passage can be found in Table 10-6.

A typical RI design was used in all three experiments. Students learned one prose passage on Day 1, and a second prose passage (interpolated material) on Day 2. For some subjects this passage contained related material of the type illustrated in Table 10-6, while other subjects learned an unrelated passage. (A passage on drug addiction was frequently used.) A retention test of the original passage was administered on Day 8.

Results from all three experiments were in keeping with interference theory predictions. The experiments did not produce identical findings, but they did indicate that the interpolated sentences which the experimenters assumed would result in interference did indeed result in retroactive inhibition whereas other sentences which the experimenters assumed would provide facilitation did indeed aid retention of the original prose passage.

Anderson and Myrow have pointed out that in order to demonstrate RI in prose learning, it is necessary to specify the similarities and differences between the original and the interpolated learning material. The inability of some of the earlier investigators to do this undoubtedly contributed to their failure to find RI operating with prose.

Although they demonstrated the operation of RI with prose, the authors have raised a basic question about the interference theory of forgetting. They have wondered how frequently forgetting analogous to RI occurs in educational settings, since students are seldom taught different answers to the same question. As a result, Anderson and Myrow have written that if RI is generated in the learning of prose only when the materials are quite similar, the efficacy of the interference model as an inclusive explanation of forgetting must be questioned. Myrow and Anderson (1972) have concluded that it seems probable that students do forget without the presence of closely similar material. The problem remains, of course, to identify these other forgetting processes.

## SUMMARY

Retention and forgetting have been basic areas of interest for traditional investigators, who have continued to use list-learning tasks consisting of words or CVCs as their experimental material. Although representing only different sides of the same coin—what is not retained is forgotten—each topic has retained a separate conceptual identity.

TABLE 10-6.   Type of original and interpolated sentences used in examining retroactive inhibition

| Kind of Sentences | Original Material | Interpolated Material |
|---|---|---|
| Facilitative | Tribe A makes beer from squash. | Tribe B makes beer from squash. |
| Interfering | Tribe A's staple food is rice. | Tribe B's staple food is wheat. |
| Neutral | Tribe A's major activity is hunting. | Tribe B lives in the hills. |

Adapted from material by Anderson and Myrow (1971).

Early experimenters of retention were interested in describing how performance declined as a function of the length of the retention interval. Ebbinghaus's retention curve, obtained in his monumental study, was considered by some to reflect the course of retention for all material. Experimenters are now aware that the slope of the retention curve is related to the specific experimental conditions employed.

A major problem in using very long retention intervals to examine retention curves is obtaining subjects. Seldom is it possible to have subjects learn material at one time and then have those same subjects available for a retention test many years later. One solution to this problem has been to use a cross-sectional approach. This procedure uses only a single retention test, which is given at approximately the same time to all subjects. Variation in the time that the material was originally learned provides the experimenter with different retention intervals. Bahrick, Bahrick, and Wittlinger (1975) were quite successful in using this procedure to examine the capacity of individuals to remember the names and faces of members of their high school graduating class with retention intervals as long as 49 years.

Experimental studies of retention have centered around the investigation of three conditions that have been demonstrated to influence retention: (1) strength of the original learning, (2) context effects, and (3) state-dependent effects. Many investigators have found that as the strength of the original learning increases, retention of the material becomes progressively better. In some situations, subjects have had learning trials continued after they have achieved perfect mastery of the material, a procedure identified as overlearning. Overlearning has been shown to play an important role in increasing retention.

Material is always learned within a particular environmental context—the time of day, method of presentation, etc. Many studies have demonstrated that retention is maximized when the environment or context is the same during recall as it was during learning.

Thus, the reinstatement of the learning environment at recall produces optimal performance.

A state-dependent effect refers to the phenomenon whereby material that was learned when the subject was under the influence of one physiological or emotional state is best remembered when the subject is in that same state. Anecdotes testifying to the existence of this phenomenon abound—e.g., a sober alcoholic cannot remember where he hid his vodka when he was drunk, but does remember when he again becomes drunk. An experimental demonstration of the state-dependent effect is found in a study conducted by Weingartner, Adefris, Eich, and Murphy (1976), who noted that when subjects learned lists of words under the condition of either sobriety or intoxication, superior recall of these words took place when subjects were again in the same state during recall.

"Why do we forget?" is a puzzling question, and over the years many psychologists have attempted to answer it. An early position posited that forgetting took place because of disuse and a decaying of the neural trace. But later studies of Jenkins and Dallenbach (1924) and Van Ormer (1932) demonstrated that there was less forgetting when the retention interval was filled with sleep than when it was filled with activity. This finding suggested that forgetting arose from activity that interfered with the material to be recalled and provided the foundation for an interference theory of forgetting. If the interfering activity had been learned prior to the original learning and subsequent recall of the experimental material, it was identified as proactive inhibition (PI). If the interfering activity had been learned during the retention interval, it was identified as retroactive inhibition (RI).

Much experimental work has centered around an examination of the characteristics of these interfering activities. One type, response competition, is assumed to occur when the subject attempts to recall one set of responses but finds interference from the other set that has been learned. Response competition has been posited to take place with both PI and RI.

A second kind of interference, called unlearning or extinction, is assumed to take place in RI studies when the subject responds with first-list responses during the learning of responses from the second list. Inasmuch as these first-list responses are incorrect and are not reinforced, they are unlearned or extinguished and not available for subsequent recall.

Response competition and unlearning have thus been posited to be the two factors that create interference and produce forgetting. A variety of experiments have been conducted in order to examine the operation of these two factors on forgetting; some have been successful but others have not, so modifications of the two-factor theory have been necessary.

Although an interference position is the most developed theoretical explanation of forgetting, this theory does have a number of problems. One problem has been that forgetting appears to take place at a relatively uniform rate, regardless of the characteristics of the material learned. Thus, low-frequency words are forgotten at about the same rate as high-frequency words, although one would assume that the kind of material learned between the original learning and the test for retention should result in differences in the amount retained for the two types of material.

A second problem has been how the time of sleep—the first four hours of sleep compared with the second four hours—contributes to the amount forgotten. It is difficult for an interference theory to explain why one sleep period contributes to greater amounts of forgetting than another. Finally, interference theory has difficulty explaining why interference effects cannot be demonstrated with recognition measures of retention.

Many investigators have been interested in the applicability of RI and PI to the forgetting of connected discourse. Although RI can be obtained when prose serves as the experimental material, the situations used to obtain these results, like their list-learning counterparts, appear to be quite artificial. Thus, the applicability of RI to the forgetting of prose seems questionable.

# CHAPTER ELEVEN

# Memory

About two decades ago, the beginnings of a new approach to the study of learning and retention could be discerned—an approach that challenged the traditional examination of learning and retention described in the two previous chapters. No single factor was responsible for this new look; rather, a series of events coalesced to provide investigators with an alternative approach to the traditional position. This new approach did not clearly differentiate learning from retention; as a result, it has been designated the area of memory. This chapter examines the nature of events that led to this different perspective.

The examination of a person's immediate memory span first became a part of psychology with the work of Jacobs (1887). A memory span task, it will be recalled, consists of presenting a number of items, typically digits, to the subject, who is asked to repeat them immediately following the presentation of the last item. Beginning with three or four digits, the experimenter increases the number presented by one until the subject is unable to correctly repeat all of the items. The subject's memory span is represented by the number of digits that can be correctly recalled. But few traditional investigators of learning and retention were interested in the operation of memory span tasks.

In the late 1940s, Hebb (1949) assumed that a basic memory process could be inferred from the findings of memory span studies. He proposed that after stimuli were perceived, for a very short time they continued to reverberate in the organism's nervous system. This short reverberation period was distinct from a second memory process that operated in traditional retention studies, where substantial intervals of time were placed between the learning of material and its subsequent recall. Hebb's dual-memory position was similar to the position of William James (1890), who had suggested that the human memory consisted of two separate components—a primary memory, which was believed to contain material that had not left the individual's consciousness, and a second memory system, which was believed to contain material that was not in the individual's consciousness but that was available if needed. The dual position proposed by Hebb and subsequently by Broadbent (1958) was contrary to the traditional point of view, which assumed the operation of only a single memory process.

Investigators were also becoming concerned and impatient about several facets of the traditional approach to learning and retention. For example, investigators believed that learning and retention should be analyzed in terms of what the subject did to the verbal material, an approach that deemphasized the role of the properties of verbal stimuli. It was also believed that the kind of material used, its presentation, and measurement should not be as constrained as they had been by earlier procedures. As a result, experimental materials were broadened to include more connected discourse and prose, as well as a variety of visual stimuli such as faces. Variations of recall and recognition measures were also introduced.

Many different types of tasks were added to the traditional serial and paired-associate tasks, although list-learning tasks continued to be used frequently. One task that came into extensive use was free recall with only a single presentation of the items to be learned followed by a single recall trial. These single presentation–single retention trial procedures invariably raised a question: Was it learning or retention that was being measured? Since the traditional distinction between these constructs could not be made, the concept of memory was used to include the operation of both processes.[1]

Finally, a different conceptual approach was adopted. Some investigators believed that the operation of human memory could be likened to the functioning of a computer, which receives information from cards and tapes and stores it for subsequent use. The information can later be retrieved either in the form of its input or in some other form, as determined by the programmer. The concepts of acquisition or encoding, storage, and retrieval were assumed to represent fundamental properties of the memory process. This approach, now called an **information processing** position, was a radical departure from traditional investigators' conceptualization of memory.

## TWO MEMORY SYSTEMS OR ONE?

An early issue stemming from the information processing approach was whether people had two memory systems or just one, as had been assumed by traditional verbal-learning inves-

tigators. Broadbent (1958), in his text *Perception and Communication,* had formally proposed a **long-term memory** (LTM) and **short-term memory** (STM) system, hypothesizing that material entering the short-term memory store formed a trace that decayed rapidly but could be maintained by rehearsal. Since all of the items could not be rehearsed simultaneously, there was a limit to the number of items that could be kept as traces by rehearsal.

The findings from several studies supported Broadbent's description of how short-term memory functioned. Miller (1956) had earlier proposed that an individual's memory span would hold only about seven items, or chunks as he termed them, a finding supportive of Broadbent's position that the capacity of STM was quite limited. In addition, an experiment by Brown (1958) and a second by Peterson and Peterson (1959) revealed that without rehearsal, information rapidly dropped out of memory. In the Peterson and Peterson study, a single CCC was presented for half a second, followed by a three digit number. Subjects were instructed to count backwards by threes or fours from this number until a cue for the recall of the trigram was provided. This response of counting backwards seriously interfered with any rehearsal of the CCC that the subject might undertake. Each subject was tested a number of times at recall intervals of 3, 6, 9, 12, 15, and 18 seconds. Correct recall, defined as a subject responding with a latency of less than 2.83 seconds, was found to be a function of the length of the retention interval. (The authors said they used the value of 2.83 seconds because the mean latency of all correct responses was 2.83.) Figure 11-1 presents these findings.

Many subsequent investigators replicated Peterson and Peterson's findings. Peterson and Peterson's (1959) examination of individual protocols revealed little evidence of proactive inhibition effects, although each of their subjects had been provided with a number of CCCs to recall during the course of the experiment. With proactive inhibition ruled out as an explanation for forgetting, a case

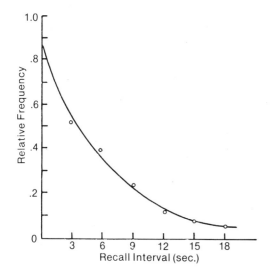

could be made for Broadbent's trace decay explanation of forgetting.

Some of the most interesting evidence bearing on the distinction between short-term and long-term memory was obtained from neurophysiology. Milner (1968) has provided an analytic examination of this dual function of memory, writing:

> Bilateral surgical lesions in the hippocampal region, on the mesial aspect of the temporal lobes, produce a remarkably severe and persistent memory disorder in human patients, the pattern of breakdown providing valuable clues to the cerebral organization of memory. Patients with these lesions show no loss of preoperatively acquired skills . . . but . . . they seemed largely incapable of adding new information to the long-term store. . . . Nevertheless, the immediate registration of new input (as measured, for example, by digit span and dichotic listening tests) appears to take place normally and material which can be encompassed by verbal rehearsal is held for many minutes without further loss than that entailed in the initial verbalization. Interruption of re-

hearsal, regardless of the nature of the distracting task, produces immediate forgetting of what went before. . . . Material already in long-term store is unaffected by the lesion, except for a certain amount of retrograde amnesia for preoperative events. (As quoted by Atkinson and Shiffrin, 1968, p. 97)

The case history of H. M., frequently cited by Milner, is an intriguing account of the memory capacity of an individual who had undergone surgery in the hippocampal region. See Box 11-1.

The effect of these lesions on memory, as reported by Milner (1968), is similar to that observed in patients who have Korsakoff's syndrome, a disease often occurring with chronic alcoholics. These patients are unable to remember recent events for even a short time, a period measured in seconds or at the most minutes. For example, they may not be able to remember a meal that they have just eaten. Carlson (1977) has indicated that recent evidence suggests that these patients, as a result of their drinking, have undergone extensive brain damage in the hippocampal region.

Drachman and Arbit (1966) experimentally demonstrated this type of finding in their systematic examination of patients who had bilateral hippocampal lesions. Twenty control subjects were used in addition to five brain-damaged patients. A digit span task was first employed—the subject had to recall five digits immediately following their presentation. The task was then expanded; a single digit was added to the list each time the subjects were able to recall all of the previously presented items. Once the number of digits was increased beyond the subject's memory span, additional trials were provided in order to enable the subject to reach a criterion of one perfect trial. Findings from this study are presented in Figure 11-2. The digit storage capacity for the control group was 20 digits or more, while no brain-damaged patient had a digit storage capacity of greater than 12 digits. The immediate memory span for both groups appeared to be about the same, but the brain-injured patients were significantly less capable of recalling more than 12 digits, regardless of the number of trials provided. Presumably,

▬▬▬ BOX 11-1 ▬▬▬▬▬▬▬▬▬▬▬▬▬▬▬▬▬▬▬▬▬▬▬▬▬▬▬▬▬▬▬▬▬

Brain operations can provide interesting and suggestive evidence, although not necessarily conclusive, concerning how memory functions. The effects of one brain operation have been reported by Milner and her colleagues in a series of studies; see Milner (1963, 1965, 1968), Milner and Teuber (1968), Milner, Corkin, and Teuber (1968). All the studies examined the residual learning capacities of H.M. following the bilateral removal of his medial temporal lobes. Prior to his operation, H.M. had severe epilepsy, suffering major convulsions about once a week, combined with many minor attacks each day. In order to alleviate this condition, an operation was performed to bilaterally remove the medial temporal lobes. Once this was done, major convulsions were almost entirely eliminated, while minor seizures were reduced to one or two a day. But the improved physical condition was accompanied by an unusual memory deficit. H.M. could not remember information obtained after the operation. He was unable, for example, to recognize people who became close neighbors or family friends, or to remember the address of the house to which his family had moved after the operation. He revealed little awareness of major national or international events. Laboratory testing involving memory functions, as reported by Milner, Corkin, and Teuber (1968), confirmed this type of memory loss.

But H.M.'s memory deficit was not accompanied by any general intellectual loss. Prior to his operation he had an IQ of 104; two years after his operation, his IQ was 112; seven years later, it was 118. Moreover, the operation did not appear to change H.M.'s capacity to recall remote events antedating his operation. He was able to remember incidents from his early school years and positions that he had held during his late teens and early twenties. His interaction with individuals in social settings revealed that he had not lost any of the social graces he had acquired in his youth.

▬▬▬▬▬▬▬▬▬▬▬▬▬▬▬▬▬▬▬▬▬▬▬▬▬▬▬▬▬▬▬▬▬▬▬▬▬▬▬▬▬▬▬▬▬

this failure reflects the inability of the subject to transfer material from short-term to long-term memory.

### Difficulties with the STM-LTM Distinction

All psychologists have not been convinced that short-term and long-term memory represent two functionally and conceptually different constructs. Melton (1963) rejected the STM-LTM distinction and argued for the desirability of considering these two memory systems as representing a continuum. Lewis (1979), in his review and careful evaluation of the evidence, has also supported the position that a distinction between STM and LTM cannot be made. But what is the nature of the evidence?

Hebb (1949) and Broadbent (1958) had theorized that forgetting in STM arose from the memory trace decaying over time. It will be recalled that Peterson and Peterson (1959)

had provided experimental support for this position by not being able to obtain proactive inhibition effects in their STM study. However, Keppel and Underwood (1962) and subsequent experimenters—see Wickens, Born, and Allen (1963) or Wickens and Clark (1968)—were able to demonstrate that proactive inhibition did contribute to the forgetting of material in short-term memory experiments. Other investigators lent support for the role of interference in STM by demonstrating that the kind of material that intervened between the presentation of material and the test for retention in the STM experiment was important in determining the amount of forgetting. Wickelgren (1965), for example, found both proactive and retroactive inhibition in STM when he used interfering consonant-vowel units acoustically similar to those the subjects had originally learned.

The neurological evidence that had been used to support a two-memory system, upon

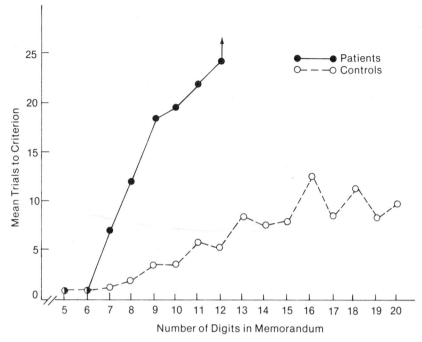

FIGURE 11-2.   Extended digit span: mean trials to criterion for subspan and supraspan memoranda. Patients with hippocampal lesions require many more trials than controls to achieve criterion with supraspan memoranda; no patient successfully recalled more than 12 digits. Adapted from D. A. Drachman and J. Arbit, "Memory and the hippocampal complex, II." *Archives of Neurology*, 1966, 15, 52–61. Copyright 1966, American Medical Association.

closer scrutiny, seemed suspect. Drachman and Arbit's (1966) study did indicate that brain-damaged patients were able to recall material that was beyond memory span length, thus suggesting that some information that had been placed in short-term memory was transferred to long-term memory. Corkin's (1968) further examination of H.M. has indicated the involvement of long-term memory in his acquisition of motor skills. See Box 11-2. In addition to these findings, other investigators have reported amnesic patients learning and placing in long-term memory other types of responses, such as visual discrimination responses (Sidman, Stoddard, and Mohr, 1968), and classical conditioning of the eyeblink (Weiskrantz and Warrington, 1979).

In summary, the experimental evidence supporting a dual-memory system now seems weak. But we should acknowledge that many psychologists have accepted an operational distinction between the two constructs. Short-term memory—or **working memory**, as it has been called more recently—has been operationally defined as the presentation of within-memory span material, with a retention interval measured in seconds. Long-term memory is defined as the presentation of beyond–memory span material, with the retention interval measured in minutes or hours. Again it should be emphasized that these terms identify a *particular experimental methodology* and do *not* reflect the position that different memory systems are operating when such procedures are used.

■■■ BOX 11-2 ■■■■■■■■■■■■■■■■■■■■■■■■■■■■■■■■■■■■■■■■■■

Corkin's (1968) examination of H.M. has revealed that H.M. could acquire a motor skill even when training sessions were distributed over days, thus suggesting a continuity between short-term and long-term memory for this type of task. On two different motor skill tasks, rotary pursuit and bimanual tracking, performance increased significantly over the daily trials. In the interest of brevity, we shall just report H.M.'s acquisition of the rotary pursuit. The subject was instructed to hold a stylus between the thumb and index finger of the preferred hand and to rest the tip of the stylus on a small metal target placed on a revolving turntable. The subject was to attempt to keep the stylus in contact with the target as it rotated, with time on target being the response measure. See page 249 for a picture of this apparatus. H.M. was provided with eight trials per session, with two sessions per day being conducted on the first two days and one session per day for the next five days. One week after the first training session, a retention test was provided.

The figure below shows rotary pursuit scores for H.M. and also the mean scores obtained from seven normal control subjects. There was a significant increase in H.M.'s time on target from the first session to the last, while his retention of the skill had not deteriorated over a week's time. Clearly H.M. was able to retain this skill, although his performance was significantly poorer than that of the control subjects.

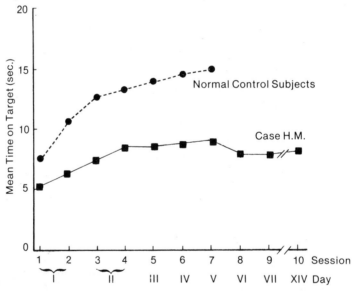

BOX FIGURE 11-1.   Rotary pursuit: time scores. Reprinted with permission from *Neuropsychologia*, 1968, 6, 255–265. Corkin, S., "Acquisition of motor skill after bilateral medial temporal-lobe excision." Copyright © 1968, Pergamon Press, Ltd.

## CONCEPTUAL FRAMEWORK OF THE INFORMATION PROCESSING POSITION

The information processing position, in addition to stimulating a variety of theories, has provided a general conceptual framework that many experimenters have used to guide their research. This position assumes that three processes contribute to memory—namely, encoding, storage, and retrieval. More specifically, when verbal material is received by the experimental subject, it is first encoded, then stored, and subsequently retrieved. The following sections will discuss some of the experiments that have been conducted in an effort to help the reader understand better how these processes operate.

*A Caution:* This book's separate consideration of encoding, storage, and retrieval may provide the impression that the operation of an independent variable in an experiment can be readily identified as contributing to one of these processes. Unfortunately, such identification must be done with utmost caution, because investigators are working with only two observables: (a) the stimulus condition or characteristics of the material that is to be placed in memory and (b) some performance or response measure from which the presence of a memory has been inferred. But the processes of encoding, storage, and retrieval have been assumed to operate serially and between the two observables. Thus, it is not possible to examine the operation of just one of these processes separate and apart from the other two.

We prefer to think of the processes of encoding, storage, and retrieval as metaphors; they are representations of what many theorists believe is taking place when material is presented to be learned and later recalled. The identification of any one given independent variable as contributing to just one of these processes cannot be done experimentally but depends on the experimenter's theoretical position or judgment as to the locus of the effects.

## Encoding

Our view of encoding is that certain processes, which shall be called **encoding processes,** are responsible for transforming external stimuli into internal information, or a representation of the external stimuli in the memory system.[2] Although the identification and operation of these processes has stimulated a great deal of research, a basic problem has been how to categorize the different ways that encoding has been employed. There is no taxonomy of encoding operations, but some of the basic conditions that have been identified as contributing to the encoding process can be enumerated.

**Rehearsal**  One of the most basic encoding procedures is **rehearsal**—the overt or covert repetition of material that the subject desires to remember.

Examining the findings from the Peterson and Peterson (1959) type of short-term memory experiment, one finds that preventing the rehearsal of the trigram produces a performance decrement. Moreover, as Dillon and Reid (1969) have shown, the amount of decrement is a function of the type of interfering task used. Complex interfering tasks appear to prevent rehearsal of the experimental material more effectively than simple interfering tasks, resulting in greater recall decrement.

Many investigators have found that an active rehearsing of the items to be learned contributes to performance when long-term memory operations are employed. Rundus and Atkinson (1970) and Rundus (1971) asked their subjects to rehearse aloud so that the experimenters could analyze the nature of the rehearsed responses after the experiment had been completed. The investigators presented lists of 20 unrelated nouns, with each noun exposed for five seconds. During this time, subjects were asked to study the list by rehearsing—repeating aloud any items from the list that they wished. Restrictions were not placed on the choice of items or on the rate of overt responding. A tape recorder was used to obtain rehearsal protocols for the subjects. After each presentation of the list—there were usually three—the subject was asked to recall as many of the nouns as possible.

The characteristics and role of the rehearsed responses were examined by looking at a rehearsal set. A rehearsal set was defined as all of the overt responses that the subject made during the five second interval during which each word was presented. Thus, the second rehearsal set comprised those responses that were rehearsed when the second noun on the list was shown; the third rehearsal set included those responses that were rehearsed when the third noun on the list was being presented; etc. Rundus (1971) found that with the exception of the first rehearsal set, the number of rehearsed items in each set remained relatively constant, ranging from 4.0 to 4.9. The number of *different* items that were rehearsed in a set increased until the fourth item was presented, at which point it stabilized except for the last few items. When the probability of recalling an item is plotted as a function of the mean number of rehearsals of that item, the relationship is quite high for the first 15 items on the list. See Figure 11-3. It may also be noted that the last items of the list are recalled quite well in spite of relatively few rehearsals—a finding undoubtedly resulting from the fact that subjects were able to keep these items in their memory span until they had the opportunity to write them down. Rundus and Atkinson (1970) and Rundus (1971) concluded that overt rehearsal aids recall. This has been supported by other investigators; see Nelson (1977), Glenberg, Smith, and Green (1977).

When investigators use overt rehearsal in their experiments, they make an implicit as-

sumption that this procedure is similar to what is taking place when the subject is permitted to rehearse covertly. This assumption has been confirmed by Horton (1976) and Murdock and Metcalfe (1978). Both studies were unable to demonstrate any differences in performance when covert and overt rehearsal procedures were compared.

An interesting difference between overt and covert rehearsal has been noted, however, by Kellas, McCauley, and McFarland (1975). These investigators could not find performance differences with the two procedures, thus supporting the findings of Horton (1976) and Murdock and Metcalfe (1978). They did note that when a self-paced condition was used, the overt rehearsal group chose to look at the presented items twice as long as the covert group. This increased looking time suggested, in spite of the finding of no perfor-

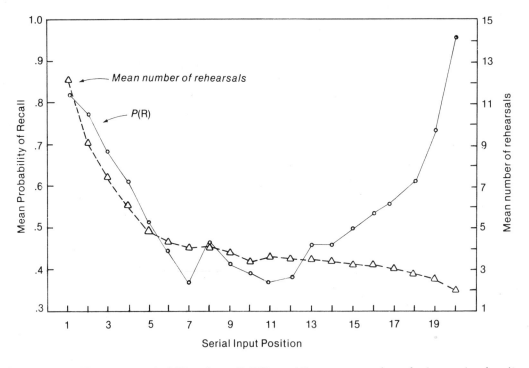

FIGURE 11-3.   The mean probability of recall, P(R), and the mean number of rehearsals of an item as a function of its serial input position. Adapted from D. Rundus, "Analysis of rehearsal processes in free recall." *Journal of Experimental Psychology*, 1971, 89, 63–67. Copyright © 1971 by the American Psychological Association. Reprinted by permission.

mance differences between the groups, that these different rehearsal procedures resulted in different encoding strategies.

Some investigators have been interested in manipulating what they have designated as rehearsal with the "memory" aspect of the experiment masked. In one study, Darley and Glass (1975) indicated to their subjects that they were conducting a visual search experiment. Subjects were to search a left-hand column of 16 words to find a target word. The target word was shown on the right side of the page. The searching of sixteen of these word column–target word pages comprised the experimental task. The location of the target word within the word column was varied, with locations classified as first, second, third, or fourth quarter of the column. Table 11-1 illustrates the task.

The authors assumed that the subjects, when performing the search task, would rehearse each target word until it was located in the column, at which time they would go on to the next page. It would then be expected that the amount of rehearsal would be related to where the target word was found in the

TABLE 11-1. Sample page of experimental task

| | |
|---|---|
| animal | |
| chief | |
| destroy | |
| valley | |
| thousand | |
| school | |
| neighbor | |
| paint | |
| journal | dollar |
| health | |
| ranch | |
| escape | |
| finger | |
| dollar | |
| round | |
| record | |

The word on the right serves as a target word; the column of words on the left must be searched in order to find the target word. In this illustration, the target word is found in the fourth quarter of the column. With other pages, the target word would be placed in the first, second, or third quarter of the list.

word column. Assuming that recall was related to the amount of rehearsal, the probability of recalling a target word that was located among Words 1–4 of the column would be smaller than when the target word was among Words 5–8, etc. Findings proved this to be true—the position of the target in the column of words was a significant factor in determining ease of recall.

A subsequent study (Experiment 1) by Maki and Schuler (1980) also masked the memory aspect of the task. Their subjects were asked to participate in a "reaction time" experiment. A word was presented on a screen for two seconds, after which a set of 8 words was shown on the screen and subjects were asked to determine if the set contained the target word. The time taken to decide whether or not the target word was among those shown was recorded. Subjects were required to search through one, two, three, or four sets of words in order to find the target word. Once the target word was found among the set, a new target word was shown, followed by presentations of more word sets, etc. At the conclusion of the presentation of all of the target words and their appropriate word sets, subjects were asked to recall as many of the target words as possible. Results, in keeping with those obtained by Darley and Glass (1975), indicated that the probability of recalling the target word was a function of the number of sets of words that were searched. The larger the number of sets searched for a particular target word, the greater the probability was that the subjects would recall that word. The authors reasoned that as the amount of time that the subjects kept in mind (rehearsed) the target word increased, the probability of recall increased. Two additional experiments by the same authors supported these findings.

Most of the experimental evidence suggests that some kind of rehearsal contributes to recall, although a few investigators have reported findings contrary to this conclusion; see Meunier, Ritz, and Meunier (1972), Craik and Watkins (1973).

It has been generally assumed that rehearsal reflects a basic encoding process. But the concept of rehearsal presents a problem, since the word has been defined in a variety of ways. Darley and Glass (1975) have suggested that the overt repetition of a word while the subject is attending to and engaged in some other task be termed "echoing," pointing out that it is possible to echo words while solving a simple arithmetic problem in the head. A second type of overt rehearsal has been identified as **attending**; here the subject pays attention to the words that are being overtly rehearsed (Darley and Glass, 1975).

The definition of covert rehearsal appears to pose even greater problems, since it generally refers to any activity that the subject desires to engage in when being presented with the experimental material. It may include, therefore, not only the covert repetition of the to-be-recalled items but also a variety of other encoding operations that are typically not described by the subjects. To these considerations of overt and covert rehearsal can be added the inference of rehearsal from specific activities engaged in by the subject; see Darley and Glass (1975), Maki and Schuler (1980).

**Other Encoding Processes** A current way of examining the encoding process is for the experimenter to provide the subject with specific instructions as to what should be done with the experimental material. By examining the instructions and the subject's performance, the investigator can make some inferences about the nature of the encoding process that has taken place.

This approach has been adopted by Jenkins and his associates; see Hyde and Jenkins (1969, 1973), Walsh and Jenkins (1973), Till and Jenkins (1973). The Hyde and Jenkins (1973) study, described in Chapter 9, illustrates the kind of instructions that have been used as well as the kind of findings that have been obtained. In the experimenters' task, five groups of subjects recalled a list of 24 words, which were orally presented at intervals of three seconds. Prior to the presentation of the words, each group received a different set of task instructions; subjects were asked to "process" the words in one of the following ways:

1. Rate each word as to how pleasant or unpleasant it was.
2. Rate each word as to how frequently it was used.
3. Determine if either an E or a G or both of these letters appeared in the word.
4. Identify the part of speech of each word.
5. Determine whether the word fit (or did not fit) into the frame "It is _____," or "It is the _____."

Each group was subdivided into (1) an intentional learning group—subjects in this group were informed that they would be asked to recall the words at the end of the session—and (2) an incidental learning group—subjects did not receive these instructions. A sixth group, serving as a control, was instructed to listen and attempt to recall the words.

The results of the Hyde and Jenkins (1973) experiment are shown in Table 11-2. The incidental versus intentional learning conditions resulted in little difference in performance, regardless of the type of orienting instructions. Of greater concern for an examination of the encoding process was the performance difference found between the first two sets of instructions (rating words for pleasantness or unpleasantness, and for frequency of

TABLE 11-2.    Mean number of words recalled as a function of the type of processing

| Condition | Learning Intentional | Incidental |
|---|---|---|
| Rating words for pleasantness | 12.7 | 11.2 |
| Rating words for frequency of usage | 10.4 | 10.2 |
| Identifying words as a part of speech | 8.1 | 8.1 |
| Checking of letters E and G | 8.2 | 6.6 |
| Does word fit into sentence frame? | 6.2 | 6.6 |
| Control | 10.9 | |

Adapted from Hyde and Jenkins (1973).

use) and the last three. These first two types of instructions produced greater recall scores; the authors assumed these instructions produced a semantic type of processing or encoding. Such processing was assumed to be qualitatively different from the nonsemantic type of processing occasioned by the last three types of instructions.

A different approach to encoding is found in a series of studies conducted by Wickens and his associates. This approach emphasized the attributes of the stimuli that are perceived by the subject while he/she is encoding the material for subsequent recall. An early study by Wickens, Born, and Allen (1963) illustrates the methodology, experimental findings, and general rationale. Using the Peterson and Peterson (1959) procedure, experimental and control subjects were presented with a CCC for half a second. Following a retention interval of 11 seconds, all subjects were asked to recall the syllable. Three presentations, or trials, each involving a different CCC, were provided. On the fourth trial, control subjects continued to be presented with still another CCC; experimental subjects, however, were presented with a three digit number. Results indicated a gradual performance decrement for both groups over the first three trials. On the fourth trial, it was noted that performance continued to decline for the control group but increased for the experimental group.

The recall decrement, observed in the control group over all four trials and in the experimental group over the first three trials, was attributed to proactive inhibition. The authors explained the performance increment noted on the fourth trial for the experimental group as a release from the effects of proactive inhibition. Figure 11-4 presents the kind of results obtained with this type of study.

Wickens and his associates have assumed that the interference generated over the three trials for both groups of subjects is specific to the type of material used. The fact that a performance increment is obtained when the material is changed supports this position. The encoding attribute is identified from an

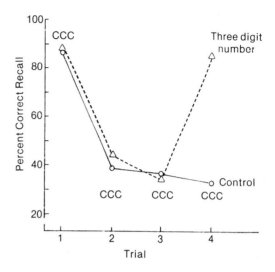

FIGURE 11-4.   Illustration of release from PI. Both experimental and control groups are presented with CCCs on the first three trials; on the fourth trial, the experimental group is presented with a three digit number while control subjects are presented with another CCC.

examination of the characteristics of the triad of items that are used as the experimental material. For example, the obtaining of a performance increment (release from PI) when a noun printed in the *upper case* follows the presentation of three *lower case* nouns suggests that the encoding attribute in this experiment has to do with the physical characteristics of the material.

Wickens (1972) summarized an extensive series of experiments conducted in his laboratory and identified at least three major classes of encoding attributes: (1) semantic features, as indicated by the use of three words, followed by a shift to a three digit number; (2) physical features, as indicated by the use of words printed in upper case, followed by a shift to a word in lower case; and (3) syntactic features, as indicated by the use of three verbs, followed by a shift to a noun. Other encoding attributes such as word frequency and imagery have also been identified.

Another procedure for identifying encoding attributes is the visual search task—subjects are presented with target letters or words and then are asked to find these same items "hidden" among a large number of distractors. By manipulating the relationship of the characteristics of the distractors to the target items, the experimenter can make inferences about the encoded attribute of the target item. These studies have revealed semantic as well as physical encoding attributes, thus confirming the findings of Wickens. Neisser (1963) found evidence for physical encoding; he found that burying angular target letters (e.g., X) among the angular distractors (e.g., Y) resulted in a slower visual search than when the distractor letters were round (e.g., B). A semantic attribute has been noted by Graboi (1975), who found that when subjects were asked to visually search for a target word such as *bird*, semantic distractors such as *fly*, *nest*, and *robin* resulted in a greater amount of search time than if the distractors were not related semantically.

**Level of Processing**  By the early 1970s, a dual theory of memory with two conceptual categories (or structural features), one related to short-term memory and the other to long-term, was an integral aspect of most information processing positions. But, as mentioned earlier, investigators were beginning to realize the difficulty of making a distinction between the two categories. Craik and Lockhart (1972) proposed an alternative way of looking at memory.

These authors suggested that the persistence of the memory trace (amount remembered) was a function of how the individual processed (or encoded) the information received, with longer-lasting and stronger traces being associated with deeper levels of processing. Two types of processing were proposed. Type I consisted of only recirculation or rehearsal of the material—a keeping of the information in consciousness. Type II processing, however, involved a deeper analysis of the material and resulted in a more durable trace.

Craik and Lockhart (1972) proposed that the use of different orienting tasks, as shown by Jenkins and his associates, was an appropriate way to manipulate processing; encoding the material in different ways would produce different amounts of material being retained. However, the encoding process was assumed to be hierarchical, proceeding through a series of stages or levels and stopping upon attainment of a level of encoding that was in keeping with the kind of task provided by the experimenter.

The study by Hyde and Jenkins (1969) was used to support the position that differential levels of processing resulted in different recall performances. It will be recalled that this study indicated that estimating the number of letters in a word or determining whether words contained specified letters resulted in poorer recall for those words than did rating the same words for pleasantness. The experimental findings of Tulving (1966) and Craik and Watkins (1973) that repetition or rehearsal did not improve performance were also in keeping with Craik and Lockhart's position that rehearsal represented a low level of processing that contributed very little to performance.

The level-of-processing position related memory to the activity of the organism—what the individual was doing—rather than identifying memory with a physical or conceptual location, as the dual theory of memory had proposed. But just as difficulties were discovered with the dual theory, problems have been noted with the level of processing position.

*Level of Processing Difficulties*  One problem is that many investigators—e.g., Rundus (1971), Nelson (1977), Glenberg, Smith, and Green (1977)—have found that repetition of material does influence retention, a finding contrary to Craik and Lockhart's (1972) hypothesis that memory was not influenced by repetition provided that the depth of processing remained constant.

Three experiments were conducted by Nelson (1977); his third study confirmed the results of his first two and illustrates his procedure and experimental findings. In this experiment, depth of processing was measured by having the subjects use either phonemic processing ("Does the word contain an r sound?") or semantic processing ("Does the item represent a living thing?"). Subjects received either one or two repetitions of a list of 30 words. Subjects were then given three retention tests: (a) uncued recall, (b) cued recall, and (c) recognition. Nelson's findings, indicated in Figure 11-5, demonstrate that the repetition of the experimental material at either level of processing does influence retention.

Using an entirely different and most innovative experimental procedure, Glenberg, Smith, and Green (1977) also found that repetition, as measured by overt rehearsal, influences retention. The procedure utilized in the three experiments was similar to the methodology employed in the Peterson and Peterson (1959) short-term retention study. In Glenberg, Smith, and Green's Experiment 2, which clearly reveals the effect of repetition, subjects were visually presented with a four digit number for 3 seconds, after which either one or three words were shown for 2 seconds, followed by a blank screen. During an interval of 2, 6, or 18 seconds, the subjects were required to verbally repeat the words that had been presented. If just one word was exposed, verbalization consisted of either 3, 7, or 27

repetitions, while if three words were exposed, verbalization consisted of 1, 3, or 9 repetitions. Following such rehearsal, subjects were asked to recall the four digit number. Since the subjects were told that the overt rehearsal task was used to prevent them from rehearsing the digits, the experimenters assumed that Craik and Lockhart's (1972) Type I processing (rehearsal) was in effect and not contaminated by any attempt on the part of the subjects to provide a higher level of processing. Sixty presentations or trials of the digits and word distractors were provided, with the first three and last three trials excluded from the analysis. A recognition test was given in which the words appeared amid appropriate distractors. It revealed that performance increased as a function of the number of overt rehearsals, with the effect being demonstrated when both one and three words were used.

In addition to raising the experimental difficulties indicated, Postman, Thompkins, and Gray (1978) questioned whether the varying types of orienting tasks or questions provided in experiments on depth of processing can be used to make inferences about processing level. They doubt, for example, that

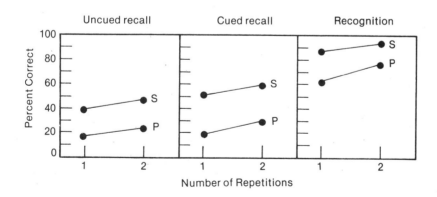

FIGURE 11-5.  Percentage correct on three memory tests as joint function of (a) number of repetitions (one versus two) and (b) depth of processing (semantic versus phonemic). Adapted from T. O. Nelson, "Repetition and depth of processing." *Journal of Verbal Learning and Verbal Behavior,* 1977, 16, 151–171.

adults ever restrict their processing of words to the nonsemantic or physical level, pointing out that substantial amounts of retention have been observed in many experiments even though only nonsemantic processing had presumably taken place.

A second conceptual problem touched on by Postman, Thompkins, and Gray (1978) is that there has been no adequate way to (1) define what is meant by processing or (2) measure processing depth. For example, Loftus, Greene, and Smith (1980) examined recognition memory using a series of color slides of natural outdoor scenes as the experimental material. They had one group of subjects "process" this material by contemplating the "meaning of life." These investigators found that recognition performance by this group was as high as that of a second group of subjects who had been provided standard intentional learning instructions. Performance by the first group was superior to that of a third experimental group asked to process the material by estimating the percentage of each slide that was taken up by the sky. Most experimenters, however, have been content to use orienting instructions or kinds of questions from which just two or three levels of processing have been inferred. But certainly the encoding process is more complex than this, and as Nelson (1977) has pointed out, no algorithm for ordering different kinds of processing in terms of levels or depth has emerged.

## STORAGE: IS MEMORY PERMANENT?

Storage refers to the holding or storing of information that has been received or encoded by the individual. The tapes in a musical library are stored representations of concerts that took place years ago, but nonetheless are available when one wishes to listen to them. Storage has been generally thought of as a passive process; it has been conceptualized as consisting of traces or **engrams**, neurological correlates of the stimulus events as encoded or perceived by the subject, which can be subsequently retrieved by the subject.

Questions concerning the nature of the storage process and the characteristics of the neural trace have probably been asked as long as people have been interested in the area of memory. Thus many of the issues raised by current information processing theorists have had a long experimental history. One of these issues has been whether the memory trace is permanent. That is, once laid down, does the trace remain until death as a part of the organism's neural structure?

This question may appear foolish, since it is obvious that there are many occasions on which one is unable to remember material that had once been learned. But failure to remember an event at a particular time does not mean that the memory of that event has been lost, since the event may come to mind perhaps an hour or a day later. Clearly, the earlier failure to remember cannot be used as evidence that the event has been irretrievably lost or that the memory trace was transient; such failure to remember can be traced to a problem with the retrieval process rather than storage. This illustration reveals the basic problem that confronts investigators in attempting to determine whether memory is permanent. Failure to remember may not reflect the fact that the appropriate memory trace has been erased or has decayed; it may simply reflect an inability of the individual to retrieve the information at a particular time. Until appropriate physiological evidence is obtained, it is impossible to answer this question. That is, no one can demonstrate that memories are not permanent, since all failures to remember can be attributed to retrieval failure. Nonetheless, there is some interesting clinical evidence that bears on the problem.

**The Case of S**   Chapter 10 mentioned the clinical observations of Luria (1968), who for more than 30 years systematically observed S, a man whose ability to remember vast amounts of material was truly remarkable. Luria was convinced that the capacity of S's memory was virtually unlimited—that he did not have to "memorize" the data presented but merely had to "register" an impression, which he could "read" at any subsequent point in time. Luria reports instances in which

S was able to reproduce material 10 or even 16 years after its original presentation and without apparent or obvious rehearsal of this material during the interim.

Luria has indicated that there were instances of S "forgetting" material but that such forgetting consisted of omissions of elements within the material to be remembered. But there was a simple explanation for these omissions. In "reading" off the impressions during the recall period, S might omit a particular element because it was not discernible. Luria believed that these omissions were not defects of memory but in fact defects of perception. In these instances, failure to recall could not be explained in terms of traditional explanations—the decay of memory traces, or interference provided by other material that had been learned—but rather by certain factors that influenced S's perception, such as the clarity of the perception, contrast, the amount of lighting available, etc. As Luria (1968) has written, "His errors could not be explained, then, in terms of the psychology of memory but had to do with the psychological factors that govern perception" (p. 35).

**Penfield's Conceptualization of Memory**
Physiological evidence on the permanence of memory has come from the work of Penfield (1955), a Canadian neurosurgeon. As a result of his surgical observations with patients who had epilepsy, Penfield suggested that information that has been placed in memory (storage) is localized there permanently. In the course of operations, patients were given only a local anesthetic, and when the brain was exposed, Penfield explored the cortex by applying a weak electrical current from place to place in an effort to reproduce the beginning of the patient's attack and thus verify the appropriate place to make a surgical excision. Penfield noted that when such gentle electrical stimulation was applied to the temporal lobes, it resulted in some of his patients remembering experiences from the past—a phenomenon that he defined as **psychical responses**. In some cases there was a detailed reenactment of a single experience which presumably had been unavailable for a long time to the normal recall of the patient. Such experiences in-

cluded many different elements of thought, including auditory, visual, and somatic sensations and also emotional responding. Penfield likened these psychical responses to a stream of consciousness and attempted to indicate their nature by means of the following analogy:

> Among the millions and millions of nerve cells that clothe certain parts of the temporal lobe on each side, there runs a thread. It is the thread of time, the thread that had run through each succeeding wakeful hour of the individual's past life. Think of this thread, if you like, as a pathway through an unending sequence of nerve cells, nerve fibers, and synapses. It is the pathway which can be followed again because of the continuing facilitation that has been created in the cell contacts.
>
> When, by chance, the neurosurgeon's electrode activated some portion of that thread, there is a response as though that thread were a wire recorder, or a strip of cinematographic film, on which are registered all those things of which the individual was once aware, the things he selected for his attention in that interval of time. Absent from it are the sensory impulses he ignored, the talk he did not heed.
>
> Time's strip of film runs forward, never backward, even when resurrected from the past. It seems to proceed again at time's own unchanged pace. It would seem, once one section of the strip has come alive, that a functional all-or-nothing principle steps in so as to protect the other portion of the film from activation by the electrical current. As long as the electrode is held in place, the experience of a former day goes forward. There is no holding it still, no turning back. When the electrode is withdrawn it stops as suddenly as it began. (Reprinted by permission of the publisher from "The Permanent Record of the Stream of Consciousness" by W. Penfield, *Proceedings of the Fourteenth International Congress of Psychology, Montreal, June 1954*, pp. 67–68. Copyright 1955 by Elsevier North Holland, Inc.

It is tempting to assume that Penfield's neurological findings represent the place and mechanism of storage, thus supporting the position that the memory trace is permanent. But challenges to his physiological conceptualization of memory have come from several sources. Barbizet (1970) has reported that only a small percentage of patients—less than 8 percent—provide such recollections when their temporal lobes are stimulated. Mahl, Rothenberg, Delgado, and Hamlin (1964) found that the psychical responses of one of their patients who was electrically stimulated in the temporal lobe were related to specific events that had taken place just prior to the time she received the stimulation, and were not literal recollections of earlier events. Finally, Neisser (1967) has suggested that a careful examination of recollections obtained with temporal lobe stimulation frequently reveals that they are comparable to dreams, which are generally accepted to be synthetic constructions and not literal recall of earlier events.

**Hypnosis and the Phenomenon of Age Regression**   A last bit of evidence having to do with the permanence of memory comes from the phenomenon of hypnotic age regression. Many of us are familiar with stage or parlor demonstrations of hypnosis. A hypnotist suggests to a hypnotized subject that he or she is much younger, perhaps a child of 6 or 7. Upon receiving the suggestion, the subject provides information or behaves in a way that seems characteristic of children that age. This phenomenon has been described as hypnotic age regression. The fact that an individual who is unable to respond appropriately when in a normal state is apparently able to do so when hypnotized suggests that the "forgotten" event did not decay with time but instead is permanent.

In one early clinical study of age regression, Erickson (1937) reported the experiences of a police informer who had survived a homicidal assault which had occurred two years previously. The subject had complete amnesia for virtually all of the details of this experience, including the name of the hospital to which he had been admitted. Extensive and persistent questioning of the subject, both in the ordinary deep hypnotic trance and in the normal waking state, elicited little information about the event. A different approach was then used to get at the details of this incident. The subject was placed in a trance and

induced to relive past events in a chronologically progressive fashion, beginning considerably before his traumatic experience. It was found that when the subject came to the day of the homicidal attack, he was able to recount the incident with remarkable vividness and richness of detail. The accuracy of the subject's recollections of the event were verified by inquiring at the hospital to which he had been taken; the police for whom the subject had served as an informer were also questioned and confirmed the information that he had reported about their role in this incident.

Hypnosis is currently being used by police officers as a clinical procedure to help individuals remember information that they cannot recall in the waking state. See Box 11-3.

Although case histories on age regression are interesting, other experimenters have preferred to use more than a single subject and to obtain readily confirmable information from their regressed subjects. True's (1949) study was of this type.

Fifty subjects, ages 20 to 24, were regressed through hypnosis to ages 10, 7, and then 4. At each age, they were asked to indicate on what day of the week their birthday and Christmas Day fell that year. Their answers, checked with an appropriate calendar, are presented in Table 11-3. True's findings—that subjects could remember under hypnosis material that could not be retrieved when they were awake—are impressive. Surprisingly, True found that when his subjects were regressed to 4 years of age, 62 percent of them were able to correctly remember the day of their birthday and 76 percent were able to remember on what day Christmas fell. But such a finding is suspect, since it is not likely that 4-year-olds are actually aware of the varying days of the week. Subsequent studies

TABLE 11-3.   Hypnotic age regression states of 50 subjects (40 males and 10 females)

|  | *Percent Correct by Age* | | |
| --- | --- | --- | --- |
|  | *10* | *7* | *4* |
| Birthday | 92 | 84 | 62 |
| Christmas | 94 | 86 | 76 |

Adapted from R. M. True, "Experimental Control in Hypnotic Age Regression States." *Science*, 1949, 110, 583–584.

**BOX 11-3**

On July 15, 1976, a school bus driver and 26 children disappeared from the small town of Chowchilla, California. Subsequent information indicated that the driver of the bus and the children had been kidnapped by three masked men. They had been driven to a gravel quarry located more than 100 miles away and forced to stay in an abandoned trailer truck that had been buried 6 feet underground. Eventually the driver and children were rescued unharmed, but questioning of the victims by the police gave them little information about the kidnappers. A professional hypnotist was asked to help in the case. Under hypnosis, the bus driver was able to recall all but one digit of the license plate on the white van that the kidnappers had used in committing the crime. This information was primarily responsible for the apprehension of the three suspects.

The Chowchilla incident is only one of many that illustrate the usefulness of hypnosis to the police. Schafer and Rubio (1978) have discussed 14 cases of interrogation of witnesses and victims of crimes under hypnosis in and around Orange County, California during 1972–1973. They have reported that in 10 cases, information obtained when the individual was hypnotized substantially helped investigators to solve the crime; moreover, such information was not obtainable when the victims and witnesses were in their normal waking state. Yarmey (1979) indicated that hypnotists associated with the Israeli National Police Force have reportedly solved 25 cases and assisted in 60 others between the years 1972 and 1976.

by Best and Michaels (1954) and Barber (1961), attempting to replicate True's (1949) findings, were unsuccessful. It is possible, as Barber (1962) has suggested, that since True's subjects were tested over a period of many months, there may have been some discussion of the experiment by the to-be-hypnotized subjects, who then obtained the appropriate information about these varying days prior to serving as subjects.

One of the most extensive studies was conducted by Reiff and Scheerer (1959). After a preliminary testing of more than 100 subjects, Reiff and Scheerer chose five easily hypnotized subjects. These subjects were university students aged 19 to 27. The experimental procedure consisted of regressing them to ages 10, 7, and 4, in that order. While in each regressed stage, the subjects were asked to perform six or seven different tests that the authors believed were appropriate for the age level examined. Fifteen control subjects were used, five at each age level. They were not hypnotized but were asked to simulate to the best of their ability how a child aged 4, 7, or 10 would perform on these same tests. Just two of the tests used will be described. For age 4, one test was a mud and lollipop task—sub-

jects had to make mud pies and after about five minutes were offered a lollipop. It was assumed that regressed subjects would not be disturbed about eating a lollipop with muddy, dirty hands, while control subjects would show difficulties in either accepting the offer of a lollipop or eating it with dirty hands.

A second test was a word association test, which was administered to subjects at all three regressed age levels. Norms obtained from word association studies indicated that adults and children respond differently to the same word; adults usually reply with an opposite or a superordinate, whereas children are more likely to respond with a synonym. For example, most adults would respond to *dark* with its opposite *light* or *white*; children would be more likely respond with *night* or *black*. It was assumed that regressed subjects would provide associations similar to those found on children's norms, whereas controls would provide associations similar to those found on adult norms.

Statistical evaluation of the findings from the varying tests, although not supporting differences in performance between regressed and control subjects in all instances, did provide a number of significant differences. The regressed subjects exhibited a level of behavior in keeping with the age to which they had regressed; control subjects did not. The authors have noted that the statistical evaluation of the results cannot capture the impression of genuineness and spontaneity which the regressed subjects gave, as contrasted with the forced and embarrassed behavior of the simulators.

In spite of Yates's (1961) belief that the technique of hypnotic age regression can provide a crucial test of the theory that learned responses are never "destroyed" but only supplanted, thus remaining available for activation under appropriate circumstances, the experimental findings so far cannot answer this question. Although they demonstrate improved recall in some instances, it is readily apparent that hypnotized subjects cannot remember all of the information that they have previously learned. And the reason for their failure is not clear. Contrary to the assumption of some investigators, it may be that there is a decay of the memory trace. Or, there may be a failure of the retrieval process. A ready answer is not forthcoming.

## Retrieval

Retrieval is the last category to be discussed in the information processing model of memory. After information has been encoded and placed in storage, it becomes necessary for the subject to recover it—to call it to mind. Stated differently, **retrieval** is a process of converting the trace which has been kept in storage into a covert or overt response. Some theorists have considered retrieval to be synonymous with the subject's overt responding, as measured by a retention test; more frequently, retrieval, like encoding and storage, has been considered to be a conceptual process inferred from the investigator's theoretical position and the type of independent variable manipulated.

In one type of experiment used to provide information about the retrieval process, two groups of subjects are given a list of words (or some other type of verbal material) that is to be recalled later. It is assumed that the encoding and storage of this list of words is the same for both groups. However, just prior to the recall test, the experimental group may receive specific information, such as retrieval cues, pertaining to some characteristic of the word list. If the recall scores obtained by the experimental group are superior to those of the control, investigators assume that the information provided had a facilitative effect on the retrieval process.

**The Role of Retrieval Cues**   The role of retrieval cues on retention has interested investigators for some time. A number of experimenters have demonstrated that recall can be related to the presence or absence of these cues as well as to the kind of cues provided.

In a paired-associate study by Bahrick (1969), 20 pairs of unrelated common nouns served as the material to be learned. After the subjects had reached a criterion of six correct anticipations, a retention interval of either zero or two hours, two days, or two weeks was provided, followed by a retention test in which the subjects were given the list of stimulus terms and asked to write the responses they could recall opposite the appropriate stimuli. Subjects were then told that they would be given a second trial in which retrieval cues would be presented to help them recall each response word that they had missed on the previous trial. (Bahrick called these retrieval cues prompting words.) The experimental variable that interested Bahrick was the associative relationship between the retrieval cue he presented and the response word that had been forgotten. Five progressively higher associative relationship levels were examined. At the lowest level, the retrieval cue elicited the response word approximately 4 percent of the time, as with retrieval cue *print* and response word *book*. At the highest level, the retrieval cue elicited the response word approximately 74 percent of the time, as with retrieval cue *hot* and response word *cold*.

Results indicated that regardless of the length of the retention interval (zero or two hours, two days, or two weeks), the recall of forgotten responses was aided by the presen-

TABLE 11-4. Percent correct responding as a function of the associative level between the retrieval cue and the to-be-remembered word

| Associative Level of Retrieval Cue | Retention Interval | | | | |
|---|---|---|---|---|---|
| | 0 | 2 hours | 2 days | 2 weeks | Mean |
| 1 | 18 | 16 | 13 | 14 | 15 |
| 2 | 48 | 43 | 42 | 27 | 40 |
| 3 | 49 | 55 | 58 | 50 | 53 |
| 4 | 79 | 72 | 62 | 63 | 69 |
| 5 | 86 | 80 | 70 | 80 | 79 |
| Mean | 56 | 53 | 49 | 47 | |

Adapted from H. P. Bahrick, "Measurement of memory prompted by recall." *Journal of Experimental Psychology*, 1969, 79, 213–219. Copyright © 1969 by the American Psychological Association. Reprinted by permission.

tation of retrieval cues. Moreover, as the associative level of the retrieval cue–response word increased, recall of the forgotten words also increased. Table 11-4 presents the results for the five levels of associative relationships and the duration of the retention interval.

**The Principle of Encoding Specificity** In his analysis of the role of retrieval cues, Tulving has hypothesized that cues present when the information was encoded must also be present during retrieval if they are to be effective in aiding recall. This relationship between encoding cues and retrieval cues has been called the principle of **encoding specificity**. Studies by Tulving and Pearlstone (1966) and Tulving and Osler (1968) illustrate its operation.

In the Tulving and Pearlstone (1966) study, lists of either 12, 24, or 48 words were constructed. Each list also included additional words that indicated the presence of either one, two, or four classes or categories of list words. In the oral presentation of these words, the category word would be presented, followed by the words to be recalled (CRIMES: theft, treason; WEAPONS: bomb, cannon; etc). After such a presentation, the subjects were asked to recall as many of the words as possible, either with the category words, which could serve as retrieval cues, or without them.

As can be observed from Figure 11-6, the findings indicated that cued recall was higher than noncued recall in all comparisons; moreover, the influence of cueing was greater as the length of the list increased.

In a subsequent study, Tulving and Osler (1968) examined the characteristics of the cues in relation to the words to be recalled. Rather than using category names as in the Tulving and Pearlstone (1966) study, Tulving and Osler (1968) utilized weak associates of the experimental words. For example, the cue for the to-be-remembered word *city* would be *dirty* or *village*. Instructions, similar to those provided by Tulving and Pearlstone (1966), informed the subjects that the associated cues might aid them in their subsequent recall. Their results supported earlier findings. The use of word associates as cues increased recall if the cue was present during both the original presentation of the material and the subsequent recall test; however, the cue had no effect when presented only during recall. Moreover, no effect was obtained if different cues were present during presentation and recall. For example, recall for the word *city* was not influenced if *dirty* was used when *city* was originally presented and *village* was used during the test for recall. In summary, the authors note that "specific retrieval cues facilitate recall if and only if the information about them

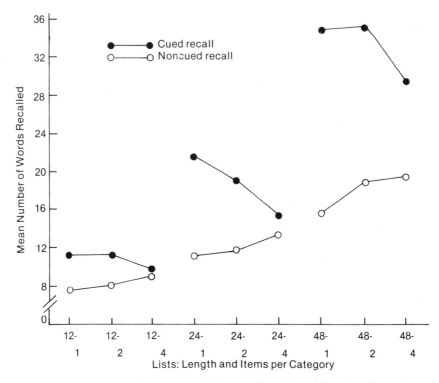

FIGURE 11-6. Mean number of words recalled as a function of list length and number of items per category. Adapted from E. Tulving and Z. Pearlstone, "Availability versus accessibility of information in memory for words." *Journal of Verbal Learning and Verbal Behavior*, 1966, 5, 381–391.

and their relation to the to-be-remembered word is stored at the same time as the information about the membership of the to-be-remembered word in a given list" (p. 593), a conclusion that has been the basis for the principle of encoding specificity. Subsequent studies by Thomson and Tulving (1970) and Tulving and Thomson (1973) have provided additional experimental support for this principle.

But all of the experimental evidence does not support Tulving's principle of encoding specificity. The retrieval cues used by Bahrick (1969) and Kochevar and Fox (1980) were not present during the original presentation of the target words, and yet the results of both studies indicated that recall was aided by their presence. Moreover, Reder, Anderson, and Bjork (1974) have found that if the target words to be learned were of very low frequency, cue words highly associated with

these target words were very effective as retrieval cues even though they were not present when the target words were originally given.

Thomson and Tulving (1970), to account for these results in terms of the encoding specificity principle, have suggested that these retrieval cues were implicitly activated during the original presentation of the target words. But as Santa and Lamwers (1974) and Baddeley (1976) have pointed out, such an explanation makes the principle untestable, since any failure to obtain the predicted result would be accounted for by positing that the retrieval cue was encoded implicitly during the presentation of the experimental material.

**Recall versus Recognition** Traditional experimenters have assumed that recall and recognition, the two most frequently used measures of retention, each tap the same storage construct, though with differing sensitivities. Recognition, as noted in Chapter 9, has been found in most studies to be the more sensitive of the two measures employed. (However, comparisons between response measures are tenuous, since both recall and recognition scores are dependent upon the experimental methodology employed.)

In contrast to the traditionalists, many information processing investigators have not accepted the differential sensitivity position; rather, they have assumed that the process involved in recall is qualitatively different from that observed in recognition. If material is to be recalled, retrieval consists of a generation and a discrimination-decision process; in contrast, if the information needs to be recognized, only the discrimination-decision process is involved.

In order to illustrate this position, assume that one is interested in remembering the numerical value of pi. In attempting to recall this value, one may generate a variety of numerical values—e.g., 3.16, 3.12, 3.19, etc. After generation of each value, a discrimination-decision process takes place whereby each value is considered and then rejected until one value is accepted as being correct. The subject overtly responds with this value. In contrast, if it is necessary only to recognize the correct value, the generation process does not take place. The correct value and several distractor values are presented to the subject; the recognition of the correct value involves only a discrimination-decision process.

Investigators, to support the qualitatively different position, have argued that if recall and recognition differ only in the sensitivity with which they measure memory, in experiments using both of these measures they should reveal similar retention scores. But this has not always been found. Although high-frequency words have been shown to be more easily recalled than low-frequency words—see Hall (1954), Bousfield and Cohen (1955)—some experimenters have found that low-frequency words are more easily recognized; see Gorman (1961), Shepard (1967), Wallace, Sawyer, and Robertson (1978). In addition, Kintsch (1968) has found that lists containing highly associated or conceptually similar words are recalled better than lists with unrelated words; on the other hand, there is no difference between such lists when retention is measured with a recognition test.[3]

Tulving and his associates have rejected the recognition-recall qualitative difference position, arguing that the retrieval process operating in both recognition and recall is the same. When a difference is found between the two measures, such a difference can be related to the number and/or characteristics of the retrieval cues present.

One kind of support for the single process has been provided by Tulving and Watkins (1973), who have demonstrated the continuity of recall and recognition. In their study, subjects were presented with five lists of 28 words, each word five letters long. One list served as a control—subjects were provided with traditional free-recall instructions. With the four experimental lists, component letters of the words were used as retrieval cues, thus providing a cued-recall test. The first two, three, four, or five letters of each word served as the retrieval cue. Results, presented in Figure 11-7, support Tulving and Watkin's (1973) position of a continuity in the retrieval process, with the amount of retention depending on the number of retrieval cues available.

Tulving has also pointed out that by appropriately manipulating retrieval cues, the experimenter should be able to demonstrate that recall can be superior to recognition. Such a finding would argue against the two-process position, which has maintained that recognition should always be superior to recall because recognition involves only one process rather than two. Using a cued-recall procedure, Tulving and Thomson (1973), Watkins (1974), Watkins and Tulving (1975), Wiseman and Tulving (1975, 1976), and Muter (1978) have all indicated that under appropriate circumstances recall is superior to recognition. The experimental procedure used in some of these cued-recall and recognition experiments was to provide the subject with a list of pairs of associatively related words, such as *hot-cold*, with one word of each pair designated as the target item or to-be-remembered word and the other word serving as a cue word. Cue words are studied by the sub-

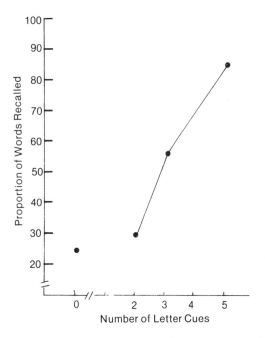

FIGURE 11-7. Proportion of words recalled as a function of number of letter cues. Adapted from E. Tulving and M. J. Watkins, "Continuity between recall and recognition." *American Journal of Psychology*, 1973, 86, 739–748. Copyright © 1973 The University of Illinois Press.

ject with the expectation that they will aid in the recall of the target item. Following the presentation of these pairs of words, the subject is given two successive retention tests. The first, a recognition test, provides only the target words and appropriate distractors. The second, a cued-recall test, provides all the cue words to help the subject recall the target words. These experiments have demonstrated that under such circumstances recall is superior to recognition.

Watkins's (1974) study illustrates the procedure as well as typical findings. Subjects were presented with 39 pairs of five letter and two letter nonsense words, such as SPANI SH, with the first five letters being designated as the A term and the second two letters as the B term. It may be noted that if each B term is added to the appropriate A term, a common word is formed. Subjects were then given a

distractor task in which 15 of the pairs of items that had been earlier presented were combined with 15 distractors; subjects were asked to recognize those pairs of items previously presented. After a 30 to 40 minute delay, subjects were presented with the 24 B terms (which had not been among those items used in the earlier recognition test), along with 24 distractor items, and asked to recognize those that had been previously presented. If 24 items were not "recognized," subjects were forced to select additional items to total 24. A cued-recall test was then provided; subjects were asked to recall the B term after having been given the A term of each pair. This procedure is somewhat complex, so Table 11-5 provides a summary of the experimental steps.

When recall was compared with the two recognition measures, results indicated that the recall condition produced vastly superior retention; the probability of a correct response was .72 for cued recall, compared with .14 for free recognition and .52 for forced recognition.

Watkins (1974) has acknowledged that his findings were atypical, writing, "It is conceded that such contrived procedures are not representative of those used in most verbal memory studies, and that the finding of recall that is better than recognition is likewise unusual" (p. 162). Nonetheless, these findings do support the position that any measure of memory is related to the method of measurement. The findings also show that any theory which posits that one measure is invariably superior to another is undoubtedly incorrect.

Rabinowitz, Mandler, and Patterson (1977) and Rabinowitz, Mandler, and Barsalou (1979) have indicated that the generation and discrimination-decision hypothesis for explaining recall, at least in its pure form, is untenable. They noted that free recall does not generally consist of the generation of candidate items coupled with a discrimination-decision phase. Unlike the situation in the example used earlier, an individual does not normally retrieve the value of pi (or any other kind of information) by a generation process. The experimental findings of Rabinowitz and

TABLE 11-5.    Experimental steps used in examining recall and recognition

1.  Thirty-nine pairs of items presented; e.g., $\dfrac{A}{EXPLO}$ $\dfrac{B}{RE}$; $\dfrac{A}{AMNES}$ $\dfrac{B}{IC}$; $\dfrac{A}{LIQUE}$ $\dfrac{B}{FY}$.

2.  Distraction task provided: subjects asked to recognize 15 "noncritical" A and B pairs of items that were on first list from 15 A and B distractor pairs.

3.  Remaining 24 B terms combined with 24 two letter distractors; subjects asked to recognize the 24 items that had been presented in the original list.

4.  Cued recall test provided: subjects asked to recall the B terms after having been given retrieval cue of the A item, such as EXPLO__; AMNES__;

his associates have suggested, however, that this process can be conceptualized as an auxiliary strategy—it is used sometimes. But the usefulness of the generation process is limited, since it is most effective when employed shortly after target items have been presented. This strategy is ineffectual if a relatively long period, such as a week, has elapsed between the presentation of the material and the test for recall. Rabinowitz, Mandler, and Barsalou (1979) have concluded that "since in the real world auxiliary retrieval strategies are typically used after some time interval and only after direct access has failed, generation-recognition seems to be a poor candidate for trying to recall the name of a town one had visited some time ago or the name of a guest at a party" (p. 70).

In summary, the recall-versus-recognition controversy has not been resolved. The evidence is clear, however, that any measure of memory is related to the method of measurement. Inasmuch as the two measures utilized different procedures, some question can be raised as to whether any comparison of them is appropriate.

## SUMMARY

Growing impatience and disaffection with the traditional approach to the study of learning and retention have caused many investigators to adopt alternative ways of studying these constructs. Since these alternative methods do not distinguish between the concepts of learning and retention, the construct of memory has been used. One such alternative, the information processing position, works with the analogy of a computer, which receives information and stores it for subsequent use.

An early controversy stemming from the new approach to the study of memory occurred over the position that human memory employed two memory processes, short-term (STM) and long-term memory (LTM) systems. James (1890) had proposed such a dual system; Hebb (1949) and Broadbent (1958) had also posited the operation of two such systems in their examination of human memory. Experimental impetus was provided by the classic studies of Brown (1958) and Peterson and Peterson (1959), who were able to demonstrate decremental retention curves for consonant syllables (CCCs) when the retention interval was measured in seconds. Peterson and Peterson (1959) found, for example, that when the presentation of a single CCC was followed by 15 to 18 seconds of counting backward, there was little retention of this syllable.

Clinical and experimental evidence appeared to support the two-memory system, but a detailed examination of this evidence revealed problems. Many investigators rejected the dual position and opted for a continuous memory process, with short-term memory at one end of the continuum and long-term memory at the other end. Current investigators have continued to use these constructs to distinguish between operations that use within-memory span material, with a retention interval measured in seconds (short-term memory), and those that use beyond-memory span material, with a retention interval measured in hours or longer (long-term memory). The information processing position places emphasis upon the three basic constructs of encoding, storage, and retrieval. Encoding refers to those processes responsible for transforming external stimuli into internal information. Although no taxonomy of encoding operations has been developed, the concept of rehearsal represents a commonly accepted encoding operation. The experimental evidence provides clear support that either covert or overt rehearsal will result in increased retention. One methodological problem is how to manipulate rehearsal, since there is no assurance that any of a variety of procedures will result in identical encoding processes.

The second construct, storage, refers to the holding or storing of information that has been received or encoded by the subject. Little experimental information is available about the operation of the storage process. Some theorists have assumed that material placed in storage remains there permanently and that difficulties in remembering arise not from a decay or deterioration of the memory trace, but from an inadequate functioning of the retrieval process. Neurological evidence obtained by Penfield (1955), who found that his surgical patients would remember forgotten events when their cortex was stimulated with a weak electrical current, suggested that the human storage system could be likened to a tape recorder, with memories being permanently held. However, other investigators have pointed to inadequacies in Penfield's speculations.

Hypnotic age regression has also been used to provide support for a permanent memory system. It has been shown that hypnotized subjects are able to remember forgotten information from an earlier age. In the last analysis, however, every human organism forgets—the question of whether or not memory is permanent is unanswerable, since any failure to remember, which presumably would negate the notion of permanence, can always be attributed to retrieval failure rather than to the impermanence of the memory trace.

Retrieval, the third memory construct posited by information processing theorists, refers to the subject recovering previously presented material from storage. It is now acknowledged that the retrieval process can be enhanced by a number of different types of probes or measures of retention. One theory of retrieval proposed by Tulving and his associates, called the principle of encoding specificity, refers to the fact that retention is maximized when the cues that were present when the material was encoded are also present during the test for retention. The inadequacy of the encoding specificity principle has been demonstrated by experiments in which retention was enhanced through presentation of specific cues that were not available during encoding.

Another retrieval issue has to do with the employment of recall and recognition measures. Considerable debate exists as to whether these measures are qualitatively or quantitatively different. The qualitative position holds that recall depends on two processes, generation and discrimination-decision, whereas recognition depends on only the discrimination-decision process. Since recall involves two processes in contrast to just one demanded by recognition, the dual position holds that recognition should always be superior to recall. In contrast, the quantitative position states that recognition and recall are merely different ways to measure the same storage content, although they differ in their sensitivity. The experimental evidence is conflicting, so a resolution of this controversy cannot be provided at this time.

## NOTES

1. Most experimenters using multi-trial presentations of material assumed that the gradual increment in performance over trials reflected the operation of a learning process. When the experimenter, after providing a series of trials, placed an interval of time between the last learning trial and a test for retention (retention interval), it was assumed that such an operation was measuring retention.
2. Some experimenters have included the registration of stimuli as an encoding process.

Here it has been assumed that stimuli may influence the organism's sense organs for a brief period of time and involve the central nervous system without necessarily becoming a part of the individual's memory. The early work of Sperling (1960) and Averbach and Coriell (1961) is representative of research conducted in this area. Sperling's (1960) work suggested that when a briefly presented stimulus is perceived, there is a short-term visual trace which suffers very rapid decay. Although some writers have included this topic in their discussion of memory, such findings are more appropriately included in the area of perception.

3.  The evidence is not completely unequivocal on this issue, since Hall (1979) has demonstrated that low-frequency words are less easily recognized than high-frequency words when appropriate distractors are used. Recognition test scores depend on the nature of the distractors utilized. Since it is necessary to use different types of distractors in the high- and low-frequency word recognition tests, it is possible that the findings of Gorman (1961) and other experimenters were related to the differences between the types of distractors used, rather than any qualitative difference existing between the two performance measures.

# CHAPTER TWELVE

# Memory for Prose and Faces

Chapter 11 pointed out that many investigators who adopted the information processing approach to the study of memory used list-learning tasks; other experimenters, however, believed that this type of task was too restrictive and that the study of memory should encompass a wider range of materials. As a result, they brought into the laboratory other commonly found materials, which can be subsumed under the rubric of verbal learning. The two of these to be discussed in this chapter are memory for prose or meaningful material and memory for faces.

## MEMORY FOR PROSE OR MEANINGFUL MATERIAL

Up until the 1960s, with the exception of the experiments conducted by Bartlett (1932), which were briefly described in Chapter 1, prose or meaningful material had been used in experiments only infrequently. Experimenters were reluctant to use this type of material because of two methodological problems. The first was the difficulty of calibrating prose. Investigators were aware that the attributes of isolated words, such as meaningfulness, imagery, etc., affected learning. It was obvious that prose materials differed in their complexity, intelligibility, etc., but the difficulty in defining these characteristics and then measuring them hindered the widespread use of such material.

A second problem was how to measure memory of a sentence or a paragraph. Generally, verbatim recall does not seem to be a viable response measure with such tasks. However, measuring recall by having the subject give the essence or gist of a sentence or paragraph allows a variety of interpretative judgments, resulting in scoring difficulties for the experimenter. These problems have not been solved, at least to the satisfaction of many experimenters, but some progress has been made.

### A Traditional Investigation of Prose

When the study of prose was undertaken by traditional investigators, the usual approach was to examine the contribution of a list-learning variable and use verbatim recall of the material.

A study by Deese and Kaufman (1957), examining the effect of serial position, illustrates this approach. In this study, 100 passages from the *World Almanac* were used, with each passage consisting of ten sentences of equal length. By a minor rewording of the sentences, it was possible to present the sentences in a number of different serial orders. The material was presented with a tape recorder, following which the subjects were asked

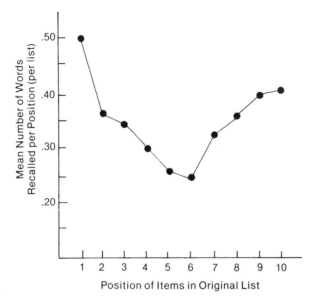

FIGURE 12-1.   Mean frequency of recall per passage per *S* for statements in textual passages as a function of position of statements in original passages. Adapted from J. Deese and R. A. Kaufman, "Serial effects in recall of unorganized and sequentially organized verbal material." *Journal of Experimental Psychology*, 1957, 54, 180–187. Copyright © 1957 by the American Psychological Association. Reprinted by permission.

to recall as many of the sentences as possible. Retention was measured by counting the number of words in each sentence recalled at each position. Figure 12-1 presents the findings, a familiar bow-shaped curve. See Box 12-1.

## Syntactics and Semantics

In the late 1950s, the linguist Noam Chomsky published the text *Syntactic Structures* (1957), in which he developed a theory of generative grammar that had an important impact on the study of memory for prose. Chomsky's theory represented a marked departure from the position that had been adopted by most linguists. Briefly, Chomsky proposed a grammar that consisted of an ordered set of rules, which could be used to generate all grammatical sentences in a language. His theory differed from the linguist's descriptive approach, which diagrammed sentences in terms of their subject, predicate, noun phrases, etc., and then, at a lower level, denoted the varying parts of speech used. This procedure has been termed parsing.

Chomsky's contribution was noteworthy because his theory took issue with the traditional psychological explanation that language was only another example of conditioned response learning. Mowrer (1954), for example, had written that the sentence is preeminently a conditioning device, and its chief effect is to produce new associations, new learning, just as any other paired presentation of stimuli would do. But such a simplistic position could not explain the enormous complexity of language. It was readily apparent that individuals articulate sentences that they have never spoken before, as well as understand sentences that they are hearing for the first time. Moreover, the traditional psychological concepts of stimulus and response appeared to have little relevance to the learning of language.

An important aspect of Chomsky's position was his analysis of sentences in terms of their surface structure, their deep structure, and the transformational rules that were responsible for relating one structure to the other. Surface structure was the physical form

**BOX 12-1**

Can the serial-position effect be demonstrated when the experimental material does not consist of a series of isolated sentences but rather is a narrative? Gentner (1976) attempted to answer this question, using a passage about the Civil War with 14 sentences and 143 facts. Gentner played a tape recording of this material for subjects four times. Subjects were instructed that after the recording was finished each time, they would be asked to tell everything they could remember from the passage. Four recall protocols were thus provided. The experimenter scored each protocol in terms of whether each fact was correct, partially correct, or absent.

Gentner noted that on the first presentation of the material, the recall of the facts did approximate a serial-position curve, with those facts presented at the beginning and at the end of the narrative being most frequently recalled. Gentner noted, however, that as the material was presented on subsequent trials, the serial-position effect was lost. In explaining his findings, Gentner has written,

> on first hearing the tape recording, the subjects perceive the passage as a collection of sentences or facts strung together in serial order, but as portions of the passage begin to "make sense," they perceive and organize the passage in a manner closer to its underlying meaning structure: The serial order loses its importance. (p. 417)

of the sentence, its syntax, and could be related to the descriptive approach of linguists. Deep structure contained the abstract and fundamental meaning that the sentence was to convey to the reader. Many have likened deep structure to the concept of semantics.

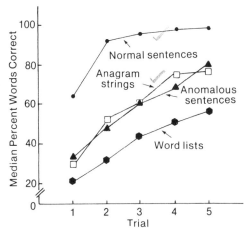

FIGURE 12-2. Median percent of words correct for each of the four types of strings over five trials. A word was counted as correct only if it appeared in its correct position in the string. Adapted from L. E. Marks and G. A. Miller, "The role of semantic and syntactic constraints in the memorization of English sentences." *Journal of Verbal Learning and Verbal Behavior*, 1964, 3, 1–5.

Chomsky's analysis gave traditional psychologists another approach for their examination of sentence memory. How is the memory of prose, for example, influenced by syntax and semantics? Early studies by Epstein (1961, 1962) and Marks and Miller (1964) examined the contribution of these variables. In the Marks and Miller (1964) experiment, the investigators used five sentences of five words each; all sentences had identical syntactic structures: (adjective) (plural noun) (verb) (adjective) (plural noun). A sample sentence would be *Fatal accidents deter careful drivers.* From these original sentences, five additional sentences were constructed by taking the first word from the first sentence, the second word from the second sentence, etc., so a sample sentence would read, *Rapid bouquets deter sudden neighbors.* The syntactic structure of these derived sentences remained identical to that of the normal sentences; that is: (adjective) (plural noun) (verb) (adjective) (plural noun). However, because of the word substitutions, the derivative sentences were semantically anomalous. In addition, two other "sentence" types were provided. The first type, specified as the anagram string, was constructed by taking each normal sentence and scrambling its word order, while the second type was formed by scrambling the word order of the anomalous sentences.

Five sentences, each representing one of the four types of material described, were presented to the subject, who listened to each of them and was then given two minutes to write down as many of them as possible. Five such trials were provided. Figure 12-2 indicates the median percent of words correct for each of the four types of material as a function of trials, and demonstrates the importance of both syntax and semantics in memory for sentences. Sentences that are semantically and syntactically correct (normal) were learned most rapidly, while strings of words were learned least rapidly. Between these two extremes were the anagram strings (sentences that were syntactically correct but did not have meaning) and anomalous sentences (those from which some meaning could be derived but which were syntactically inappropriate).

A basic shortcoming of many of these early studies was that the experimenter demanded verbatim recall, and in doing so ignored the subject's comprehension of the material. An individual who reads or listens to prose and comprehends it can do a variety of things to reflect such understanding. The individual can paraphrase or summarize the material, answer questions about it, or even translate it into another language. The representation of prose in the memory does not appear to be equivalent to the verbatim report of its component words, a position supported by the problems noted in the machine translation of a foreign language. Early attempts at such translation usually took the form of looking at each word from the input language, finding each equivalent in the output language, and then rearranging these words according to the grammatical structure appropriate in the output language. But Raphael (1976) examined such translations and wrote,

these experiments failed miserably, producing translations whose meanings differed from the original in all kinds of strange, unexpected ways. For example, when the biblical quotation, "The spirit is willing but the flesh is weak," was translated from English to Russian and then back to English, what came out of the computer was, "The wine is agreeable but the meat is spoiled." (p. 180)

# CURRENT APPROACHES TO THE STUDY OF PROSE

During the last decade, interest in studying meaningful material has grown rapidly. There are two basic approaches to an examination of how prose is represented in memory. One approach is theoretical, with a variety of models having been proposed. Since these models are quite diverse and complex, the reader should turn to a more advanced text for a discussion of them. See Kintsch (1974), Norman and Rumelhart (1975), and Frederiksen (1975).

The second approach, which will be discussed here, can be called descriptive. Investigators, building on the work of Bartlett (1932), have been interested in examining the nature of the recalled material and identifying specific processes that have been hypothesized to operate in memory.

## A Descriptive Account of the Nature of Memory for Prose

When a subject listens to or reads a paragraph or story and is then asked to recall it, how does the subject's recall of the material relate to what was originally presented? Bartlett (1932) was an early investigator of this type of question. His procedure was to present a story, such as the following:

### The War of the Ghosts

One night two young men from Egulac went down to the river to hunt seals, and while they were there it became foggy and calm. Then they heard war-cries, and they thought: "Maybe this is a war-party." They escaped to the shore, and hid behind a log. Now canoes came up, and they heard the noise of paddles, and saw one canoe coming up to them. There were five men in the canoe, and they said:

"What do you think? We wish to take you along. We are going up the river to make war on the people."

One of the young men said: "I have no arrows."

"Arrows are in the canoe," they said.

"I will not go along. I might be killed. My relatives do not know where I have gone. But you," he said, turning to the other, "may go with them."

So one of the young men went, but the other returned home.

And the warriors went on up the river to a town on the other side of Kalama. The people came down to the water, and they began to fight, and many were killed. But presently the young man heard one of the warriors say: "Quick, let us go home: that Indian has been hit." Now he thought: "Oh, they are ghosts." He did not feel sick, but they said he had been shot.

So the canoes went back to Egulac, and the young man went ashore to his house, and made a fire. And he told everybody and said: "Behold I accompanied the ghosts, and we went to fight. Many of our fellows were killed, and many of those who attacked us were killed. They said I was hit, and I did not feel sick."

He told it all, and then he became quiet. When the sun rose he fell down. Something black came out of his mouth. His face became contorted. The people jumped up and cried.

He was dead. [From Bartlett, F. C., *Remembering* (London: Cambridge University Press, 1972), p. 65.]

## The Concept of a Schema

In attempting to account for how such material was remembered, Bartlett (1932) introduced the concept of a schema. He assumed that our knowledge of the world is made up of a set of models or **schemas** derived from our past experience. New material which is perceived—as in reading a narrative, for example—is integrated into the model, so recall is related to the schema that has been generated.

It is not surprising that many current investigators examining the recall of meaningful material find the concept of a schema most attractive, since the comprehension of prose appears to be intimately related to the experience of the individual.

In some instances, Bartlett examined the repeated reproduction of the story. Here, the same subjects would attempt to recall it on several different occasions. A methodological problem with this procedure is that when the narrative is recalled more than once, it is virtually impossible to know whether subjects are basing their recall on the memory acquired

during the original presentation or on the memory of an earlier recall. But in other instances, Bartlett had different groups of subjects recall the material at retention intervals that varied in time from a few hours to many months. Methodologically, such a procedure is much sounder than the method of repeated reproductions. Two of these recall protocols are illustrated.

A subject's recall 20 hours later:

Two men from Edulac went fishing. While thus occupied by the river they heard a noise in the distance.

"It sounds like a cry," said one, and presently there appeared some men in canoes who invited them to join the party on their adventure. One of the young men refused to go, on the ground of family ties, but the other offered to go.

"But there are no arrows," he said.

"The arrows are in the boat," was the reply.

He thereupon took his place, while his friend returned home. The party paddled up the river to Kaloma, and began to land on the banks of the river. Presently some one was injured, and the cry was raised that the enemy were ghosts.

The party returned down the stream, and the young man arrived home feeling none the worse for his experience. The next morning at dawn he endeavoured to recount his adventure. While he was talking something black issued from his mouth. Suddenly he uttered a cry and fell down. His friends gathered round him.

But he was dead. (p. 66)

A subject's recall six months later:

Four men came down to the water. They were told to get into the boat and to take arms with them. They inquired "What arms?" and were answered "Arms for battle." When they came to the battlefield they heard a great noise and shouting, and a voice said, "The black man is dead." And he was brought to the place where they were, and laid on the ground. And he foamed at the mouth. (pp. 71–72)

However, a basic problem has been to determine precisely what schema means. Generally, it has been considered to be a prototype or norm. Wickelgren (1979), illustrating a schema for words, has written that the word *give* primes the reader or listener to expect a "giver," a "receiver," and a "gift." A schema for a face would contain all the essential elements found in a face: two eyes, two ears, a nose, and a mouth. But a schema generally encompasses much more than a word or a face. It can include some prototypical behaviors found, for instance, when going to a restaurant to eat a meal, or to an airport to catch a plane. Table 12-1 provides an example of a schema used by Kintsch (1977) in taking a bus from Boulder, Colorado, to the airport. In this instance, it may be noted that the schema is hierarchical in that it consists of a number of activities, each subdivided into subactivities, etc.

Thorndyke and Hayes-Roth (1979) have described some of the properties that they believe characterize a schema. These authors have indicated that

1. A schema represents a basic abstraction of the complex concept it represents. For example, as indicated earlier, a schema for a face would undoubtedly contain all of the essential elements—two eyes, a nose, a mouth, and two ears.
2. A schema is derived from past experiences which provide numerous examples of the concept it represents. Presumably, the concept of a face is abstracted after many of them have been seen.
3. A schema can guide the organization of incoming information into clusters of knowledge that are examples of the schema.
4. When one of the constituent concepts of a schema is missing in the input, its features are usually inferred. If a face is in shadow and one cannot see the mouth, one may still infer that it has two lips.

Studies by Dooling and Lachman (1971) and Sulin and Dooling (1974) have demonstrated the importance of providing the reader with a schema—some general clue to aid comprehension of connected discourse. In the Dooling and Lachman (1971) study, subjects were provided with a metaphorical passage that was related to (1) Christopher Columbus Discovering America or (2) The First Space Trip to the Moon. The Columbus passage is reproduced below to indicate the nature of this material.

WITH HOCKED GEMS FINANCING HIM/ OUR HERO BRAVELY DEFIED ALL SCORNFUL LAUGHTER/ THAT TRIED TO PREVENT HIS SCHEME/ YOUR EYES DECEIVE/ HE HAD SAID/ AN EGG/ NOT A TABLE/ CORRECTLY TYPIFIES THIS UNEXPLORED PLANET/ NOW THREE STURDY SISTERS SOUGHT PROOF/ FORGING ALONG SOMETIMES THROUGH CALM VASTNESS/ YET MORE OFTEN OVER TURBULENT PEAKS AND VALLEYS/ DAYS BECAME WEEKS/ AS MANY DOUBTERS SPREAD FEARFUL RUMORS ABOUT THE EDGE/ AT LAST/ FROM NOWHERE/ WELCOME WINGED CREATURES APPEARED/ SIGNIFYING MOMENTOUS SUCCESS (p. 217)

Dooling and Lachman found that presenting the title immediately prior to the reading of the passage produced 18 percent greater recall than when the title was omitted. Moreover, it was found that when subjects were asked to write out the story in their own words, more than 65 percent of those subjects who had been told the title were judged able to do an acceptable job in contrast to less than 3 percent of those who had not been told the title.

A frequently used educational practice has been to give students an overview of the material to be covered in a class or lecture; this can be considered an application of the concept of a schema. Some educational psychologists advocate the use of advanced organizers—sets of ideas that aid students both in organizing knowledge that they have and in facilitating the organization of material to be acquired. Such organizers are provided in a systematic way for specific materials and thus differ from "natural" schema that evolve through experience.

### Reproductive and Constructive Processes

Besides positing the existence of a schema, which occupied a central place in his examination of the recall of prose, Bartlett (1932) also analyzed his subjects' recall protocols

## TABLE 12-1. An example of a schema

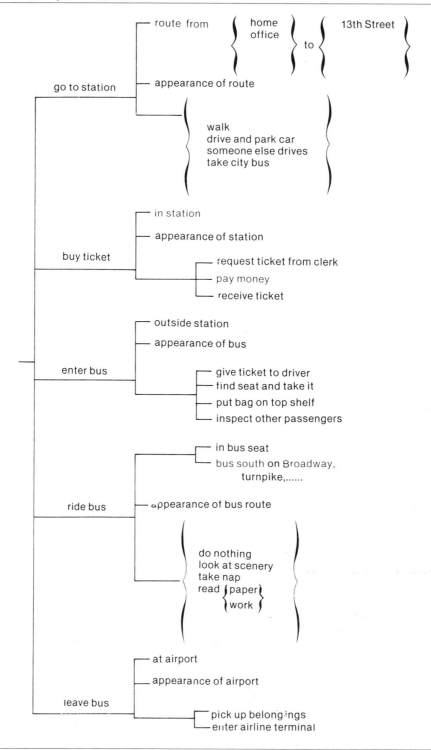

Adapted from W. Kintsch, *Memory and Cognition* (New York: John Wiley and Sons, 1977).

and found two basic changes in the protocols as compared with the original material. One change he identified as omissions; here, specific information about the story was no longer available. A second change he termed rationalization, which meant that information was added to the story in order to make it more meaningful and eliminate apparent inconsistencies and incongruities. Current investigators, building on Bartlett's early work, have considered these changes as reflecting two memory processes and have identified them as: (1) a **reproductive** or abstractive process and (2) a **constructive** process.

**The Reproductive Process**   One can see from Bartlett's protocols, as well as from many current studies, that an individual is able to recall only a portion of the prose that is presented. But what is the nature of the material that is placed in memory? In an attempt to answer this question, Gomulicki (1956) examined the recall of 37 prose passages, which varied in length from 13 to 95 words. The recall of each passage was requested immediately after its presentation—subjects were instructed to repeat orally as much as they could recall. Gomulicki noted that as the prose passage increased in length, omissions increased. Thus, the amount of material that was omitted increased from single adjectives to short descriptive phrases and then to longer phrases. In the longest passages, whole sentences or even paragraphs were eliminated.

Gomulicki recognized that what was omitted was not determined by a random selection by the subject. Rather, there was some selectivity in the determination of the omitted material. The material placed in memory appeared to be ordered in terms of relative importance, with enough of the least important material eliminated to bring the content of the passage within the scope of the subject's recall. This topic of the importance of linguistic units will be covered further in a later section.

*Syntactics and Semantics Revisited*   The work of Marks and Miller (1964), reviewed earlier, suggested that the syntactic attribute made a contribution in the acquisition of

strings of words similar to prose. When narrative material is place in memory, is its syntax a part of this representation? Sachs (1967) has examined this question. In her classic study, students listened to 28 passages of prose, one of which is reproduced below:

> There is an interesting story about the telescope. In Holland, a man named Lippershey was an eye-glass maker. One day his children were playing with some lenses. They discovered that things seemed very close if two lenses were held about a foot apart. Lippershey began experimenting and his "spyglass" attracted much attention. *He sent a letter about it to Galileo, the great Italian scientist.* Galileo at once realized the importance of the discovery and set about to build an instrument of his own. He used an old organ pipe with one lens curved out and the other in. On the first clear night he pointed the glass toward the sky. He was amazed to find the empty dark spaces filled with brightly gleaming stars! Night after night Galileo climbed to a high tower, sweeping the sky with his telescope. One night he saw Jupiter, and to his great surprise discovered near it three bright stars, two to the east and one to the west. On the next night, however, all were to the west. A few nights later there were four little stars. (From Sachs, J. S., "Recognition memory for syntactic and semantic aspects of connected discourse." *Perception and Psychophysics*, 1967, 2, 438–439.)

Following the presentation of the passage, a test sentence related to the italicized sentence was presented. Subjects were asked to indicate whether the test sentence was identical to the one originally heard or whether it had been changed. Different test sentences were used with different subjects. These test sentences were of four types. Some were identical to the sentence used in the original passage. Some were semantically different, as in *Galileo, the great Italian scientist, sent him a letter about it.* Two other types were syntactically different, although the meaning was the same as in the original sentence. One syntactic change was to make the test sentence passive; thus, *A letter about it was sent to Galileo, the great Italian scientist.* The other syntactic change was identified as formal, since only the words were rearranged; thus, *He sent Galileo, the great Italian scientist, a letter about it.*

Sachs also was interested in determining how the amount of material presented between the critical sentence and its subsequent recall influenced retention. Either 0, 80, or 160 syllables were presented after the critical sentence had been heard and before the test sentence was presented. Results are indicated in Figure 12-3.

Note that when the test sentence was presented immediately following the critical sentence, performance with all test sentences was quite good. When 80 or 160 syllables were interpolated between listening to the critical sentence and the test for retention, memory for syntax was reduced almost to chance level. On the other hand, semantic memory, as indicated by the subjects' recognition that

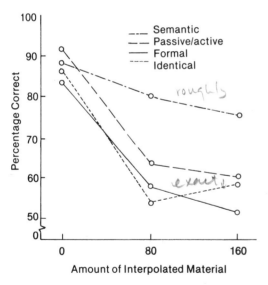

FIGURE 12-3. Percentage of judgments *identical* and *changed* that were correct for each test type. Adapted from J. S. Sachs, "Recognition memory for syntactic and semantic aspects of connected discourse." *Perception and Psychophysics*, 1967, 2, 437–442. Reprinted by permission of the Psychonomic Society.

the test sentence, *Galileo, the great Italian scientist, sent him a letter about it*, did not appear in the passage, continued to remain high. Sachs's (1967) findings have been replicated by others. Perfetti and Garson (1973), for example, found that the syntactic structure of material obtained from popular magazines was lost within 30 minutes of the presentation.

*The Nature of the Semantic Attribute* The fact that the semantic attribute or meaning of prose, rather than its grammatical form, is represented in memory is intuitively reasonable. But how can the semantic attribute or the construct of meaningfulness be manipulated? Perfetti (1969) suggested that one facet of this attribute could be called **lexical density**—the number of nouns, adjectives, adjective and noun variables, adverbs, and main verbs that are found in a sentence. A large number of these parts of speech would indicate a sentence high in lexical density, as illustrated by the sentence "The police watched nearly every move of the clever thief." In contrast, the sentence "The family has accepted an offer to purchase the house," having a smaller number of these specific parts of speech, would be categorized as being low in lexical density.

In an experiment examining this variable, Perfetti (1969) constructed 64 sentences, with 10 words each, to represent two levels of lexical density. Both sets of sentences were similar in articulation length of syllables and word frequency. After an oral presentation of one sentence, the subject performed a short addition task and then attempted a verbatim recall of the sentence. Results, as measured by perfectly recalled sentences, indicated that sentences with high lexical density were recalled less frequently than those with low lexical density.

Perfetti's use of a verbatim recall measure neglects the issue of comprehension, which is basic to the problem of meaningfulness. Does the verbatim recall of low lexical density prose mean that such material is better understood or comprehended than prose that has high lexical density? Perhaps, but an experiment should be conducted in order to determine whether or not such is the case.

A different approach to the problem of defining the semantic attribute was undertaken by Kintsch and Monk (1972). Instead of using single sentences as Perfetti (1969) did, the experimenters used paragraphs, designated as "simple" or "complex." Sentences in the "simple" paragraph were expressed as directly as possible, whereas in the "complex" paragraph the sentences were transformed both syntactically and semantically. Examples of the two types of paragraphs are as follows:

Simple:

The council of elders in the land of Syndra meets whenever a stranger arrives. If the council meets and if the stranger presents the proper gifts to the council, he is not molested by the natives. The explorer Portmanteau came to Syndra without any valuable gifts. (p. 27)

Complex:

The arrival of strangers in the land of Syndra, like the explorer Portmanteau, who did not bring valuable gifts, always resulted in a meeting of the council of elders, which insured that the stranger was not molested by the natives upon receipt of the proper gifts. (p. 27)

Retention, as measured by having subjects answer questions about what they had read, revealed superior memory for the material found in the simple paragraphs. King and Greeno (1974) conducted a similar study and replicated these findings.

*The Importance and Hierarchical Structure of Linguistic Units*  A prose passage is composed of a number of linguistic units or sentences; an experimental subject attempting to remember such material does not consider all of them to be equally important. Generally, there is a hierarchical arrangement of the units, with some units basic to the overall theme of the passage and others of secondary or tertiary importance. A broadly conceptualized theory of prose must include the role of the hierarchical structure of linguistic units.

Johnson (1970) was an early investigator of this variable. His general procedure was to divide a prose passage into linguistic units and then obtain measures of the importance of these units to the overall study. He used Bartlett's (1932) "The War of the Ghosts" with subjects, first dividing the narrative into "pause acceptability" units. A pause was defined as a temporary suspension of the voice designed to allow readers to catch their breath and to give emphasis to the story or enhance meaning. These varying units were then given to other subjects, who were asked to eliminate the unimportant ones without destroying the essence of the story. A rating of the importance of each unit was obtained by determining the number of times each unit was retained by subjects as essential to the story. Six levels of importance were derived from the ratings. Another group of subjects was then asked to read the complete story twice at their normal reading rate. After retention intervals of either 15 minutes, 7 days, 21 days, or 63 days, these subjects were asked to recall the story as accurately as possible. Recall as a function of the structural importance of the linguistic units is plotted in Figure 12-4. Findings demonstrate the importance of the hierarchical unit as a basic variable in the recall of prose. Two additional experiments using other material and controlling reading time replicated these findings.

The role of hierarchical structure in prose was also examined by Meyer and McConkie (1973). Two prose passages were obtained from articles found in a popular magazine. Judges then selected the most important idea in each of the paragraphs; secondary and tertiary ideas that described or provided additional information about the main idea were also designated. Each idea unit selected was assumed to be a single meaningful piece of information. The logical interrelationship among these idea units was then demonstrated by arranging them hierarchically—main ideas at the top, units of lesser importance under the main ideas, and then units of still lesser importance under these. From this hierarchical structure, a depth score was obtained for each

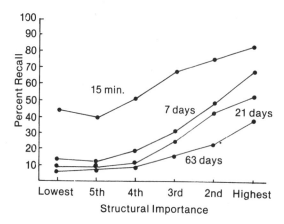

FIGURE 12-4. Percentage of recall of linguistic subunits of "Ghosts" as a function of levels of structural importance. Adapted from R. E. Johnson, "Recall of prose as a function of the structural importance of the linguistic units." *Journal of Verbal Learning and Behavior*, 1970, 9, 12–20.

of the idea units. Experimental subjects were presented with the first passage and then asked to recall as much of the material as possible. The second passage was then presented and recalled. Results indicated that the proportion of idea units recalled was a function of the hierarchical depth score of the idea units. More main ideas were recalled than idea units of either medium or low value.

A somewhat more theoretical approach to an examination of the semantic attribute or the problem of meaning has been provided by Kintsch (1972, 1974, 1977). Briefly, Kintsch has related the meaning of prose to what he has termed its text base. [A complete description of Kintsch's work can be found in Kintsch (1974).] This base consists of a sequence of propositions, with each proposition consisting of one relational term, typically a main verb, and one or more arguments, frequently nouns, that are related to the verb by means of an agent, object, instrument, or goal. For example, in the proposition *George hit John*, the verb or relational term is *hit*, with two arguments, *George* and *John*. An important feature of Kintsch's model is that textual material differs from a series of unrelated sentences in that the propositions are interconnected

through the repetition of arguments. Such interconnections result in a hierarchical structure in which there is a topical proposition, with other propositions subordinate to it forming a second level, followed by other propositions at a lower level, etc. This hierarchical structure is similar to that proposed by Meyer and McConkie (1973), which was described earlier.

Kintsch and Keenan (1973) have examined the effects of the number of propositions and the hierarchical structure on reading time and recall. In one part of their study, the experimental material was composed of ten sentences, 16–17 words long (Set A). The number of propositions contained in each sentence varied between four and nine. Two sample sentences illustrate the kind of experimental material used. One sentence, *Romulus, the legendary founder of Rome, took the women of the Sabine by force,* contains just four propositions and two hierarchical levels. On the other hand, the sentence *Cleopatra's downfall lay in her foolish trust in the fickle political figures of the Roman world* contains eight propositions and four hierarchical levels.

Two procedures were used to manipulate reading time. With one, subjects were instructed to read and study the slides at their own speed (each slide presenting one sentence). With the second, each slide was shown for just five seconds. Following the presentation of each slide, subjects attempted to recall the sentence. Recall protocols for the ten sentences were scored for the recall of the propositions, with paraphrases of the original wording accepted as correct. Kintsch and Keenan's (1973) procedure of demanding recall immediately following the presentation of each sentence is not in keeping with most prose presentation-recall procedures, in which the complete narrative is read prior to a test for recall. Nonetheless, the authors' finding—that reading time (and presumably processing time) was positively related to the number of propositions provided in the sentence—is thought provoking. This kind of finding suggests that the context of prose is stored in memory in propositional form. Findings also indicated that the longer the subject studied a sentence, the better recall was. Finally, the authors found that the probability of recall was related to hierarchical structure, a finding that supported the earlier results of Meyer and McConkie (1973) and that was also confirmed in a subsequent study by Kintsch, Kozminsky, Streby, McKoon, and Keenan (1975).

**The Constructive Process**  It will be recalled that Bartlett (1932) found that his subjects frequently introduced new material into their recall protocols, apparently in order to have the folktale that they had read make sense. He termed this process rationalization. Current investigators have identified it as constructive.

What kind of evidence do we have to support the operation of such a process? An interesting illustration is reported by Kintsch (1977), who presented to his experimental subjects the biblical story of Joseph and his brothers. Kintsch found that if a retention test immediately followed presentation, his subjects' recall faithfully followed the presented material. But if the recall test was delayed for 24 hours, Kintsch found that his subjects were unable to differentiate between what he had presented and their general knowledge of Joseph. Many individuals wrote down just about all of the information that they had about Joseph's life.

In Kintsch's study, the new information that was incorporated into the subject's recall protocol had been in the individual's memory prior to the presentation of the original study. But it is possible to demonstrate the operation of a constructive process by providing the subject with new information between the original presentation of the meaningful material and the subsequent test of recall. A series of studies by Loftus and her associates has demonstrated such an effect.

The procedure and the kind of findings obtained are illustrated by Loftus's (1975) Experiment 2. In this experiment, students were shown a three minute videotape depicting the disruption of a school classroom by 8 demonstrators. At the end of the videotape presentation, the subjects received one of two questionnaires, each containing 19 filler questions and 1 key question. One form of the key question asked, "Was the leader of the 4 demonstrators who entered the classroom a male?" The other form asked the question "Was the leader of the 12 demonstrators who entered the classroom a male?" One week later, all subjects answered a series of 20 questions about the disruption, with the critical question being, "How many demonstrators did you see entering the classroom?" Results from those subjects who had been previously asked the question presupposing 12 demonstrators averaged 8.85 individuals, while for those subjects who had been asked the question presupposing 4 demonstrators the average was 6.40 people. The difference between the two values was statistically significant.

The same basic effect—that additional information influences a subsequent reporting of an event—was obtained in another study in which students viewed a brief videotape of an automobile accident and then answered a questionnaire that presupposed that there was (or was not) a barn in the picture. One week after seeing this film, the subjects were asked if they had seen the barn. Again, results indicated that by providing information about the previously perceived event, one could influence the subsequent reporting of what had taken place.

The Loftus (1975) study raises several questions, some theoretical, others procedural. In the studies reported, the subjects were presented with a *visual* event and were asked to *verbally* remember it. But does the transformation from a visual presentation to a verbal response contribute to the experimental findings? Did the subjects actually "see" the barn in the slide? Moreover, was it not possible that Loftus's experimental subjects, although actually seeing 8 demonstrators or not seeing the barn, "went along" with the experimenter, assuming that what was presented in the questionnaire was correct?

A series of experiments by Loftus, Miller, and Burns (1978) attempted to answer these questions. Their procedure consisted of presenting a series of 30 color slides depicting successive stages of an automobile-pedestrian accident. One key slide featured a sign located at the intersection. For half of the subjects it was a stop sign, while for the remaining subjects it was a yield sign. The usual questionnaire was administered, in which the key question presupposed either a stop sign or a yield sign. Following an interval of 20 minutes, the subjects were given a forced-choice recognition test in which 15 pairs of slides were presented, with subjects asked to select the slide that had previously been presented. Choices made by the subjects on the pair of slides which depicted the stop sign on one slide and a yield sign on the other provided the basic data. The data supported earlier findings; the interpolated questionnaire predisposed subjects to select the slide of the kind of sign that had been indicated on the key questionnaire.

In other experiments, the investigators found that most subjects actually encoded or "saw" the sign in the slide. Thus, when they were asked to draw in the details of the accident rather than choose the appropriate slide, a majority of them actually sketched in the presence of a yield sign (Experiment 4). This did not appear to be a result of either confusion on the part of the subjects or a desire to please the experimenter. When experimental subjects were given a "debriefing" questionnaire in which they were asked to indicate if there was a discrepancy between what they had seen in the slide and what the questionnaire indicated, only 12 percent stated that they had noted the difference (Experiment 2). Finally, in an effort to determine when misleading information should be provided in order to maximize the effect, the questionnaire was presented either immediately following the presentation of the original slides depicting the accident or immediately preceding the recognition test, with the interval between the slide presentation and the recognition test being either 20 minutes, 1, 2, or 7 days. Results indicated that the questionnaire had a larger impact on retention if it was introduced just prior to the recognition test rather than immediately following the slide presentation (Experiment 3).

The studies of Kintsch (1977), Loftus (1975), and Loftus, Miller, and Burns (1978) have demonstrated the operation of a constructive process in recall. However, most often this process is not found; recall protocols indicate the presence of only an abstraction or reproduction of the experimental material. Spiro (1977, 1980) has identified two conditions that he believes can at least partially account for the failure of experimenters to find the constructive process.

He has hypothesized that this process should most frequently operate in natural or practically relevant situations where the material to be remembered is not carefully separated by the experimental subject from general knowledge available about that same topic. In such instances, the individual fails to separate the two sources of knowledge. Thus, although only the presented material is supposed to be remembered, material from the general source is found in the recall protocol. The reason many laboratory studies of memory have difficulty in demonstrating the constructive process is because experimenters have utilized artificial passages of material, permitting the subject to encode this material separately from other information. There is little opportunity for earlier knowledge to become part of or be incorporated into the schema or totality of the material to be remembered.

A second condition that Spiro believes contributes to the development of a constructive process is contradictory information in the material to be recalled. In instances where contradictory material appears, the subject will add material to the recall protocol to reconcile the contradiction, a construction process that Spiro has termed accommodative reconstruction. A lengthy and complex experimental study conducted by Spiro (1977) has provided support for his assumptions.

## FACIAL RECOGNITION

"I can't recall your name but I do remember your face" is an embarrassing expression we have frequently heard and have undoubtedly used ourselves. It is a simple illustration of the important role that facial recognition plays in our daily lives, and yet few early psychologists were interested in examining memory for the human face. Many current experimenters, however, believe that any study of memory should encompass this type of stimulus material. In fact, some investigators have indicated that the face is a unique stimulus, pointing to the clinical condition identified as "prosopagnosia" in which individuals have difficulty in recognizing faces even of close relatives, although their ability to recognize other objects appears to be normal.

In the study of facial memory, it is possible to have subjects provide a verbal description of a face that had been viewed earlier, thus providing a measure of recall. However, this is generally an unsatisfactory response measure, since people are often unable to use a verbal report to capture the distinctiveness of the remembered face. The result has been that virtually all experimenters studying facial memory have used some type of recognition measure. This measure suggests that memory for faces is unusually good. For instance, as discussed in Chapter 10, a study by Bahrick, Bahrick, and Wittlinger (1975) showed that facial recognition remained extraordinarily high even after retention intervals of more than 30 years.

### Recognition for Inverted Faces

One early investigator interested in facial recognition was Köhler (1940); he speculated that inverted faces were more difficult to recognize than upright ones. It remained for Brooks and Goldstein (1963), Goldstein (1965), and Hochberg and Galper (1967) to experimentally demonstrate that Köhler's speculation was correct. All of these investigators found that recognizing a previously presented inverted face among other inverted faces is much more difficult than recognizing a previously presented upright face among other upright faces.

But is this an unusual finding? Would not other inverted visual stimuli produce similar recognition difficulty? A series of experiments conducted by Yin (1969) was designed to answer this question. In one experiment using pictures of houses, airplanes, stick figures, and faces, Yin found that faces were more easily recognized than any of the other visual

materials presented when tested in an upright position. However, when these stimulus materials were presented and tested in an inverted position, the recognition of faces was the most difficult.

Yin's finding led to the hypothesis that the pictorial material that was easiest to recognize upright was most difficult to recognize when inverted. This did not prove to be the case. Yin found that faceless figures clothed in different period costumes were more easily recognized than human faces when both sets of stimuli were presented upright. But contrary to his hypothesis, the easily recognized faceless figure stimulus was not the most difficult to recognize when inverted—the human face continued to be the most difficult to recognize. Perhaps, as has been suggested earlier, the human face represents a unique type of stimulus material.

## CURRENT APPROACHES TO THE INVESTIGATION OF FACIAL RECOGNITION

Some individuals have considered the recognition of inverted faces as a kind of esoteric enterprise, since, as they have pointed out, few of us view others standing on their heads. The more common approach has been to examine the recognition of upright faces as a function of the manipulation of specific stimulus variables.

### Recognition as Related to Facial Features

A logical approach to the study of facial recognition is to examine how the specific features that make up the face contribute to such recognition. But when individuals are questioned about how they remember a face, they generally do not specify any particular facial feature as being most important, except, of course, in those cases in which one feature dominates all of the others, such as a very large nose. This has led some investigators to examine facial recognition by covering either the lower or upper part of the face. An early study by Howells (1938) indicated that faces were more difficult to recognize when the *lower* part of the face was covered rather than the upper, a finding that contrasts with a common practice of thieves, who cover the upper part of the face in order to avoid identification. But the more recent studies of Goldstein and Mackenberg (1966) and McKelvie (1976) have indicated that thieves are right after all—recognition is poorest when the upper portion of the face is masked. In the McKelvie (1976) study, experimental subjects examined 27 faces and then were asked to identify each of the previously presented photographs, now placed with new photographs (distractors). For one group of subjects, the test photograph that was placed among the distractors was the same as that which had been previously presented; for a second group, the test photograph had the eyes masked; for the third group, the test photograph had the mouth masked. Recognition errors were significantly larger for those photographs in which the eyes rather than the mouth were masked, causing McKelvie to suggest that the eyes appear to be the most important part of facial representation in memory.

### The Role of Disguises

Another method for examining recognition of facial features is to show the experimental subject faces with varying disguises. In a very extensive examination of the role of disguises, Patterson and Baddeley (1977) found the not so surprising result that (a) a change in hair style, (b) the addition or removal of glasses, and (c) the addition or removal of a beard and/or moustache each resulted in a drastic decline in recognition performance.

### Attractiveness and Distinctiveness as Facial Attributes

Often one describes a face as attractive, distinctive, etc., without attempting to provide a further analysis of what is meant by each of these descriptive terms. Some investigators have been interested in examining how such general descriptions of the face can be related to facial memory. It has been noted often that

faces that have been given a high rating on one of these general descriptors are more readily recognized than faces that have been provided lower ratings.

Cross, Cross, and Daly (1971) found that subjects were better at recognizing faces that had been previously identified as "attractive" than faces that had not been so described. Shepherd and Ellis (1973) partially confirmed these findings, but also found that faces that were rated as "low" in attractiveness would provide superior recognition as well. In their study, 97 photographs of female faces were rated for attractiveness on a nine-point scale, following which 54 of these were selected to serve as the experimental material. These 54 photographs represented the entire range of rankings, with 18 being considered most attractive, 18 least attractive, and the remaining 36 representing intermediate attractiveness. One set of 27 photographs (9 high, 9 intermediate, 9 low) was presented to experimental group A to memorize; the other 27 photographs were presented to experimental group B with similar instructions.

Immediately following the presentation, a recognition test was provided. In this test, the experimenters paired 9 of the previously presented faces (3 from each level of attractiveness) with faces of similar attractiveness. This pairing procedure produced a two-choice recognition test with 9 items. Subjects were asked to identify the photograph that had been presented previously. Second and third recognition tests, with each test consisting of 9 different previously presented photographs paired with a photograph of similar attractiveness, were provided 6 and 35 days later.

Figure 12-5 reveals that significant differences in facial recognition were not found among the three levels of attractiveness at either of the first two testing sessions; however, at the third testing session, recognition scores were significantly lower for faces rated as intermediate in attractiveness than for faces of either high or low attractiveness. It is interesting that memory for faces in these latter two categories did not reveal a retention decrement over an interval of 35 days.

Another facial attribute is uniqueness or distinctiveness. Going and Read (1974) had a

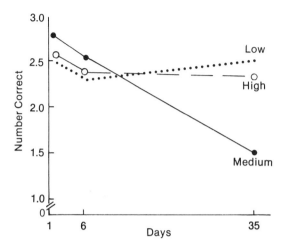

FIGURE 12-5.   Recognition scores for stimuli of high, medium, and low levels of attractiveness at three testing intervals; each point represents the mean of the scores of 36 subjects. Adapted from J. W. Shepherd and H. D. Ellis, "The effect of attractiveness on recognition memory for faces." *American Journal of Psychology*, 1973, 86, 627–633. Copyright © 1973 the University of Illinois Press.

group of students first rate 140 full-face photographs of males and females on a seven-point scale of uniqueness. From these pictures, 56 were selected, 28 of which had been rated highly unique and 28 of which had been rated low on this facial attribute. One experimental group of subjects was then shown the 28 high-rated photographs, and a second experimental group was shown the 28 low-rated photographs. Following the presentation, both groups viewed the same 112 pictures and had to select those faces that had been previously presented. Results indicated that those faces that had been judged to be highly unique were recognized more frequently (72 percent correct) than those faces that had been rated low in uniqueness (53 percent).

## Context Effects

Another variable of interest to investigators of facial memory has been the role of context. The experimental findings of Watkins, Ho, and Tulving (1976) and Winograd and Rivers-Bulkeley (1977) have indicated that changing the context of facial stimuli produces a memory decrement, a finding similar to one obtained with verbal material (see Chapter 10). In the Watkins, Ho, and Tulving (1976) study (Experiment 1), 80 pairs of faces were presented. Subjects were instructed to study the faces as pairs, and afterwards were given a recognition test. Instructions to the subjects indicated that their primary task was to recognize which *right-hand* members of the test pairs had been previously presented in the study list, regardless of whether the left-hand faces were the same or different. The test series consisted of 16 right-hand faces that had not been seen previously (distractors) and 64 right-hand faces that had appeared previously in this position in the study list. Of these 64 target faces, 32 were paired with the same face as used in the study list, thus forming the Same Context condition. The other 32 were randomly re-paired to form a Changed Context condition. Results indicated that recognition in the Same Context condition was statistically superior to that in the Changed Context condition, although the difference was modest—73 percent correct for the Same Context condition and 68 percent for the Changed Context condition. Winograd and Rivers-Bulkeley (1977) have confirmed these findings.

## The Role of Race Membership

Members of the white race have frequently claimed that they have difficulty in identifying blacks or orientals; members of these other racial groups have expressed a similar difficulty in distinguishing among whites. These personal observations suggest that race membership may be a significant variable contributing to facial recognition, but is this difficulty in identifying members of another race grounded in sound experimental evidence? Some experimenters have suggested that it is.

Malpass and Kravitz (1969) recruited subjects from the University of Illinois, whose enrollment consists of mostly white students, and from Howard University, whose enrollment is mostly black. The experimental material consisted of photographs of 40 black and 40 white males of college age. Each subject saw a random arrangement of photographs of 10 blacks and 10 whites selected from the two sets of 40, with each picture being viewed for about 1½ seconds. Following the presentation of these 20 photographs, all subjects where shown all 80 facial photos and asked to recognize those pictures that had previously been presented. Malpass and Kravitz's findings indicated that white subjects were better able to recognize the photographs of white students than those of black students. The evidence obtained with black subjects, however, was equivocal. Blacks attending the University of Illinois were able to correctly recognize more photographs of members of their own race than those of whites. Black subjects attending Howard University found white photographs easier to recognize. Table 12–2 presents these recognition data for the four groups of subjects.

The results provided by Howard University black students may be suspect, since several investigators have indicated that black subjects were able to recognize facial photographs of members of their own race better than facial photographs of whites; see Luce (1974), Shepherd, Deregowski, and Ellis (1974), Chance, Goldstein, and McBride (1975), and Ellis, Deregowski, and Shepherd (1975).

For example, Chance, Goldstein, and McBride (1975) had 48 black and 48 white student subjects view pictures of 10 white, 10 black, and 10 Japanese male faces, with each face projected on the screen for about 3 seconds. A recognition test immediately followed—each of the 10 previously viewed faces of a particular racial group was presented along with 30 other faces of the same race (distractors). Each subject was asked to indicate whether a particular face had been "seen before" or "not seen before." Results, provided in Table 12-3, confirm the usual finding that white subjects are able to recognize the facial photographs of whites better than those of blacks. They also indicate that black subjects are able to recognize the facial photographs of blacks better than those of whites. The recognition of Japanese faces was poorest for both black and white experimental subjects.

Additional support for the general hypothesis that the recognition of own-race faces is superior to that of other-race faces is found in Luce's (1974) study. Luce reported that Asian-American subjects are better able to recognize the photographs of other Asian-Americans than the photographs of whites or blacks.

A basic question has to do with the reason for the superior recognition of own-race faces. Probably the most often suggested explanation is differential experience. It is well known, for example, that zoologists and animal psychologists who work with primates learn to recognize each individual animal. To the uninitiated, however, all of these animals look alike. The role of experience seems critical in allowing these laboratory workers to identify each of their experimental animals. It is suggested that humans' ability to recognize faces of individuals of their own race stems from their extensive experience with them,

TABLE 12-2. Correct recognitions of black and white photographs by black and white experimental subjects at two universities

| | Photographs | |
| | Black | White |
| --- | --- | --- |
| University of Illinois | | |
| Black Subjects | 7.38 | 6.77 |
| White Subjects | 6.08 | 7.92 |
| | | |
| Howard University | | |
| Black Subjects | 6.14 | 7.14 |
| White Subjects | 5.57 | 6.14 |

Adapted from R. S. Malpass and J. Kravitz, "Recognition for faces of own and other race." *Journal of Personality and Social Psychology*, 1969, 13, 330–334. Copyright © 1969 by the American Psychological Association. Reprinted by permission.

TABLE 12-3. Mean numbers of correct recognitions for white, black, and Japanese faces

| | Oriental | Black | White |
| --- | --- | --- | --- |
| Black subjects | 4.33 | 6.04 | 4.99 |
| White subjects | 4.54 | 5.54 | 6.75 |

Adapted with permission from J. Chance, A. G. Goldstein, and L. McBride, "Differential experience and recognition memory for faces." *Journal of Social Psychology*, 1975, 97, 243–253.

whereas their failure to recognize other-race faces arises from a lack of contact or experience. Intuitively this seems reasonable, since most individuals live in racially homogeneous areas and associate more frequently with members of their own race than with individuals from other races.

The study of Malpass and Kravitz (1969), cited earlier, has not supported the experience hypothesis. These investigators administered questionnaires to their black and white subjects to measure each subject's previous contact with members of the other race. Results indicated that the amount of contact was not related to recognition performance. Cross, Cross, and Daly (1971), who defined contact as whether an individual lived in a racially segregated or racially integrated neighborhood, were also unable to find that this type of experience was related to recognition performance. Finally, Luce (1974), in examining the contribution of contact to the facial recognition of white, black, and oriental photographs, has written,

> We found no relationship between experience with other races and the ability to recognize specific faces. The black subjects had difficulty recognizing all photographs except those of blacks, even though they had had extensive contact with whites. . . . The white students who had no previous contact with Asian-Americans, recognized them almost as easily as they did white faces, but they had trouble identifying blacks, in spite of their previous associations with them. . . . the Asian-Americans could recognize other Asian-Americans easily . . . but they had some difficulty in identifying blacks, and a great deal of difficulty identifying whites. . . . These results mean that simple exposure to other groups does not ensure recognition of individuals who differ from us racially. (pp. 106–107)

It has been acknowledged that "exposure" or mere contact may not contribute to the improvement of other-face recognition, but other kinds of experience do appear to have some influence. Lavrakas, Buri, and Mayzner (1976), for example, reported that white subjects who indicated that they had black friends (at least one of their five closest

friends was black) were better able to recognize photographs of black faces than other white subjects who reported having either gone to school with blacks or grown up in an integrated neighborhood. In addition, Seeleman (1940) and Galper (1973) have suggested that an individual's attitude may play a role in determining how easy other-race facial recognition is. Both of these investigators found that subjects who indicated a positive attitude toward blacks were significantly better at recognizing photographs of black faces than were white subjects who held less positive attitudes toward members of the black race.

### Interference Effects

Investigators who have adopted the traditional approach to the study of learning and retention have demonstrated that specific characteristics of facial photographs may contribute to the ease of recognition. The traditional position would also suggest that interference effects could be introduced by manipulating the number and/or characteristics of the distractors provided in the retention test.

Laughery, Alexander, and Lane (1971) conducted one such study (Experiment 1). The experimental subject viewed target stimuli consisting of four slides presenting a single face in different positions, following which 150 test faces were presented in a recognition test. The target face was placed at either the 40th or 140th position. Results indicated superior recognition performance for subjects who viewed the target item in the 40th in contrast to the 140th position, thus suggesting that the number of distractor faces placed between first sight of the target item and a subsequent recognition test contributed to recognition performance.

The similarity of the distractor faces to the target face is a second variable that appears to contribute to recognition performance. In two experiments (Experiments 2b, 2c) conducted by Laughery, Fessler, Lenorovitz, and Yoblick (1974), the similarity of the distractor faces to the target face affected recognition performance. The general procedure used in these two experiments was similar to that in the previously reported study, with the target face presented in four slides, followed by a series of distractors varying in facial similarity (high or low) to the target face. The procedure designed to measure distractor similarity varied. In one experiment, ratings were obtained from a large number of subjects as to how similar each distractor was to the target face; in the second experiment, it was based upon matching nine physical characteristics, such as hair color, eye color, glasses, beard, etc., in the target and distractor photographs. If the target and a distractor face had eight or nine of these attributes in common, the distractor face was considered to be highly similar; if there were four or fewer attributes in common, the distractor was considered to have low similarity.

The two experiments also differed in terms of the number of distractors used and the position of the target item among the distractors. These variations in experimental procedure, however, made little difference; the findings from both studies indicated that recognition performance was improved when low-similarity distractors were used. As the authors have written, "the greater the similarity between a target and the decoys preceding it, the lower the probability that the target will be correctly identified" (p. 495).

The findings obtained from the studies of Laughery and his associates are in keeping with an interference theory of forgetting. But Davies, Shepherd, and Ellis (1979) have indicated that any simple interference explanation for the recognition decrement found with memory for faces cannot account for the results of their facial recognition experiment. These investigators have suggested that an important consideration in facial recognition appears to be the kind of information processing undertaken by the subject. In the Davies, Shepherd, and Ellis experiment, subjects viewed a 1½ minute videotape of three men playing cards, with the tape providing a close-up picture of each man. Subjects were informed that they would be asked to recognize these men at a later time. Varying types of interpolated activity were then provided to four groups of subjects:

1. A face-rating group was asked to rate 100 faces for pleasantness–unpleasantness (the target faces did not appear among these 100 faces).
2. A standard search group viewed these same 100 faces but was required to decide whether or not each face was one of the three men they had previously seen.
3. An informed group was treated the same way as the standard group except that prior to being exposed to the test series of photos, each subject was informed that none of the 100 faces shown would be the target faces.
4. Finally, a control group did not view any faces but listened to a recording.

Following these varying interpolated activities, all four groups were asked to select the target faces out of 36 test faces. The target items appeared in the seventh, eighteenth, and thirty-fourth positions.

The standard search condition group, which viewed the 100 interpolated faces prior to viewing the 36 test items, had the *poorest* recognition test score, a result that apparently supported an interference position. However, the group that rated the 100 interpolated faces for pleasantness was tied with the control group for the *best* recognition score. The authors have suggested that viewing the interpolated faces in a way that presumably requires a different type of processing has no discernable effect on recognition test performance.

### The Processing of Facial Memories

It is not surprising that, as the Davies, Shepherd, and Ellis (1979) study has indicated, investigators should look to an information processing position to provide another theoretical framework for investigating facial memory. The studies of Bower and Karlin (1974) and Warrington and Ackroyd (1975) have attempted to demonstrate that a shallow level of processing faces will result in poorer recognition memory than if a deeper processing level is achieved.

In Bower and Karlin's (1974) study, 72 faces obtained from a college yearbook were used, with subjects instructed to judge each face on the basis of either (1) sex, (2) honesty, or (3) likeableness. The task was divided into 12 faces per block, with subjects informed at the start of each block as to the characteristics on which the faces were to be rated. Subjects were led to believe that the experimenters were interested in how fast a judgment could be made and were instructed to depress one of two buttons which presumably measured the time it took them to make a decision. (Actually, no time was recorded.) When sex was judged, one button indicated male, the other female; with the other characteristics, one button indicated that the face was above average in honesty or likeableness, the other button indicated that the face was below average in these attributes. Subjects were *not* told that they should try to remember the faces for a subsequent recognition test.

After this presentation, subjects were asked to view 144 faces and to indicate whether or not the face had been previously presented. A second experiment was conducted in which the procedure followed was identical to the first except that subjects were told to study each picture carefully so that they would be able to recognize the pictures in the subsequent task. It may be noted that Experiment 1 was an incidental learning task, whereas Experiment 2 was one of intentional learning. The results of both experiments are shown in Table 12-4. It is quite apparent that recognition accuracy was significantly higher when the subjects were rating the photographs

TABLE 12-4. Recognition memory for faces as a function of depth of processing and incidental or intentional learning

|  | Incidental Learning (Experiment 1) | Intentional Learning (Experiment 2) |
|---|---|---|
|  | Percent Correct | Percent Correct |
| Honesty | 81 | 76 |
| Likeableness | 75 | 80 |
| Sex | 60 | 56 |

Adapted from G. H. Bower and M. B. Karlin, "Depth of processing pictures of faces and recognition memory." *Journal of Experimental Psychology*, 1974, 103, 751–757. Copyright © 1974 by the American Psychological Association. Reprinted by permission.

for honesty and likeableness than when the subjects were determining the sex of the subjects. In keeping with the findings obtained with verbal materials, the kind of processing undertaken by the subject made a significant contribution to what was remembered, with intentional versus incidental learning being of little significance.

Warrington and Ackroyd (1975) were also able to demonstrate that subjects who were provided a relevant orienting task when viewing faces (instructions to categorize each face as pleasant or unpleasant) made significantly fewer errors than subjects who were given either no orienting instructions (instructions to attend to each stimulus) or irrelevant instructions (instructions to categorize each face as being tall or short).

### Practical Concerns

The experimental investigations of facial recognition have an obvious practical significance, since recognition plays a pervasive role in everyday situations. Nowhere does it seem more important than in police detection work and courts of law, where the identification of suspects and eyewitness testimony are of paramount importance.

Some of the material discussed in this section is relevant to these practical concerns. The hundreds of photographs that are viewed by a victim in an effort to identify the criminal would appear to reduce recognition accuracy, although it is difficult to know how to modify this procedure in order to minimize such interference. We are aware that other-race recognition is considerably poorer than own-race recognition, so facial recognition testimony of a witness who is not of the same race as the suspect must be viewed with caution. But much remains to be done. One glaring problem is found in the methodology typically used in laboratory studies in which the photograph used in the retention test is identical to the photograph used as the target face. This is certainly not the case when a witness attempts to identify the face of a criminal from a mugshot, since generally the criminal's appearance when the crime was committed differs considerably from his or her appearance when the mugshot was taken.

## SUMMARY

Many experimenters in the verbal learning area have extended their investigations to an examination of prose or connected discourse and facial recognition. Traditional investigators using prose have examined experimental variables that they had found made a contribution to the learning of lists, such as serial position. Current investigators have taken as their point of departure the early work of Bartlett (1932), who in his studies of subjects learning prose suggested that memory for this material was related to the use of a schema, as well as two basic memory processes, (1) abstractive or reproductive and (2) constructive.

A schema can be thought of as a basic abstraction of a complex concept, derived from past experience, which guides the organization of incoming material that is to be recalled. A number of investigators have demonstrated the importance of providing the experimental subject with a schema that effectively facilitates the remembering of material.

Abstraction refers to a process in which the number of omissions in recall increases as the amount of connected discourse increases. But what is the nature of the material that is placed in memory? Inspired by the work of Chomsky, who analyzed sentences in terms of their surface structure or syntactical arrangement and deep structure or meaning, investigators attempted to determine if the representation of prose in memory reflected both of these attributes. Experimental findings have indicated that the syntactical characteristics of prose are not remembered, only the semantic attribute.

In their examination of the semantic attribute, many experimenters have divided connected discourse into linguistic units or ideas, hierarchically arranged with respect to their relationship to the main theme of the narrative. When this has been done, it has been found that as the linguistic unit grows more distant or remote from the main idea, memory for such material declines.

A second construct that operates in memory for prose has been called the constructive process. Bartlett noted that many of his subjects introduced new material into the recall protocols in order to have the story make sense. Current investigators see this process as being responsible for the experimental subject inserting additional information into the material to-be-remembered. In many instances, this additional material is information about the same subject that had been acquired previously; in other instances, as Loftus and her associates have indicated, the added material arises from information that is provided between the original presentation of the to-be-remembered material and a subsequent test for retention.

There has been some difficulty in demonstrating the constructive process in laboratory studies. Spiro (1977) has suggested that one reason may be that experimenters use artificial material, permitting the subject to encode this material separately from other information. Spiro has also pointed out that the constructive process seems to operate when the experimental subject must reconcile contradictory information in a recall protocol.

Facial recognition is a second area that has interested current investigators. Many experimenters have attempted to identify specific stimulus aspects of the face and relate them to memory for faces. It has been found that covering the upper part of the face, in contrast to the lower, results in poorer recognition and the adoption of varying disguises also reduces the efficiency of recognition. Other investigators have been interested in examining general facial characteristics such as attractiveness and uniqueness. These characteristics have also been shown to contribute to facial memory. A variable of considerable interest has been race membership. Almost all experimenters have found that own-race recognition of faces is superior to other-race recognition, with the experimental evidence suggesting that the individual's experience with the race is an important contributor to this result.

The information process approach has been adopted by some investigators in their examination of facial recognition. Their findings suggest that the level of processing contributes to memory for faces.

# CHAPTER THIRTEEN

# The Learning of Motor Skills

This last chapter is concerned with the learning of motor skills—a topic of basic importance for all humans since it is necessary to use motor skills of one variety or another all of our lives. Walking, handling a knife and fork, riding a bicycle, typing, driving an automobile, operating a lathe, and playing golf and tennis are only a few of the large number of motor skills that individuals may acquire in their lifetimes. Tasks involving motor skills appear to differ markedly from the conditioning and verbal-learning tasks examined earlier; hence our separate consideration of them in this chapter.

Bryan and Harter's (1897, 1899) study of the acquisition of the telegraphic language was conducted at about the same time that Pavlov and Thorndike were investigating animal learning, and only shortly after Ebbinghaus had published his work on verbal learning. But for some reason, motor-skills learning never generated a great deal of interest and enthusiasm among psychologists. Up until the late 1930s, the investigation of motor-skills learning was confined largely to studies describing the acquisition of a particular skill.

Events of the early 1940s brought about a marked increase in interest. The need to select thousands of inductees for pilot training in World War II resulted in psychologists making extensive studies of motor skills in order to aid in this selection process. The fact that psychologists who worked on these programs returned to university research after the war, as well as the extensive research support provided by the Air Force during the post-war years, provided the impetus for the motor-skills area to assume much greater importance than ever before.

## A DEFINITION OF MOTOR-SKILLS LEARNING

When a motor-skills task is examined, the experimenter is interested in determining how the organism's overt responses change as a function of the subject's experience or practice. The novice golfer does not know how to swing a golf club correctly; similarly, the aspiring quarterback lacks the skills to throw an adequate forward pass. It is only after long hours of practice that proficiency in these skills is acquired.

The acquisition of series of specific muscular movements, which define motor-skills learning, contrasts with the kind of learning that generally characterizes classical and instrumental conditioning as well as verbal learning and memory. With the latter types of tasks, the organism has the response already available in its repertoire. As a result, learning consists of establishing associative relationships (or connections) between varying events—a stimulus and a response. As Miller (1959) states, learning psychologists have concentrated on determining the laws governing the connections of responses to stimuli.

A formal definition of motor-skills learning has been provided by Fitts et al. (1959). They indicate that the learning of a motor-skills task emphasizes the acquisition of a temporal-spatial organization of muscular movement in a precise and consistent manner. "Spatial" organization refers to the fact that appropriate muscles must be selected and used in a graded manner in skilled performance, while "temporal" organization refers to muscular contraction and/or relaxation which must occur at the precise moment. Fitts et al. have further pointed out that motor-skills learning places emphasis on three specific conditions: (1) response latency, (2) timing and anticipation, and (3) feedback.

**Response constancy** means that on successive occasions the individual is able to select, from a number of available response patterns, the specific response that will enable him/her to achieve a uniform outcome. The student is able to throw crumpled pieces of paper into a wastepaper basket using a variety of throwing motions and from different places in the room—and is able to hit the target consistently. Or one can vary the size of one's signature as the occasion demands, yet legibility is not lost and all of one's signatures reveal a basic similarity. In brief, response constancy enables an individual to employ different response patterns to achieve the same result.

A second condition is **timing and anticipation.** Appropriate timing is obviously a critical aspect of the muscle pattern that characterizes skilled motor activities. In describing a good golf swing, for example, the golf instructor emphasizes the proper timing of the action of the hands, arms, shoulders, hips, etc. But timing, at least with externally paced tasks, is impossible unless one can anticipate the pattern of the stimulus events to be presented; anticipation thus becomes an important correlate to timing.

The last condition is **feedback.** Most skilled performance provides the individual with some sensory feedback—that is, the individual obtains information from the action of his/her muscles, as well as other sense organs. Feedback provides the subject with cues or internal stimuli which can make an important contribution to the learning process.

## MOTOR-SKILLS TASKS

An examination of current research reveals experimenter interest in two general categories of motor-skills tasks. The first category includes those tasks which, for the most part, are found in our normal everyday experiences. Obvious examples are learning to operate a typewriter, drive an automobile, or play a musical instrument. Because of the pervasiveness of such tasks, it is not surprising that they have been of interest to many experimenters, particularly those in physical education. There is little value in describing these tasks, since they are familiar to everyone.

The second category of learning tasks can be described as laboratory-designed tasks, and a survey of the motor-skills literature reveals a bewildering array of them. We shall look at a few of the more frequently used.

**Line Drawing and Linear Movement**   In an early study, Thorndike (1927) asked blindfolded subjects to draw a straight line of a given length. The instructions were quite simple: "Draw a three inch line." The subject then proceeded to draw a line that he/she believed was of this length.

Investigators have long been interested in how linear movements are made with the hand and arm. One type of apparatus used to examine this response consists of a knob or handle which slides along a long metal bar. The task of the subject, who is blindfolded, is to grasp the knob with his or her preferred hand and move it along the bar for a distance that the subject believes matches the distance asked for by the experimenter. By using such a simple task, the experimenter can focus interest on the operation of specific motor-skills variables, such as muscular feedback and knowledge of results, which contribute to the individual becoming better in judging the extent of movement.

**Tracking Tasks**    Another laboratory task requires the subject to track a moving target —the rotary pursuit is an excellent example of this kind of motor-skills task. Here, the subject attempts to keep a hinged stylus on a small brass target that revolves on a turntable at a constant speed. See Figure 13-1.

**Gross Motor Tasks**    The two tasks just described require reasonably fine motor coordination. Some investigators have been interested in using tasks requiring gross muscular activity. One of these involves the stabilimeter. The subject stands on a small platform and attempts to maintain body balance for a fixed interval of time (trials). The extent of the subject's movement in maintaining balance is recorded. See Figure 13-2.

**Complex Tasks**    The tasks described so far are for the most part relatively simple, and near asymptotic performance is reached with a relatively small amount of practice. Some experimenters, however, have been interested in using more complex types of tasks, many of which had their origins in the United States Air Force psychology program for pilot selection. The Mashburn Complex Coordinator (Melton, 1947), or a modification of it (Lewis and Shephard, 1950), simulates a cockpit. It is composed of three double banks of lights: a slightly curved upper bank, a vertical bank, and a lower horizontal bank. Each bank contains a row of red and a row of green pilot lamps, 13 per row. When lighted, the red lamps serve as stimuli, while the green lights can be separately illuminated by the subject through the movement of a hand stick and a foot bar—movements that simulate control of the aileron, elevator, and rudder of an airplane. In a trial, three red lights are lighted, one in each of the three double banks of lights,

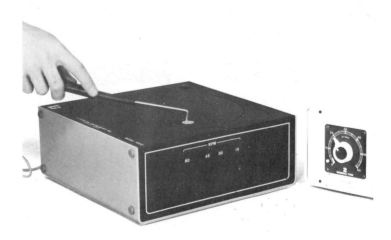

FIGURE 13-1.    Rotary pursuit apparatus. The subject attempts to keep the stylus on the small metal disk that revolves with the turntable. Contact time is recorded on a clock. The stylus is hinged to prevent the subject from exerting pressure on the disk. Courtesy of Lafayette Instrument Company.

FIGURE 13-2.   Stability platform. This instrument is used to evaluate the individual's ability to maintain bodily balance or equilibrium over a period of time. Courtesy of Lafayette Instrument Company.

and the subject is required to manipulate the controls so that the green lights match the red ones. When a match is made, a new combination of red lights is presented. See Figure 13-3.

## THE COURSE OF
## MOTOR-SKILLS LEARNING

Many of the motor-skills tasks performed in our everyday environment or studied in the laboratory are reasonably complex, requiring a long time for someone to attain proficiency. Intuitively, it appears that in learning such a skill one moves through a number of steps or transitions. Beginning as only a crude approximation of the desired skill, the responses become more coordinated and appropriate to the task as practice continues, finally evolving into the smooth, coordinated set of muscular responses that characterizes skilled performance. These steps or transitions, also called stages, were first investigated by Bryan and Harter (1897).

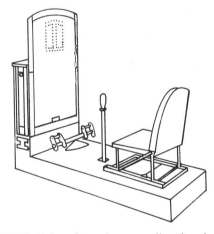

FIGURE 13-3.   Complex coordination instrument. The stick and pedals are used by the subject to match a pattern of lights displayed on the panel. Adapted from E. A. Fleishman, "A comprehensive study of aptitude patterns in unskilled and skilled pyschomotor performance." *Journal of Applied Psychology*, 1957, 41, 263–272. Copyright © 1957 by the American Psychological Association. Reprinted by permission.

## Stages of Acquisition

Bryan and Harter (1897) noted an interesting phenomenon in their study of students learning to use Morse Code. After observing a steady improvement in their subjects' receiving of the code, they found "a long period [in] which the student can feel no improvement and when objective tests show little or none." This was the discovery of the **plateau phenomenon**—defined as a period of no change in performance that has been preceded by and is followed by learning increments.

The authors hypothesized that in the learning of a complex skill, there is a hierarchy of habits that must be mastered by the subject. During certain phases of learning a skill, it is necessary to replace lower-order habits with higher-order ones if performance increments are to continue. Bryan and Harter's interpretation of the plateau in the learning curve was that lower-order habits were approaching their maximum efficiency but were not yet sufficiently automatic to leave the individual free to attack the higher-order habits. Not all psychologists have agreed that the plateau phenomenon is bona fide; some believe that in many instances it appears simply because the method of measuring learning is not sufficiently sensitive to indicate that progress is being made. Most have, however, accepted the position that the acquisition of a complex motor skill appears to take place in different stages.

Fitts and Posner (1967) have described three stages in the acquisition of a skill—a cognitive stage, an associative stage, and an autonomous stage. They posited that in the early stages of learning any new motor skill, the primary task of the subject is to understand the problem and learn what needs to be done. During this phase, the subject attends to a variety of cues, many of which will be subsequently ignored. Considerable cognitive activity is manifest, since the subject must not only try to remember how similar responses were made in the past, but also make verbal responses to guide the motor activity. For example, the novice golfer, in preparing to hit the ball, may verbalize, "bend your knees," "head down," "keep your left arm straight," etc.

The second, or associative, stage consists of trying out new responses; it is during this stage that most of the erroneous responses are eliminated. Schmidt (1975) has described this phase as the individual shifting from learning "what to do" to "how to do it." How long this intermediate phase lasts depends on the complexity of the skill and the extent to which it demands new subroutines and new integrations.

In the third phase, an automatic or autonomous one, the subject responds efficiently with errors greatly reduced and a relatively high level of proficiency. What is involved during this stage of learning? Behaviorally, the subject does not have to pay as much attention to the task as he or she had to previously in order to perform at an acceptable level of proficiency. There is some consensus that during this transition the subject's behavior comes under the control of proprioceptive stimulation, so that attention formerly directed to the task at hand can now be directed to other kinds of stimulation.

Learning to drive an automobile illustrates the operation of these stages. In the first stage, the individual learns what must be done to operate a car, while the second stage is one of learning how to do it. The individual often guides his or her behavior vis-a-vis self-instructions. Moreover, a variety of external stimuli control the individual's responding. The speedometer must be looked at in order to determine at what speed the clutch must be depressed and the gear shift moved, etc. The subject's attention is directed to all of the external stimuli that are a part of the driver's environment, and there is little time to listen to the radio or engage in conversation or other activities that frequently accompany driving. Finally, the third stage is one in which the individual's driving responses are virtually automatic. The subject is able to engage in a variety of behaviors at the same time that he or she is driving.

## Stages of Practice and Ability

The fact that there appear to be different stages in the learning of a complex motor skill suggests the possibility that the abilities the subject uses to maximize performance early in practice are not the same as those that result in optimal performance late in practice. In a series of studies, Fleishman and his associates have demonstrated this to be the case; see Fleishman and Hempel (1954, 1955), Fleishman (1957, 1960), and Fleishman and Parker (1962).

An experiment by Fleishman and Hempel (1955) illustrates this finding, although it should be acknowledged that these investigators did not use a task demanding a graded muscular response on the part of their experimental subjects. In the first part of their study, the experimenters used a discrimination reaction-time test in which the subject had to make different manual responses (pushing one of four toggle switches) to different visual patterns. These visual patterns were made by four lamps arranged in a square, with the upper left and lower right lamps being red, and the upper right and lower left lamps being green. Different combinations of red and green lamps were presented, requiring different switches to be pushed; the subject's reaction time was the response measure. Twenty stimulus patterns were presented on each trial, with all subjects receiving 16 trials. The score for each trial was the total time taken to make a correct response to each of the 20 stimulus presentations. Results revealed that although the mean amount of time for the first trial was .45 minutes, reaction time on the fifteenth and sixteenth trials was reduced to approximately .25 minutes/trial—a marked improvement in responding over the course of the trials provided.

The second part of the study was to measure abilities that were believed to have some relevance to the subject's performance on the discrimination task. The experimenters used 9 different printed tests as well as 10 apparatus tests. Discrimination-task performance on Trials 1, 3, 5, 7, 9, 11, 13, and 15 was correlated with scores obtained on each of the 19 tests, and these findings were then subjected to a factor analysis. The results revealed nine general factors (or abilities) that contributed to discrimination-task performance.

Figure 13-4 shows the amount various factors contributed at different stages of practice. It may be noted that some of the abilities important early in practice became less so later on, and vice versa. For example, early in the training trials it was necessary for the subject to be able to identify the patterns, which were arranged spatially, so a spatial-relations factor made a large and important contribution to performance on these early trials; the subject's speed of movement and reaction time, on the other hand, made a negligible contribution at this time. Late in training, however, the subject's reaction time and speed of responding made a basic contribution to performance, while spatial-relations ability declined in importance.

Sage (1977) has written that these findings have some interesting implications for coaches, since some of them assume that initial performance is related to ultimate proficiency and the rate at which it will be attained. He has pointed out that some athletic coaches have selected their teams on the basis of player performance on a few practice sessions because they believe that the best performers at that point had the best potential for further improvement. The findings, however, consistently show that the abilities which underlie this early superiority are not necessarily the abilities which underlie later proficiency levels. As a result, coaches should pause before they quickly dismiss the poorly skilled.

## VARIABLES CONTRIBUTING TO MOTOR-SKILLS LEARNING

The experimental variables operating with conditioning and verbal-learning tasks provide a convenient framework around which to organize those conditions that contribute to the learning of motor skills. Stimulus and motivational variables have been the major areas of interest for most investigators.

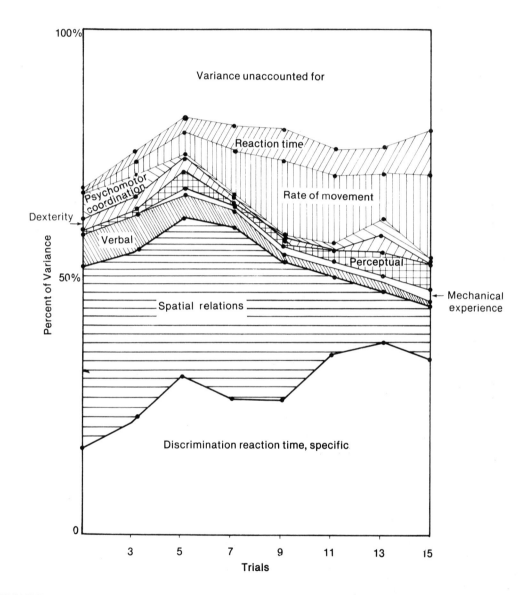

FIGURE 13-4.    Percentage of variance represented by loadings on each factor at different stages of practice on the discrimination reaction-time task. Note: Percentage of variance is represented by the size of the shaded areas for each factor. Adapted from E. A. Fleishman and W. E. Hempel Jr., "The relation between abilities and improvement with practice in a visual discrimination reaction task." *Journal of Experimental Psychology*, 1955, 49, 301–312. Copyright © 1955 by the American Psychological Association. Reprinted by permission.

## Task or Stimulus Variables

Two task or stimulus variables that have had a long experimental history are related to the conditions of practice. The first is how practice sessions should be scheduled, while the second is whether the task should be practiced in its totality—or whether it should be broken up into its component parts, with practice devoted to each of the parts. A third stimulus variable which has had a much shorter experimental history is stimulus-response compatibility.

**Massed versus Distributed Practice**   When one is giving trials or practice periods to subjects who are learning a skill, it is possible to vary the interval of time placed between trials. The terms **massed** and **distributed** are general descriptions of the length of the intertrial interval used in such experiments. The term massed is used when trials or practice sessions are continuous, while the term distributed trials means that some time interval has been placed between the trials.

A survey of the literature on motor-skills learning reveals that hundreds of experiments have been conducted on a variety of tasks performed under massed and distributed practice. A most extensive study using the rotary pursuit task was undertaken by Ammons (1950). Intertrial intervals of either 0, 20, or 50 seconds, 2, 5, or 12 minutes, or 24 hours were used with practice periods of 20 seconds. Data from 36 trials disclosed that the massed group performed most poorly. But an examination of the varying distributed practice groups revealed no systematic relationship between the length of the intertrial interval and performance level. See Figure 13-5.

This finding has been reflected in most studies; almost all investigators have found that some type of distributed practice is superior to massed practice. But when the kinds of distributed practice sessions are examined for best performance, the findings are so mixed that it is impossible to arrive at any general conclusion concerning the optimal length of the intertrial interval.

**Part versus Whole Method**   When the subject is learning a task by the whole method, the entire task is presented to the subject. In contrast, the part method divides the task into smaller units, each of which is learned independently of the others. The units or parts are then combined to form the complete task. Results of early studies did not demonstrate that one method was best. This inability to find a "best method" undoubtedly contributed to the fact that most current psychologists exhibit little interest in the topic.

Investigators of sport skills, however, have shown a continuing interest in the problem of part versus whole methods. Beginning with Cozens's (1931) work on track and field events, a variety of skills have been investigated in an effort to determine the superior method—these include gymnastics and tumbling (Shay, 1934, Wickstrom, 1958), three-ball juggling (Knapp and Dixon, 1952), golf (Purdy and Stallard, 1967), swimming, badminton, and volleyball (Neimeyer, 1959).

But the experimental findings on sport skills have been so mixed that few conclusions can be drawn. This state of affairs can be illustrated by Neimeyer's (1959) experiment. Neimeyer was interested in the effects of the whole or part method on the learning of swimming, volleyball, and badminton. Results indicated that the use of the part method resulted in significantly better learning for volleyball, whereas the whole method was superior for the learning of swimming. No difference between the two methods was noted in the learning of badminton.

The mixed findings dictate that a more analytical approach to the problem be undertaken. In keeping with this point of view, it has been suggested that if the parts or components that comprise the task are relatively independent of one another, it is better to practice each component separately. Adams and Hufford (1962) found that learning a series of discrete acts—for instance, the parts of the total task of flying an airplane—made a significant contribution to mastery of whole task operations. An obvious advantage of such part practice sessions is that easily

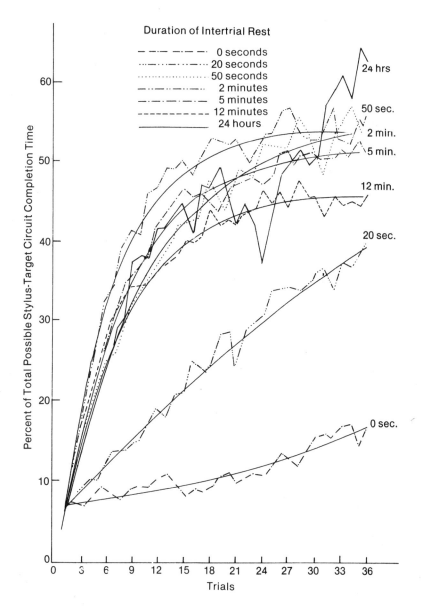

FIGURE 13-5. Performance as a function of the intertrial interval. Adapted from R. B. Ammons, "Acquisition of motor skill: III. Effects of initially distributed practice on rotary pursuit performance." *Journal of Experimental Psychology,* 1950, 40, 777–787. Copyright © 1950 by the American Psychological Association. Reprinted by permission.

learned components need not be repeated and the learner can devote most of his or her practice time to the most difficult parts of the task. Seymour (1954) examined part versus whole methods in training individuals to operate the capstan lathe. He found the part method superior because it enabled the subject to concentrate on those parts of the task that were most difficult to perform.

In contrast, investigators have expressed the belief that training by the whole method is most efficient if the task involves some synchrony among its components—if the speed and timing of one part are critical to the operation of another. Their reasoning has been that the integration of the parts is an important aspect of learning the task and the practice of these parts in isolation neglects this integrative aspect. The basketball jump shot and the golf swing are composed of almost inseparable links of muscular movements, with one link blending into and providing cues for the next link in a sequential manner. To practice only a part of such activities ignores the timing relationship existing among parts, which must be learned if optimal performance is to be achieved.

It must be acknowledged that the suggestions as to when part in contrast to whole methods of practice should be used are only speculative. A more definitive answer to the problem will come when it is possible to provide a logical division of the "parts" that comprise a particular task.

**Stimulus-Response Compatibility** A more recently investigated task variable is stimulus-response compatibility. This concept is used to describe the fact that some S-R sequences can be learned much more rapidly than others by nearly all of the general population. In brief, it is a kind of habitual responding or behavioral stereotype.

A commonplace example of such compatibility is found with the use of the turn signal found in automobiles. When environmental stimuli dictate that a right turn should be made, the individual responds by pushing the turn signal to the right, whereas a proposed left turn is followed by a push of the turn sig-

nal to the left. The operation of the turn signal appears to be an obvious kind of mechanism, but it is surprising the number of times that controls devised for moving vehicles have produced stimulus-response incompatibility, with accidents a common result.

A number of experimental studies have revealed the importance of stimulus-response compatibility. One of the earliest was conducted by Fitts and Deininger (1954). The subject placed a stylus in contact with a small metal button located at the intersection of eight pathways, which radiated from this point like the spokes on a wheel. The angle between each pair of adjacent paths was 45°. Figure 13-6 illustrates the apparatus. With the presentation of a specific stimulus, the subject moved the stylus in one of eight directions; reaction time was measured from the onset of the stimulus movement until the time when the stylus was moved into the appropriate pathway.

FIGURE 13-6. Schematic of the apparatus. The example shows a stimulus from the symbolic set and a response, down and to the right, which represents maximum S-R correspondence for this stimulus. (The stimulus numeral is not drawn to scale.) Adapted from P. M. Fitts and R. L. Deininger, "S-R compatibility: Correspondence among paired elements within stimulus and response codes." *Journal of Experimental Psychology*, 1954, 48, 483–492. Copyright © 1954 by the American Psychological Association. Reprinted by permission.

Although a number of stimulus sets—stimuli to which the subject had to respond in an appropriate way—were used, just two of these have interest for us. One can be described as spatial, the other as symbolic. Within each of these two stimulus sets, stimulus-response correspondence, or compatibility, can be described as (a) maximum, (b) mirrored, or (c) random. The two sets, along with three types of S-R compatibility, are illustrated in Figure 13-7.

Results (see Figure 13-8) are in keeping with what one would expect. Spatial stimuli that were congruent with or corresponded to the direction of the correct response yielded optimal performance. Similarly, symbolic stimuli, presented in terms of clockface num-bers, also resulted in maximum performance. Both of these relationships could be described as being S-R compatible. On the other hand, poorest performance arose when there was random correspondence between the stimuli and the appropriate responses. Interestingly, the spatial stimulus sets resulted in significantly better performance than the symbolic ones.

An interesting aspect of compatibility involves the role of stress. It has been hypothesized that if a subject is trained to make a response that is not in keeping with the behavioral stereotype, or that is not S-R compatible, the subject may regress to the stereotyped response when placed under stress. Fitts et al. (1959) report that Miquelon and Briggs have obtained some experimental support for this

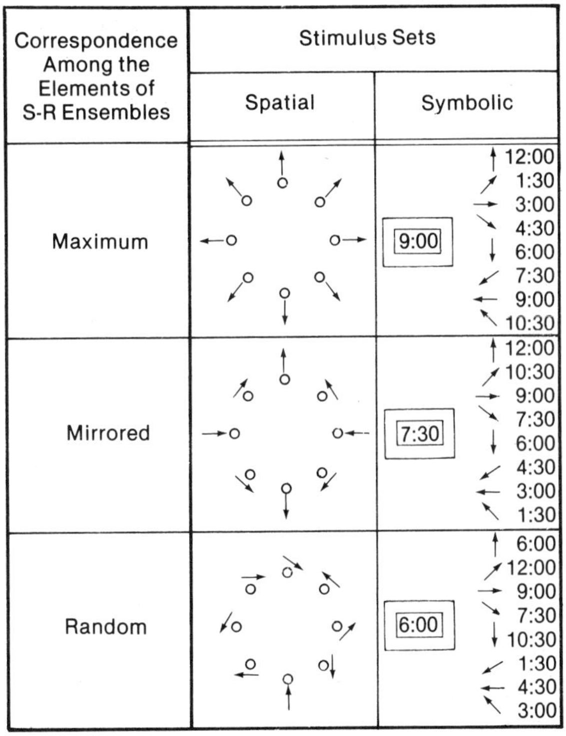

FIGURE 13-7.   The S-R ensembles investigated. The arrows indicate the directions of response movement designated by each stimulus. Response directions were different for each subject in the case of random S-R pairing. Adapted from P. M. Fitts and R. L. Deininger, "S-R compatibility: Correspondence among paired elements within stimulus and response codes." *Journal of Experimental Psychology*, 1954, 48, 483–492. Copyright © 1954 by the American Psychological Association. Reprinted by permission.

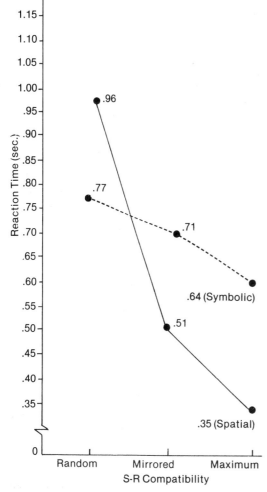

FIGURE 13-8.   Performance as measured by reaction time as a function of varying types of S-R compatibility. Plotted from data obtained from Fitts and Deininger (1954).

position. First, they trained subjects in a tracking task that required subjects to respond to targets moving either at a constant rate or with constant acceleration. Early performance on this task indicated that the subjects responded to the position of the target in space, rather than to where it would be based on its rate of movement. After training, however, the subjects learned to respond to the rate or acceleration of movement of the target. When

a secondary task was introduced, making tracking more difficult and inducing stress, the experimenters noted that the subjects regressed to their early stage of training and responded to target position. This kind of finding is relevant to the accumulating evidence indicating that pilots make a number of reversal errors in interpreting their aircraft flight instruments when they are under stress; see Fitts et al. (1959).

**Motivational Variables**   Motivational variables used in animal learning studies, such as hours of food or water deprivation and amount of reward, have rarely been examined in human learning experiments. But if the concept of motivation is expanded, two motivation-like constructs have generated considerable experimental interest among investigators of motor-skills learning. One of these has been called **knowledge of results** (KR). Here, the subject obtains information from the experimenter about the outcome of an act or a response. Such information could be as simple as the word "right" or "wrong," or in other instances could be much more complex.

The second construct is **feedback**, which provides subjects with information about the characteristics of their responding. Most frequently, interest in feedback has centered on proprioceptive stimulation—stimulation received from the muscles and joints of the body, arising from the subject's response—but visual and auditory stimulation can provide feedback as well. The similarity of knowledge of results and feedback suggests that these constructs be considered together, although certainly some investigators would not agree that feedback is a motivational variable.

**Knowledge of Results (KR)**   The operation of knowledge of results can be best described by citing one of Thorndike's (1927) studies in which he asked blindfolded subjects to draw lines either three, four, five, or six inches long. If the line was drawn within one-eighth inch of the correct length in the case of three inch lines, or within one-fourth inch of the correct length in the case of the other three lengths, the experimenter said "right." When the length of the line did not meet this criterion, the experimenter said "wrong." Subjects were required to draw all four lines, with the number of successive repetitions of a single length varying between four and eight. Six hundred lines were drawn in all, 150 of each length. Other subjects were tested without any feedback. Results indicated that the experimenter's statement of "right" or "wrong" significantly improved the subject's accuracy, whereas the control group's performance did not improve.

Thorndike's study was responsible for investigators becoming interested in determining how the frequency, precision, and delay of knowledge of results contribute to performance.

*Frequency*  It is not surprising to find that motor-skills performance can be improved by increasing the frequency with which KR is provided. A number of investigators have demonstrated this effect; see Bilodeau and Bilodeau (1958), and Bilodeau, Bilodeau, and Schumsky (1959).

In the Bilodeau and Bilodeau (1958) study, subjects were asked to move a lever for a distance of approximately 33° of arc. Since a force of 20 pounds against the lever handle was necessary to move the lever, the response provided the subject with considerably more proprioceptive stimulation than one would expect to find in the frequently used line-drawing studies. Subjects were not informed of the specific distance they were required to move the lever, but only that their task was to find out how far the lever had to be moved in order to get a "hit." On trials where KR was provided, the subject was given a verbal report of the magnitude of the error. The procedure consisted of providing 100 trials, with four groups of subjects receiving KR either every trial or every third, fourth, or tenth trial. The authors found that learning, as measured by reduction in error, was related to the frequency with which KR was provided.

*Amount and Precision*  Trowbridge and Cason (1932), modeling their experimental procedure after Thorndike's (1927) line-drawing experiment, found that precise and infor-

mative KR materially aided performance. A variety of current investigators have confirmed these findings, demonstrating that by providing a greater amount of or more precise KR, it is possible to improve performance. Smode (1958) used a tracking task as his experimental apparatus. He instructed subjects to move the control knob so as to keep the needle of the tracking display on the zero mark at all times. Group 1 subjects were provided a large amount of (or precise) KR in the form of clicks in their earphones at the rate of one for each .5 second of cumulative time-on-target; in addition, visual information was provided by a bank of small lights, with the presentation of each light indicating that the subject had been on target for .5 second. In contrast, Group 2 was told of time-on-target only after the trial had been completed. At the end of 11 training trials, each 90 seconds long, Group 1 had significantly more time-on-target. Figure 13-9 presents these findings.

*Delay*  The last KR variable is the role of delay of KR. In a study by Lorge and Thorndike (1935), subjects were required to throw a ball at a target for 40 trials, with delays of zero, one, two, four, or six seconds interpolated between the subjects' throwing of the ball and securing of KR. Results indicated that the length of the delay period did not have any influence on performance. Thus, a delay of zero seconds did not result in performance superior to that found when a delay of six seconds was utilized. This is a most surprising finding, since delay of reinforcement in animal learning studies does contribute to poorer performance. This finding has been confirmed, however, by many investigators; see Saltzman, Kanfer, and Greenspoon (1955), Bilodeau and Bilodeau (1958), McGuigan (1959), Bilodeau and Ryan (1960), Schmidt and Shea (1976).

Although Lorge and Thorndike (1935) found that the length of the delay interval did not influence performance, they did find that if the KR referred to a previous toss, rather than to the just-completed ball toss, performance was quite poor. A later demonstration of this effect is found in an experiment (Exper-

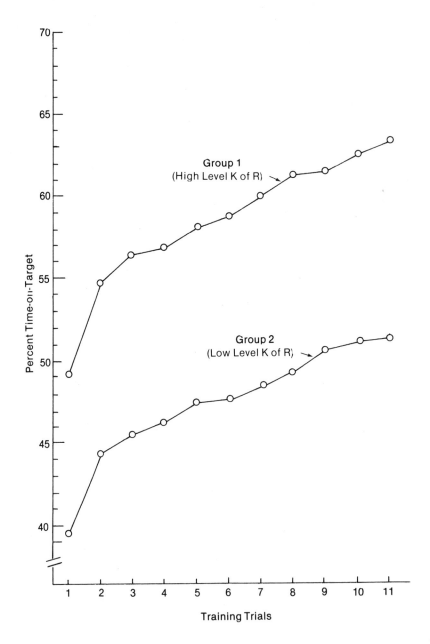

FIGURE 13-9.   Percentage of time-on-target for the two different KR conditions. Adapted from A. F. Smode, "Learning and performance in a tracking task under two levels of achievement information feedback." *Journal of Experimental Psychology*, 1958, 56, 297–304. Copyright © 1958 by the American Psychological Association. Reprinted by permission.

iment II) by Bilodeau (1956), who had subjects pull a lever for approximately 33° of arc. The time for each trial was approximately 20 seconds, with 5 seconds between the "ready" and "pull" signals, 4 seconds for the response, and approximately 11 seconds between the end of the response and the next "ready" signal. Knowledge of results was provided 5 seconds prior to each signal. However, the experimental procedure consisted of providing either a zero, two, or five *trial* KR delay. Thus, a two trial KR delay meant that the score for the first response was not given until

after the third response was made; for those subjects receiving a five trial delay, KR was provided after the sixth response had been made. Thirty KR trials were provided. The results (see Figure 13-10) point out the influence of the delay of KR on performance. What is perhaps remarkable is that any learning at all took place for the five-trial condition.

It is obvious, however, that with the "trials-delay" procedure, the sources of performance decrement are difficult to identify. As a result, several investigators have been interested in interpolating different types of

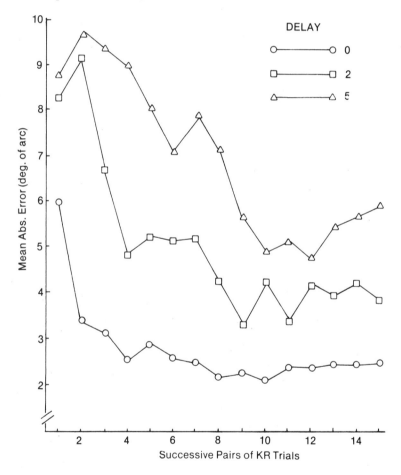

FIGURE 13-10.    Mean absolute error in lever placement for successive pairs of KR trials. (Each data point is the mean of the mean errors of the pair of trials.) Adapted from I. M. Bilodeau, "Accuracy of a simple positioning response with variation in the number of trials by which knowledge of results is delayed." *American Journal of Psychology*, 1956, 69, 434–437. Copyright © 1956 the University of Illinois Press.

activities between trials in an effort to determine the influence of these activities on performance.

A study by Shea and Upton (1976) has demonstrated that specific motor responses made during the KR delay interval can result in performance decrement. In this study, blindfolded subjects were asked to move a handle along a pair of steel rods for a distance of 100 mm. After they returned the handle to the starting place, they were asked to move the handle again, this time for a distance of 200 mm. The handle was then returned to the starting place. For control subjects, a delay interval of 30 seconds was then provided during which the subjects rested, following which the experimenter indicated to the subject first how many millimeters the subject's movement of the handle had deviated from 100 mm and then how many millimeters the subject's response had deviated from 200 mm. Five seconds later, the next trial commenced. During the delay interval of 30 seconds, subjects in the experimental group were asked to make two movements: (a) first move the handle to a stop position and return it to the start position, and (b) then move the handle to a second stop position and return it. The two distances determined by the stops were chosen so that they were either 4 cm greater or 4 cm less than the subjects' last two movements in the experimental task. Twenty trials were provided. As Figure 13-11 indicates, when the delay interval before receipt of KR was filled with additional movements, performance was much poorer than when such activity was not provided.

In summary, the experimental evidence suggests that the provision of competing responses during the KR delay interval produces performance decrements.

**Feedback**  What role does proprioceptive stimulation play in the control and learning of motor skills? The belief that such stimulation, or sensory after-effect, plays an important role in motor behavior can be traced to William James (1890), who wrote that "in action grown habitual, what instigates each new muscle contraction to take place in its appointed order is not a thought or a perception,

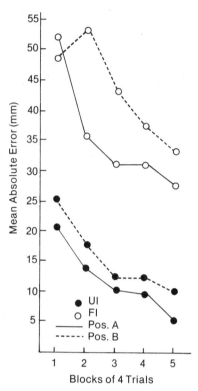

FIGURE 13-11.   Mean absolute error scores computed over trial blocks for acquisition (KR trials) and retention trials (no KR trials). (UI = unfilled interval, FI = filled interval.) Adapted from Shea and Upton (1976). Reprinted by permission of Heldref Publications, 4000 Albemarle St., N.W., Washington, D.C. 20016.

but the sensation occasioned by the muscular contraction just finished" (p. 115). Subsequently, Watson (1919) and other stimulus-response psychologists adopted a similar position in accounting for serial or sequential activity. It was hypothesized that the specific responses that comprise a serial task were chained together by proprioceptive stimulation; this response-chaining hypothesis became an early explanation for how such learning took place.

Not all psychologists agreed that the response-chaining hypothesis was correct. Lashley (1917) observed a man with a spinal injury who had almost complete anesthesia in one leg. Although there were some inadequacies in his responding, he did have normal accuracy in the direction and extent of movement of the affected leg. Lashley reasoned that since the injury had eliminated proprioceptive feedback and yet there was normal movement in the leg, such movement was controlled by the brain and unrelated to proprioceptive stimulation. Lashley's position was termed a centralist point of view.

In early experimental work, he attempted to demonstrate the inadequacies of the response-chaining hypothesis. In one of these experiments (Lashley and Ball, 1929), rats learned a maze with eight blind alleys. Following such learning, portions of the rats' spinal cord that conducted proprioceptive stimulation to the brain were sectioned. In maze running after the operation, performance was almost unimpaired, although the motor coordination of the animal was poor. Lashley and Ball concluded that the ability of the animals to traverse the maze was not influenced by the observed sensory defect; on the other hand, the authors accounted for the animals' maze running in terms of "some intraneural mechanism capable of producing an integrated sequence of movements in the absence of directive sensory cues" (p. 100).

The two points of view have evolved into what current psychologists have designated as closed- versus open-loop positions. The closed-loop position proposes that during the performance of skilled, sequential movements, sensory feedback is responsible for controlling, as well as correcting and modifying, the continuing response. One analogy for the closed-loop hypothesis is provided by the thermostatically controlled furnace. The thermostat is set for a particular temperature, and the heat from the furnace is fed back into the house until the heat of the room reaches the setting of the thermostat. At that point, the furnace cuts off and does not start again until there is another discrepancy between the thermostat setting and room temperature.

In contrast, the open-loop position hypothesizes that a motor program is structured in the brain before the movement sequence begins. This program permits the entire sequence of movements to be carried out, uninfluenced by the sensory feedback that arises from the subject's responding. Unlike the closed-loop position, this position does not specify the mechanism for correcting errors.

What kind of evidence has been brought to bear on this controversy? The closed-loop position is supported by the behavior of individuals who have tabes dorsalis, a disease that prevents them from receiving proprioceptive feedback from the limbs. As a result, walking becomes very difficult unless they are guided by visual stimulation. The individual has to literally see where to place his or her feet. The use of a procedure called delayed auditory feedback (DAF) also provides support for the closed-loop position. Under normal circumstances, auditory feedback is received as one speaks, with such feedback making a contribution to further speech. But Lee (1950, 1951) found that delaying feedback to his experimental subjects by about a half a second caused a marked deterioration of speech fluency. More specifically, the subjects slowed down their speech, with some slurring and a kind of stuttering. This effect has been frequently replicated, as a review by Yates (1963) indicates.

But open-loop theorists have also obtained evidence to support their position. A basic argument they have made is that with some activities, particularly those involving a rapid series of movements, the speed and complexity of the skilled response is too high for the subject to receive and use the proprioceptive stimulation to guide further responding. Lashley (1951) has pointed out that a pianist's fingers can move at a rate of 16 movements per second in passages that call for a definite and changing order of successive finger movements. Such a succession of movements is too rapid even for visual reaction time. And Lenneberg (1967) has reported that single muscular events occur in the speech apparatus during speech production at a rate of several hundred events per second. It is obvious that the activation of so many muscles in such a short time span cannot depend upon the reception of proprioceptive stimulation prior to each muscular response. Rather, there must be some complete train of events that is programmed and run off automatically.

Take the simple case of a subject, beginning with the hand at rest, who initiates a movement via an abrupt acceleration, and then slows the hand down so that it comes to rest on a target 10 cm away, all within a movement time of 100 milliseconds or less. The problem: From where do the deceleration instructions arise? It is argued that subjects use proprioceptive feedback for information about where their hands are. But by the time such instructions could be issued and get to the muscles involved in stopping the hand, the hand is already at rest. Clearly, the instructions to stop the movement must be planned prior to the beginning of the movement. Such planning is assumed to arise from a motor program—defined as a set of prestructured muscle commands permitting movement to be carried out, uninfluenced by peripheral feedback.

Perhaps the strongest support for the open-loop position has been obtained from biological studies. These experiments, as Delcomyn's (1980) review has indicated, have demonstrated that the central nervous system does not require feedback from the sense organs in order to generate sequenced, repetitive behavior. A variety of behavior patterns exhibited in many different experimental subjects all have been shown to operate independently of sensory feedback; these include walking in the cat and cockroach, hopping in the rabbit and toad, swimming in the eel and shark, or flying in the dragonfly and locust.

In these studies, the experimenters' objective has been to isolate the organism's nervous system from all possible sources of sensory feedback, and then to demonstrate that appropriate stimulation will elicit the normal pattern of rhythmic bursts in the motor neurons, and therefore in its muscles. Several procedures have been used to achieve this experimental objective, one of these being deafferentation. With this procedure, all or some of the sensory nerves that carry information into the nervous system are severed. The effect of this operation on the capacity of the nervous system to produce the rhythmic

behavior is then examined. Wilson's (1961) study illustrates the procedure and experimental findings. Wilson used the desert locust as his experimental subject, since it can be induced to fly in the laboratory for extended periods of time and has almost constant cyclical and coordinate movements of its two pairs of wings. Wilson found that removal of portions of the insect's wings, or in fact one whole wing, had no effect on the patterning of movement of the remaining wings—a finding that would not be predicted if proprioceptive feedback played an important role in determining the patterning or sequencing of wing movement. Wilson concluded that "the evidence presented here supports strongly the notion that there is an innate central pattern for the production of flight movements in the locust" (p. 487).

The closed-loop theorists' rebuttal to this kind of evidence has been to acknowledge that sequential rhythmic behavior in lower animals is controlled by the central nervous system but to refute that sequential behavior in humans operates in the same way. Adams (1976) has written that some feedback in the human can take place in as little as ten milliseconds, so that "feedback neural circuitry seems far faster than we have believed. Perhaps Lashley's pianist is a closed-loop, feedback-determined system after all" (p. 216).

*The Dual-Position Model*   An examination of the evidence marshalled to support either the closed- or the open-loop position suggests that neither of these theoretical accounts of how motor-skills learning takes place can successfully account for all of the findings. The answer to the problem would be to recognize that there is both peripheral and central control of movement, depending on the nature of the task and the level of skill. It seems reasonable to assume that during the early stages of learning a motor skill, primary control over the sequencing of response rests with sensory stimulation, although not necessarily kinesthetic. As the organism becomes more skilled, control is gradually shifted over to a motor program. Since very simple skills are learned rapidly, it is obvious that with such skills dependence on sensory stimulation is soon lost; in contrast, more complex tasks that take much longer to learn depend on sensory stimulation for a longer period of time. Thus, Glencross (1977) proposed a two-stage model of human motor-skills learning. In the first stage, a control system depends on feedback, while the second stage incorporates an open-loop system in the form of a motor program which, once initiated, will normally run its full course without the need for feedback.

It is quite difficult to examine the role of open- and closed-loop positions, primarily because feedback, especially proprioception, is difficult to control with human subjects.[1]

A few experiments, such as Pew's (1966) study, have suggested that the acquisition of a skill depends on both sensory stimulation *and* some type of motor program, thus supporting Glencross's (1977) two-stage model. Pew's apparatus consisted of a cathode ray display in which a target moved continuously from right to left of a midpoint. It was the subject's task to keep the target at midpoint by proper timing of alternating presses on a right- and left-hand response key. The speed of the target was one variable that the experimenter manipulated; as one might anticipate, as target speed increased, performance in keeping the target at midpoint became poorer. What Pew also found was that subjects developed two different strategies over the course of the practice trials. Early in practice, responding was slow, with the subject depending on feedback from responses made to the movement of the target. For example, the right-hand key would be depressed and the subject would wait for feedback concerning the effectiveness of the response. This would then be followed by a corrective left response, etc. A closed-loop position would best describe such movement, since responding depended on feedback from the subject observing the position of the target. Later in practice, however, a different kind of strategy developed—the subject responded continuously with both the right and left keys. If the target drifted to the left, the subject could continue to maintain dual responding by increasing the length of time the right key was active relative to the left.

Through a series of alternating responses, the subject could make the target drift back toward the center. This strategy, in contrast to the one adopted earlier in practice, would be in keeping with an open-loop program, since the subject was responding at a more rapid rate than would have been possible if such responding depended on feedback.

## SUMMARY

The acquisition of motor skills represents another major area of interest for learning psychologists. To learn a motor skill one must acquire a temporal-spatial organization of muscular movement, which takes place in a precise and consistent manner. Motor-skills tasks demand a graded response with emphasis on (a) response latency, (b) timing and anticipation, and (c) feedback.

Investigators have been interested in describing how motor-skills tasks are acquired. It appears that the individual goes through three stages in learning many such tasks. First is a cognitive stage in which the learner develops understanding of the task, and perhaps uses verbal responses to guide the motor activity. In the second or associative stage, the subject tries out new responses and eliminates old and inefficient ones. In the third or autonomous stage, the subject responds with a high level of proficiency. Often, the subject's behavior comes under the control of proprioceptive stimulation so that it is possible for him or her to engage in other activities while performing the task. One finding derived from the stage analysis is that the contribution of a specific condition or variable to performance may depend on the subject's stage of practice.

As with other learning paradigms, experimenters have been interested in identifying the specific variables that contribute to learning and performance. Three stimulus variables have been (a) massed versus distributed practice, (b) part versus whole methods of training, and (c) stimulus-response compatibility. The findings from studies examining massed versus distributed practice and part versus whole methods of training have been quite controversial, and few generalizations can be provided. Whether or not one of these conditions contributes to performance appears to depend primarily on the specific characteristics of the task. Stimulus-response compatibility, however, does contribute to learning.

Knowledge of results and feedback are two motivation-like variables of interest to experimenters. Knowledge of results consists of the subject receiving information about the outcome of a response required by the experimenter. As might be anticipated, increasing the frequency and amount or precision of KR has been shown to maximize performance. Feedback is related to the role that proprioceptive stimulation or sensory feedback plays in motor learning. Closed-loop theorists hold that during the performance of skilled sequential movements, sensory feedback is responsible for controlling as well as correcting and modifying the continuous response. In contrast, the open-loop theorist hypothesizes that a motor program is structured in the brain before the movement sequence begins. This program permits the entire sequence of movements to be carried out, uninfluenced by the sensory feedback that arises from the subject's responding.

Arguments and evidence have been marshalled to support both positions. It now appears that a position incorporating both the closed-loop and open-loop positions is necessary to successfully account for all of the findings. Thus, it has been suggested that both peripheral and central factors may contribute, depending on the nature of the task and the level of skill.

### NOTE

1. One procedure which has been used is the ischemic nerve block technique, whereby the continued application of a pressure cuff to a limb blocks sensory information. Lazlo and her colleagues have made extensive use of this procedure in examining the closed-loop and open-loop positions; see Laszlo (1966, 1967), Laszlo, Shamoon, and Sanson-Fisher (1969), Laszlo and Bairstow (1971). But Glencross and Oldfield (1975) and Scott-Kelso and Stelmach (1974) have reported that this technique results in extensive motor impairment as well as sensory loss. Glencross (1977) has written that "the motor deficit observed following ischemic nerve block is not solely the result of blocked kinesthetic sensation, and thus its relevance to the issue of central versus peripheral control of movement cannot be directly assessed" (p. 21).

# References

Abra, J. C. List-1 unlearning and recovery as a function of the point of interpolated learning. *Journal of Verbal Learning and Verbal Behavior*, 1969, *8*, 494–500.

Abramson, L. Y., Seligman, M. E. P., and Teasdale, J. D. Learned helplessness in humans: Critique and reformulation. *Journal of Abnormal Psychology*, 1978, *87*, 49–74.

Ackill, J. E., and Mellgren, R. L. Stimulus preexposure and instrumental learning. *Psychonomic Science*, 1968, *11*, 339.

Adamic, R., and Melzack, R. The role of motivation and orientation in sensory preconditioning. *Canadian Journal of Psychology*, 1970, *24*, 230–239.

Adams, J. A. *Learning and memory: An introduction.* Homewood, Ill.: Dorsey, 1976.

Adams, J. A., and Hufford, L. E. Contributions of a part task trainer to the learning and relearning of a time-shared flight maneuver. *Human Factors*, 1962, *4*, 159–170.

Adams, J. A., McIntyre, J. S., and Thorsheim, H. I. Natural language mediation and interitem interference in paired-associate learning. *Psychonomic Science*, 1969, *16*, 63–64.

Alloy, L. B., and Seligman, M. E. P. On the cognition of learned helplessness and depression. In Bower, G. H., (Ed.), *The psychology of learning and motivation.* New York: Academic Press, 1979.

Ammons, R. B. Acquisition of motor skill: III. Effects of initially distributed practice on rotary pursuit performance. *Journal of Experimental Psychology*, 1950, *40*, 777–787.

Amsel, A. The role of frustrative nonreward in noncontinuous reward situations. *Psychological Bulletin*, 1958, *55*, 102–119.

Amsel, A. Behavioral habituation, counterconditioning, and a general theory of persistence. In Black, A., and Prokasy, W. K. (Eds.), *Classical conditioning II.* New York: Appleton-Century-Crofts, 1972.

Amsel, A., Hug, J. J., and Surridge, C. T. Number of food pellets, goal approaches, and the partial reinforcement effect after minimal acquisition. *Journal of Experimental Psychology*, 1968, *77*, 530–534.

Anderson, J. R., and Bower, G. H. *Human associative memory.* New York: Wiley, Halstead Press, 1973.

Anderson, R. C., and Carter, J. F. Retroactive inhibition of meaningful learned sentences. *American Educational Research Journal*, 1972, *9*, 443–448.

Anderson, R. C., and Myrow, D. L. Retroactive inhibition of meaningful discourse. *Journal of Educational Psychology*, 1971, *62*, 81–94.

Anisfeld, M., and Knapp, M. Association, synonymity, and directionality in false recognition. *Journal of Experimental Psychology*, 1968, *77*, 171–179.

Annau, Z., and Kamin, L. J. The conditioned emotional response as a function of intensity of the US. *Journal of Comparative and Physiological Psychology*, 1961, *54*, 428–432.

Archer, E. J. Re-evaluation of the meaningfulness of all possible CVC trigrams. *Psychological Monographs*, 1960, *74*, No. 10.

Armus, H. L. Effect of magnitude of reinforcement on acquisition and extinction of a running response. *Journal of Experimental Psychology*, 1959, *58*, 61–63.

Ashida, S., and Birch, D. The effects of incentive shift as a function of training. *Psychonomic Science*, 1964, *1*, 201–202.

Atkinson, R. C., and Shiffrin, R. M. Human memory: A proposed system and its control processes. In Spence, K. W., and Spence, J. T. (Eds.), *The psychology of learning and motivation*. New York: Academic Press, 1968.

Ausubel, D., Robbins, K., and Blake, F., Jr. Retroactive inhibition and facilitation in the learning of school materials. *Journal of Educational Psychology*, 1957, *48*, 334–343.

Averbach, E., and Coriell, A. S. Short-term memory in vision. *Bell System Technical Journal*, 1961, *40*, 309–328.

Ayllon, T., and Azrin, N. H. Reinforcement and instructions with mental patients. *Journal of the Experimental Analysis of Behavior*, 1964, *7*, 327–331.

Ayllon, T., and Azrin, N. H. The measurement and reinforcement of behavior of psychotics. *Journal of the Experimental Analysis of Behavior*, 1965, *8*, 357–383.

Bacon, W. E. Partial-reinforcement extinction following different amounts of training. *Journal of Comparative and Physiological Psychology*, 1962, *55*, 998–1003.

Baddeley, A. D. The psychology of memory. New York: Basic Books, 1976.

Bahrick, H. P. Incidental learning under two incentive conditions. *Journal of Experimental Psychology*, 1954, *47*, 170–172.

Bahrick, H. P. Measurement of memory by prompted recall. *Journal of Experimental Psychology*, 1969, *79*, 213–219.

Bahrick, H. P., Bahrick, P. O., and Wittlinger, R. P. Fifty years of memory for names and faces: A cross-sectional approach. *Journal of Experimental Psychology: General*, 1975, *104*, 54–75.

Baker, R. A., and Lawrence, D. H. The differential effects of simultaneous and successive stimuli presentation on transposition. *Journal of Comparative and Physiological Psychology*, 1951, *44*, 378–382.

Bandura, A. *Principles of behavior modification*. New York: Holt, Rinehart and Winston, 1969.

Banks, R. K. Generality of persistence: The role of stimulus and response factors in persistence to punishment. *Learning and Motivation*, 1973, *4*, 218–228.

Barber, T. X. Experimental evidence for a theory of hypnotic age-regression. *International Journal of Clinical and Experimental Hypnosis*. 1961, *9*, 181–193.

Barber, T. X. Hypnotic age regression: A critical review, *Psychosomatic Medicine*, 1962, *24*, 286–299.

Barbizet, J. *Human memory and its pathology*. San Francisco: Freeman, 1970.

Barker, L. M. CS duration, amount, and concentration effects in conditioning taste aversions. *Learning and Motivation*, 1976, *7*, 265–273.

Barnes, J. M., and Underwood, B. J. "Fate" of first-list associations in transfer theory. *Journal of Experimental Psychology*, 1959, *58*, 97–105.

Barrett, T. R., and Ekstrand, B. R. Effect of sleep on memory: III. Controlling for time-of-day effects. *Journal of Experimental Psychology*, 1972, *96*, 321–327.

Bartlett, F. C. *Remembering*. London: Cambridge University Press, 1932.

Bass, M. J., and Hull, C. L. The irradiation of a tactile conditioned reflex in man. *Journal of Comparative Psychology*, 1934, *17*, 47–65.

Baum, M. Paradoxical effect of alcohol on the resistance to extinction of an avoidance response. *Journal of Comparative and Physiological Psychology*, 1969, *69*, 238–240.

Baum, M. Extinction of avoidance responding through response prevention (flooding) in rats. *Psychological Bulletin*, 1970, *74*, 276–284.

Benedict, J. O., and Ayres, J. J. B. Factors affecting conditioning in the truly random control procedure in the rat. *Journal of Comparative and Physiological Psychology*, 1972, *78*, 323–330.

Berger, B. D., Yarczower, M., and Bitterman, M. E. Effect of partial reinforcement on the extinction of a classically conditioned response in the goldfish. *Journal of Comparative and Physiological Psychology*, 1965, *59*, 399–405.

Bernard, L. L. *Instinct: A study in social psychology*. New York: Holt, 1924.

Bernstein, I. I. Learned taste aversions in children receiving chemotherapy. *Science*, 1978, *200*, 1302–1303.

Berrian, R. W., Metzler, D. P., Kroll, N. E. A., and Clark-Meyers, G. M. Estimates of imagery, ease of definition, and animateness for 328 adjectives. *Journal of Experimental Psychology: Human Learning and Memory*, 1979, *5*, 435–447.

Best, H. L., and Michaels, R. M. Living out "future" experience under hypnosis. *Science*, 1954, *120*, 1077.

Bevan, W., and Steger, J. A. Free recall and abstractness of stimuli. *Science*, 1971, *172*, 597–599.

Biel, W. C., and Force, R. C. Retention of nonsense syllables in intentional and incidental learning. *Journal of Experimental Psychology*, 1943, *32*, 52–63.

Bilodeau, E. A., and Bilodeau, I. M. Variations of temporal intervals among critical events in five studies of knowledge of results. *Journal of Experimental Psychology*, 1958, *55*, 603–612.

Bilodeau, E. A., Bilodeau, I. M., and Schumsky, D. A. Some effects of introducing and withdrawing knowledge of results early and late in practice. *Journal of Experimental Psychology*, 1959, *58*, 142–144.

Bilodeau, E. A., and Ryan, F. J. A test for interaction of delay of knowledge of results and two types of interpolated activity. *Journal of Experimental Psychology*, 1960, *59*, 414–419.

Bilodeau, I. M. Accuracy of a simple positioning response with variation in the number of trials by which knowledge of results is delayed. *American Journal of Psychology*, 1956, *69*, 434–437.

Bindra, D. How adaptive behavior is produced: A perceptual-motivational alternative to response-reinforcement. *The Behavioral and Brain Sciences*, 1978, *1*, 41–52.

Birch, D. Discrimination learning as a function of the ratio of nonreinforced to reinforced trials. *Journal of Comparative and Physiological Psychology*, 1955, *48*, 371–374.

Black, A. H. Heart rate changes during avoidance learning in dogs. *Canadian Journal of Psychology*, 1959, *13*, 229–242.

Blodgett, H. C. The effect of the introduction of reward upon the maze performance of rats. *University of California Publications in Psychology*, 1929, *4*, 113–134.

Bolles, R. C. Species-specific defense reactions and avoidance learning. *Psychological Review*, 1970, *77*, 1, 32–48.

Bolles, R. C. *Learning theory*. New York: Holt, Rinehart and Winston, 1979.

Bolles, R. C., and deLorge, J. Explorations in a Dashiell maze as a function of prior deprivation, current deprivation, and sex. *Canadian Journal of Psychology*, 1962, *16*, 221–227.

Bolles, R. C., Moot, S. A., and Grossen, N. E. The extinction of shuttlebox avoidance. *Learning and Motivation*, 1971, *2*, 324–333.

Boneau, C. A. Paradigm regained? Cognitive behaviorism restated. *American Psychologist*, 1974, *29*, 297–309.

Bousfield, W. A. The occurrence of clustering in the recall of randomly arranged associates. *Journal of General Psychology*, 1953, *49*, 229–240.

Bousfield, W. A., and Cohen, B. H. The occurrence of clustering in the recall of randomly arranged words of different frequencies of usage. *Journal of General Psychology*, 1955, *52*, 83–95.

Bousfield, W. A., and Wicklund, D. A. Rhyme as a determinant of clustering. *Psychonomic Science*, 1969, *16*, 183–184.

Bower, G. H. Partial and correlated reward in escape learning. *Journal of Experimental Psychology*, 1960, *59*, 126–130.

Bower, G. H. A contrast effect in differential conditioning. *Journal of Experimental Psychology*, 1961, *62*, 196–199.

Bower, G. H. Chunks as interference units in free recall. *Journal of Verbal Learning and Verbal Behavior*, 1969, *8*, 610–613.

Bower, G. H. Interference paradigms for meaningful propositional memory. *American Journal of Psychology*, 1978, *91*, 575–585.

Bower, G. H., and Karlin, M. B. Depth of processing pictures of faces and recognition memory. *Journal of Experimental Psychology*, 1974, *103*, 751–757.

Bower, G. H., Monteiro, K. P., and Gilligan, S. G. Emotional mood as a context for learning and recall. *Journal of Verbal Learning and Verbal Behavior*, 1978, *17*, 573–585.

Brady, J. P., and Rieger, W. Behavior treatment of anorexia nervosa. In Thompson, T., and Dockens, W. S. (Eds.), *Applications of behavior modification*. New York: Academic Press, 1975.

Braud, W. G. Effectiveness of "neutral," habituated, shock-related and food-related stimuli as CSs for avoidance learning in goldfish. *Conditional Reflex*, 1971, *6*, 153–156.

Braveman, N. S. Formation of taste aversion in rats following prior exposure to sickness. *Learning and Motivation*, 1975, *6*, 512–534.

Breland, J., and Hothersall, D. Heart rate control under conditions of augmented sensory feedback. *Psychophysiology*, 1966, *3*, 23–28.

Breland, K., and Breland, M. The misbehavior of organisms. *American Psychologist*, 1961, *16*, 681–684.

Brener, J., and Hothersall, D. Paced respiration and heart rate control. *Psychophysiology*, 1967, *4*, 1–6.

Broadbent, D. D. *Perception and communication.* New York: Pergamon, 1958.

Broadhurst, P. L. Emotionality and the Yerkes-Dodson law. *Journal of Experimental Psychology*, 1957, *54*, 345–352.

Brogden, W. J. Sensory pre-conditioning. *Journal of Experimental Psychology*, 1939, *25*, 323–332.

Brogden, W. J. Acquisition and extinction of a conditioned avoidance response in dogs. *Journal of Comparative and Physiological Psychology*, 1949, *42*, 296–302.

Brogden, W. J., Lipman, E. A., and Culler, E. The role of incentive in conditioning and extinction. *American Journal of Psychology*, 1938, *51*, 109–117.

Brooks, C. I. Frustration to nonreward following limited reward experience. *Journal of Experimental Psychology*, 1969, *81*, 403–405.

Brooks, C. I. Frustration considerations of the small-trials partial reinforcement effect: Experience with nonreward and intertrial reinforcement. *Journal of Experimental Psychology*, 1971, *89*, 362–371.

Brooks, C. I. Effect of prior nonreward on subsequent incentive growth during brief acquisition. *Animal Learning and Behavior*, 1980, *8*, 143–151.

Brooks, R. M., and Goldstein, A. G. Recognition of children of inverted photographs of faces. *Child Development*, 1963, *34*, 1033–1040.

Brown, J. Some tests of the decay theory of immediate memory. *Quarterly Journal of Experimental Psychology*, 1958, *10*, 12–21.

Brown, J. S. Generalization and discrimination. In Mostofsky, D. (Ed.), *Stimulus generalization.* Stanford: Stanford University Press, 1965.

Brown, J. S., and Bass, B. The acquisition and extinction of an instrumental response under constant and variable stimulus conditions. *Journal of Comparative and Physiological Psychology*, 1958, *51*, 499–504.

Brown, J. S., Bilodeau, E. A., and Baron, M. R. Bidirectional gradients in the strength of a generalized voluntary response to stimuli on a visual-spatial dimension. *Journal of Experimental Psychology*, 1951, *41*, 52–61.

Brown, P. L., and Jenkins, H. M. Auto-shaping of the pigeon's key peck. *Journal of the Experimental Analysis of Behavior*, 1968, *11*, 1–8.

Brown, R. T., and Wagner, A. R. Resistance to punishment and extinction following training with shock or nonreinforcement. *Journal of Experimental Psychology*, 1964, *68*, 503–507.

Bruner, J. S., Goodnow, J. J., and Austin, G. A. *A study of thinking.* New York: Wiley, 1960.

Bryan, W. L., and Harter, N. Studies in the physiology and psychology of the telegraphic language. *Psychological Review*, 1897, *4*, 27–53.

Bryan, W. L., and Harter, N. Studies on the telegraphic language: The acquisition of a hierarchy of habits. *Psychological Review*, 1899, *6*, 345–375.

Bugelski, B. R. Images as mediators in one-trial paired-associate learning. II. Self-timing in successive lists. *Journal of Experimental Psychology*, 1968, *77*, 328–334.

Bugelski, B. R., Kidd, E., and Segmen, J. Images as a mediator in one-trial paired-associate learning. *Journal of Experimental Psychology*, 1968, *76*, 69–73.

Burtt, H. E. An experimental study of early childhood memory. *Journal of Genetic Psychology*, 1932, *40*, 287–295.

Burtt, H. E. A further study of early childhood memory. *Journal of Genetic Psychology*, 1937, *50*, 187–192.

Burtt, H. E. An experimental study of early childhood memory: Final report. *Journal of Genetic Psychology*, 1941, *58*, 435–439.

Butter, C. M., and Thomas, D. R. Secondary reinforcement as a function of the amount of primary reinforcement. *Journal of Comparative and Physiological Psychology*, 1958, *51*, 346–348.

Calkins, M. W. Association. *Psychological Review*, 1894, *1*, 476–483.

Calkins, M. W. Association: An essay analytic and experimental. *Psychological Review Monograph Supplements*, 1896, *2*.

Campbell, B. A., and Masterson, F. A. Psychophysics of punishment. In Campbell, B. A., and Church, R. M. (Eds.), *Punishment and aversive behavior.* New York: Appleton-Century-Crofts, 1969.

Campbell, D., Sanderson, R. E., and Laverty, S. G. Characteristics of a conditioned response in human subjects during extinction trials following a single traumatic conditioning trial. *Journal of Abnormal and Social Psychology*, 1964, *68*, 627–639.

Campbell, P. E., Batsche, C. J., and Batsche, G. M. Spaced-trials reward magnitude effects in the rat: Single versus multiple food pellets. *Journal of Comparative and Physiological Psychology*, 1972, *81*, 360–364.

Campbell, P. E., Knouse, S. B., and Wroten, J. D. Resistance to extinction in the rat following regular and irregular schedules of partial reward. *Journal of Comparative and Physiological Psychology*, 1970, *72*, 210–215.

Capaldi, E. J. The effect of different amounts of training on the resistance to extinction of different patterns of partially reinforced responses. *Journal of Comparative and Physiological Psychology*, 1958, *51*, 367–371.

Capaldi, E. J. Partial reinforcement: A hypothesis of sequential effects. *Psychological Review*, 1966, *73*, 495–477.

Capaldi, E. J. A sequential hypothesis of instrumental learning. In Spence, K. W., and Spence, J. T. (Eds.), *The psychology of learning and motivation.* New York: Academic Press, 1967.

Capaldi, E. J. Memory and learning: A sequential viewpoint. In Honig, W. K., and James, P. H. R. (Eds.), *Animal memory.* New York: Academic Press, 1971.

Capaldi, E. J. Effects of schedule and delay of reinforcement on acquisition speed. *Animal Learning and Behavior*, 1978, *6*, 330–334.

Capaldi, E. J., and Hart, D. Influence of a small number of partial reinforcement training trials on resistance to extinction. *Journal of Experimental Psychology*, 1962, *64*, 166–171.

Capaldi, E. J., and Kassover, K. Sequence, number of nonrewards, anticipation, and intertrial interval in extinction. *Journal of Experimental Psychology*, 1970, *84*, 470–476.

Capaldi, E. J., Lanier, A. T., and Godbout, R. C. Reward schedule effects following severely limited acquisition training. *Journal of Experimental Psychology*, 1968, *78*, 521–524.

Capaldi, E. J., and Waters. R. W. Conditioning and nonconditioning interpretations of small-trial phenomena. *Journal of Experimental Psychology*, 1970, *84*, 518–522.

Carlson, N. R. *Physiology of behavior.* Boston: Allyn and Bacon, 1977.

Cason, H. Specific serial learning: A study of backward association. *Journal of Experimental Psychology*, 1926, *9*, 195–227.

Cautela, J. R. Treatment of compulsive behavior by covert sensitization. *Psychological Record*, 1966, *16*, 33–41.

Cautela, J. R. Covert sensitization. *Psychological Reports*, 1967, *20*, 459–468.

Cegavske, C. F., Thompson, R. F., Patterson, M. M., and Gormezano, I. Mechanisms of efferent neuronal control of the reflex nictitating membrane response in rabbit (Oryctolagus cuniculus). *Journal of Comparative and Physiological Psychology*, 1976, *90*, 411–423.

Chance, J., Goldstein, A. G., and McBride, L. Differential experience and recognition memory for faces. *Journal of Social Psychology*, 1975. *97*, 243–253.

Chapin, M., and Dyck, D. G. Persistence in children's reading behavior as a function of N length and attribution retraining. *Journal of Abnormal Psychology*, 1976, *85*, 511–515.

Chase, S. Selectivity in multidimensional stimulus control. *Journal of Comparative and Physiological Psychology*, 1968, *66*, 787–792.

Chomsky, N. *Syntactic structures.* The Hague: Mouton, 1957.

Church, R. M. Aversive behavior. In Kling, J. W., and Riggs, L. A. (Eds.), *Woodworth and Schlosberg's Experimental Psychology.* New York: Holt, Rinehart and Winston, 1971.

Church, R. M. The internal clock. In Hulse, S. H., Fowler, H., and Honig, W. K. (Eds.), *Cognitive processes in animal behavior.* Hillsdale, N. J.: Erlbaum, 1978.

Church, R. M., Brush, F. R., and Solomon, R. L. Traumatic avoidance learning: The effects of CS-US interval with a delayed-conditioning procedure in a free-responding situation. *Journal of Comparative and Physiological Psychology*, 1956, *49*, 301–308.

Church, R. M., Getty, D. J., and Lerner, N. D. Duration discrimination by rats. *Journal of Experimental Psychology: Animal Behavior Processes*, 1976, *2*, 303–312.

Clark, F. C. The effect of deprivation and frequency of reinforcement on variable interval responding. *Journal of the Experimental Analysis of Behavior*, 1958, *1*, 221–228.

Clifford, T. Extinction following continuous reward and latent extinction. *Journal of Experimental Psychology*, 1964, *68*, 456–465.

Clifford, T. Runway length and the failure of expected rewards: The OEE. *Canadian Journal of Psychology*, 1968, *22*, 417–426.

Cofer, C. N., and Appley, M. H. *Motivation: Theory and research.* New York: Wiley, 1964.

Cofer, C. N., and Bruce, D. R. Form-class as the basis for clustering in the recall of nonassociated words. *Journal of Verbal Learning and Verbal Behavior*, 1965, *4*, 386–389.

Cofer, C. N., Failie, N. F., and Horton, D. L. Retroactive inhibition following reinstatement or maintenance of first-list responses by means of free recall. *Journal of Experimental Psychology*, 1971, *90*, 197–205.

Cohen, D. H. Effect of conditioned stimulus intensity on visually conditioned heart rate change in the pigeon: A sensitization mechanism. *Journal of Comparative and Physiological Psychology*, 1974, *87*, 495–499.

Collier, G., and Marx, M. H. Changes in performance as a function of shifts in the magnitude of reinforcement. *Journal of Experimental Psychology*, 1959, *57*, 305–309.

Collins, K. H., and Tatum, A. L. A conditioned reflex established by chronic morphine poisoning. *American Journal of Physiology*, 1925, *74*, 14–26.

Cook, S. W., and Harris, R. E. The verbal conditioning of the galvanic skin reflex. *Journal of Experimental Psychology*, 1937, *21*, 202–210.

Coppage, E. W., and Harcum, E. R. Temporal vs. structural determinants of primacy in strategies of serial learning. *Journal of Verbal Learning and Verbal Behavior*, 1967, *6*, 487–490.

Corkin, S. Acquisition of motor skill after bilateral medial temporal-lobe excision. *Neuropsychologia*, 1968, *6*, 255–265.

Corson, J. A. Observational learning of a lever pressing response. *Psychonomic Science*, 1967, *7*, 197–198.

Coughlin, R. C. Frustration effect and resistance to extinction as a function of percentage of reinforcement. *Journal of Experimental Psychology*, 1970, *84*, 113–119.

Cowles, J. T. Food tokens as incentives for learning by chimpanzees. *Comparative Psychological Monographs*, 1937, *14*, No. 5.

Cowles, J. T., and Nissen, H. W. Reward expectancy in delayed responses of chimpanzees. *Journal of Comparative Psychology*, 1937, *24*, 345–358.

Cox, J. K., and D'Amato, M. R. Disruption of overlearning discriminative behavior in monkeys (Cebus apella) by delay of reward. *Animal Learning and Behavior*, 1977, *5*, 93–98.

Cozens, F. W. Three research studies in physical education. II. A comparative study of two methods of teaching class work in track and field events. *Research Quarterly*, 1931, *2*, 75–79.

Craik, F. I. M., and Lockhart, R. S. Levels of processing: A framework for memory research. *Journal of Verbal Learning and Verbal Behavior*, 1972, *11*, 671–684.

Craik, F. I. M., and Tulving, E. Depth of processing and the retention of words in episodic memory. *Journal of Experimental Psychology: General*, 1975, *104*, 268–294.

Craik, F. I. M., and Watkins, M. J. The role of rehearsal in short-term memory. *Journal of Verbal Learning and Verbal Behavior*, 1973, *12*, 599–607.

Crespi, L. P. Quantitative variation of incentive and performance in the white rat. *American Journal of Psychology*, 1942, *55*, 467–517.

Crisler, G. Salivation is unnecessary for the establishment of the salivary conditioned reflex induced by morphine. *American Journal of Physiology*, 1930, *84*, 553–556.

Cross, J. F., Cross, J., and Daly, J. Sex, race, age, and beauty as factors in recognition of faces. *Perception and Psychophysics*, 1971, *10*, 393–396.

Culbertson, J. L. Effects of brief reinforcement delays on acquisition and extinction of brightness discrimination in rats. *Journal of Comparative and Physiological Psychology*, 1970, *70*, 317–325.

Cumming, W. W., and Eckerman, D. A. Stimulus control of a differentiated operant. *Psychonomic Science*, 1965, *3*, 313–314.

Daly, H. B. Learning as a hurdle-jump response to escape cues paired with reduced reward or frustrative nonreward. *Journal of Experimental Psychology*, 1969, *79*, 146–157.

D'Amato, M. R. Secondary reinforcement and magnitude of primary reinforcement. *Journal of Comparative and Physiological Psychology*, 1955, *48*, 378–380.

D'Amato, M. R. Delayed matching and short-term memory in monkeys. In Bower, G. H. (Ed.), *The psychology of learning and motivation*. New York: Academic Press, 1973.

D'Amato, M. R., and Schiff, D. Further studies of overlearning and position reversal learning. *Psychological Reports*, 1964, *14*, 380–382.

Darley, C. F., and Glass, A. L. Effects of rehearsal and serial list position on recall. *Journal of Experimental Psychology: Human Learning and Memory*, 1975, *104*, 455–458.

Davenport, D. G., and Olson, R. D. A reinterpretation of extinction in discriminated avoidance. *Psychonomic Science*, 1968, *13*, 5–6.

Davenport, J. W. Species generality of within-subjects reward magnitude effects. *Canadian Journal of Psychology*, 1970, *24*, 1–7.

Davies, G., Shepherd, J., and Ellis, H. Effects of interpolated mugshot exposure on accuracy of eyewitness identification. *Journal of Applied Psychology*, 1979, *64*, 232–237.

Dawson, M. E. Cognition and conditioning: Effects of masking the CS-UCS contingency on human GSR classical conditioning. *Journal of Experimental Psychology*, 1970, *85*, 389–396.

Dawson, M. E., and Biferno, N. A. Concurrent measurement of awareness and electrodermal classical conditioning. *Journal of Experimental Psychology*, 1973, *101*, 55–62.

Dawson, M. E., and Grings, W. W. Comparison of classical conditioning and relational learning. *Journal of Experimental Psychology*, 1968, *76*, 227–231.

Dawson, M. E., and Satterfield, J. H. Can human GSR conditioning occur without relational learning? *Proceedings of the 77th Annual Convention of the American Psychological Association*, 1969, *4*, 69–70.

Deane, G. E. Human heart rate responses during experimentally induced anxiety. *Journal of Experimental Psychology*, 1961, *61*, 489–493.

Deese, J., and Hardman, G. W., Jr. An analysis of errors in retroactive inhibition of rote verbal learning. *American Journal of Psychology*, 1954, *67*, 299–307.

Deese, J., and Kaufman, R. A. Serial effects in recall of unorganized and sequentially organized verbal material. *Journal of Experimental Psychology*, 1957, *54*, 180–187.

Delcomyn, F. Neural basis of rhythmic behavior in animals. *Science*, 1980, *210*, 492–498.

Dement, W., and Kleitman, N. The relation of eye movement during sleep to dream activity: An objective method for the study of dreaming. *Journal of Experimental Psychology*, 1957, *53*, 339–346.

Dennenberg, V. H., and Karas, G. C. Supplementary report: The Yerkes-Dodson law and shift in task difficulty. *Journal of Experimental Psychology*, 1960, *59*, 429–430.

DeVilliers, P. A. Choice in concurrent schedules and a quantitative formulation of the law of effect. In Honig, W. K., and Staddon, J. E. R. (Eds.), *Handbook of operant behavior*. Englewood Cliffs, N.J.: Prentice-Hall, 1977.

Dews, P. B. The effect of multiple SΔ periods on responding on a fixed-interval schedule. *Journal of the Experimental Analysis of Behavior*, 1962, *5*, 369–374.

DiCara, L. V., and Miller, N. E. Changes in heart rate instrumentally learned by curarized rats as avoidance responses. *Journal of Comparative and Physiological Psychology*, 1968, *65*, 1–7.

Dickinson, A., and Mackintosh, N. J. Classical conditioning in animals. In Rosenzwieg, M. R., and Porter, L. W. (Eds.), *Annual Review of Psychology*. Palo Alto, Calif.: Annual Reviews, Inc., 1978.

Dillon, R. F., and Reid, L. S. Short-term memory as a function of information processing during the retention interval. *Journal of Experimental Psychology*, 1969, *81*, 261–269.

Dinsmoor, J. A. *Operant conditioning: An experimental analysis of behavior*. Dubuque, Iowa: W. C. Brown Co., 1970.

Doleys, D. M. Behavioral treatments for nocturnal enuresis in children: A review of the recent literature. *Psychological Bulletin*, 1977, *84*, 30–54.

Dooling, D. J., and Lachman, R. Effects of comprehension on retention of prose. *Journal of Experimental Psychology*, 1971, *88*, 216–222.

Drachman, D. A., and Arbit, J. Memory and the hippocampal complex, II. *Archives of Neurology*, 1966, *15*, 52–61.

Dragoin, W. B. Conditioning and extinction of taste aversions with variations in intensity of the CS and UCS in two strains of rats. *Psychonomic Science*, 1971, *22*, 303–304.

Dubin, W. J., and Levis, D. J. Generalization of extinction gradients: A systematic analysis. *Journal of Experimental Psychology*, 1973, *100*, 403–412.

Dyal, J. S., and Holland, T. A. Resistance to extinction as a function of the number of reinforcements. *American Journal of Psychology*, 1963, *76*, 332–333.

Dyck, D. G., Mellgren, R. L., and Nation, J. R. Punishment of appetitively reinforced instrumental behavior: Factors affecting response persistence. *Journal of Experimental Psychology*, 1974, *102*, 125–132.

Ebbinghaus, H. *Memory: A contribution to experimental psychology* (Translated by Ruger, H. A., and Bussenius, C. E.). New York: Teachers College, Columbia University, 1913.

Egeland, B. Effects of errorless training on teaching children to discriminate letters of the alphabet. *Journal of Applied Psychology*, 1975, *60*, 533–536.

Ehrenfreund, D. An experimental test of the continuity theory of discrimination learning with pattern vision. *Journal of Experimental Psychology*, 1948, *41*, 408–422.

Ehrenfreund, D., and Badia, P. Response strength as a function of drive level and pre- and postshift incentive magnitude. *Journal of Experimental Psychology*, 1962, *63*, 468–471.

Eibl-Eibesfeldt, I. *Ethology: The biology of behavior.* New York: Holt, Rinehart and Winston, 1970.

Eiserer, L. A., and Hoffman, H. S. Priming of duckling's response by presenting an imprinted stimulus. *Journal of Comparative and Physiological Psychology,* 1973, *82,* 345–359.

Ekstrand, B. R. To sleep, perchance to dream (about why we forget). In Duncan, C. P., Sechrest, L., and Melton, A. W. (Eds.), *Human memory: Festschrift in honor of Benton J. Underwood.* New York: Appleton-Century-Crofts, 1972.

Ekstrand, B. R., and Underwood, B. J. Free learning and recall as a function of unit-sequence and letter-sequence interference. *Journal of Verbal Learning and Verbal Behavior,* 1965, *4,* 390–396.

Ellis, H. D., Deregowski, J. B., and Shepherd, J. W. Descriptions of white and black faces by white and black subjects. *International Journal of Psychology,* 1975, *10,* 119–123.

Engel, B. T., and Hansen, S. P. Operant conditioning of heart rate slowing. *Psychophysiology,* 1966, *3,* 176–187.

Epstein, W. The influence of syntactical structure on learning. *American Journal of Psychology,* 1961, *74,* 80–85.

Epstein, W. A further study of the influence of syntactical structure on learning. *American Journal of Psychology,* 1962, *75,* 121–126.

Erdelyi, M. H., and Kleinbard, J. Has Ebbinghaus decayed with time? The growth of recall (Hypermnesia) over days. *Journal of Experimental Psychology: Human Learning and Memory,* 1978, *4,* 275–289.

Erickson, M. H. Development of apparent unconsciousness during hypnotic reliving of a traumatic experience. *Archives of Neurology and Psychiatry,* 1937, *38,* 1282–1288.

Erickson, R. L. Relational isolation as a means of producing the von Restorff effect in paired-associate learning. *Journal of Experimental Psychology,* 1963, *66,* 111–119.

Estes, B. W., Miller, L. B., and Curtin, M. E. Supplementary report: Monetary incentive and motivation in discrimination learning—sex differences. *Journal of Experimental Psychology,* 1962, *63,* 320.

Estes, W. K. Introduction to volume 2. In Estes, W. K. (Ed.), *Handbook of learning and cognitive processes, Vol. 2, Conditioning and behavior theory.* Hillsdale, N. J.: Erlbaum, 1975.

Estes, W. K., and Skinner, B. F. Some quantitative properties of anxiety. *Journal of Experimental Psychology,* 1941, *29,* 390–400.

Fagan, J. F. Clustering of related but nonassociated items in free recall. *Psychonomic Science,* 1969, *16,* 92–93.

Fantino, E., Kasdon, D., and Stringer, N. The Yerkes-Dodson law and alimentary motivation. *Canadian Journal of Psychology,* 1970, *24,* 77–84.

Fehrer, E. Effects of amount of reinforcement and of pre- and postreinforcement delays on learning and extinction. *Journal of Experimental Psychology,* 1956, *52,* 167–176.

Finkelman, D. Science and psychology. *American Journal of Psychology,* 1978, *91,* 179–199.

Fitts, P. M., Bahrick, H. P., Briggs, G. E., and Noble, M. E. *Skilled performance* (Technical Report, Project No. 7707, Contract No. AF 41 (657)-70). Ohio: Wright-Patterson Air Force Base, 1959.

Fitts, P. M., and Deininger, R. L. S-R compatibility: Correspondence among paired elements within stimulus and response codes. *Journal of Experimental Psychology,* 1954, *48,* 483–492.

Fitts, P. M., and Posner, M. I. *Human performance.* Belmont, Calif.: Brooks-Cole, 1967.

Fitzgerald, R. D. Effects of partial reinforcement with acid on the classically conditioned salivary response in dogs. *Journal of Comparative and Physiological Psychology,* 1963, *56,* 1056–1060.

Fitzwater, M. E. The relative effect of reinforcement and nonreinforcement in establishing a form discrimination. *Journal of Comparative and Physiologcal Psychology,* 1952, *45,* 476–481.

Fleishman, E. A. A comprehensive study of aptitude patterns in unskilled and skilled psychomotor performance. *Journal of Applied Psychology,* 1957, *41,* 263–272.

Fleishman, E. A. Abilities at different stages of practice in rotary pursuit performance. *Journal of Experimental Psychology,* 1960, *60,* 162–171.

Fleishman, E. A., and Hempel, W. E., Jr. Changes in factor structure of a complex psychomotor test as a function of practice. *Psychometrika,* 1954, *18,* 239–252.

Fleishman, E. A., and Hempel, W. E., Jr. The relation between abilities and improvement with practice in a visual discrimination reaction task. *Journal of Experimental Psychology,* 1955, *49,* 301–312.

Fleishman, E. A., and Parker, J. F. Factors in the retention and relearning of a perceptual-motor skill. *Journal of Experimental Psychology,* 1962, *64,* 215–226.

Fouts, R. S. Use of guidance in teaching sign language to a chimpanzee. *Journal of Comparative and Physiological Psychology,* 1972, *80,* 515–522.

Fouts, R. S. Ameslan in Pan. In Bourne, G. H. (Ed.), *Progress in ape research.* New York: Academic Press, 1977.

Fowler, H. Cognitive associations as evident in the blocking effects of response-contingent CSs. In Hulse, S. H., Fowler, H., and Honig, W. K. (Eds.), *Cognitive processes in animal behavior.* Hillsdale, N.J.: Erlbaum, 1978.

Fowler, H., and Trapold, M. A. Escape performance as a function of delay of reinforcement. *Journal of Experimental Psychology,* 1962, *63,* 464–467.

Franklin, B. *The autobiography of Benjamin Franklin.* New York: Heritage Press, 1951.

Frederiksen, C. H. Representing logical and semantic structure of knowledge acquired from discourse. *Cognitive Psychology,* 1975, *7,* 371–458.

Freund, J. S., and Underwood, B. J. Storage and retrieval cues in free recall learning. *Journal of Experimental Psychology,* 1969, *81,* 49–53.

Frey, P. W. Within- and between-session CS intensity performance effects in rabbit eyelid conditioning. *Psychonomic Science,* 1969, *17,* 1–2.

Frezza, D. A., and Holland, J. G. Operant conditioning of the human salivary response. *Psychophysiology,* 1971, *8,* 581–587.

Frincke, G. Word characteristics, associative-relatedness, and the free recall of nouns. *Journal of Verbal Learning and Verbal Behavior,* 1968, *7,* 366–372.

Frisch, K., von. *The dance language and orientation of bees* (Translated by Chadwick, L.) Cambridge: Harvard University Press, 1967.

Frisch, K., von. *Bees, their vision, chemical senses, and language.* Ithaca: Cornell University Press, 1972.

Frisch, K., von. Decoding the language of the bee. *Science,* 1974, *185,* 663–668.

Furedy, J. J., and Poulos, C. X. Short-interval classical SCR conditioning and the stimulus-sequence-change-elicited OR: The case of the empirical red herring. *Psychophysiology,* 1977, *14,* 351–359.

Galper, R. E. Functional race membership and recognition of faces. *Perceptual and Motor Skills,* 1973, *37,* 455–462.

Gamzu, E., and Schwam, E. Autoshaping and automaintenance of a key-press response in squirrel monkeys. *Journal of the Experimental Analysis of Behavior,* 1974, *21,* 361–371.

Gamzu, E. R., and Williams, D. R. Associative factors underlying the pigeon's key pecking in auto-shaping procedures. *Journal of the Experimental Analysis of Behavior,* 1973, *19,* 225–232.

Garcia, J., and Kimmeldorf, D. J. Temporal relationship within the conditioning of saccharin aversion through radiation exposure. *Journal of Comparative and Physiological Psychology.* 1957, *50,* 180–183.

Garcia, J., Kimmeldorf, D. J., and Koelling, R. A. Conditioned aversion to saccharin resulting from exposure to gamma radiation. *Science,* 1955, *122,* 157–158.

Garcia, J., and Koelling, R. A. Relation of cue to consequence in avoidance learning. *Psychonomic Science,* 1966, *4,* 123–124.

Gardiner, J. M., and Watkins, M. J. Remembering eventful and uneventful word presentations. *Bulletin of the Psychonomic Society,* 1979, *13,* 108–110.

Gardner, B. T., and Gardner, R. A. Comparing the early utterances of child and chimpanzee. *Minnesota symposium on child psychology, Vol. 8.* Minneapolis: University of Minnesota Press, 1974.

Gardner, R. A., and Gardner, B. T. Teaching sign language to a chimpanzee. *Science,* 1969, *165,* 664–672.

Gardner, R. A., and Gardner, B. T. Two-way communication with an infant chimpanzee. In Schrier, A. M., and Stollnitz, F. (Eds.), *Behavior of non-human primates, Vol. 4.* New York: Academic Press, 1971.

Garskof, B. E., and Sandak, J. M. Unlearning in recognition memory. *Psychonomic Science,* 1964, *1,* 197–198.

Gatling, F. P. Study of the continuity of the learning process as measured by habit reversal in the rat. *Journal of Comparative and Physiological Psychology,* 1951, *44,* 78–83.

Gentner, D. R. The structure and recall of narrative prose. *Journal of Verbal Learning and Verbal Behavior,* 1976, *15,* 411–418.

Gibbs, C. M., Latham, S. B., and Gormezano, I. Classical conditioning of the rabbit membrane response: Effects of reinforcement schedule on response maintenance and resistance to extinction. *Animal Learning and Behavior,* 1978, *6,* 209–215.

Glanzer, M., and Cunitz, A. R. Two storage mechanisms in free recall. *Journal of Verbal Learning and Verbal Behavior,* 1966, *5,* 351–360.

Glanzer, M., and Peters, S. C. Re-examination of the serial position effect. *Journal of Experimental Psychology,* 1962, *64,* 258–266.

Glaze, J. A. The association value of nonsense syllables. *Journal of Genetic Psychology*, 1928, *35*, 255–269.

Glenberg, A., Smith, S. M., and Green, C. Type I rehearsal: Maintenance and more. *Journal of Verbal Learning and Verbal Behavior*, 1977, *16*, 339–352.

Glencross, D. J. Control of skilled movements. *Psychological Bulletin*, 1977, *84*, 14–29.

Glencross, D. J., and Oldfield, S. R. The use of ischemic nerve block procedures in the investigation of the sensory control of movements. *Biological Psychology*, 1975, *2*, 165–174.

Godbout, R. C., Ziff, D. R., and Capaldi, E. J. Effect of several reward exposure procedures on the small trial PRE. *Psychonomic Science*, 1968, *13*, 153–154.

Godden, D. R., and Baddeley, A. D. Context-dependent memory in two natural environments: On land and underwater. *British Journal of Psychology*, 1975, *66*, 325–331.

Goesling, W. J., and Brener, J. Effects of activity and immobility conditioning upon subsequent heart-rate conditioning in curarized rats. *Journal of Comparative and Physiological Psychology*, 1972, *81*, 311–317.

Going, M., and Read, J. D. Effects of uniqueness, sex of subject, and sex of photograph on facial recognition. *Perceptual and Motor Skills*, 1974, *39*, 109–110.

Goldstein, A. G. Learning of inverted and normally oriented faces in children and adults. *Psychonomic Science*, 1965, *3*, 447–448.

Goldstein, A. G., and Mackenberg, E. J. Recognition of human faces from isolated facial features: A development study. *Psychonomic Science*, 1966, *6*, 149–150.

Goldstein, D. S. Instrumental cardiovascular conditioning: A review. *The Pavlovian Journal of Biological Science*, 1979, *14*, 108–127.

Goldstein, H., and Spence, K. W. Performance in differential conditioning as a function of variation in magnitude of reward. *Journal of Experimental Psychology*, 1963, *65*, 86–93.

Gomulicki, B.R. Recall as an abstractive process. *Acta Psychologica*, 1956, *12*, 77–94.

Goodall, J. My life among wild chimpanzees. *National Geographic Magazine*, 1963, *125*, 272–308.

Goodrich, K. P. Performance in different segments of an instrumental response chain as a function of reinforcement schedule. *Journal of Experimental Psychology*, 1959, *57*, 57–63.

Goodrich, K. P. Running speed and drinking rate as functions of sucrose concentration and amount of consummatory activity. *Journal of Comparative and Physiological Psychology*, 1960, *53*, 245–250.

Goodrich, K. P., and Zaretsky, H. Running speed as a function of concentration of sucrose incentive during pre-training. *Psychological Reports*, 1962, *11*, 463–468.

Goodwin, D. W., Powell, B., Bremer, B., Hoine, H., and Stern, J. Alcohol and recall: State-dependent effects in man. *Science*, 1969, *163*, 1358–1360.

Gorman, A. M. Recognition memory for nouns as a function of abstractness and frequency. *Journal of Experimental Psychology*, 1961, *61*, 23–29.

Gormezano, I. Investigators of defense and reward conditioning in the rabbit. In Black, A. H., and Prokasy, W. F. (Eds.), *Classical conditioning II: Current research and theory*. New York: Appleton-Century-Crofts, 1972.

Gormezano, I., Schneiderman, N., Deaux, E., and Fuentes, I. Nictitating membrane: Classical conditioning and extinction in the albino rat. *Science*, 1962, *138*, 33–34.

Graboi, D. G. The effects of physical shape and meaning on the rate of visual search. *Dissertation Abstracts International*, 1975, *35*, 5665.

Grant, D. A., and Schipper, L. M. The acquisition and extinction of conditioned eyelid responses as a function of the percentage of fixed-ratio random reinforcement. *Journal of Experimental Psychology*, 1952, *43*, 313–320.

Grant, D. A., Schipper, L. M., and Ross, B. M. Effect of intertrial interval during acquisition on extinction of the conditioned eyelid response following partial reinforcement. *Journal of Experimental Psychology*, 1952, *44*, 303–310.

Greene, J. E. Magnitude of reward and acquisition of a black-white discrimination habit. *Journal of Experimental Psychology*, 1953, *46*, 113–119.

Grice, G. R. The relation of secondary reinforcement to delayed reward in visual discrimination learning. *Journal of Experimental Psychology*, 1948, *38*, 1–16.

Grice, G. R. Stimulus intensity and response evocation. *Psychological Review*, 1968, *75*, 359–373.

Grice G. R. Conditioning and a decision theory of response evocation. In Bower, G. H. (Ed.), *The psychology of learning and motivation*. New York: Academic Press, 1972.

Grice, G. R., and Hunter, J. J. Stimulus intensity effects depend upon the type of experimental design. *Psychological Review*, 1964, *71*, 247–256.

Grice, G. R., and Saltz, E. The generalization of an instrumental response to stimuli varying in the size dimension. *Journal of Experimental Psychology*, 1950, *40*, 702–708.

Griffin, D. R. *The question of animal awareness.* New York: Rockefeller University Press, 1976.

Grindley, G. C. Experiments on the influence of the amount of reward on learning of young chickens. *British Journal of Psychology*, 1929, *20*, 173–180.

Grings, W. W. Orientation, conditioning, and learning. *Psychophysiology*, 1977, *14*, 343–350.

Grings, W. W., and Lockhart, R. A. Effects of "anxiety-lessening" instructions and differential set development on the extinction of GSR. *Journal of Experimental Psychology*, 1963, *66*, 292–299.

Grosslight, J. H., Hall, J. F., and Murnin, J. Patterning effect in partial reinforcement. *Journal of Experimental Psychology*, 1953, *46*, 103–106.

Grosslight, J. H., and Radlow, R. Patterning effect on the nonreinforcement-reinforcement sequence in a discrimination situation. *Journal of Comparative and Physiological Psychology*, 1956, *49*, 524–546.

Grosslight, J. H., and Radlow, R. Patterning effect of the nonreinforcement-reinforcement sequence involving a single nonreinforced trial. *Journal of Comparative and Physiological Psychology*, 1957, *50*, 23–25.

Gumenik, W. E., and Levitt, J. The von Restorff effect as a function of difference in the isolated item. *American Journal of Psychology*, 1968, *81*, 247–252.

Gustavson, C. R., Garcia, J., Hankins, W. G., and Rusiniak, K. W. Coyote predation control by aversive conditioning. *Science*, 1974, *184*, 581–583.

Guthrie, E. R. *The psychology of learning.* New York: Harper, 1935.

Guttman, N. Operant conditioning, extinction, and periodic reinforcement in relation to concentration of sucrose used as reinforcing agent. *Journal of Experimental Psychology*, 1953, *46*, 213–224.

Guttman, N., and Kalish, H. I. Discriminability and stimulus generalization. *Journal of Experimental Psychology*, 1956, *51*, 79–88.

Haggard, D. F. Acquisition of a simple running response as a function of partial and continuous schedules of reinforcement. *Psychological Record*, 1959, *9*, 11–18.

Hall, J. F. Learning as a function of word frequency. *American Journal of Psychology*, 1954, *67*, 138–140.

Hall, J. F. Retroactive inhibition in meaningful material. *Journal of Educational Psychology*, 1955, *46*, 47–52.

Hall, J. F. A note on the relationship between the Thorndike-Lorge and Underwood-Schulz frequency counts. *Journal of Verbal Learning and Verbal Behavior*, 1967, *6*, 771–772.

Hall, J. F. *Classical conditioning and instrumental learning: A contemporary approach.* Philadelphia: Lippincott, 1976.

Hall, J. F. Recognition as a function of word frequency. *American Journal of Psychology*, 1979, *92*, 497–505.

Hall, J. F., and Kobrick, J. L. The relationship among three measures of response strength. *Journal of Comparative and Physiological Psychology*, 1952, *45*, 280–282.

Hammes, J. A. Visual discrimination learning as a function of shock-fear and task difficulty. *Journal of Comparative and Physiological Psychology*, 1956, *49*, 481–484.

Hanson, H. M. Effects of discrimination on stimulus generalization. *Journal of Experimental Psychology*, 1959, *58*, 321–334.

Hanson, H. M. Stimulus generalization following three-stimulus discrimination training. *Journal of Comparative and Physiological Psychology*, 1961, *54*, 181–185.

Hara, K., and Warren, J. M. Stimulus additivity and dominance in discrimination performance in cats. *Journal of Comparative and Physiological Psychology*, 1961, *54*, 86–90.

Harcum, E. R., and Coppage, E. W. Explanation of serial learning errors within Deese-Kresse categories. *Journal of Experimental Psychology*, 1969, *81*, 489–496.

Harlow, H. F. Studies in discrimination learning in monkeys: V. Initial performance by experimentally naive monkeys on stimulus-object and pattern discrimination. *Journal of General Psychology*, 1945, *33*, 3–10.

Harlow, H. F. The formation of learning sets. *Psychological Review*, 1949, *56*, 51–65.

Harlow, H. F., Gluck, J. P., and Suomi, S. J. Generalization of behavioral data between nonhuman and human animals. *American Psychologist*, 1972, *27*, 709–716.

Harlow, H. F., and Hicks, L. H. Discrimination learning theory: Uniprocess vs. duo-process. *Psychological Review*, 1957, *64*, 104–109.

Harris, A. H., and Brady, J. V. Animal learning—visceral and autonomic conditioning. In Rosenzweig, M. R., and Porter, L. W. (Eds.), *Annual Review of Psychology.* Palo Alto, Calif.: Annual Reviews, Inc., 1974.

Harris, P., and Nygaard, J. E. Resistance to extinction and number of reinforcements. *Psychological Reports*, 1961, *8*, 233–234.

Harvey, B., and Wickens, D. D. Effect of instructions on responsiveness to the UCS in GSR conditioning. *Journal of Experimental Psychology*, 1971, *87*, 137–140.

Harvey, C. B., and Wickens, D. D. Effects of cognitive control processes on the classically conditioned galvanic skin response. *Journal of Experimental Psychology*, 1973, *101*, 278–282.

Hatzenbuehler, L. C., and Schroeder, H. E. Desensitization procedures in the treatment of childhood disorders. *Psychological Bulletin*, 1978, *85*, 831–844.

Hearst, E. The classical-instrumental distinction: Reflexes, voluntary behavior, and categories of associative learning. In Estes, W. K. (Ed.), *Handbook of learning and cognitive processes; Vol. 2, Conditioning and behavior theory.* Hillsdale, N.J.: Erlbaum, 1975.

Hearst, E., and Koresko, M. B. Stimulus generalization and amount of prior training on variable interval reinforcement. *Journal of Comparative and Physiological Psychology*, 1968, *66*, 133–138.

Hebb, D. O. *The organization of behavior.* New York: Wiley, 1949.

Heinemann, E. G., and Chase, S. Stimulus generalization. In Estes, W. K. (Ed.), *Handbook of learning and cognitive processes, Vol. 2, Conditioning and behavior theory.* Hillsdale, N.J.: Erlbaum, 1975.

Helson, H. Adaptation-level as a basis for a quantitative theory of frames of reference. *Psychological Review*, 1948, *55*, 297–313.

Helson, H. *Adaptation-level theory: An experimental and systematic approach to behavior.* New York: Harper, 1964.

Herbert, M. J. and Harsh, C. M. Observational learning in cats. *Journal of Comparative and Physiological Psychology*, 1944, *37*, 81–95.

Herman, L. M., and Arbeit, W. R. Stimulus control and auditory discrimination learning sets in the bottlenose dolphin. *Journal of the Experimental Analysis of Behavior*, 1973, *19*, 379–394.

Hermann, J. A., de Montes, A. I., Dominguez, B., Montes, F., and Hopkins, B. L. Effects of bonuses for punctuality on the tardiness of industrial workers. *Journal of Applied Behavior Analysis*, 1973, *6*, 563–570.

Herrnstein, R. J. Relative and absolute strength of response as a function of frequency of reinforcement. *Journal of the Experimental Analysis of Behavior*, 1961, *4*, 267–272.

Herrnstein, R. J. Acquisition, generalization, and discrimination reversal of a natural concept. *Journal of Experimental Psychology: Animal Behavior Processes*, 1979, *5*, 116–129.

Herrnstein, R. J., and Loveland, D. H. Complex visual concept in the pigeon. *Science*, 1964, *146*, 549–551.

Herrnstein, R. J., Loveland, D. H., and Cable, C. Natural concepts in pigeons. *Journal of Experimental Psychology: Animal Behavior Processes*, 1976, *2*, 285–302.

Hess, E. H. *Imprinting: Early experience and the developmental psychology of attachment.* Princeton, N.J.: Van Nostrand-Reinhold, 1973.

Heth, C. D., and Rescorla, R. A. Simultaneous and backward fear conditioning in the rat. *Journal of Comparative and Physiological Psychology*, 1973, *83*, 434–443.

Hilgard, E. R. Methods and procedures in the study of learning. In Stevens, S. S. (Ed.), *Handbook of experimental psychology.* New York: Wiley, 1951.

Hilgard, E. R., and Marquis, D. G. *Conditioning and learning.* New York: Appleton-Century-Crofts, 1940.

Hill, F. A. Effects of instructions and subjects' need for approval on the conditioned galvanic skin response. *Journal of Experimental Psychology*, 1967, *73*, 461–467.

Hill, W. F., and Wallace W. P. Effects of magnitude and percentage of reward on subsequent patterns of runway speed. *Journal of Experimental Psychology*, 1967, *73*, 544–548.

Hiroto, D. S. Locus of control and learned helplessness. *Journal of Experimental Psychology*, 1974, *102*, 187–193.

Hiroto, D. S., and Seligman, M. E. P. Generality of learned helplessness in man. *Journal of Personality and Social Psychology*, 1975, *31*, 311–327.

Hobson, G. N. Effects of UCS adaptations upon conditioning in low and high anxiety men and women. *Journal of Experimental Psychology*, 1968, *76*, 360–363.

Hochberg, J., and Galper, R. E. Recognition of faces: I. An exploratory study. *Psychonomic Science*, 1967, *9*, 610–620.

Hochhauser, M., and Fowler, H. Cue effects of drive and reward as a function of discrimination difficulty: Evidence against the Yerkes-Dodson law. *Journal of Experimental Psychology: Animal Behavior Processes*, 1975, *1*, 261–269.

Hockman, C. H., and Lipsitt, L. P. Delay-of-reward gradients in discrimination learning with children for two levels of difficulty. *Journal of Comparative and Physiological Psychology*, 1961, *54*, 24–27.

Hoffeld, D. R., Thompson, R. F., and Brogden, W. J. Effect of stimuli time relations during preconditioning training upon the magnitude of sensory pre-conditioning. *Journal of Experimental Psychology*, 1958, *56*, 437–442.

Hoffman, H. S. Experimental analysis of imprinting and its behavioral effects. In Bower, G. H. (Ed.), *The psychology of learning and motivation*. New York: Academic Press, 1978.

Hoffman, H. S., and Fleshler, M. Aversive control with the pigeon. *Journal of Experimental Analysis of Behavior*, 1959, *2*, 213–218.

Hoffman, H. S., Searle J. L., Toffey, S., and Kozma, F., Jr. Behavioral control by an imprinted stimulus. *Journal of the Experimental Analysis of Behavior*, 1966, *9*, 177–189.

Hoffman, R. R., and Senter, R. J. Recent history of psychology: Mnemonic techniques and the psycholinguistic revolution. *The Psychological Record*, 1978, *28*, 3–15.

Holland, P. C., and Rescorla, R. A. The effect of two ways of devaluing the unconditioned stimulus after first-and second-order appetitive conditioning. *Journal of Experimental Psychology: Animal Behavior Processes*, 1975, *1*, 355–363.

Honig, W. K. Generalization of extinction on the spectral continuum. *Psychological Record*, 1961, *11*, 269–278.

Honig, W. K. Studies of working memory in the pigeon. In Hulse, S. H., Fowler, H., and Honig, W. K. (Eds.), *Cognitive processes in animal behavior*, Hillsdale N.J.: Erlbaum, 1978.

Horton, K. D. Phonemic similarity, overt rehearsal, and short-term store. *Journal of Experimental Psychology: Human Learning and Memory*, 1976, *2*, 244–251.

Hovland, C. I. The generalization of conditioned responses. I. The sensory generalization of conditioned responses with varying frequencies of tone. *Journal of General Psychology*, 1937, *17*, 125–148 (a).

Hovland, C. I. The generalization of conditioned responses. II. The sensory generalization of conditioned responses with varying intensities of tone. *Journal of Genetic Psychology*, 1937, *51*, 279–291 (b).

Hovland, C. I. The generalization of conditioned responses. III. Extinction, spontaneous recovery, and disinhibition of conditioned and of generalized responses. *Journal of Experimental Psychology*, 1937, *21*, 47–62 (c).

Hovland, C. I. The generalization of conditioned responses. IV. The effects of varying amounts of reinforcement upon the degree of generalization of conditioned responses. *Journal of Experimental Psychology*, 1937, *21*, 261–276 (d).

Hovland, C. I. Experimental studies in rote-learning theory: III. Distribution of practice with varying speeds of syllable presentation. *Journal of Experimental Psychology*, 1938, *23*, 172–190.

Howells, T. H. A study of ability to recognize faces. *Journal of Abnormal and Social Psychology*, 1938, *33*, 124–127.

Hull, C. L. A functional interpretation of the conditioned reflex. *Psychological Review*, 1929, *36*, 498–511.

Hull, C. L. The conflicting psychologies of learning—a way out. *Psychological Review*, 1935, *42*, 491–516.

Hull, C. L. *Principles of behavior*. New York: Appleton-Century-Crofts, 1943.

Hull, C. L. Stimulus intensity dynamism (V) and stimulus generalization. *Psychological Review*, 1949, *56*, 67–76.

Hulse, S. H., Jr. Amount and percentage of reinforcement and duration of goal confinement in conditioning and extinction. *Journal of Experimental Psychology*, 1958, *56*, 48–57.

Hulse, S. H., Fowler, H., and Honig, W. K. *Cognitive processes in animal behavior*. Hillsdale, N.J.: Erlbaum, 1978.

Humphreys, L. G. The effect of random alternation of reinforcement on the acquisition and extinction of conditioned eyelid reactions. *Journal of Experimental Psychology*, 1939, *25*, 141–158.

Hunt, E., and Love, T. How good can memory be? In Melton, A. W., and Martin, E. (Eds.), *Coding processes in human memory*. Washington: V. H. Winston & Sons, 1972.

Hunt, H. F., and Brady, J. V. Some effects of electro-convulsive shock on a conditioned emotional response ("anxiety"). *Journal of Comparative and Physiological Psychology*, 1951, *44*, 88–98.

Hupka, R. B., Kwaterski, S., and Moore, J. W. Conditioned diminution of the UCR: Differences between the human eyeblink and the rabbit nictitating membrane response. *Journal of Experimental Psychology*, 1970, *83*, 45–51.

Hutton, R. A., Woods, S. C., and Makous, W. L. Conditioned hypoglycemia: Pseudoconditioning controls. *Journal of Comparative and Physiological Psychology*, 1970, *71*, 198–201.

Hyde, T. S., and Jenkins, J. J. The differential effects of incidental tasks on the organization of recall of a list of highly associated words. *Journal of Experimental Psychology*, 1969, *82*, 472–481.

Hyde, T. S., and Jenkins, J. J. Recall for words as a function of semantic, graphic, and syntactic orienting tasks. *Journal of Verbal Learning and Verbal Behavior*, 1973, *12*, 471–480.

Irwin, F. W. *Intentional behavior and motivation: A cognitive theory.* Philadelphia: J. B. Lippincott, 1971.

Ison, J. R. Experimental extinction as a function of number of reinforcements. *Journal of Experimental Psychology*, 1962, *64*, 314–317.

Ison, J. R., and Cook, P. E. Extinction performance as a function of incentive magnitude and number of acquisition trials. *Psychonomic Science*, 1964, *1*, 245–246.

Jackson, T. A., and Jerome, E. Studies of the transposition of learning by children: IV. A preliminary study of patternedness in discrimination learning. *Journal of Experimental Psychology*, 1940, *26*, 432–439.

Jacobs, J. Experiments on "prehension." *Mind*, 1887, *12*, 75–79.

Jacobson, E. *Progessive relaxation.* Chicago: University of Chicago Press, 1938.

Jacoby, K. E., and Dawson, M. E. Observation and shaping learning: A comparison using Long Evans rats. *Psychonomic Science*, 1969, *16*, 257–258.

Jaffe, J. H. Drug addiction and drug abuse. In Goodman, L., and Gilman, A. (Eds.), *The pharmacological basis of therapeutics.* New York: Macmillan, 1970.

Jakubowski, E., and Zielinski, K. Stimulus intensity effects on acute extinction of the CER in rats. *Acta Neurobiologiae Experimentalis*, 1978, *38*, 1–10.

James, J. P. Latent inhibition and the preconditioning interval. *Psychonomic Science*, 1971, *24*, 97–98.

James, W. *Principles of psychology.* New York: Holt, 1890.

Janda, L. H., and Rimm, D. C. Covert sensitization in the treatment of obesity. *Journal of Abnormal Psychology*, 1972, *80*, 37–42.

Jenkins, J. G., and Dallenbach, K. M. Obliviscence during sleep and waking. *American Journal of Psychology*, 1924, *35*, 605–612.

Jensen, A. R. The von Restorff effect with minimal response learning. *Journal of Experimental Psychology*, 1962, *64*, 123–125.

Johnson, D. F., and Cumming, W. W. Some determiners of attention. *Journal of the Experimental Analysis of Behavior*, 1968, *11*, 157–166.

Johnson, R. E. Recall of prose as a function of the structural importance of the linguistic units. *Journal of Verbal Learning and Verbal Behavior*, 1970, *9*, 12–20.

Jones, F. M., and Jones, M. H. Vividness as a factor in learning lists of nonsense syllables. *American Journal of Psychology*, 1942, *55*, 96–101.

Justensen, D. R., Braun, E. W., Garrison, R. G., and Pendleton, R. B. Pharmacological differentiation of allergic and classically conditioned asthma in the guinea pig. *Science*, 1970, *170*, 864–866.

Kalish, H. I. The relationship between discriminability and generalization: A re-evaluation. *Journal of Experimental Psychology*. 1958, *55*, 637–644.

Kamin, L. J. The delay-of-punishment gradient. *Journal of Comparative and Physiological Psychology*, 1959, *52*, 434–437.

Kamin, L. J. Temporal and intensity characteristics of the conditioned stimulus. In Prokasy, W. F. (Ed.), *Classical conditioning.* New York: Appleton-Century-Crofts, 1965.

Kamin, L. J., and Brimer, C. J. The effects of intensity of conditioned and unconditioned stimuli on a conditioned emotional response. *Canadian Journal of Psychology*, 1963, *17*, 194–198.

Kamin, L. J., Brimer, C. J., and Black, A. H. Conditioned suppression as a monitor of fear of the CS in the course of avoidance training. *Journal of Comparative and Physiological Psychology*, 1963, *56*, 497–501.

Kamin, L. J., and Schaub, R. E. Effects of conditioned stimulus intensity on the conditioned emotional response. *Journal of Comparative and Physiological Psychology*, 1963, *56*, 502–507.

Kamman, R., and Melton, A. W. Absolute recovery of first-list responses from unlearning during 26 minutes filled with easy or difficult information processing task. *Proceedings from the 75th Annual Convention, of the American Psychological Association, 1967, 2,* 63–64.

Kappauf, W. E., and Schlosberg, H. Conditioned responses in the white rat. III. Conditioning as a function of the length of the period of delay. *Journal of Genetic Psychology*, 1937, *50*, 27–45.

Kazdin, A. E. *History of behavior modification.* Baltimore: University Park Press, 1978.

Keesey, R. Intracranial reward delay and the acquisition rate of a brightness discrimination. *Science,* 1964, *143,* 702.

Kellas, G., McCauley, C., and McFarland, C. E., Jr. Reexamination of externalized rehearsal. *Journal of Experimental Psychology: Human Learning and Memory,* 1975, *1,* 84–90.

Keppel, G., and Underwood, B. J. Proactive inhibition in short-term retention of a single item. *Journal of Verbal Learning and Verbal Behavior,* 1962, *1,* 153–161.

Kessen, W. Response strength and conditioned stimulus intensity. *Journal of Experimental Psychology,* 1953, *45,* 82–86.

Kimble, G. A. *Hilgard and Marquis' conditioning and learning.* New York: Appleton-Century-Crofts, 1961.

Kimble, G. A., and Dufort, R. H. Meaningfulness and isolation as factors in verbal learning. *Journal of Experimental Psychology,* 1955, *50,* 361–368.

Kimmel, E., and Kimmel, H. D. A replication of operant conditioning of the GSR. *Journal of Experimental Psychology,* 1963, *65,* 212–213.

Kimmel, H. D. Instrumental conditioning of autonomically mediated responses in human beings. *American Psychologist,* 1974, *29,* 325–335.

King, D. R. W., and Greeno, J. G. Invariance of inference times when information was presented in different linguistic formats. *Memory and Recognition,* 1974, *2,* 233–235.

Kinnaman, A. J. Mental life of two *Macacus Rhesus* monkeys in captivity. *American Journal of Psychology,* 1902, *13,* 98–148.

Kintsch, W. Recognition and free recall of organized lists. *Journal of Experimental Psychology,* 1968, *78,* 481–487.

Kintsch, W. The structure of semantic memory. In Tulving, E., and Donaldson, W. (Eds.), *The organization of memory.* New York: Academic Press, 1972.

Kintsch, W. *The representation of meaning in memory.* Hillsdale, N.J.: Erlbaum, 1974.

Kintsch, W. *Memory and cognition.* New York; Wiley, 1977.

Kintsch, W., and Keenan, J. M. Reading rate and retention as a function of the number of propositions in the base structure of sentences. *Cognitive Psychology,* 1973, *5,* 257–274.

Kintsch, W., Kozminsky, E., Streby, W. J., McKoon, G., and Keenan, J. M. Comprehension and recall of text as a function of content variables. *Journal of Verbal Learning and Verbal Behavior,* 1975, *14,* 196–214.

Kintsch, W., and Monk, D. Storage of complex information in memory: Some implications of the speed with which inferences can be made. *Journal of Experimental Psychology,* 1972, *94,* 25–32.

Klein, D. C., and Seligman, M. E. P. Reversal of performance in learned helplessness and depression. *Journal of Abnormal Psychology,* 1976, *85,* 11–26.

Kling, J. W. Generalization of extinction of an instrumental response to stimuli varying in size dimension. *Journal of Experimental Psychology,* 1952, *44,* 339–346.

Kling, J. W. Learning: Introductory survey. In Kling, J. W. and Riggs, L. A. (Eds.), *Woodworth & Schlosberg's Experimental Psychology.* New York: Holt, Rinehart and Winston, 1971.

Knapp, C. G., and Dixon, W. R. Learning to juggle: II. A study of whole and part methods. *Research Quarterly,* 1952, *23,* 398–401.

Knapp, T. J., and Shodahl, S. A. Ben Franklin as a behavior modifier: A note. *Behavior Therapy,* 1974, *5,* 656–660.

Knouse, S. B., and Campbell, P. E. Partially delayed reward in the rat: A parametric study of delay duration. *Journal of Comparative and Physiological Psychology,* 1971, *75,* 116–119.

Kochevar, J. W., and Fox, P. W. Retrieval variables in the measurement of memory. *American Journal of Psychology,* 1980, *93,* 355–366.

Köhler, W. *Dynamics in psychology.* New York: Liveright, 1940.

Köhler, W. Simple structural functions in the chimpanzee and in the chicken. In Ellis, W. D. (Ed.), *A source book of Gestalt psychology.* London: Routledge and Kegan Paul, Ltd., 1955.

Konorski, J., and Miller, S. On two types of conditioned reflex. *Journal of General Psychology,* 1937, *16,* 264–272.

Korman, A. K. *The psychology of motivation.* Englewood Cliffs, N.J.: Prentice-Hall, 1974.

Kraeling, D. Analysis of amount of reward as a variable in learning. *Journal of Comparative and Physiological Psychology,* 1961, *54,* 560–565.

Krantz, D. S., Glass, D. C., and Snyder, M. L. Helplessness, stress level and the coronary-prone behavior pattern. *Journal of Experimental and Social Psychology,* 1974, *10,* 284–300.

Krechevsky, I. "Hypotheses" versus "chance" in the pre-solution period in sensory discrimination-learning. *University of California Publications in Psychology,* 1932, *6,* 27–44(a).

Krechevsky, I. Antagonistic visual discrimination habits in the white rat. *Journal of Comparative and Physiological Psychology*, 1932, *14*, 263–277 (b).

Krechevsky, I. A study of the continuity of the problem-solving process. *Psychological Review*. 1938, *45*, 107–133.

Krueger, W. C. F. The effect of overlearning on retention. *Journal of Experimental Psychology*, 1929, *12*, 71–78.

Kučera, H., and Francis, W. N. *Computational analysis of present-day American English*. Providence, R. I.: Brown University Press, 1967.

Lachman, R. The influence of thirst and schedules of reinforcement-nonreinforcement ratios upon brightness discrimination. *Journal of Experimental Psychology*, 1961, *62*, 80–87.

Lang, P. J., and Melamed, B. G. Avoidance conditioning of an infant with chronic ruminative vomiting. *Journal of Abnormal Psychology*, 1969, *74*, 1–8.

Lashley, K. S. The accuracy of movement in the absence of excitation from the moving organ. *American Journal of Physiology*, 1917, *43*, 169–194.

Lashley, K. S. Learning: I. Nervous-mechanisms of learning. In Murchison, C. (Ed.), *The foundations of experimental psychology*. Worcester, Mass.: Clark University Press, 1929.

Lashley, K. S. The mechanism of vision. XV. Preliminary studies of the rat's capacity for detail vision. *Journal of Genetic Psychology*, 1938, *18*, 123–193.

Lashley, K. S. The problem of serial order in behavior. In Jeffress, L. A. (Ed.), *Cerebral mechanisms in behavior*. New York: Wiley, 1951.

Lashley, K. S., and Ball, J. Spinal conduction and kinaesthetic sensitivity in the maze habit. *Journal of Comparative Psychology*, 1929, *9*, 71–106.

Lashley, K. S., and Wade, M. The Pavlovian theory of generalization. *Psychological Review*, 1946, *53*, 72–87.

Laszlo, J. I. The performance of a simple motor task with kinesthetic sense loss. *Quarterly Journal of Experimental Psychology*, 1966, *18*, 1–8.

Laszlo, J. I. Training of fast tapping with reduction of kinesthetic, tactile, visual and auditory sensations. *Quarterly Journal of Experimental Psychology*, 1967, *19*, 344–349.

Laszlo, J. I., and Bairstow, P. J. Accuracy of movement, peripheral feedback and efferent copy. *Journal of Motor Behavior*, 1971, *3*, 241–252.

Laszlo, J. I., Shamoon, J. S., and Sanson-Fisher, R. W. Reacquisition and transfer of motor skills with sensory feedback reduction. *Journal of Motor Behavior*, 1969, *1*, 195–209.

Laughery, K. R., Alexander, J. F., and Lane, A. B. Recognition of human faces: Effects of target exposure time, target position, pose position, and type of photograph. *Journal of Applied Psychology*, 1971, *55*, 477–483.

Laughery, K. R., Fessler, P. K., Lenorovitz, D. R., and Yoblick, D. A. Time delay and similarity effects in facial recognition. *Journal of Applied Psychology*, 1974, *59*, 490–496.

Lavrakas, R. J., Buri, J. R., and Mayzner, M. S. A perspective on the recognition of other-race faces. *Perception and Psychophysics*, 1976, *20*, 475–481.

Lawrence, D. H. Acquired distinctiveness of cues: I. Transfer between discriminations on the basis of familiarity with the stimulus. *Journal of Experimental Psychology*, 1949, *39*, 770–784.

Lawrence, D. H., and DeRivera, J. Evidence of relational transposition. *Journal of Comparative and Physiological Psychology*, 1954, *47*, 465–471.

Leaf, R. C. Avoidance response evocation as a function of prior discriminative fear conditioning under curare. *Journal of Comparative and Physiological Psychology*, 1964, *58*, 446–449.

Leary, R. W. Homogeneous and heterogeneous reward of monkeys. *Journal of Comparative and Physiological Psychology*, 1958, *51*, 706–710.

Lee, B. S. Effects of delayed speech feedback. *Journal of Acoustical Society of America*, 1950, *22*, 824–826.

Lee, B. S. Artificial stutter. *Journal of Speech and Hearing Disorders*, 1951, *16*, 53–55.

Lehr, R. Partial reward and positive contrast effects. *Animal Learning and Behavior*, 1974, *3*, 221–224.

Lehrman, D. S. A critique of Konrad Lorenz's theory of instinctive behavior. *Quarterly Review of Biology*, 1953, *28*, 337–363.

Lenneberg, E. H. *Biological foundations of language*. New York: Wiley, 1967.

Leonard, D. W., Fishbein, L. C., and Monteau, J. E. The effects of interpolated US alone (USa) presentations on classical membrane conditioning in rabbit (Oryctolagus cuniculus). *Conditional Reflex*, 1972, *7*, 107–114.

Lepley, W. Serial reactions considered as conditioned reactions. *Psychological Monographs*, 1934, *46*.

Lett, B. T. Delayed reward learning: Disproof of the traditional theory. *Learning and Motivation*, 1973, *4*, 237–246.

Lett, B. T. Visual discrimination learning with a 1-minute delay of reward. *Learning and Motivation*, 1974, *5*, 174–181.

Lett, B. T. Long delay learning in the T-maze. *Learning and Motivation*, 1975, *6*, 80–90.

Lewis, D., and Shephard, A. H. Devices for studying associative interference in psychomotor performance: I. The modified Mashburn apparatus. *Journal of Psychology*, 1950, *29*, 35–46.

Lewis, D. J. Partial reinforcement: A selective review of the literature since 1950. *Psychological Bulletin*, 1960, *57*, 1–28.

Lewis, D. J. Psychobiology of active and inactive memory. *Psychological Bulletin*, 1979, *86*, 1054–1083.

Lewis, D. J., and Duncan, C. P. Effect of different percentages of money reward on extinction of a lever pulling response. *Journal of Experimental Psychology*, 1956, *52*, 23–27.

Lieberman, D. A., McIntosh, D. C., and Thomas, G. V. Learning when reward is delayed : A marking hypothesis. *Journal of Experimental Psychology: Animal Behavior Processes,*1979, *5*, 224–242.

Light, J. S., and Gantt, W. H. Essential part of reflex arc for establishment of conditioned reflex. Formation of conditioned reflex after exclusion of motor peripheral end. *Journal of Comparative Psychology*, 1936, *21*, 19–36.

Linden, E. *Apes, men, and language.* New York: Saturday Review Press, E. P. Dutton, 1974.

Lindley, R. H., and Moyer, K. E. Effects of instructions on the extinction of a conditioned finger-withdrawal response. *Journal of Experimental Psychology*, 1961, *61*, 82–88.

Lippman, L. G., and Lippman, M. Z. Isolation and similarity effects in a serial reconstruction task. *American Journal of Psychology*, 1978, *91*, 35–50.

Little, L. M., and Curran, J. P. Covert sensitization: A clinical procedure in need of some explanations. *Psychological Bulletin*, 1978, *85*, 513–531.

Lockard, R. B. Reflections on the fall of comparative psychology. *American Psychologist*, 1971, *25*, 168–179.

Loftus, E. F. Leading questions and the eyewitness report. *Cognitive Psychology*, 1975, *7*, 560–572.

Loftus, E. F., Greene, E., and Smith, K. H. How deep is the meaning of life? *Bulletin of the Psychonomic Society*, 1980, *15*, 282–284.

Loftus, E. F., Miller, D. G., and Burns, H. J. Semantic integration of verbal information into visual memory. *Journal of Experimental Psychology: Human Learning and Memory*, 1978, *4*, 19–31.

Logan, F. A., and Ferraro, D. P. *Systematic analysis of learning and motivation.* New York: Wiley, 1978.

Lorayne, H., and Lucas, J. *The memory book.* New York: Ballantine Books, 1974.

Lorenz, K. Der kumpan in der umwelt des vogels. *Journal für Ornithologie*, 1935, *83*, 127–213.

Lorenz, K. The comparative method in studying innate behavior patterns. *Society for Experimental Biology*, Symposia, 1950, *4*, 221–268.

Lorenz, K. The evolution of behavior. *Scientific American*, 1958, *199*, 67–78.

Lorge, I., and Thorndike, E. L. The influence of delay in the after-effect of a connection. *Journal of Experimental Psychology*, 1935, *18*, 186–194.

Lovatt, D. J., and Warr, P. B. Recall after sleep. *American Journal of Psychology*, 1968, *81*, 253–257.

Lovejoy, E. *Attention in discrimination learning.* San Francisco: Holden-Day, 1968.

Lovibond, S. H. The mechanism of conditioning treatment of enuresis. *Behavior Research and Therapy*, 1963, *1*, 17–21.

Lubow, R. E. Latent inhibition. *Psychological Bulletin*, 1973, *79*, 398–407.

Lubow, R. E., Markham, R. E., and Allen, J. Latent inhibition and classical conditioning of the rabbit pinna response. *Journal of Comparative and Physiological Psychology*, 1968, *66*, 688–694.

Lubow, R. E., and Moore, A. U. Latent inhibition: The effect of nonreinforced pre-exposure to the conditioned stimulus. *Journal of Comparative and Physiological Psychology*, 1959, *52*, 415–419.

Luce, T. S. Blacks, whites, and yellows: They all look alike to me. *Psychology Today*, 1974, *8*, 104–106.

Luh, C. W. The conditions of retention. *Psychological Monographs*, 1922, *31*.

Luria, A. R. *The mind of a mnemonist.* New York: Basic Books, 1968.

Lutz, K., and Lutz, R. J. Effects of interactive imagery on learning: Application to advertising. *Journal of Applied Psychology*, 1977, *62*, 493–498.

Mackintosh, N. J. *The psychology of animal learning.* New York: Academic Press, 1974.

Mackintosh, N. J., and Honig, W. K. Blocking and attentional enhancement in pigeons. *Journal of Comparative and Physiological Psychology,* 1970, *73,* 78–85.

Maher, W. B., and Wickens, D. D. Effect of differential quantity of reward on acquisition and performance of a maze habit. *Journal of Comparative and Physiological Psychology,* 1954, *47,* 44–46.

Mahl, G. F., Rothenberg, A., Delgado, J. M. R., and Hamlin, H. Psychological responses in the human to intercerebral electrical stimulation. *Psychosomatic Medicine,* 1964, *26,* 337–365.

Mahoney, W. J., and Ayres, J. J. B. One-trial simultaneous and backward fear conditioning as reflected in conditioned suppression of licking in rats. *Animal Learning and Behavior,* 1976, *4,* 357–362.

Maier, S. F., and Jackson, R. L. Learned helplessness: All of us were right (and wrong): Inescapable shock has multiple effects. In Bower, G. H. (Ed.), *The psychology of learning and motivation.* New York: Academic Press, 1979.

Maier, S. F., and Seligman, M. E. P. Learned helplessness: Theory and evidence. *Journal of Experimental Psychology: General,* 1976, *105,* 3–46.

Maki, R. H., and Schuler, J. Effects of rehearsal duration and level of processing on memory for words. *Journal of Verbal Learning and Verbal Behavior,* 1980, *19,* 36–45.

Malmo, R. B. Heart rate reactions and locus of stimulation within the septal area of the rat. *Science,* 1964, *144,* 1029–1030.

Malmo, R. B. Classical and instrumental conditioning with septal stimulation as reinforcement. *Journal of Comparative and Physiological Psychology,* 1965, *60,* 1–8.

Malpass, R. S., and Kravitz, J. Recognition for faces of own and other race. *Journal of Personality and Social Psychology,* 1969, *13,* 330–334.

Maltzman, I. The orienting reflex and thinking as determiners of conditioning and generalization to words. In Kendler, H. H., and Spence, J. T. (Eds.), *Essays in neobehaviorism: A memorial volume to Kenneth W. Spence.* New York: Appleton-Century-Crofts, 1971.

Maltzman, I. Orienting in classical conditioning and generalization of the galvanic skin response to words: An overview. *Journal of Experimental Psychology,* 1977, *106,* 111–119.

Manning, A. A., Schneiderman, N., and Lordahl, D. S. Delay versus trace heart-rate classical discrimination conditioning in rabbits as a function of interstimulus interval. *Journal of Experimental Psychology,* 1969, *80,* 225–230.

Marks, I. Flooding (implosion) and allied treatment. In Agris, W. S. (Ed.), *Behavior modification: Principles and clinical applications.* Boston: Little, Brown, 1972.

Marks, I. Behavioral treatments of phobic and obsessive-compulsive disorders: A critical appraisal. In Hersen, M., Eisler, R. M., and Miller, P. M. (Eds.), *Progress in behavior modification.* New York: Academic Press, 1975.

Marks, L. E., and Miller, G. A. The role of semantic and syntactic constraints in the memorization of English sentences. *Journal of Verbal Learning and Verbal Behavior,* 1964, *3,* 1–5.

Martin, J. G. Associative strength and word frequency in paired-associate learning. *Journal of Verbal Learning and Verbal Behavior,* 1964, *3,* 317–320.

Marx, J. L. Ape-language controversy flares up. *Science,* 1980, *217,* 1330–1333.

Marx, M. H. Resistance to extinction as a function of continuous or intermittent presentation of a training cue. *Journal of Experimental Psychology,* 1958, *56,* 251–255.

Marx, M. H. Interaction of drive and reward as a determiner of resistance to extinction. *Journal of Comparative and Physiological Psychology,* 1967, *64,* 488–489.

Masserman, J. H. *Behavior and neurosis.* Chicago: University of Chicago Press, 1943.

Mathews, R. Recall as a function of the number of classificatory categories. *Journal of Experimental Psychology,* 1954, *47,* 241–247.

Maturana, H. R., Lettvin, J. Y., McCulloch, W. S., and Pitts, W. H. Anatomy and physiology of vision in the frog (Rana pipiens). *Journal of General Physiology, Supplement,* 1960, *6,* 129–275.

McAllister, W. R., and McAllister, D. E. Increase over time in the stimulus generalization of acquired fear. *Journal of Experimental Psychology,* 1963, *65,* 576–582.

McCain, G. Partial reinforcement effects following a small number of acquisition trials. *Psychonomic Monograph Supplement,* 1966, *1,* 251–270.

McCain, G. The partial reinforcement effect after minimal acquisition: Single pellet reward. *Psychonomic Science,* 1968, *13,* 151–152.

McCrary, J. W., and Hunter, W. S. Serial position curves in verbal learning. *Science,* 1953, *117,* 131–134.

McGeoch, J. A. The influence of associative value upon the difficulty of non-sense syllable lists. *Journal of Genetic Psychology*, 1930, *37*, 421–426.

McGeoch, J. A. Forgetting and the law of disuse. *Psychological Review*, 1932, *39*, 352–370.

McGeoch, J. A., and McKinney F. The susceptibility of prose to retroactive inhibition. *American Journal of Psychology*, 1934, *46*, 429–436.

McGuigan, F. J. The effect of precision, delay, and schedule of knowledge of results on performance. *Journal of Experimental Psychology*, 1959, *58*, 79–84.

McKelvie, S. J. The role of eyes and mouth in recognition memory for faces. *American Journal of Psychology*, 1976, *89*, 311–323.

McNulty, J. A. An analysis of recall and recognition processes in verbal learning. *Journal of Verbal Learning and Verbal Behavior*, 1965, *4*, 430–436.

Mellgren, R. Positive and negative contrast effects using delayed reinforcement, *Learning and Motivation*, 1972, *3*, 185–193.

Melton, A. W. (Ed.). *Apparatus tests.* Washington D. C.: U.S. Government Printing Office, 1947.

Melton, A. W. Implications of short-term memory for a general theory of memory. *Journal of Verbal Learning and Verbal Behavior*, 1963, *9*, 596–606.

Melton, A. W., and Irwin, J. M. The influence of degree of interpolated learning on retroactive inhibition and the overt transfer of specific responses. *American Journal of Psychology*, 1940, *53*, 173–203.

Menzel, E. W. Cognitive mapping in chimpanzees. In Hulse, S. H., Fowler, H., and Honig, W. K. (Eds.), *Cognitive processes in animal behavior*. Hillsdale, N.J.: Erlbaum, 1978.

Meunier, G. F., Ritz, D., and Meunier, J. A. Rehearsal of individual items in short-term memory. *Journal of Experimental Psychology*, 1972, *95*, 465–467.

Meyer, B. J. F., and McConkie, G. W. What is recalled after hearing a passage? *Journal of Educational Psychology*, 1973, *65*, 109–117.

Meyer, D. R., Cho, C., and Wesemann, A. F. On problems of conditioning discriminated leverpress avoidance responses. *Psychological Review*, 1960, *67*, 224–228.

Mikulka, P. J., and Pavlik, W. B. Deprivation level, competing responses and the PRE. *Psychological Reports*, 1966, *18*, 95–102.

Miles, C. G. Blocking the acquisition of control by an auditory stimulus with pretraining on brightness. *Psychonomic Science*, 1970, *19*, 133–134.

Miller, G. A. The magical number seven, plus or minus two: some limits on our capacity for processing information. *Psychological Review*, 1956, *63*, 81–97.

Miller, G. A., Galanter, E., and Pribram, K. H. *Plans and the structure of behavior*. New York: Holt, 1960.

Miller, I. W., III, and Norman, W. H. Learned helplessness in humans: A review and attribution-theory model. *Psychological Bulletin*, 1979, *86*, 93–118.

Miller, L. B., and Estes, B. W. Monetary reward and motivation in discrimination learning. *Journal of Experimental Psychology*, 1961, *61*, 501–504.

Miller, N. E. Liberalization of basic S-R concepts: Extensions to conflict behavior, motivation, and social learning. In Koch, S. (Ed.), *Psychology: A study of a science*. New York: McGraw-Hill, 1959.

Miller, N. E. Biofeedback and visceral learning. In Rosenzweig, M. R., and Porter, L. W. (Eds.), *Annual Review of Psychology*, Palo Alto, Calif.: Annual Reviews, 1978.

Miller, N. E., and Banuazzi, A. Instrumental learning by curarized rats of a specific visceral response, intestinal or cardiac. *Journal of Comparative and Physiological Psychology*, 1968, *65*, 1–7.

Miller, N. E., and Carmona, A. Modification of a visceral response, salivation in thirsty dogs, by instrumental training with water reward. *Journal of Comparative and Physiological Psychology*, 1967, *63*, 1–6.

Miller, N. E., and DiCara, L. Instrumental learning of heart-rate changes in curarized rats: Shaping, and specificity to discriminative stimulus. *Journal of Comparative and Physiological Psychology*, 1967, *63*, 12–19.

Miller, N. E., and DiCara, L. Instrumental learning of urine formation in rats; changes in renal blood flow. *American Journal of Physiology*, 1968, *215*, 677–683.

Miller, N. E., and Dworkin, B. R. Visceral learning: Recent difficulties with curarized rats and significant problems for human research. In Obrist, P. A., Black, A. H., Brener, J., and DiCara, L. V. (Eds.), *Cardiovascular psychophysiology: Current issues in response mechanisms, biofeedback, and methodology*. Chicago: Aldine, 1974.

Milner, B. Effects of different brain lesions on card sorting. *Archives of Neurology*, 1963, *9*, 90–100.

Milner, B. Visually-guided maze learning in man: Effects of bilateral hippocampal, bilateral frontal, and unilateral cerebral lesions. *Neuropsychologia*, 1965, *3*, 317–338.

Milner, B. Neuropsychological evidence for differing memory processes. Abstract for the symposium on short-term and long-term memory. *Proceedings of the Eighteenth International Congress of Psychology*, Moscow, 1966. Amsterdam: North-Holland Publishers, 1968.

Milner, B., Corkin, S., and Teuber, H. L. Further analysis of the hippocampal-amnesia syndrome, 14 year follow-up of H. M. *Neuropsychologia*, 1968, *6*, 215–234.

Milner, B., and Teuber, H. L. Alternation of perception and memory in man: Reflections on methods. In Weiskrantz, L. (Ed.), *Analysis of behavioral change.* New York: Harper and Row, 1968.

Mineka, S. The role of fear in theories of avoidance learning, flooding, and extinction. *Psychological Bulletin*, 1979, *86*, 985–1010.

Mis, R. W., and Moore, J. W. Effects of preacquisition UCS exposure on classical conditioning of the rabbit's nictitating membrane response. *Learning and Motivation*, 1973, *4*, 108–114.

Moore, B. R. The role of directed Pavlovian reaction in simple instrumental learning in the pigeon. In Hinde, R. A., and Stevenson, J. (Eds.), *Constraints on learning.* New York: Academic Press, 1973.

Moore, R., and Goldiamond, I. Errorless establishment of visual discrimination using fading procedures. *Journal of the Experimental Analysis of Behavior*, 1964, *7*, 269–272.

Morgan, J. J. B., and Witmer, F. J. The treatment of enuresis by conditioned reaction technique. *Journal of Genetic Psychology*, 1939, *55*, 59–65.

Mountjoy, P. P., and Malott, M. K. Wave-length generalization curves for chickens reared in restricted portions of the spectrum. *Psychological Record*, 1968, *18*, 575–583.

Mowrer, O. H. Preparatory set (expectancy)—a determinant in motivation and learning. *Psychological Review*, 1938, *45*, 62–91.

Mowrer, O. H. On the dual nature of learning—a reinterpretation of "conditioning" and "problem-solving." *Harvard Educational Review*, 1947, *17*, 102–148.

Mowrer, O. H. *Learning theory and personality dynamics.* New York: Ronald Press, 1950.

Mowrer, O. H. The psychologist looks at language. *American Psychologist*, 1954, *9*, 660–692.

Mowrer, O. H. *Learning theory and behavior.* New York: Wiley, 1960.

Mowrer, O. H. Enuresis: The beginning work—what really happened. *Journal of the History of the Behavioral Sciences*, 1980, *16*, 25–30.

Mowrer, O. H., and Jones, H. M. Habit strength as a function of the pattern of reinforcement. *Journal of Experimental Psychology*, 1945, *35*, 293–311.

Mowrer, O. H., and Mowrer, W. M. Enuresis: A method for its study and treatment. *American Journal of Orthopsychiatry*, 1938, *8*, 436–459.

Murdock, B. B. The serial position effect of free recall. *Journal of Experimental Psychology*, 1962, *64*, 482–488.

Murdock, B., and Metcalfe, J. Controlled rehearsal in single-trial free recall. *Journal of Verbal Learning and Verbal Behavior*, 1978, *17*, 309–324.

Muter, P. Recognition failure of recallable words in semantic memory. *Memory and Recognition*, 1978, *6*, 9–12.

Myers, R. D., and Mesker, D. C. Operant responding in a horse under several schedules of reinforcement. *Journal of the Experimental Analysis of Behavior*, 1960, *3*, 161–164.

Myrow, D. L., and Anderson, R. C. Retroactive inhibition of prose as a function of the type of test. *Journal of Educational Psychology*, 1972, *63*, 303–308.

Nachmias, J., Gleitman, H., and McKenna, V. V. The effect of isolation of stimuli and responses in paired associates. *American Journal of Psychology*, 1961, *74*, 452–456.

Nation, J. R., and Massad, P. Persistence training: A partial reinforcement procedure for reversing learned helplessness and depression. *Journal of Experimental Psychology: General*, 1978, *107*, 436–451.

Nation, J. R., and Woods, D. J. Persistence: The role of partial reinforcement in psychotherapy. *Journal of Experimental Psychology: General*, 1980, *109*, 175–207.

Neimeyer, R. Part versus whole methods and massed versus distributed practice in the learning of selected large muscle activities. *Proceedings of the College of Physical Education Association for Men*, 1959, *62*, 122–125. Washington, D.C.: American Association for Health, Physical Education, and Recreation.

Neisser, U. Decision-time without reaction-time: Experiments in visual scanning. *American Journal of Psychology*, 1963, *76*, 376–385.

Neisser, U. *Cognitive psychology.* New York: Appleton, 1967.

Nelson, M. N., and Ross, L. E. Effects of masking tasks on differential eyelid conditioning: A distinction between knowledge of stimulus contingencies and attentional or cognitive activities involving them. *Journal of Experimental Psychology*, 1974, *102*, 1–9.

Nelson, T. O. Savings and forgetting from long-term memory. *Journal of Verbal Learning and Verbal Behavior*, 1971, *10*, 568–576.

Nelson, T. O. Repetition and depth of processing. *Journal of Verbal Learning and Verbal Behavior*, 1977, *16*, 151–171.

Nelson, T. O. Detecting small amounts of information in memory: Savings for nonrecognized items. *Journal of Experimental Psychology: Human Learning and Memory*, 1978, *4*, 453–468.

Nelson, T. O., Fehling, M. R., and Moore-Glascock, J. The nature of semantic savings for items forgotten from long-term memory. *Journal of Experimental Psychology: General*, 1979, *108*, 225–250.

Nelson, T. O., and Rothbart, R. Acoustic savings for items forgotten from long-term memory. *Journal of Experimental Psychology*, 1972, *93*, 357–360.

Nevin, J. A. The maintenance of behavior. In Nevin, J. A. (Ed.), *The study of behavior.* Glenview, Ill.: Scott, Foresman, 1973.

Newman, E. B. Forgetting of meaningful material during sleep and waking. *American Journal of Psychology*, 1939, *52*, 65–71.

Newman, S. E. *Paired-associate learning as a function of stimulus term and response term isolation.* Paper read at Psychonomics meeting, St. Louis, August 30, 1962.

Newman, S. E., and Saltz, E. Isolation effects: Stimulus and response generalization as explanatory concepts. *Journal of Experimental Psychology*, 1958, *55*, 467–472.

Newton, J. M., and Wickens, D. D. Retroactive inhibition as a function of the temporal position of the interpolated learning. *Journal of Experimental Psychology*, 1956, *51*, 149–154.

Nicholls, M. F., and Kimble, G. A. Effect of instructions upon eyelid conditioning. *Journal of Experimental Psychology*, 1964, *67*, 400–402.

Noble, C. E. The role of stimulus meaning (*m*) in serial verbal learning. *Journal of Experimental Psychology*, 1952, *43*, 437–446 (a).

Noble, C. E. The analysis of meaning. *Psychological Review*, 1952, *59*, 421–430 (b).

Noble, C. E. The meaning-familiarity relationship. *Psychological Review*, 1953, *60*, 89–98.

Noble, C. E. Emotionality (*e*) and meaningfulness (*m*). *Psychological Reports*, 1958, *4*, 16.

Noble, C. E. Measurements of association value (*a*), rated associations (*a'*), and scaled meaningfulness (*m'*) for the 2100 CVC combinations of the English alphabet. *Psychological Reports*, 1961, *8*, 487–521.

Noble, C. E., and McNeely, D. A. The role of meaningfulness (*m*) in paired-associate verbal learning. *Journal of Experimental Psychology*, 1957, *53*, 16–22.

Noble, C. E., Stockwell, F. E., and Pryer, M. W. Meaningfulness (*m'*) and association value (*a*) in paired-associate syllable learning. *Psychological Reports*, 1957, *3*, 441–452.

Noble, M., and Adams, C.K. Conditioning in pigs as a function of the interval between CS and US. *Journal of Comparative and Physiological Psychology*, 1963, *56*, 215–219.

Noble, M., Gruender, A., and Meyer, D. R. Conditioning in fish (Molienisia Sp.) as a function of the interval between CS and US. *Journal of Comparative and Physiological Psychology*, 1959, *52*, 236–239.

Norman, D. A., and Rumelhart, D. E. *Explorations in cognition.* San Francisco: Freeman, 1975.

North, A. J., and Stimmel, D. T. Extinction of an instrumental response following a large number of reinforcements. *Psychological Reports*, 1960, *6*, 227–234.

Notterman, J. M., Schoenfeld, W. N., and Bersh, P. J. Conditioned heart rate responses in human beings during experimental anxiety. *Journal of Comparative and Physiological Psychology*, 1952, *45*, 1–8.

Obrist, P. A., Webb, R. A., Sutterer, J. R., and Howard, J. L. The cardiac-somatic relationship: Some reformulations. *Psychophysiology*, 1970, *6*, 569–587.

Olds, J., and Milner, P. Positive reinforcement produced by electrical stimulation of septal area and other regions of the rat brain. *Journal of Comparative and Physiological Psychology*, 1954, *47*, 419–427.

Ost, J. W. P., and Lauer, D. W. Some investigations of classical salivary conditioning in the dog. In Prokasy, W. F. (Ed.), *Classical conditioning: A symposium.* New York: Appleton-Century-Crofts, 1965.

Ottenberg, P., Stein, M., Lewis, J., and Hamilton, C. Learned asthma in the guinea pig. *Psychosomatic Medicine,* 1958, *20,* 395–400.

Page, H. A., and Hall, J. F. Experimental extinction as a function of the prevention of the response. *Journal of Comparative and Physiological Psychology,* 1953, *46,* 33–34.

Paivio, A. Abstractness, imagery, and meaningfulness in paired-associate learning. *Journal of Verbal Learning and Verbal Behavior,* 1965, *4,* 32–38.

Paivio, A. A factor-analytic study of word attributes and verbal learning. *Journal of Verbal Learning and Verbal Behavior,* 1968, *7,* 41–49.

Paivio, A., Yuille, J. C., and Madigan, S. A. Concreteness, imagery, and meaningfulness values for 925 nouns. *Journal of Experimental Psychology, Monograph Supplement,* 1968, *76,* 1–25.

Passey, G. J., and Possenti, R. G. The effect of conditioned stimulus intensity upon a single running response. *Journal of Genetic Psychology,* 1956, *89,* 27–33.

Patrick, J. R. Studies in rational behavior and emotional excitement. II. The effect of emotional excitement on rational behavior in human subjects. *Journal of Comparative Psychology,* 1934, *18,* 153–195.

Patterson, F. Conversations with a gorilla. *National Geographic,* 1978, *154,* 438–465.

Patterson, K. E., and Baddeley, A. D. When face recognition fails. *Journal of Experimental Psychology: Human Learning and Memory,* 1977, *3,* 406–417.

Patterson, M. M., Cegavske, C. F., and Thompson, R. F. Effects of a classical conditioning paradigm on hind-limb flexor nerve response in immobilized spinal cats. *Journal of Comparative and Physiological Psychology,* 1973, *84,* 88–97.

Paul, G. L. Outcome of systematic desensitization. I: Background, procedures and uncontrolled reports of individual treatment. II. Controlled investigations of individual treatment, technique variations, and current status. In Franks, C. M. (Ed.), *Behavior therapy: Appraisal and status.* New York: McGraw-Hill, 1969.

Pavlov, I. P. *Conditioned reflexes* (Translated by Anrep, G. V.). New York: Dover Publications, 1927.

Pendry, M., and Maltzman, I. Instructions and the orienting reflex in "semantic conditioning" of the galvanic skin response in an innocuous situation. *Journal of Experimental Psychology: General,* 1977, *106,* 120–140.

Pendry, M., and Maltzman, I. Verbal conditioning and extinction of the GSR index of the orienting reflex. *Physiological Psychology,* 1979, *7,* 185–192.

Penfield, W. The permanent record of the stream of consciousness. *Proceedings of the Fourteenth International Congress of Psychology, Montreal, June 1954.* Amsterdam: North-Holland Publishing Co., 1955.

Perfetti, C. A. Sentence retention and the depth hypothesis. *Journal of Verbal Learning and Verbal Behavior,* 1969, *8,* 718–724.

Perfetti, C. A., and Garson, B. Forgetting linguistic information after reading. *Journal of Educational Psychology,* 1973, *65,* 136–140.

Perin, C. T. Behavior potentiality as a joint function of the amount of training and the degree of hunger at the time of extinction. *Journal of Experimental Psychology,* 1942, *30,* 93–113.

Perin, C. T. A quantitative investigation of the delay of reinforcement gradient. *Journal of Experimental Psychology,* 1943, *32,* 37–51.

Perkins, C. C., Jr., and Weyant, R. G. The interval between training and test trials as a determiner of the slope of generalization gradients. *Journal of Comparative and Physiological Psychology,* 1958, *51,* 596–600.

Perry, S. L., and Moore, J. W. The partial-reinforcement effect sustained through blocks of continuous reinforcement in classical eyelid conditioning. *Journal of Experimental Psychology,* 1965, *69,* 158–161.

Peterson, G. B., Ackill, J. E., Frommer, G. P., and Hearst, E. Conditioned approach and contact between signals for food or brain stimulation reinforcement. *Science,* 1962, *136,* 774–775.

Peterson, L. R., and Peterson, M. J. Short-term retention of individual items. *Journal of Experimental Psychology,* 1959, *58,* 193–198.

Peterson, N. Effect of monochromatic rearing on the control of responding by wavelength. *Science,* 1962, *136,* 774–775.

Pew, R. W. Acquisition of a hierarchical control over the temporal organization of a skill. *Journal of Experimental Psychology,* 1966, *71,* 764–771.

Postman, L. Extra-experimental interference and the retention of words. *Journal of Experimental Psychology,* 1961, *61,* 97–110.

Postman, L. The effect of language habits on the acquisition and retention of verbal associations. *Journal of Experimental Psychology,* 1962, *64,* 7–19 (a).

Postman, L. Retention as a function of degree of overlearning. *Science,* 1962, *135,* 666–667 (b).

Postman, L. Studies of learning to learn. II. Changes in transfer as a function of practice. *Journal of Verbal Learning and Verbal Behavior,* 1964, *3,* 437–447.

Postman, L. Interference theory revisited. In Brown, J. (Ed.), *Recall and recognition.* London: Wiley, 1976.

Postman, L., Adams, P. A., and Phillips, L. W. Studies in incidental learning: II. The effects of association value and of the method of testing. *Journal of Experimental Psychology,* 1955, *49,* 1–10.

Postman, L., and Gray, W. D. Response recall and retroactive inhibition. *American Journal of Psychology,* 1978, *91,* 3–22.

Postman, L., and Rau, L. Retention as a function of the method of measurement. *University of California Publications in Psychology,* 1957, *8,* 217–270.

Postman, L., Stark, K., and Fraser, J. Temporal changes in interference. *Journal of Verbal Learning and Verbal Behavior,* 1968, *7,* 672–694.

Postman, L., Thompkins, B. A., and Gray, W. D. The interpretation of encoding effects in retention. *Journal of Verbal Learning and Verbal Behavior,* 1978, *17,* 681–705.

Postman, L., and Underwood, B. J. Critical issues in interference theory. *Memory and Cognition,* 1973, *1,* 19–40.

Powell, R. W., and Curley, M. Instinctive drift in nondomesticated rodents. *Bulletin of the Psychonomic Society,* 1976, *8,* 175–178.

Premack, D. Language in chimpanzees? *Science,* 1971, *172,* 808–822.

Prokasy, W. F. Developments with the two-phase model applied to human eyelid conditioning. In Black, A. H., and Prokasy, W. F. (Eds.), *Classical conditioning II: Current research and theory.* New York: Appleton-Century-Crofts, 1972.

Prokasy, W. F. First interval skin conductance responses: Conditioned orienting responses? *Psychophysiology,* 1977, *14,* 360–367.

Prokasy, W. F., and Gormezano, I. The effect of US omission in classical aversive and appetitive conditioning of rabbits. *Animal Learning and Behavior,* 1979, *7,* 80–88.

Prokasy, W. F., and Harsanyi, M. A. Two-phase model for human classical conditioning. *Journal of Experimental Psychology,* 1968, *78,* 359–368.

Prokasy, W. F., and Williams, W. C. Information processing and the decremental effect of intermittent reinforcement schedules in human conditioning. *Bulletin of the Psychonomic Society,* 1979, *14,* 57–60.

Purdy, B. J., and Stallard, M. L. Effect of two learning methods and two grips on the acquisition of power and accuracy in the golf swing of college women. *Research Quarterly,* 1967, *38,* 480–484.

Purtle, R. B. Peak shift: A review. *Psychological Bulletin,* 1973, *80,* 408–421.

Putney, R. T., Erwin, T. J., and Smith, S. T., Jr. The facilitation of conditioned alpha blocking with an overt response. *Psychonomic Science,* 1972, *26,* 16–18.

Rabinowitz, J. C., Mandler, G., and Barsalou, L. W. Generation-recognition as an auxiliary retrieval strategy. *Journal of Verbal Learning and Verbal Behavior,* 1979, *18,* 57–72.

Rabinowitz, J. C., Mandler, G., and Patterson, K. E. Determinants of recognition and recall: Accessibility and generation. *Journal of Experimental Psychology: General,* 1977, *106,* 302–329.

Rachman, S. Systematic desensitization. *Psychological Bulletin,* 1967, *67,* 93–103.

Rachman, S., and Teasdale, J. *Aversion therapy and behavior disorders: An analysis.* Coral Gables, Fla.: University of Miami Press, 1969.

Ramsay, A. O., and Hess, E. H. A laboratory approach to the study of imprinting. *Wilson Bulletin,* 1954, *66,* 196–206.

Randich, A., and LoLordo, V. M. Preconditioning exposure to the unconditioned stimulus affects the acquisition of a conditioned emotional response. *Learning and Motivation,* 1979, *10,* 245–277.

Raphael, B. *The thinking computer.* San Francisco: Freeman, 1976.

Razran, G. H. S. A quantitative study of meaning by a conditioned salivary technique (semantic conditioning). *Science,* 1939, *90,* 89–90.

Razran, G. H. S. The dominance-contingency theory of the acquisition of classical conditioning. *Psychological Bulletin,* 1957, *54,* 1–46.

Razran, G. H. S. *Mind in evolution.* Boston: Houghton Mifflin, 1971.

Reder, L. M., Anderson, J. R., and Bjork, R. A. A semantic interpretation of encoding specificity. *Journal of Experimental Psychology,* 1974, *102,* 648–656.

Reiff, R., and Scheerer, M. *Memory and hypnotic age regression.* New York: International University Press, 1959.

Renner, K. E. Delay of reinforcement: A historical review. *Psychological Bulletin*, 1964, *61*, 341–361.

Rescorla, R. A. Pavlovian conditioning and its proper control procedures. *Psychological Review*, 1967, *74*, 71–80.

Restorff, H. von. Uber die Wirkung vin Bereichbildungen im Spurenfeld (Analyse von Vorgangen in Spurenfeld). *Psychologie Forschung*, 1933, *18*, 299–342.

Revusky, S. The role of interference in association over a delay. In Honig, W. K., and James, P. H. R. (Eds.), *Animal memory*. New York: Academic Press, 1971.

Revusky, S. H., and Bedarf, E. W. Association of illness with prior ingestion of novel foods. *Science*, 1967, *155*, 219–220.

Revusky, S. H., and Garcia, J. Learned associations over long delays. In Bower, G. H., and Spence, J. T. (Eds.), *The psychology of learning and motivation: Advances in research and theory*. New York: Academic Press, 1970.

Reynolds, B. The acquisition of black-white discrimination habit under two levels of reinforcement. *Journal of Experimental Psychology*, 1949, *39*, 760–769.

Reynolds, G. S. Attention in the pigeon. *Journal of the Experimental Analysis of Behavior*, 1961, *4*, 203–208.

Reynolds, W. F., and Pavlik, W. B. Running speed as a function of deprivation period and reward magnitude. *Journal of Comparative and Physiological Psychology*, 1960, *53*, 615–618.

Richter, C. P. A behavioristic study of the rat. *Comparative Psychological Monographs*, 1922, *1*, No. 2.

Richter, C. P. Animal behavior and internal drives. *Quarterly Review of Biology*, 1927, *2*, 307–343.

Riess, B. F. Genetic changes in semantic conditioning. *Journal of Experimental Psychology*, 1946, *36*, 143–152.

Riley, D. A. *Discrimination learning*. Boston: Allyn and Bacon, 1968.

Riley, D. A., and Lamb, M. R. Stimulus generalization. In Pick, A. D. (Ed.), *Perception and its development: A tribute to E. J. Gibson*. Hillsdale, N.J.: Erlbaum, 1979.

Riley, D. A., and Leuin, T. C. Stimulus-generalization gradients in chickens reared in monochromatic light and tested with a single wavelength value. *Journal of Comparative and Physiological Psychology*, 1971, *75*, 399–402.

Rilling, M. Stimulus control and inhibitory processes. In Honig, W. K., and Staddon, J. E. R.

(Eds.), *Handbook of operant behavior*. Englewood Cliffs, N.J.: Prentice-Hall, 1977.

Rilling, M., and Caplan, H. J. Extinction-induced aggression during errorless discrimination learning. *Journal of the Experimental Analysis of Behavior*, 1973, *20*, 85–92.

Rilling, M., Caplan, H. J., Howard, R. C., and Brown, C. H. Inhibitory stimulus control following errorless discrimination learning. *Journal of the Experimental Analysis of Behavior*, 1975, *24*, 121–133.

Rilling, M., Richards, R. W., and Kramer, T. J. Aversive properties of the negative stimulus during learning with and without errors. *Learning and Motivation*, 1973, *4*, 1–10.

Ritchie, B. V., Ebeling, E., and Roth, W. Evidence for continuity in the discrimination of vertical and horizonal patterns. *Journal of Comparative and Physiological Psychology*, 1950, *43*, 168–180.

Rizley, R. C., and Rescorla, R. A. Associations in second-order conditioning and sensory preconditioning. *Journal of Comparative and Physiological Psychology*, 1972, *81*, 1–11.

Roberts, W. A. A further test of the effect of isolation in serial learning. *American Journal of Psychology*, 1962, *75*, 134–139.

Roberts, W. A. Resistance to extinction following partial and consistent reinforcement with varying magnitudes of reward. *Journal of Comparative and Physiological Psychology*, 1969, *67*, 395–400.

Roberts, W. A. Failure to replicate visual discrimination learning with delayed reward. *Learning and Motivation*, 1976, *8*, 136–139.

Rosenzweig, M. R. Salivary conditioning before Pavlov. *American Journal of Psychology*, 1959, *72*, 628–633.

Ross, J., and Lawrence, K. A. Some observations on memory artifice. *Psychonomic Science*, 1968, *13*, 107–108.

Ross, L. E. The decremental effects of partial reinforcement during acquisition of the conditioned eyelid response. *Journal of Experimental Psychology*, 1959, *57*, 74–82.

Ross, S. M., Ross, L, E., and Werden, D. Trace and delay differential classical eyelid conditioning in human adults. *Bulletin of the Psychonomic Society*, 1974, *3*, 224–226.

Roth, S., and Bootzin, R. R. Effects of experimentally induced expectancies of external control: An investigation of learned helplessness. *Journal of Personality and Social Psychology*, 1974, *29*, 253–264.

Roth, S., and Kubal, L. The effects of noncontingent reinforcement on tasks of differing importance: Facilitation and learned helplessness effects. *Journal of Personality and Social Psychology*, 1975, *32*, 680–691.

Rozin, P., and Kalat, J. W. Specific hungers and poison avoidance as adaptive specializations of learning. *Psychological Review*, 1971, *78*, 459–486.

Rudel, R. G. Transposition of response by children trained in intermediate-size problems. *Journal of Comparative and Physiological Psychology*, 1957, *50*, 292–295.

Rudolph, R. I., Honig, W. K., and Gerry, J. E. Effects of monochromatic rearing on the acquisition of stimulus control. *Journal of Comparative and Physiological Psychology*, 1969, *67*, 50–57.

Rumbaugh, D. M. *Language learning by a chimpanzee: the LANA project.* New York: Academic Press, 1977.

Rundus, D. Analysis of rehearsal processes in free recall. *Journal of Experimental Psychology*, 1971, *89*, 63–77.

Rundus, D., and Atkinson, R. C. Rehearsal processes in free recall: A procedure for direct observation. *Journal of Verbal Learning and Verbal Behavior*, 1970, *9*, 99–105.

Sachs, J. S. Recognition memory for syntactic and semantic aspects of connected discourse. *Perception and Psychophysics*, 1967, *2*, 437–442.

Sage, G. H. *Introduction to motor behavior: A neuropsychological approach.* Reading, Mass.: Addison-Wesley, 1977.

Saltz, E., and Modigliani, V. Response meaningfulness in paired associates: T-L frequency, *m*, and number of meanings (*dm*). *Journal of Experimental Psychology*, 1967, *75*, 313–320.

Saltzman, I. J., Kanfer, F. H., and Greenspoon, J. Delay of reward and human motor learning. *Psychological Reports*, 1955, *1*, 139–142.

Santa, J. L., and Lamwers, L. L. Encoding specificity: Fact or artifact. *Journal of Verbal Learning and Verbal Behavior*, 1974, *13*, 412–423.

Scavio, M. J., Jr., and Gormezano, I. CS intensity effects on rabbit nictitating membrane conditioning, extinction and generalization. *Pavlovian Journal of Biological Science*, 1974, *9*, 25–34.

Schafer, D. W., and Rubio, R. Hypnosis to aid the recall of witnesses. *The International Journal of Clinical and Experimental Hypnosis*, 1978, *26*, 81–91.

Schmidt, R. A. *Motor skills.* New York: Harper and Row, 1975.

Schmidt, R. A., and Shea, J. B. A note on delay of knowledge of results in positioning responses. *Journal of Motor Behavior*, 1976, *8*, 129–131.

Schneiderman, N. Interstimulus interval function of the nicitating membrane response of the rabbit under delay versus trace conditioning. *Journal of Comparative and Physiological Psychology*, 1966, *62*, 397–402.

Schneiderman, N., Fuentes, I., and Gormezano, I. Acquisition and extinction of the classically conditioned eyelid response in the albino rabbit. *Science*, 1962, *136*, 650–652.

Schneiderman, N., and Gormezano, I. Conditioning of the nictitating membrane of the rabbit as a function of the CS-US interval. *Journal of Comparative and Physiological Psychology*, 1964, *57*, 188–195.

Schnur, P., and Ksir, C. J. Latent inhibition in human eyelid conditioning. *Journal of Experimental Psychology*, 1969, *80*, 388–389.

Schnur, P., and Lubow. R. E. Latent inhibition: The effects of ITI and CS intensity during preexposure. *Learning and Motivation*, 1976, *7*, 540–550.

Schrier, A. M., and Harlow. H. F. Effect of amount of incentive on discrimination learning in monkeys. *Journal of Comparative and Physiological Psychology*, 1956, *49*, 117–125.

Schroeder, S. R., and Holland, J. G. Reinforcement of eye movement with concurrent schedules. *Journal of the Experimental Analysis of Behavior*, 1969, *12*, 897–903.

Schulman, J. L., Suran, B. G., Stevens, T. M., and Kupst, M. J. Instructions, feedback, and reinforcement in reducing activity levels in the classroom. *Journal of Applied Behavior Analysis*, 1969, *12*, 441–447.

Schusterman, R. J. Transfer effects of successive discrimination-reversal training in chimpanzees. *Science*, 1962, *137*, 422–423.

Schwartz, B. On going back to nature: A review of Seligman and Hager's biological boundaries of learning. *Journal of the Experimental Analysis of Behavior*, 1974, *21*, 183–198.

Scott-Kelso, J. A., and Stelmach, G. E. Behavioral and neurological parameters of the nerve compression block. *Journal of Motor Behavior*, 1974, *6*, 179–190.

Seeleman, V. The influence of attitude upon the remembering of pictorial material. *Archives of Psychology*, 1940, *36*, 1–64.

Seidenberg, M. S., and Petitto, L. A. Signing behavior in apes: A critical review. *Cognition,* 1979, *7,* 177–215.

Seligman, M. E. P. On the generality of laws of learning. *Psychological Review,* 1970, *77,* 406–418.

Seligman, M. E. P. *Helplessness: On depression, development and death.* San Francisco: Freeman, 1975.

Seligman, M. E. P., and Maier, S. F. Failure to escape traumatic shock. *Journal of Experimental Psychology,* 1967, *74,* 1–9.

Senkowski, P. C. Variables affecting the overtraining extinction effect in discrete-trial lever pressing. *Journal of Experimental Psychology: Animal Behavior Processes,* 1978, *4,* 131–143.

Senter, R. J., and Hoffman, R. R. Bizarreness as a nonessential variable in mnemonic imagery: A confirmation. *Bulletin of the Psychonomic Society,* 1976, *7,* 163–164.

Seward, J. P., and Levy, H. Latent extinction: Sign learning as a factor in extinction. *Journal of Experimental Psychology,* 1949, *39,* 660–668.

Seymour, W. D. Experiments on the acquisition of industrial skills. *Occupational Psychology,* 1954, *28,* 77–89.

Shanab, M. E., and Spencer, R. E. Positive and negative contrast effects obtained following shifts in delayed water reward. *Bulletin of the Psychonomic Society,* 1978, *12,* 199–202.

Shay, C. Part versus whole methods of learning in gymnastics. *Research Quarterly,* 1934, *5,* 62–67.

Shea, J. B., and Upton, G. The effects on skill acquisition of an interpolated motor short-term memory task during the KR-delay interval. *Journal of Motor Behavior,* 1976, *8,* 277–281.

Sheffield, V. F. Extinction as a function of partial reinforcement and distribution of practice. *Journal of Experimental Psychology,* 1949, *39,* 511–526.

Shepard, R. N. Recognition memory for words, sentences, and pictures. *Journal of Verbal Learning and Verbal Behavior,* 1967, *6,* 156–163.

Shepherd, J. W., Deregowski, J. B., and Ellis, H. D. A cross-cultural study of recognition memory for faces. *International Journal of Psychology,* 1974, *9,* 205–211.

Shepherd, J. W., and Ellis, H. D. The effect of attractiveness on recognition memory for faces. *American Journal of Psychology,* 1973, *86,* 627–633.

Shimp, C. P. Probabilistically reinforced choice behavior in pigeons, *Journal of the Experimental Analysis of Behavior,* 1966, *9,* 443–455.

Sidman, M. Two temporal parameters of the maintenance of avoidance behavior in the white rat. *Journal of Comparative and Physiological Psychology,* 1953, *46,* 253–261.

Sidman, M., and Fletcher, F. G. A demonstration of auto-shaping with monkeys. *Journal of the Experimental Analysis of Behavior,* 1968, *11,* 307–309.

Sidman, M., Stoddard, L. T., and Mohr, J. P. Some additional qualitative observations of immediate memory in a patient with bilateral hippocampal legions, *Neuropsychologia,* 1968, *6,* 245–254.

Siegel, S. Conditioning of insulin-induced glycemia. *Journal of Comparative and Physiological Psychology,* 1972, *78,* 233–241.

Siegel, S. Flavor preexposure and "learned safety." *Journal of Comparative and Physiological Psychology,* 1974, *87,* 1073–1082.

Siegel, S. Conditioning insulin effects. *Journal of Comparative and Physiological Psychology,* 1975, *89,* 189–199.

Siegel, S., and Wagner, A. R. Extended acquisition training and resistance to extinction. *Journal of Experimental Psychology,* 1963, *66,* 308–310.

Silver, C. A., and Meyer, D. R. Temporal factors in sensory preconditioning. *Journal of Comparative and Physiological Psychology,* 1954, *47,* 57–59.

Silverstein, A., and Dienstbier, R. A. Rated pleasantness and association value of 101 English nouns. *Journal of Verbal Learning and Verbal Behavior,* 1968, *7,* 81–86.

Skinner, B. F. *The behavior of organisms.* New York: Appleton-Century-Crofts, 1938.

Skinner, B. F. A case history in scientific method. In Koch, S. (Ed.), *Psychology: A study of science.* New York: McGraw-Hill, 1959.

Skinner, B. F. *About behaviorism.* New York: Knopf, 1974.

Small, W. S. Notes on the psychic development of the young white rat. *American Journal of Psychology,* 1899, *11,* 80–100.

Small, W. S. An experimental study on the mental processes of the rat. *American Journal of Psychology,* 1900, *11,* 133–165.

Smith, J. C., and Birkle, R. Conditioned aversion to sucrose in rats using X-rays as the unconditioned stimulus. *Psychonomic Science,* 1966, *5,* 271–272.

Smith, J. C., and Roll, D. L. Trace conditioning with x-rays as an aversive stimulus. *Psychonomic Science,* 1967, *9,* 11–12.

Smith, M. C. CS-US interval and US intensity in classical conditioning of the rabbit's nictitating membrane response. *Journal of Comparative and Physiological Psychology*, 1968, *66*, 679–687.

Smith, O. A., Jr., McFarland, W. L., and Taylor, E. Performance in shock-avoidance conditioning situation interpreted as pseudo-conditioning. *Journal of Comparative and Physiological Psychology*, 1961, *54*, 154–157.

Smith, R. F., and Keller, F. R. Free-operant avoidance in the pigeon using a treadle response. *Journal of the Experimental Analysis of Behavior*, 1970, *13*, 211–214.

Smith, S. M. Remembering in and out of context. *Journal of Experimental Psychology*, 1979, *5*, 460–471.

Smith, S. M., Glenberg, A., and Bjork, R. A. Environmental context and human memory. *Memory and Recognition*, 1978, *6*, 342–353.

Smode, A. F. Learning and performance in a tracking task under two levels of achievement information feedback. *Journal of Experimental Psychology*, 1958, *56*, 297–304.

Snyder, C., and Noble, M. Operant conditioning of vasoconstriction. *Journal of Experimental Psychology*, 1968, *77*, 263–268.

Solomon, R. L., Kamin, L. J., and Wynne, L. C. Traumatic avoidance learning: The outcomes of several extinction procedures with dogs. *Journal of Abnormal and Social Psychology*, 1953, *48*, 281–302.

Solomon, R. L., and Turner, L. H. Discriminative classical conditioning in dogs paralyzed by curare can later control discriminative avoidance responses in the normal state. *Psychological Review*, 1962, *69*, 202–219.

Spalding, D. A. Instinct with original observation on young animals. *MacMillans Magazine*, 1873, *27*, 282–283 (reprinted in *British Journal of Animal Behavior*, 1954, *2*, 1–11).

Spence, K. W. The nature of discrimination learning in animals. *Psychological Review*, 1936, *43*, 427–449.

Spence, K. W. Analysis of the formation of visual discrimination habits in chimpanzee. *Journal of Comparative Psychology*, 1937, *23*, 77–100 (a).

Spence, K. W. The differential response in animals to stimuli varying within a single dimension. *Psychological Review*, 1937, *44*, 430–444 (b).

Spence, K. W. An experimental test of the continuity and noncontinuity theories of discrimination learning. *Journal of Experimental Psychology*, 1945, *35*, 253–266.

Spence, K. W. *Behavior theory and conditioning.* New Haven: Yale University Press, 1956.

Spencer, R. E., and Shanab, M. E. Contrast effects as a function of delay and shifts in magnitude of water reward in thirsty rats. *Bulletin of the Psychonomic Society*, 1979, *13*, 93–96.

Sperling, G. The information available in brief visual presentations. *Psychological Monographs*, 1960, *74*.

Spiro, R. J. Remembering information from text: The "state of schema" approach. In Anderson, R. C., Spiro, R. J., and Montague, W. E. (Eds.), *Schooling and the acquisition of knowledge.* Hillsdale, N.J.: Erlbaum, 1977.

Spiro, R. J. Accommodative reconstruction in prose recall. *Journal of Verbal Learning and Verbal Behavior*, 1980, *19*, 84–95.

Squire, L. R., and Slater, P. C. Forgetting in very long-term memory as assessed by an improved questionnaire technique. *Journal of Experimental Psychology: Human Learning and Memory*, 1975, *1*, 50–54.

Stephens, T. A., and Burroughs, W. A. An application of operant conditioning to absenteeism in a hospital setting. *Journal of Applied Psychology*, 1978, *63*, 518–521.

Stern, J. A., and Walrath, L. C. Orienting responses and conditioning in electrodermal responses. *Psychophysiology*, 1977, *14*, 334–342.

Stern, S. D., and Frey, P. W. Backward conditioning of the rabbit eyelid response: A test using second order conditioning. *Bulletin of the Psychonomic Society*, 1978, *11*, 231–234.

Strong, T. N., Jr. Activity in the white rat as a function of apparatus and hunger. *Journal of Comparative and Physiological Psychology*, 1957, *50*, 596–600.

Sulin, R. A., and Dooling, D. J. Intrusion of a thematic idea in retention of prose. *Journal of Experimental Psychology*, 1974, *103*, 255–262.

Sutherland, N. S., and Mackintosh, N. J. *Mechanisms of animal discrimination learning.* New York: Academic Press, 1971.

Swenson, R. P., and Hill, F. A. Effects of instruction and interstimulus interval in human GSR conditioning. *Psychonomic Science*, 1970, *21*, 369–370.

Tarpy, R. M., and Koster, E. D. Stimulus facilitation of delayed-reward learning in the rat. *Journal of Comparative and Physiological Psychology*, 1970, *71*, 147–151.

Taylor, J. A., and Spence, K. W. The relationship of anxiety level to performance in serial learning. *Journal of Experimental Psychology*, 1952, *44*, 61–64.

Terrace, H. S. Discrimination learning with and without "errors." *Journal of the Experimental Analysis of Behavior*, 1963, *6*, 1–27 (a).

Terrace, H. S. Errorless transfer of a discrimination across two continua. *Journal of the Experimental Analysis of Behavior*, 1963, *6*, 223–232 (b).

Terrace, H. S. By-products of discrimination learning. In Bower, G. H. (Ed.), *The psychology of learning and motivation.* New York: Academic Press, 1972.

Terrace, H. S., Petitto, L. A., Sanders, R. J., and Bever, J. T. Can an ape create a sentence? *Science*, 1979, *206*, 891–902.

Terrell, G., and Ware, R. Role of delay of reward in speed of size and form discrimination learning in childhood. *Child Development*, 1961, *32*, 409–415.

Theios, J. The partial reinforcement effect sustained through blocks of continuous reinforcement. *Journal of Experimental Psychology*, 1962, *64*, 1–6.

Thomas, D. R., and DeCapito, A. Role of stimulus labeling in stimulus generalization. *Journal of Experimental Psychology*, 1966, *71*, 913–915.

Thomas, D. R., and Jones, C. G. Stimulus generalization as a function of the frame of reference. *Journal of Experimental Psychology*, 1962, *64*, 77–80.

Thomas, D. R., and Lopez, L. J. The effects of delayed testing on generalization slope. *Journal of Comparative and Physiological Psychology*, 1962, *55*, 541–544.

Thomas, D. R., and Mitchell, K. The role of instructions and stimulus categorizing in a measure of stimulus generalization. *Journal of the Experimental Analysis of Behavior*, 1962, *5*, 375–381.

Thomas, D. R., and Williams, J. L. A further study of stimulus generalization following three-stimulus training. *Journal of the Experimental Analysis of Behavior*, 1963, *6*, 171–176.

Thompson, C. R., and Church, R. M. An explanation of the language of a chimpanzee. *Science*, 1980, *208*, 313–314.

Thompson, R. F. The neural basis of stimulus generalization. In Mostofsky, D. I. (Ed.), *Stimulus generalization.* Stanford, Calif.: Stanford University Press, 1965.

Thompson, R. F. Sensory preconditioning. In Thompson, R. F., and Voss, J. F. (Eds.), *Topics in learning and performance.* New York: Academic Press, 1972.

Thomson, D. M., and Tulving, E. Associative encoding and retrieval: Weak and strong cues. *Journal of Experimental Psychology*, 1970, *86*, 255–262.

Thorndike, E. L. Animal intelligence. *Psychological Review Monograph Supplement*, 1898, *2*, No. 4.

Thorndike, E. L. *Animal Intelligence.* New York: Macmillan, 1911.

Thorndike, E. L. The law of effect. *American Journal of Psychology*, 1927, *39*, 212–222.

Thorndike, E. L., and Lorge, I. *The teacher's word book of 30,000 words.* New York: Columbia University Press, 1944.

Thorndyke, P. W., and Hayes-Roth, B. The use of schemata in the acquisition and transfer of knowledge. *Cognitive Psychology*, 1979, *11*, 82–106.

Thornton, J. W., and Jacobs, P. D. Learned helplessness in human subjects. *Journal of Experimental Psychology*, 1971, *87*, 367–372.

Till, R. E., and Jenkins, J. J. The effects of cued orienting tasks on the free recall of words. *Journal of Verbal Learning and Verbal Behavior*, 1973, *12*, 489–498.

Tinbergen, N. *The study of instinct.* Oxford: Clarendon Press, 1951.

Tinklepaugh, O. L. An experimental study of representative factors in monkeys. *Journal of Comparative Psychology*, 1928, *8*, 197–236.

Toglia, M. P., and Battig, W. F. *Handbook of semantic word norms.* Hillsdale, N.J.: Erlbaum, 1978.

Tolman, E. C. *Purposive behavior in animals and men.* New York: Appleton-Century-Crofts, 1932.

Tombaugh, T. N. Resistance to extinction as a function of the interaction between training and extinction delays. *Psychological Reports*, 1966, *19*, 791–798.

Tombaugh, T. N. A comparison of the effects of immediate reinforcement, constant delay of reinforcement, and partial delay of reinforcement on performance. *Canadian Journal of Psychology*, 1970, *24*, 276–288.

Topping, J. S., and Parker, B. K. Constant and variable delay of reinforcement effects on probability learning by pigeons. *Journal of Comparative and Physiological Psychology*, 1970, *70*, 141–147.

Tracy, W. K. Wave length generalization and preference in monochromatically reared ducklings. *Journal of the Experimental Analysis of Behavior*, 1970, *13*, 163–178.

Trapold, M. A., and Fowler, H. Instrumental escape performance as a function of the intensity of noxious stimulation. *Journal of Experimental Psychology*, 1960, *60*, 323–326.

Treichler, F. R., and Hall, J. F. The relationship between deprivation weight loss and several measures of activity. *Journal of Comparative and Physiological Psychology*, 1962, *55*, 346–349.

Trowbridge, M. H., and Cason, H. An experimental study of Thorndike's theory of learning. *Journal of General Psychology*, 1932, *7*, 245–258.

Trowill, J. A. Instrumental conditioning of the heart rate in the curarized rat. *Journal of Comparative and Physiological Psychology*, 1967, *63*, 7–11.

True, R. M. Experimental control in hyponotic age regression states. *Science*, 1949, *110*, 583–584.

Tulving, E. Subjective organization in free recall of "unrelated" words. *Psychological Review*, 1962, *69*, 344–354.

Tulving, E. Subjective organization and effects of repetition in multi-trial free-recall learning. *Journal of Verbal Learning and Verbal Behavior*, 1966, *5*, 193–197.

Tulving, E., McNulty, J. A., and Ozier, M. Vividness of words and learning to learn in free-recall learning. *Canadian Journal of Psychology*, 1965, *19*, 242–252.

Tulving, E., and Osler, S. Effectiveness of retrieval cues in memory for words. *Journal of Experimental Psychology*, 1968, *77*, 593–601.

Tulving, E., and Pearlstone, Z. Availability versus accessibility of information in memory for words. *Journal of Verbal Learning and Verbal Behavior*, 1966, *5*, 381–391.

Tulving, E., and Thomson, D. M. Encoding specificity and retrieval processes in episodic memory. *Psychological Review*, 1973, *80*, 352–373.

Tulving, E., and Watkins, M. J. Continuity between recall and recognition, *American Journal of Psychology*, 1973, *86*, 739–748.

Twitmyer, E. B. A study of the knee jerk. Ph.D. dissertation, University of Pennsylvania, 1902. Reprinted in the *Journal of Experimental Psychology*, 1974, *103*, 1947–1066.

Tyler, D. W., Wortz, E. C., and Bitterman, M. E. The effect of random and alternating partial reinforcement on resistance to extinction in the rat. *American Journal of Psychology*, 1953, *66*, 57–65.

Uhl, C. N., and Young, A. G. Resistance to extinction as a function of incentive, percentage of reinforcement, and number of nonreinforced trials. *Journal of Experimental Psychology*, 1967, *73*, 556–564.

Underwood, B. J. Retroactive and proactive inhibition after five and forty-eight hours. *Journal of Experimental Psychology*, 1948, *38*, 29–38 (a).

Underwood, B. J. "Spontaneous recovery" of verbal associations. *Journal of Experimental Psychology*, 1948, *38*, 429–439 (b).

Underwood, B. J. Studies of distributed practice: XII. Retention following varying degrees of original learning. *Journal of Experimental Psychology*, 1954, *47*, 294–300.

Underwood, B. J. Interference and forgetting. *Psychological Review*, 1957, *64*, 49–60.

Underwood, B. J. Stimulus selection in verbal learning. In Cofer, C. N., and Musgrave, B. S. (Eds.), *Verbal behavior and learning.* New York: McGraw-Hill, 1963.

Underwood, B. J. False recognition produced by implicit verbal responses. *Journal of Experimental Psychology*, 1965, *70*, 122–129.

Underwood, B. J., and Ekstrand, B. R. An analysis of some shortcomings in the interference theory of forgetting. *Psychological Review*, 1966, *73*, 540–549.

Underwood, B. J., and Ekstrand, B. R. Linguistic associations and retention. *Journal of Verbal Learning and Verbal Behavior*, 1968, *7*, 126–171.

Underwood, B. J., Ekstrand, B. R., and Keppel, G. An analysis of intralist similarity in verbal learning with experiments on conceptual similarity. *Journal of Verbal Learning and Verbal Behavior*, 1965, *4*, 447–462.

Underwood, B. J., Ham, M., and Ekstrand, B. R. Cue selection in paired-associate learning. *Journal of Experimental Psychology*, 1962, *64*, 405–409.

Underwood, B. J., and Postman, L. Extraexperimental sources of interference in forgetting. *Psychological Review*, 1960, *67*, 73–95.

Underwood, B. J., and Schulz, R. W. *Meaningfulness and verbal learning.* Philadelphia: Lippincott, 1960.

Vandercar, D. H., and Schneiderman, N. Interstimulus interval functions in different response systems during classical discrimination conditioning of rabbits. *Psychonomic Science*, 1967, *9*, 9–10.

Van Ormer, E. B. Sleep and retention. *Psychological Bulletin*, 1932, *30*, 415–439.

Vinogradova, O. S. On the dynamics of the OR in the course of closure of a conditioned connection. In Voronin, L. G., Leontiev, A. N., Luria,

A. R., Sokolov, E. N., and Vinogradova, O. S. (Eds.), *Orienting reflex and exploratory behavior.* Washington, D.C.: American Institute of Biological Sciences, 1965.

Vom Saal, W., and Jenkins, H. M. Blocking the development of stimulus control. *Learning and Motivation*, 1970, *1*, 52–54.

Wagner, A. R. Effects of amount and percentage of reinforcement and number of acquisition trials on conditioning and extinction. *Journal of Experimental Psychology*, 1961, *62*, 234–242.

Wagner, A. R., Siegel, L. S., and Fein, G. G. Extinction of conditioned fear as a function of percentage of reinforcement. *Journal of Comparative and Physiological Psychology*, 1967, *63*, 160–164.

Wagner, A. R., Siegel, S., Thomas, E., and Ellison, G. D. Reinforcement history and the extinction of a conditioned salivary response. *Journal of Comparative and Physiological Psychology*, 1964, *58*, 354–358.

Wahlsten, D. L., and Cole, M. Classical and avoidance training of leg flexion in the dog. In Black, A. H., and Prokasy, W. F. (Eds.), *Classical conditioning II: Current research and theory.* New York: Appleton-Century-Crofts, 1972.

Walker, E. Eyelid conditioning as a function of intensity of conditioned and unconditioned stimuli. *Journal of Experimental Psychology*, 1960, *59*, 303–311.

Walker, E. L. Action decrement and its relation to learning. *Psychological Review*, 1958, *65*, 129–142.

Wallace, W. P. Review of the historical, empirical and theoretical status of the von Restorff phenomenon. *Psychological Bulletin*, 1965, *63*, 410–424.

Wallace, W. P. Recognition failure of recallable words and recognizable words. *Journal of Experimental Psychology: Human Learning and Memory*, 1978, *4*, 441–452.

Wallace, W. P. On the use of distractors for testing recognition memory. *Psychological Bulletin*, 1980, *88*, 696–704.

Wallace, W. P., Sawyer, T. J., and Robertson, L. C. Distractors in recall, distractor-free recognition, and the word-frequency effect. *American Journal of Psychology*, 1978, *9*, 295–304.

Walsh, D. A., and Jenkins, J. J. Effects of orienting tasks on free recall in incidental learning: "Difficulty," "effort," and "process" explanations. *Journal of Verbal Learning and Verbal Behavior*, 1973, *12*, 481–488.

Ward, L. B. Reminiscence and rote learning. *Psychological Monographs*, 1937, *49*.

Warden, C. L., and Jackson, T. A. Imitative behavior in the Rhesus monkey. *Journal of Genetic Psychology*, 1935, *46*, 103–125.

Warren, J. M., and Kolb, B. Generalizations in neuropsychology. In Finger, S. (Ed.), *Brain damage.* New York: Plenum, 1978.

Warrington, E. K., and Ackroyd, C. The effect of orienting tasks on recognition memory. *Memory and Cognition*, 1975, *3*, 140–142.

Wasserman, E. A., Deich, J. D., Hunter, N. B., and Nagamatsu, L. S. Analyzing the random control procedure: Effects of paired and unpaired CSs and USs on autoshaping the chick's key peck with heat reinforcement. *Learning and Motivation*, 1977, *8*, 467–487.

Watkins, M. J. When is recall spectacularly higher than recognition? *Journal of Experimental Psychology*, 1974, *102*, 161–163.

Watkins, M. J., Ho, E., and Tulving, E. Context effects in recognition memory. *Journal of Verbal Learning and Verbal Behavior*, 1976, *15*, 505–518.

Watkins, M. J., and Tulving, E. Episodic memory: When recognition fails. *Journal of Experimental Psychology: General*, 1975, *104*, 5–29.

Watson, J. B. The place of the conditioned reflex in psychology. *Psychological Review*, 1916, *23*, 89–117.

Watson, J. B. The effect of delayed feeding upon learning. *Psychobiology*, 1917, *1*, 51–60.

Watson, J. B. *Psychology from the standpoint of a behaviorist.* Philadelphia: Lippincott, 1919.

Watson, J. B. *Behaviorism.* New York: Norton, 1924.

Watson, J. B., and Rayner, R. Conditioned emotional reactions. *Journal of Experimental Psychology*, 1920, *3*, 1–14.

Wayner, M. J., and Carey, R. J. Basic drives. In Mussen, P. H., and Rosenzweig, M. R. (Eds.), *Annual Review of Psychology.* Palo Alto, Calif.: Annual Reviews, Inc., 1973.

Webber, S. M., and Marshall, P. H. Bizarreness effects in imagery as a function of processing level and delay. *Journal of Mental Imagery*, 1978, *2*, 291–300.

Weiner, B. *Theories of motivation: From mechanism to cognition.* Chicago: Markham Publishing Co., 1972.

Weingartner, H., Adefris, W., Eich, J. E., and Murphy, D. L. Encoding-imagery specificity in alcohol state–dependent learning. *Journal of Experimental Psychology*, 1976, *2*, 83–87.

Weinstock, S. Acquisition and extinction of a partially reinforced running response at a 24-hour intertrial interval. *Journal of Experimental Psychology*, 1958, *56*, 151–158.

Weiskrantz, L., and Warrington, E. K. Conditioning in amnesic patients. *Neuropsychologica*, 1979, *17*, 187–194.

Wendt, G. R. An interpretation of inhibition of conditioned reflexes as competition between reaction systems. *Psychological Review*, 1936, *43*, 258–281.

Wickelgren, W. A. Acoustic similarity and intrusion errors in short-term memory. *Journal of Experimental Psychology*, 1965, *70*, 102–108.

Wickelgren, W. A. *Cognitive psychology.* Englewood Cliffs, N.J.: Prentice-Hall, 1979.

Wickens, D. D. Characteristics of word encoding. In Melton, A. W., and Martin, E. (Eds.), *Coding processes in human memory.* Washington, D.C.: V. H. Winston and Sons, 1972.

Wickens, D. D., Allen, C. K., and Hill, F. A. Effect of instructions and UCS strength on extinction of the conditioned GSR. *Journal of Experimental Psychology*, 1963, *66*, 235–240.

Wickens, D. D., Born, D. G., and Allen, C. K. Proactive inhibition and item similarity in short-term memory. *Journal of Verbal Learning and Verbal Behavior*, 1963, *2*, 440–445.

Wickens, D. D., and Briggs, G. E. Mediated stimulus generalization as a factor in sensory pre-conditioning. *Journal of Experimental Psychology*, 1951, *42*, 197–200.

Wickens, D. D., and Clark, S. Osgood dimensions as an encoding class in short-term memory. *Journal of Experimental Psychology*, 1968, *78*, 580–584.

Wickstrom, R. L. Comparative study of methodologies for teaching gymnastics and tumbling stunts. *Research Quarterly*, 1958, *29*, 109–115.

Wike, E. L., and Chen, J. S. Runway performance and reward magnitude. *Psychonomic Science*, 1971, *21*, 139–140.

Wike, E. L., and McWilliams, J. Duration of delay, delay-box confinement, and runway performance. *Psychological Reports*, 1967, *21*, 865–870.

Wikler, A. Conditioning factors in opiate addiction and relapse. In Wilner, D. M., and Kassebaum, G. G. (Eds.), *Narcotics.* New York: McGraw-Hill, 1965.

Wikler, A. Some implications of conditioning theory for problems of drug abuse. In Blackly, P. H. (Ed.), *Abuse data and debate.* Springfield, Ill.: Charles C. Thomas, 1970.

Wilcoxin, H. C., Dragoin, W. B., and Kral, P. A. Illness-induced aversions in rat and quail: Relative salience of visual and gustatory cues. *Science*, 1971, *171*, 826–828.

Wilkie, D. M., and Masson, M. E. Attention in the pigeon: A reevaluation. *Journal of the Experimental Analysis of Behavior*, 1976, *26*, 207–212.

Williams, C. D. The elimination of tantrum behavior by extinction procedures. *Journal of Abnormal and Social Psychology*, 1959, *59*, 269.

Williams, D. R., and Williams, H. Auto-maintenance in the pigeon: Sustained pecking despite contingent non-reinforcement. *Journal of the Experimental Analysis of Behavior*, 1969, *12*, 511–520.

Williams, S. Resistance to extinction as a function of the number of reinforcements. *Journal of Experimental Psychology*, 1938, *23*, 506–522.

Wilson, D. M. The central nervous control of flight in a locust. *Journal of Experimental Biology*, 1961, *48*, 471–490.

Wilson, M. P. Periodic reinforcement interval and number of periodic reinforcements as parameters of response strength. *Journal of Comparative and Physiological Psychology*, 1954, *47*, 51–56.

Winograd, E., and Rivers-Bulkeley, N. T. Effects of changing context on remembering faces. *Journal of Experimental Psychology*, 1977, *3*, 397–405.

Wiseman, S., and Tulving, E. A test of confusion theory of encoding specificity. *Journal of Verbal Learning and Verbal Behavior*, 1975, *14*, 370–381.

Wiseman, S., and Tulving, E. Encoding specificity: Relation between recall superiority and recognition failure. *Journal of Experimental Psychology: Human Learning and Memory*, 1976, *2*, 349–361.

Wolfle, H. M. Time factors in conditioning finger-withdrawal. *Journal of General Psychology*, 1930, *4*, 372–378.

Wolfle, H. M. Conditioning as a function of the interval between the conditioned and the original stimulus. *Journal of General Psychology*, 1932, *7*, 80–103.

Wollen, K. A., Weber, A., and Lowry, D. H. Bizarreness versus interaction of mental images as determinants of learning. *Cognitive Psychology*, 1972, *3*, 518–523.

Wolpe, J. The formation of negative habits: A neurophysiological view. *Psychological Review*, 1950, *57*, 19–26.

Wolpe, J. Experimental neurosis as learned behavior. *British Journal of Psychology,* 1952, *43,* 243–268.

Wolpe, J. *Psychotherapy by reciprocal inhibition.* Stanford, Calif.: Stanford University Press, 1958.

Wolpe, J. The systematic desensitization treatment of neurosis. *Journal of Nervous and Mental Disease,* 1961, *132,* 189–203.

Wong, P. T. P. A behavior field approach to instrumental learning in the rat: II. Training parameters and a stage model of extinction. *Animal Learning and Behavior,* 1978, *6,* 82–93.

Wood, G., and Bolt, M. Mediation and mediation time in paired associate learning. *Journal of Experimental Psychology,* 1968, *78,* 15–20.

Woods, S. C., Makous, W., and Hutton, R. A. A new technique for conditioned hypoglycemia. *Psychonomic Science,* 1968, *10,* 389–390.

Woods, S. C., Makous, W., and Hutton, R. A. Temporal parameters of conditioned hypoglycemia. *Journal of Comparative and Physiological Psychology,* 1969, *69,* 301–307.

Woodward, W. T. Classical respiratory conditioning in the fish: CS intensity. *American Journal of Psychology,* 1971, *84,* 549–554.

Woodworth, R. S., and Schlosberg, H. *Experimental psychology.* New York: Holt, 1954.

Yarmey, A. D. *The psychology of eyewitness testimony.* New York: The Free Press, 1979.

Yarmey, A. D., and Paivio, A. Further evidence on the effects of word abstractness and meaningfulness in paired-associate learning. *Psychonomic Science,* 1965, *2,* 307–308.

Yaroush, R., Sullivan, M. J., and Ekstrand, B. R. Effect of sleep on memory. II. Differential effect of the first and second half of the night.

*Journal of Experimental Psychology,* 1971, *88,* 361–366.

Yates, A. J. Hypnotic age regression. *Psychological Bulletin,* 1961, *58,* 429–440.

Yates, A. J. Delayed auditory feedback. *Psychological Bulletin,* 1963, *60,* 213–232.

Yates, F. A. *The art of memory.* Chicago: University of Chicago Press, 1966.

Yehle, A. L. Divergencies among rabbit response systems during three-tone classical discrimination conditioning. *Journal of Experimental Psychology,* 1968, *77,* 468–473.

Yerkes, R. M., and Dodson, J. D. The relation of strength of stimulus to rapidity of habit-formation. *Journal of Comparative Neurology and Psychology,* 1908, *18,* 459–482.

Yin, R. K. Looking at upside-down faces. *Journal of Experimental Psychology,* 1969, *81,* 141–145.

Young, R. A., Cegavske, C. F., and Thompson, R. F. Tone-induced changes in excitability of abducens motoneurons and of the reflex path of nictitating membrane response in rabbit (*Oryctolagus cuniculus*). *Journal of Comparative and Physiological Psychology,* 1976, *90,* 424–434.

Zeaman, D. Response latency as a function of the amount of reinforcement. *Journal of Experimental Psychology,* 1949, *39,* 466–483.

Zeaman, D., and House, B. J. The role of attention in retardate discrimination learning. In Ellis, N. R. (Ed.), *Handbook of mental deficiency: Psychological theory and research.* New York: McGraw-Hill, 1963.

Zielinski, K., and Walasek, G. Stimulus intensity and conditioned suppression magnitude: Dependence upon the type of comparison and stage of training. *Acta Neurobiologica Experimentalis,* 1977, *37,* 299–309.

# Author Index

Going, M., 240
Goldiamond, I., 78
Goldstein, A. G., 239, 240
Goldstein, D. S., 69
Goldstein, H., 52
Gomulicki, B. R., 233
Goodall, J., 136
Goodnow, J. J., 132
Goodrich, K. P., 45, 50, 52
Goodwin, D. W., 185
Gorman, A. M., 156, 221, 225
Gormezano, I., 25, 26, 38, 40, 43, 44, 101, 102, 111
Graboi, D. G., 212
Grant, D. A., 43, 98, 101, 102, 111
Gray, W. D., 194, 213, 214
Green, C., 208, 212, 213
Greene, E., 214
Greene, J. E., 81
Greeno, J. G., 235
Greenspoon, J., 259
Grice, G. R., 38, 39, 82, 118, 119, 133
Griffin, D. R., 66
Grindley, G. C., 50
Grings, W. W., 36, 85, 106, 107
Grossen, N. E., 108
Grosslight, J. H., 104
Gruender, A., 39
Gumenik, W. E., 162, 163
Gustavson, C. R., 56
Guthrie, E. R., 104
Guttman, N., 50, 119, 120, 121, 133

Haggard, D. F., 45
Hall, J. F., 19, 21, 41, 69, 104, 106, 110, 156, 157, 197, 221, 225
Ham, M., 165, 166
Hamilton, C., 27
Hamlin, H., 216
Hammes, J. A., 81
Hankins, W. G., 56
Hansen, S. P., 68
Hanson, H. M., 124, 125, 126
Hara, K., 76
Harcum, E. R., 162
Hardman, G. W., Jr., 197
Harlow, H. F., 74, 76, 77, 81, 86, 87, 94, 142
Harris, A. H., 68
Harris, P., 99
Harris, R. E., 61

Harsanyi, M. A., 44
Harsh, C. M., 6
Hart, D., 112, 116
Harter, N., 4, 247, 250, 251
Harvey, C. B., 62
Hatzenbuehler, L. C., 144
Hayes-Roth, B., 231
Hearst, E., 16, 123, 124
Hebb, D. O., 201, 204, 223
Heinemann, E. G., 73
Helson, H., 39
Hempel, W. E., 252, 253
Herbert, M. J., 6
Herman, L. M., 87
Hermann, J. A., 147, 148
Herrnstein, R. J., 49, 75
Hess, E. H., 138, 139
Heth, C. D., 20
Hicks, L. H., 77
Hilgard, E. R., 6, 14, 28, 29, 30, 35, 36
Hill, F. A., 62, 106
Hill, W. F., 50
Hiroto, D. S., 65
Ho, E., 241
Hobson, G. N., 42
Hochberg, J., 239
Hochhauser, M., 82
Hockman, C. H., 84
Hoffeld, D. R., 71
Hoffman, H. S., 138, 139, 140
Hoffman, R. R., 168, 169
Hoine, H., 185
Holland, J. G., 49, 68
Holland, P. C., 19
Holland, T. A., 99
Honig, W. K., 63, 93, 121, 122, 130
Hopkins, B. L., 147, 148
Horton, D. L., 194
Horton, K. D., 208
Hothersall, D., 68
House, B. J., 93
Hovland, C. I., 118, 119, 121, 124, 132, 159
Howard, J. L., 70
Howard, R. C., 95
Howells, T. H., 240
Hufford, L. E., 254
Hug, J. J., 113
Hull, C. L., 9, 38, 39, 88, 89, 90, 91, 94, 97, 105, 106, 115, 118, 129, 130, 131, 132, 133, 135, 161
Hulse, S. H., 63, 98

Humphreys, L. G., 43, 100, 101
Hunt, E., 176
Hunt, H. F., 25
Hunter, J. J., 38, 39
Hunter, N. B., 23
Hunter, W. S., 159, 160
Hupka, R. B., 41
Hutton, R. A., 26
Hyde, T. S., 164, 210, 212

Irwin, F. W., 72
Irwin, J. M., 190
Ison, J. R., 98, 100

Jackson, R. L., 72
Jackson, T. A., 90
Jacobs, J., 201
Jacobs, P. D., 65
Jacobson, E., 144
Jacoby, K. E., 6
Jaffe, J. H., 27
Jakubowski, E., 38
James, J. P., 106
James, W., 201, 223, 262
Janda, L. H., 146
Jenkins, H. M., 34, 93
Jenkins, J. G., 188, 196, 199
Jenkins, J. J., 164, 210, 212
Jensen, A. R., 160, 163
Jerome, E., 90
Johnson, D. F., 92
Johnson, R. E., 235, 236
Jones, C. G., 127, 128
Jones, F. M., 162
Jones, H. M., 110, 111
Jones, M. H., 162
Justensen, D. R., 27

Kalat, J. W., 56, 57, 141
Kalish, H. I., 119, 120, 121, 123, 133
Kamin, L. J., 29, 38, 43, 45, 108, 109, 110
Kamman, R., 191
Kanfer, F. H., 259
Kappauf, W. E., 39
Karas, G. C., 81
Karlin, M. B., 244, 245
Kasdon, D., 82
Kassover, K., 112
Kaufman, R. A., 226, 227
Kazdin, A. E., 110, 150
Keenan, J. M., 236, 237
Keesey, R., 82
Kellas, G., 208

# Subject Index